pre-co... ...ay

DAVID KERR
Associate Professor of English
University of Botswana

James Currey
LONDON

N...IROBI

David Philip
CAPE TOWN

Baobab

D1334784

James Currey Ltd
54b Thornhill Square, Islington
London N1 1BE

Heinemann
A division of Reed Elsevier Inc
361 Hanover Street
Portsmouth, New Hampshire 03801-3959

East African Educational Publishers
PO Box 45314
Nairobi

David Philip Publishers (Pty) Ltd
PO Box 23408
Claremont 7735
Cape Town

Baobab Books
PO Box 1559
Harare

© David Kerr 1995
First published 1995
1 2 3 4 5 99 98 97 96 95

British Library Cataloguing in Publication Data
Kerr, David
  African Popular Theatre : From Pre-colonial
  Times to the Present Day. – (Studies in
  African Literature)
  I. Title   II. Series
  792.096

ISBN 0-85255-534-2 (James Currey Cloth)
ISBN 0-85255-533-4 (James Currey Paper)

Library of Congress Cataloging-in-Publication Data
Kerr, David.
  African popular theatre : from pre-colonial times to the present
day / David Kerr.
    p. cm. -- (Studies in African literature. New series)
  Includes bibliographical references and index.
  ISBN 0-435-08967-6 (Heinemann : cloth). -- ISBN 0-435-08969-2
(Heinemann : paper)
  1. Theater--Africa. Sub-Saharan--History. 2. Theater--Political
aspects--Africa, Sub-Saharan. 3. Theater and society--Africa. Sub
-Saharan. I. Title. II. Series.
PN2969.K47   1995
792'.0967--dc20   95-10210
                                                   CIP

Typeset by
Long House Publishing Services, Cumbria, UK
in 9/10 Palatino
Printed by
Villiers Publications Ltd.,
London N3

Contents

List of Illustrations with Acknowledgements   *vii*

Preface   *xi*

1. *Pre-colonial*
    African Popular Theatre   1

2. *Colonialism*
    & Theatre   16

3. *The Reaction of Indigenous*
    African Theatre to Colonialism   41

4. *Syncretic Popular Theatre:*
    Militaristic Mime   59

5. *Syncretic Popular Theatre:*
    Concert Party & Yoruba Opera   72

6. *Literary Drama*
    & Popular Theatre   105

7. The Travelling Theatre
   Movement   133

8. Theatre for Development   149

9. Popular Theatre
   & Macro-Media   172

10. Populist Theatre
    & National Ideology in Modern Africa   196

11. Popular Theatre
    & the Struggle for Liberation
    in Southern Africa   209

12. Towards a Theatre
    of Popular Struggle   240

Bibliography   257

Index   271

List of
Illustrations
with Acknowledgements

The author and publishers acknowledge with thanks the sources listed below for the pictures in this book. While every effort has been made to trace the ownership of all the pictures used, so far we have failed to trace the owners of some of the pictures on pages 3, 13, 24, 27, 43, 157, 206, 218, 226, 229, 238, 245, 252.

Chapter One

Audience for *Okumkpa* masquerade of the Afikpo follows the shape   3
of village architecture, creating difficult sightlines, thereby giving rise
to a need for play leaders to interpret the action. (S. Ottenberg, *Masked Rituals of Afikpo*,
University of Washington Press, 1975)

Bamana *Kote-tlon* performance. (Photo: James Brink in *African Arts*, 10/4, 1977)   3

Play leaders observing an *Okumkpa* skit prior to interpreting it for the audience.   8
(S. Ottenberg, *Masked Rituals of Afikpo*, University of Washington Press, 1975)

Formal audience arrangement for dance by chief Okongu of the Mangbetu   10
people. (Photo: Herbert Lang; reproduced with permission of the American
Museum of Natural History)

Whirling cloths of sacred elder *Egungun* (R. Farris Thompson, *African Art in*   10
Motion, UCLA Press, 1974)

Satirical *Egungun* mask representing a prostitute. (H.J. Drewal, in *African Arts*,   13
11/3, 1978)

Chapter Two

F. Horniman's private ethnographic museum, showing Africana in London,   17
1891. Horniman is second on the left. (Photo: reproduced with permission of
the Horniman Museum, London)

The Windybrow Theatre, Johannesburg, showing clear architectural   17
nostalgia for Europe.

The Bantu Dramatic Society's performance of Oscar Wilde's   24
Lady Windermere's Fan, Johannesburg, 1934. (T. Couzens, *The New African:*
A Study of the Life and Work of H.I.E. Dhlomo, Ravan Press, 1983)

'Darkest Africa'. Advertisement for Hollywood serial film, set in Africa   24
during the 1950s.

Colonial ethnographic film-making. Jean Rouch making an   27
anthropological film in Niger. (*Cinéaste*)

Family listening to Central African Broadcasting Services on a cheap   27
'saucepan special' radio. (HMSO)

Chapter Three

Makisi masquerade of the Mbunda people, with toes showing through the sisal   43
costume. (Photo: André Vrydagh, in *African Arts*, 10/4, 1977)

List of Illustrations

Odwira festival, Ghana. (J. Scott Kennedy, *In Search of African Theatre*,   47
Charles Scribner's Sons, New York, 1973; reprinted with the permission of
Scribner, an imprint of Simon & Schuster. Copyright ©1973, J. Scott Kennedy)

Satirical *Apidan* masks of European District Officer and his wife. (S.   48
Ottenberg, *Masked Rituals of Afikpo*, University of Washington Press, 1975)

Nyau 'Simon' mask, in action during a *Gule wa Mkulu* performance at Tembuna   51
village, near Chipata, Zambia, July 1975 (Photo: D. Kerr)

The British Prince of Wales inspecting an animal mask from the Gold Coast, 1925.   51

A reconstruction (based on a drawing by Harry Johnston) of the *Egungun*   53
performance (including satirical mask of a white man) for Clapperton
at King Mansola's court. (H. Johnston, *Pioneers in West Africa*, The Gresham
Publishing Co., London, 1912)

Chapter Four

Chigubu, or gourd trumpet, used in *Malipenga* as a substitute for Western   63
commercial trumpet. (W. P. Koma-Koma, *M'ganda Kapena Malipenga*, Malawi
Publications and Literature Bureau, 1965)

Uniformed musicians using marching steps and simultaneously playing   63
the drum in *Muganda*. (W. P. Koma-Koma, *M'ganda Kapena Malipenga*, Malawi
Publications and Literature Bureau, 1965)

Beni group performing at a democracy rally at Ntaja in Malawi, June 1993.   63
(Photo: D. Kerr)

Chapter Five

Floor plan for *Anansesem* performance.   73

Bob Johnson in 'black-face' make-up, during an early Concert Party stand-up   75
comedy routine. (Photo: Willis Bell, in E. Sutherland, *The Original Bob: The Story of
Bob Johnson, Ghana's Ace Comedian*, Anowuo Educational Publications, 1970)

The Axim Trio during the early 1930s. Bob Johnson is on the left. (Photo: Willis   77
Bell, in E. Sutherland, *The Original Bob: The Story of Bob Johnson, Ghana's Ace Comedian*,
Anowuo Educational Publications, 1970)

Typical minibus (with adverts) for Concert Party touring. (Photo: John Collins/   80
BAPMAF (Bokoor African Popular Music Archives Foundation)

Some Concert Party stereotyped roles. (Photo: John Collins, BAPMAF (Bokoor   80
African Popular Music Archives Foundation)

Obra Ye Ko (Life is War): a scene from a 1965 production by the Ghana Brigade   83
Group in the Concert Party style. (J. Scott Kennedy, *In Search of African Theatre*,
Charles Scribner's Sons, New York, 1973; reprinted with permission of Scribner,
an imprint of Simon & Schuster. Copyright ©1973, J. Scott Kennedy)

A scene from Ogunde's *Bread and Bullet* (1950). (E. Clark, *Hubert Ogunde: The*   83
Making of Nigerian Theatre, University Press, Ibadan, 1979)

Chapter Six

Kenyan National Theatre, Nairobi. (I. Björkman, *Mother, Sing for Me: People's*   107
Theatre in Kenya, Zed Books, London, 1989)

A scene from *Carrefour*, Dakar. (R. Cornevin, *Le Théâtre en Afrique noire et*   107
à Madagascar, Le Livre Africaine, Paris, 1970)

A production of the Nigerian play *Shaihu Umar* by Umaru Ladun and   116
Dexter Lyndersay, showing the prominent role played by chiefs in African
literary drama with a historical setting. (Photo: Dexter Lyndersay, in Umaru
Ladun and Dexter Lyndersay, *Shaihu Umar*, Longman, 1970)

A scene from Ola Rotimi's *Ovanramven Nogbaisi*. (Interview with   116
Margaret Folarin, in *New Theatre* magazine, Vol. 12, No. 2, 1973)

Storyteller and Ananse in Efua Sutherland's *The Marriage of Anansewa*.   120
(Photo: Willis Bell, in E. Sutherland, *The Marriage of Anansewa*, Longman, 1975)

List of Illustrations

A scene from Saka Acquaye's *The Lost Fishermen*. (J. Scott Kennedy, *In Search of*   120
African Theatre, Charles Scribner's Sons, New York, 1973; reprinted with permission of
Scribners, an imprint of Simon & Schuster. Copyright ©1973, J. Scott Kennedy)
A scene from *Kongi's Harvest* by Wole Soyinka. (Guy Hennebelle, *Les Cinémas*   122
africains en 1972, Société Africain d'Edition, Dakar, 1972; reproduced with
permission of l'Afrique litteraire, Paris)

Chapter Seven
A scene from an UNZADRAMS production of *The Trial of Zwangendaba* by David   140
Kerr and Solomon Mbuzi, at Chikwakwa Theatre, Lusaka, 1976. (Photo: D. Kerr)
A fund-raising appeal for Chikwakwa Theatre, Lusaka. (*Chikwakwa Review*,   141
Issue 1, 1969)
A bare minimalist travelling theatre production on a simple proscenium   146
arch stage in Changalume community hall, Malawi, 1984. (Photo: D. Kerr)
An in-the-round open-air travelling theatre production in Silele village,   146
Zambia, 1975. (Photo: D. Kerr)

Chapter Eight
Puppet theatre show with developmental message as part of a packaged   150
programme on nutrition in Zambia. (Food and Nutrition Commission, Lusaka)
A page from a 'How-to' manual on Theatre for Development, published for   150
the *Laedza Batanani* campaign. (Popular Theatre Committee, *Laedza Batanani:
Organising Popular Theatre*, University of Botswana, Gaborone, 1978)
Villagers preparing an impromptu theatre for a developmental drama   157
production in Mulangali, Malawi, 1988. (Photo: D. Kerr)
Masquerade figure of a hyperdermic needle in a carnival on the theme   157
of Vaccination for Health, Guinea Bissau, 1987. (Photo: Bernard Brandham in
African Arts, 26/3, 1993)
Theatre for Development play about Primary Health Care in Malawi, 1988.   164
(Photo: D. Kerr)

Chapter Nine
A radio drama performance in Gabon. (Photo: Maurice Dercraiene, in   174
Robert Cornevin, *Le Théâtre en Afrique noire et à Madagascar*, Le Livre
Africain, Paris, 1970)
A scene from *Diankha-bi* directed by Mhama Traoré. (Guy Hennebelle,   174
Les Cinémas africains en 1972, Société Africain d'Edition, Dakar, 1972; reproduced with
permission of l'Afrique litteraire, Paris)
A scene from Wole Soyinka's *Kongi's Harvest*, directed by Ossie Davis   187
for the Calpenny Company. (Guy Hennebelle, *Les Cinémas africains en 1972*,
Société Africain d'Edition, Dakar, 1972; reproduced with permission of l'Afrique
litteraire, Paris)
A scene from *Mandabi* (*Le Mandat*) directed by Ousmane Sembène.   190
(Guy Hennebelle, *Les Cinémas africains en 1972*, Société Africain d'Edition,
Dakar, 1972; reproduced with permission of l'Afrique litteraire, Paris)
A scene from Ousmane Sembène's film, *Emitai*. (Guy Hennebelle,   190
Les Cinémas africains en 1972, Société Africain d'Edition, Dakar, 1972; reproduced
with permission of l'Afrique litteraire, Paris)

Chapter Ten
Malawian *Mbumba* dance in a stadium for President Banda. (Ministry of   203
Information, Malawi)
Programme cover for *Chikhakhali*, a dance-drama created by a Malawian   203
national theatre group for performance to delegates at an international
conference. (Malawi Ministry of Information)
Dancers from Zairean National Dance Theatre. (ICA, Dakar)   206

Athletic dancers of Sierra Leone National Dance Theatre performing on a   206
proscenium arch stage. (Photo: Sylvester Ekunbuyo Rowe in *African Arts*, 9/1, 1978)

Chapter Eleven
A township dance sequence from *King Kong*. (H. Bloom and P. Williams,   218
King Kong, Collins, 1961)
A scene from *Woza Albert!* by Barney Simon, Mbongeni Ngema and Percy Mtwa.   226
(B. Simon, M. Ngema and P. Mtwa, *Woza Albert!*, Methuen, London, 1983)
A scene from Maishe Maponya's *Umongikazi*. (Polypoton, 1983)   229
A scene from Matsemela Manaka's *Egoli*.   229
The Soyikwa players singing to the audience in a production of *Size*,   234
performed in urban and rural venues in South Africa during 1988.
(Photo: Gordon Metz, reprinted with permission of The Mayibuye Centre, Cape Town)
A scene from *Katshaa!*, a collaborative play created by Zambuko/Izibuko from   234
Zimbabwe in solidarity with the South African liberation struggle. (Robert McClaren,
Katshaa! The Sound of the AK, Zambuko/Izibuko, Harare, 1985)
Dancers from Smali Ndaba's 1993 musical *Ubuntu Bomhlaba*.   238
(Photo: Karina Turok, in *The Weekly Mail*, Johannesburg, June 1993)

Chapter Twelve
Kamiriithu Theatre before its destruction in 1982. (Photo: Niels Juul Bush, 1982)   245
A scene from *Maitu Njugira* by Ngugi wa Thiong'o and the Kamiriithu Theatre.   245
(I. Björkman, *Mother Sing for Me: People's Theatre in Kenya*, Zed Books, London, 1989)
Cover for a class-conscious pidgin play from Nigeria. (Adena Publishers,   252
Benin City, 1980s)
Mime dancer imitating President Banda at a pro-democracy rally in Nsanje,   252
Malawi, October 1993. (Photo: D. Kerr)

Acknowledgements

I would like to thank the following people who helped me (perhaps without realizing it themselves) either through access to materials or through discussing ideas: Salihu Bappa, Karin Barber, Emevwo Biakolo, Stephen Chifunyise, Fay Chung, Michael Etherton, James Gibbs, Jacques-Noel Gouat, Ibrahim Hussein, John Iliffe, Christopher Kamlongera, Ross Kidd, T. Kitenge-Ngoy, Robert McClaren, John McCracken, Jack Mapanje, Kofi Mensah, Penina Mlama, Sam Mtamba, Mapopa Mtonga, Dickson Mwansa, Mike Nambote, Lewis Nkosi, Alex Pongweni, Adrian Roscoe and Landeg White.

I would like to thank, in particular, Ngugi wa Mirii, with whom I wanted to collaborate on the book, if the exigencies of African politics had not made communication between us impossibly difficult; George Matoga who typed the manuscript; Szilard Biernaczky, who encouraged me to finish *African Popular Theatre*; and my mother, Anne, my late father, Eric, my children Lewis, Rachel, Sammy and Tamya, and my wife, Nyandovi, who all endured the turmoil involved at various stages of the book's creation.

Preface

It requires a certain amount of gall to write a book you know must be full of oversimplifications and half truths. Yet I believe *African Popular Theatre* is a work of necessary hubris, if only to provoke researchers into greater accuracy than I have been able to achieve. The need to make the attempt arises from the lack, as I am writing, of a general introduction to varieties of African popular theatre. My experience of popular theatre work in adult education in Africa has made me realize the particular need for a theoretical work which could link popular theatre practice to conditions of production.

The word 'overview' is much abused, but I can find no better to describe the attempt in this book to trace some of the different forms of popular theatre in Africa since pre-colonial times to the present. The reader should look at this synthesis as a rough framework for constructing a total model of African popular theatre, so that the separate insights provided by different researchers may be put into perspective.

The effort of all this synthesis is to create certain structural constraints in the book which need to be acknowledged here.

Unfortunately, as with all surveys, I have relied heavily on secondary sources. I expect that many future corrections to *African Popular Theatre* will come from scholars noting the discrepancies between the theories here and the facts revealed by further primary research. One way of cutting down on inspired guesswork deriving from speculative reading of secondary sources is to concentrate on those regions of Africa which are familiar to me. For that reason, apart from Chapters One, Four and Nine, there is a heavy, but by no means exclusive emphasis on examples from East, Central and Southern Africa. Examples from the Maghreb and Madagascar have been totally excluded because of my ignorance, not for any methodological reasons.

The relatively large number of quotations in the book is deliberate. Many of the sources of information are fairly obscure, and it seemed like a service to the reader to allow those sources to speak for themselves as often as space permitted.

Nevertheless, *African Popular Theatre* is emphatically not a book of literary criticism or textual analysis. The bulk of African popular theatre does not exist in script form – it has to be reconstructed by analysing oral or written descriptions. Instead, the book attempts to give a roughly chronological account of the development of African popular theatre along with an examination of its economic, social and political background, linked to the conditions of production.

Because the book uses a dialectical framework I found it convenient to use the past tense even of quite recent works, the results of which are still very much present at the time of writing. Another effect of this perspective is that I have tried to group different popular theatre forms according to the dialectic of their historical moments. This leads to a certain amount of over-simplified categorizing; I am very aware that, in practice, many of the theatre forms which in this book are treated under separate chapter headings were in historical fact overlapping.

Another stylistic feature of the book which requires even greater apology is the absence of strict orthographic accuracy (especially in accenting) in the quotations of titles from such languages as Yoruba and Kikuyu. This was dictated purely by motive of material print resources and not by any wish to denigrate those languages.

While in danger of offending those readers with detailed knowledge of specific African theatre modes, I may not escape the wrath of theorists of African culture. In particular, my reluctance (for the sake of saving innocent paper from endless debate) to tussle with definitions of Culture, Class and Ideology may seem a form of escapism. The only contentious word I want to refer to in this introduction is 'popular'. A strong tradition in the theorizing about African theatre is to distinguish between 'popular' theatre and 'people's' theatre, on the grounds that 'people's' theatre is flawed by false consciousness and that only a 'popular' theatre which self-consciously projects the aspirations and practice of the people in contesting racial or class oppression is a true reflection of the people's culture.

I have much sympathy with that view, and it tended to be a guiding principle in conceiving the book. In practice, however, the search for ideological purity can become almost masochistically self-indulgent. I found it necessary to use 'popular' to cover a broad spectrum of genres, ranging from those which were 'populist' in that they mystified the people through offering them escapist forms of entertainment or atavistic ritual, to those which the people self-consciously adopted as ideological weapons in the struggle against imperialism or neo-colonialism.

A similar imprecision applies to my terminology for describing the 'people'. Sometimes it is possible to use relatively precise terms like 'peasant' or 'proletarian'; but frequently the eclecticism of African audiences demands a more general term, for which I have normally used Gramsci's useful phrase, 'subaltern classes'.

While painfully aware of the above inadequacies and convinced that the book is not the definitive work on the subject, I still trust that *African Popular Theatre* may provoke productive debate and thought about the linkages between popular theatre and the economic/social forms engaged by the subaltern classes at different stages of African history.

1

Pre-Colonial
African Popular Theatre

Writing a chapter about pre-colonial African theatre in the colonial language of English gives rise not only to irony but to confusion. There has been heated debate as to whether drama did or did not exist in pre-colonial Africa, and to what extent it could or should be distinguished from rituals. I believe that much of this confusion is caused by using English words like 'drama', 'theatre' and 'ritual', which are loaded with meanings derived from European rather than African culture.

Eventually Africanists may develop a way of describing pre-colonial performing arts in Africa by reference to indigenous aesthetic terms.[1] Until those terms are researched, agreed upon at a Pan-African level and widely understood, we have to make do with the European terms. This makes my omnibus adjective 'pre-colonial' a necessary, but ahistorical imprecision. However, I hope not to get too diverted by arguments about terminology, inadequate though the terms may be. Briefly, drama refers to displays of actions to an audience, in which there is an imitation of events in the real or supernatural world and there is an element or story or suspense. Although denied by some scholars,[2] undoubtedly pre-colonial African theatre forms, such as the Mandingo and Bamana comic sketches and many forms of masquerade, fit this definition. Ritual refers to an action which is undertaken to give homage to, obtain assistance from, or in some way intercede with supernatural forces. This may or may not involve dramatic representation. I use the word theatre in a very wide sense to cover drama, many forms of ritual, dance, and other performing arts such as acrobatics, mime and semi-dramatized narratives. This wide reference avoids having to use rather clumsy words like paradrama or metatheatre which have sometimes been used to cover the wide variety of African pre-colonial performing arts.

My main interest is less in distinguishing between different genres and

1

modes of pre-colonial African theatre than in examining the way pre-colonial theatre mediated a) indigenous economic and social systems, b) class formation and historical change.

In one fairly short chapter it is impossible to cover the whole rich variety of African pre-colonial theatre. Instead I concentrate on a few West African theatre forms as a way of correcting what I feel to be general biases in the way indigenous African theatre has normally been analysed by previous scholars. One major bias arises from the fact that pre-colonial theatre has not been very thoroughly researched. Compared, for example, with African pre-colonial history of state formation, there has been little use in theatre studies of such evidence as archaeology or oral sources. Much of the information we do have comes from reconstructions and hypotheses made by colonial anthropologists and Africanists. The problem with those sources is not only that they tended to have values alien to African culture, but also that they had an ideological bias which distorted the image of African theatre.

Many of the colonial Africanists shared a view of African pre-colonial culture as almost unchanging for many centuries. This view suited colonial ideology because it made African culture seem outside of the dynamic process of history, thereby rationalizing the increased dependency of African economies on Europe.[3]

Surprisingly, this image of Africa has proved quite durable even after independence. In the Negritude philosophy of the 1930s and 1940s African intellectuals turned colonial ideology inside out, retaining the static view of African history but praising it in contrast to the dynamic but destructive sterility of European culture. That philosophy had an important impact on post-independence views of African culture. Many African academics and government spokesmen tended to endorse the conception of a classless innocent, unchanging African pre-colonial culture.

The notion of a communal, sharing, pre-colonial society has found a theatrical equivalent in an aesthetic emphasis on African theatre's anonymous, participatory qualities. Even anthropologically inclined studies from the late colonial era commented on the participatory quality of indigenous African theatre. For example, in a study of the *Okumkpa* masked plays among Nigeria's Afikpo people, Ottenberg explains how the absence of raked seating caused problems with sightlines. As a result, play leaders had to move around the audience interpreting the play for the audience. Ottenberg comments that this caused 'a slackening in dramatic tension but increased audience–player interaction'.[4]

Post-independence African scholars have given a polemical thrust to the participatory element in African theatre. A good example is this description of indigenous Ugandan theatre by Mukotani Rugyendo:

> In the course of the performance, all the spectators could participate as they liked by clapping, shouting or whistling, all in appreciation, and actually contributing to the force of the performance by joining beautifully with the performers.[5]

Rugyendo's account emphasizes the collectivity of pre-colonial African theatre by contrast with the divisive individualism of colonial Western theatre. The aim of his paper is to urge modern post-independence African theatre practitioners to return to the collective 'socialist' ethos of pre-colonial African theatre.

2

Audience for *Okumkpa*
masquerade of the Afikpo
follows the shape of village
architecture, creating difficult
 sightlines, thereby giving rise to
a need for play leaders to
interpret the action

Bamana *Kote-tlon* performance

There are clear homologies here with political theories urging a return to pre-colonial communocratic values (as seen for example in Nyerere's philosophy of Ujamaa). I believe a danger in such theories is that they tend to discount the changing dynamic within indigenous forms of African culture, a neglect which has something in common with functionalist models of pre-colonial culture espoused as the dominant view of colonial anthropologists.

My analysis tries to show that class formation and social innovation were very much part of pre-colonial history, and were reflected intimately in the performing arts.

One crucial relationship which I feel needs analysis is the one between mode of production and popular theatre. The way in which pre-colonial African societies organized their labour to create the necessities of life was mediated in an intimate way by popular theatre. A good example of this is the *Kote-tlon* theatre of the Bamana people in Mali.

In the fourteenth and fifteenth centuries a great Bamana kingdom arose in ancient Mali in which feudal lords exacted tribute from slaves and bonded agriculturalists in order to build the wealth needed for maintaining the kingdom. The wealth also allowed the development of specialized crafts such as metal and leather work and textiles. In the sixteenth century this kingdom collapsed into fragmented states. They were still dominated, however, by military, religious and merchant aristocracies which were linked by a system of tribute to the agriculturalists in what P. Francis calls the 'tributary mode of production'.[6]

The social system created by the tributary mode of production was a very complex one which combined elements of an archaic communal cooperative agriculture system along with more hierarchical institutions, such as *Byam* (domestic slavery). Nevertheless, farming techniques in pre-colonial Mali were advanced – with shifting cultivation, deep hoeing and ridging for millet, and irrigation for vegetables and other special crops. The agricultural system was maintained by a network of village headmen, who, with their council of elders, were extremely powerful; they divided and allocated land, either for individual cultivation or for collective youth projects (*ton*).

Ideological factors were extremely important for suppressing emergent contradictions in the economic system. Elaborate masked rituals associated with the initiation grades of *N'dama*, *Kama*, *Tyi Wara*, *Nama* and *Kore* ensured that the farming tasks which had to be undertaken by the youths were linked to creation myths and other ritualized symbols. The religious rituals served to legitimize the agricultural tasks and the subordination of the youths to the elders.

The theatre form I am going to examine was a more secular unmasked drama known as the *Kote-tlon*. The *Kote-tlon* were improvised young men's comedies which frequently moralized on techniques of agricultural production by holding up to ridicule anti-social elements in the community. James Brink, who studied the form, lists several common stereotypes: 'unfaithful wives, lovers, greedy persons, morons and others are punished as vices and made to look absurd'.[7] Such stereotypes reinforced the conformity to ethics and health standards necessary in a commmunity where the productivity of society depended less on the tools of production than on the human instrumentality of the labour force. The commonest target in the Bamana plays was that of wicked or lazy millet farmers. In almost all

4

societies where economic survival depends upon organizing labour power into the productive force, art forms express abhorrence of laziness.

A particularly interesting feature of the *Kote-tlon* theatre is the clear relationship between the organization of the theatrical performances and the organization of agricultural work teams. Bamana labour teams were organized through age-grade associations known as *ton*. The *ton* was called *ngonson ton* when it acted as a collective agricultural labour force, or was used on public work projects initiated by the council of elders; the same group, under the age-set leadership, called *flamekew*, operated as an entertainment society, known as *koteba ton*, for the production of theatrical performances.

The close structural relationship between the economic unit and cultural unit ensured a very tight ideological relationship between the two. For example, the age-set structure of Bamana society, which was an essential feature of the Bamana relations of production, was reflected in the *fere* (arena) and individualistic acrobatics (*baduka*). The *Kote-tlon* started with skits called *kaka* by very young boys. When the *Kote-tlon* proper got under way the skits were presented strictly by age sets, starting with the younger teams (in their teens) and progressing to the older groups (in their late twenties). The older groups preferred the more artistically complex plays; the respect they received parallels the increased power which men obtained in Bamana society as they grew older, until they reached the stage of becoming full adults.

Another ideological feature of Bamana *Kote-tlon* was the way the solidarity of the *ngonson ton* was reinforced by the theatrical activities of the *koteba ton*. Brink describes the close harmony of movement which characterized the *bamuko* dance which opened the *koteba*. 'Choreographic unity', he suggests, 'expresses *ton* solidarity'.[8]

Despite the obvious ways theatre supported the mode of production in pre-colonial Bamana society, we also need to be aware of the ways the *Kote-tlon* performances pointed to contradictions within the relations of production. The power which the chiefs and elders had in allocating land and jobs produced 'latent contradictions involving elders who controlled land and the young men who provided collective labour'.[9] The labour exploitation was exacerbated by a system whereby elders enforced late marriage on young men. The resulting frustration accounts for the prominence of satire on sexual themes, aimed at unfaithful wives, impotent old men and cuckolds. There is an ambiguous impetus to make individuals conform to the norms of society, along with a good-humoured but identifiable rebellion against the domination of the elders. Brink gives a splendidly fantastic example of a farce in which a woman loses her vagina in a river, causing consternation to her husband and family. Such ribald satire in some ways reinforced conformity to sexual codes in order to preserve group solidarity, but at the same time it allowed youths to vent their sexual frustration in an uninhibited manner.

It was particularly the skits of the *koreduga* (buffoons) which were capable of expressing youthful dissatisfaction against the tributary mode of production, as can be seen by this *koreduga* song:

Each year we prepare the fields for planting, but there are no wives for us;
At the beginning of the dry season there are no wives for us;

The road to the cemetery is well-travelled, but no one returns from there;
There is no way to pay for a person's soul.[10]

The singers link their sexual frustration to the time spent (or ln their eyes wasted) in hard work for the elders.

The *koreduga* were able to get away with such criticism of the system because of the special role performers had in Bamana society. The *Kote-tlon* actors were recognized as having a special gift known as *nyankoro*, the ability to recognize comic situations and reproduce them through mimicry; the possession of *nyankoro* gave performers a status in society which was a combination of privilege and marginality. Brink comments: 'Actors pay little attention to their dress and demeanour in public situations, and they ... have the reputations as drunkards, playboys, lazy farmers and thieves.'[11] There is an obvious irony in the actors being considered lazy farmers when they satirized lazy farmers in their skits.

Contradictions between the marginal status of performers and the stabilizing ideology which their performance content sometimes presented were common in pre-colonial theatre and point to their potentially liberating role. The critical privilege which performers held and their non-conformist role in society generated the moral insecurity needed for any change of consciousness. In pre-colonial theatre performers tended 'to be both admired and feared – admired for their artistic skill ... feared because of the potential they represent for subverting and transforming the status quo'.[12] The ambiguous status artists had of being both despised and feared, of apparently supporting yet simultaneously undermining authority, can be found repeatedly in pre-colonial theatre.[13]

It is not very surprising to find a sceptical attitude and implicit resistance among performers of *Kote-tlon*. Unmasked performers tended to be more innovative than masked. This was because masquerades were usually based on ancestor worship where the ancestral figures provided ideological support for the status quo. For example, among the Dogon in Mali, a people closely related to the Bamana, the 'ancestor figures ... [were] essential to support a system of status authority over the command of resources and their allocation, and some labour command for one segment of the population, the clan elders'.[14]

Nevertheless, even masked forms of African popular theatre were able to respond to innovation and economic transformation in pre-colonial African society. The masked Bamana dances, for instance, tended to become more secular as the economic values implicit in the ideological structure of the plays became more apparent to the performers. One scholar, Pascal Imperato, notes that the *Tyi Wara* masquerade 'assumed a non-religious character in that it was performed to encourage the members of the *ton* to be good farmers'.[15] The process was one whereby agricultural methods were gradually delinked from spiritual mystification. Imperato notes that his aged informants, whose oral 'memories' went back several generations, were sure that secularization started to take place before any contact with colonialism, urban values or the cash nexus.

Secularization was accompanied by several other cultural effects. One was a tendency for theatre performances to attract an increasing aesthetic interest among audiences somewhat divorced from the religious origins. With the Dogon masquerades, for example, 'little by little ... from being attentive to the progression of the rite, the crowd becomes attentive to the spectacle'.[16] It is not that the aesthetic element was previously absent, but that it became more self-conscious when delinked from ritual.

Another cultural effect accompanying secularization was the increased use of topical satire and dramatic stereotyping. A good example of a pre-colonial masquerade which developed a sophisticated system of satirical caricature was the *Okumkpa* drama of the Afikpo from Nigeria's Cross River region.

The *Okumkpa* masquerades, like those of Bamana, were related to all-male ancestral cults controlled by the elders in Afikpo society. It was particularly the wealthy, titled, male elders who displayed their influence over the *Okumkpa* by acting as patrons for the plays, either through direct support to the performing troupes, or by 'dashing' the actors during arrangements for the plays. 'The elders and more prominent male members of the audience [sat] in the shade of a tree or in the men's resthouse in the main common. Women and children [sat] elsewhere, often in the hot sun.'[17] The audience distinctions reflected the domination of the wealthy elders in Afikpo society, as well as social divisions based on the sexual division of labour.

Women were not allowed to have any contact with *Okumkpa* and so could not vent their grievance against a male-dominated society, but young men could express their resentment against elders, despite the respect given to elders in the theatrical mode of production. To start with, the timing of the performances (in the dry season after the harvest) was one of economic adjustment, when prominent farmers wished to show their wealth. It was also a period of great public mingling, when the *Okumkpa* players had a special licence to create satirical songs and dances. The ritual origins of the masquerade survived in a ceremony whereby the players retired to the *Ajaba* (prayer and changing room) before the performance, and ritually allowed themselves to be possessed by the spirit *mma* when they donned their masks. According to Afikpo culture this possession gave the players licence to criticize and lampoon anyone in society, however respectable he might be.

The satire was achieved through the creation of masks, songs and topical skits and through commentaries made to the audience by the leaders (*odudo*) and leaders' assistants (*odudo eguru ale*). The leaders helped to monitor the participation of the audience by giving a running commentary on the play to those members of the huge audience who were unable to see the action properly. The sketches and songs were made up during secret rehearsals in the bush.

Sometimes the satires referred to general targets, especially members of alien groups such as Muslims; in this *Okumkpa* reinforced Afikpo solidarity for group survival. More often, however, they referred to specific individuals in society. Since the whole community attended the performances those individuals witnessed the satires, but were not expected to show displeasure. There were two favourite groups of targets: women who intruded on the all-male privacy of the cult, and greedy, selfish or ineffective elders. The stereotypes were backed up by stylization of masking, costume and props.

Ottenberg suggests that the *Okumkpa* plays represented a temporary reversal of the normal authority relations in Afikpo society:

> It is the players who are active, who develop and imitate and create. The elders and others in the audience are relatively passive, more or less accepting the comments

Play leaders observing an *Okumkpa* skit prior to interpreting it for the audience

of the players whether they like them or not, as younger persons do of actions of the elders in everyday life.[18]

Although the performers had considerable licence to criticize the elders, their own position in society, like that of the Bamana actors, was marginal. They were not politically influential, or wealthy, nor did they take high titles in society. In fact their power probably arose as much from their marginality as from ancestral licence. Through the temporary reversal of power relations, popular *Okumkpa* theatre acted as a weapon in the hands of the younger and less influential sections of the community – not to overthrow the elders' power, but at least to control it.

The class conflicts expressed in the performances of the Bamana and Afikpo were of a fairly embryonic kind, disguised by the social cement of religion, gender divisions and kinship systems. But in societies which were destabilized by strong internal contradictions theatrical forms expressed more open class conflict. One such art form was the spirit masquerade of the Dan people from the modern Liberia/Ivory Coast region. This is a society which developed a repressive system of domestic slavery, partly as a consequence of its articulation with the eighteenth-century international slave economy. One scholar explains that 'wealthy chiefs who profited from agriculture and hunting activities surrounded themselves with young warriors who protected them and their possessions'.[19] The warriors danced as terrifying ancestral spirits. For instance, the warrior caste used the *kaogle* (monkey mask) to protect their chief and assert their own strength, through intimidating the commoners and slaves into a state of subservience.

Another focus of pre-colonial conflict which performing arts helped to mediate was that of tension between the chief's desire for centralized control and commoners' tendencies to cut themselves off from the royal palace. The rebelliousness in the peripheral areas was often given cultural expression by the creation of secret societies in which rituals and dances mediated divisive tendencies at the edges of newly-formed states. Such tension can be seen in the early nineteenth-century state of Benin, where the conflict between the 'pure' metropolitan Bini people, loyal to the autocratic Oba, and the peripheral Ekpo community of ex-slaves was expressed in the performing arts. The rituals of the Bini people centred on the semi-divine Oba who controlled the judiciary, the system of tribute, patronage and the granting of titles; the theatrical elements at court constantly reintegrated the Bini people into that power nexus. Among the Ekpo, however, myths and rituals emerged which celebrated a culture hero, Agboghidi (represented in wooden masks), who became the source of a mythic ideolory whereby the Ekpo identified themselves with youth and cleanliness in opposition to the ruling elders in the capital.[20]

The problem with the examples we have chosen is that many of them deal with late periods of African theatre history when pre-colonial states had already made some contact with colonalism through trade. Moreover, the description of the pre-colonial theatre forms has been built up partly by guesswork from the way the forms have survived into the colonial period.

By contrast, it is worth looking at a theatre form which has had a clearly identifiable existence over a long period of time. The Yoruba *Egungun* theatre has been traced, and to some extent documented, from the fifteenth century to modern times through lineage histories.

Formal audience arrangement for dance by chief Okongu of the Mangbetu people
Whirling cloths of sacred elder *Egungun*

The origins of *Egungun* are obscure but most sources suggest that the cult was a transplant from other cultures. A dominant Yoruba oral tradition suggests that the Nupe people brought *Egungun* either when they invaded and ruled the main Yoruba town of Oyo for a short period in the early sixteenth century, or earlier still when Oya, the Nupe wife of the semi-divine Oba, Sango, introduced it in the fourteenth century. An alternative tradition states that *Egungun* was introduced to the Yoruba at Kushu when Alaafin Onigbogi went into exile among the Borgu people in the sixteenth century. All accounts would suggest that it was an aristocratic cult. However, *Egungun* was almost certainly connected with a widespread and much older tradition of masquerades found all over West Africa and derived from communalistic ancestral cults. Myths about *Egungun* say it came from the union between a monkey and a woman; the monkey is still a sacred animal in the cult. Yet other myths stress the sacred role of the python. All these indicate that the pre-feudal origins of *Egungun* derive from a rural culture where animals were very important, perhaps relating to a hunting economy.

The Yoruba cultural diversity reflects a history of extreme ethnic fluidity and syncretism. In the town of Owo to the east of Oyo, traditions show a whole variety of *Egungun* cults, some, such as *Omolaka*, *Elinodi*, and *Eluori*, derived from aristocratic immigrants from as early as the fourteenth century, whereas others (such as *Uka* and *Ora*) could be traced back to slaves captured in the seventeenth and eighteenth centuries. In other words, the Owo *Egungun* cults represent a multi-layered culture with different class and historical traditions.[21]

The structure of the Yoruba kingdom encouraged such diversity. Although Oyo achieved a certain domination from the sixteenth to eighteenth centuries, the Yoruba 'empire' was basically a confederation of semi-autonomous city states, each with varying religious and cultural traditions. In general, we are probably dealing with a pre-feudal rural tradition of masquerade, associated with ancestor worship, which became appropriated by urban semi-feudal princes (Oba) through the creation of a high priest (Alagba) and a hierarchy of lesser priests loyal to the royal court.

The different class origins of the various *Egungun* cults can be seen in the masquerade types. Because *Egungun* was a lineage-based cult the class origins of cults were preserved for centuries, with distinctions between aristocratic lineages, bonded labourers (who became bonded through the *iwofa* system of pawning labour to raise capital) and captive slaves. In Iganna, for example, there was a distinction between aristocratic *Egungun* cults (*baba-alago*) and slave cults (*eru-eegun*). The status distinctions were expressed by the length of cloth, with short cloths for the *eru-eegun* and cloths so long for the *baba-alago* that they needed an assistant to carry them.[22]

The wide variety of mask types in *Egungun* made it a particularly suitable theatre for innovation. The most solemn and sacred cult mask, the elder *Egungun*, used whirling, brightly coloured cloth with saw-tooth patterns as a symbolic representation of ancestral forces in order to terrify non-initiates (particularly women) and to purify the community from disease, death and misfortune. The performances of these elder *Egungun* were strictly religious, restricted either to the annual festival or to funerals.

Some of the more common masks, however, such as the trickster *Egungun*, the *onidan* (miracle worker) or the *olokiti* (tumblers), were more oriented towards entertainments which were spectacular (such as acrobatics and displays of conjuring tricks) or satirical (through the lampooning poetry of the chants and through stereotyped, semi-representational masks). In actual performance, since the Yoruba, as Adedeji says, 'do not draw a sharp dividing line between the sacred and the profane', the fierce elder *Egungun*, who came to judge the world, intermingled with the more profane comic *Egungun*, who came to entertain it.[23]

All the same, over the years, the satirical masks, while never totally divorced from their ritual origins, developed secular overtones which gave scope to strong representational qualities. Since *Egungun* were meant to cleanse the Yoruba communities from physical and psychological disorders, many of the stereotypes used grotesque masks to portray such physical, psychic or social aberrations as leprosy, goitre, club-foot, small-pox, drunkenness, insanity and prostitution. Fairly representational costumes, like plaited hair and artificial teeth for the prostitute, reinforced the stereotypes. Another common stereotype was that of the outsider, such as the Nupe, Hausa or Dahomean; these often referred back to wars with other peoples (like the Dahomean wars of the nineteenth century).

Because the satirical masquerades were, to a certain extent, impromptu, they were able to adapt to almost any topical social or political context. The *Ora Ofe* masquerades, for example, included 'invocation and self authorization, curse, prophecy, allusion to sexual conduct and morality, comment on foreign and domestic politics. as well as remarks on religion, hierarchy, history and funeral commemoration'.[24] The wide variety of theatrical themes was a step towards a secular theatre capable of questioning traditional ideologies; but real progress in that direction only took place when performers became separated from specific *Egungun* festivals and funeral rites. *Egungun* in Iwi, for example, contained a special mask type, the *Onidan*, which were not restricted to a specific festival or season, but could perform all year round.

It was out of such specialized *Egungun* groups that professional semi-secular Yoruba theatre emerged, variously called *oloje, oje* and *apidan*. A particularly well-researched professional Yoruba theatre form is that of *Alarinjo,* which has been studied by Adedeji.[25] According to his (admittedly speculative) research, *Alarinjo* started in Oyo at the court of Alaafin Ogbolu in about 1590, with six *Egungun* characters representing such stock physical deformities as the hunchback, albino, dwarf and leper, under the leadership of an *Egungun* singer, Ologbin Ologbojo. In its origin, therefore, the *Alarinjo* was a courtly entertainment under the patronage of the Alaafin. By the early seventeenth century, however, *Alarinjo* had widened its appeal; the troupe leader, Esu Ogbin, 'took the theatre to the masses, the grassroots'.[26] At about the same time, different lineages from that of Ologbojo set up theatre troupes, some specializing in acrobatics, some in dance/poetry, others in satirical sketches, and each seeking patronage from different Alaafin.

With increasing professionalism, the form of the *Alarinjo* theatre became rather more defined. A chorus (*akunyungba*) played the role of singing, praising the troupe, commenting on the action and filling gaps in the scenario, and forming an intimate link with the audience. The *Egungun* cult leaders attempted to keep some control over the *Alarinjo* professional offshoots, but the *Alarinjo* performers showed their independence by satirizing some of the

12

Satirical *Egungun* mask representing a prostitute

solemnities of the cult. Adedeji records audiences being amazed 'when they saw the restrictions of the *Egungun* society trampled upon in the arena of play, and laughed when their revered gods were revealed in sketches as caricatures'.[27]

During its early period, performances of *Alarinjo* were restricted to the palace courtyard of the Alaafin. However, with the popularization of the theatre in the seventeenth century the companies became more commercial and travelled each dry season, sometimes playing in aristocratic courtyards, at other times on more popular stages in urban squares or rural marketplaces.

In the early nineteenth century, when, under pressure from the Fulani, and after internecine civil wars in the Yoruba nation, the centre of the Yoruba confederation moved from Oyo south to Ibadan, the traditional feudal courts began to lose their control of *Alarinjo*, and the performances became more like a professional travelling theatre. In the process, the performers became even more marginalized. As with the young men who performed *Kote-tlon* or *Okumkpa*, they were stigmatized as unreliable, happy-go-lucky, lecherous and rather dangerous. With the *Alarinjo* performers, this dangerous reputation was enhanced by their being travelling troupes, not responsible to the authority of the Alaafin or elders in a community.

The *Alarinjo* troupes' marginal status gave them the opportunity for making scurrilous satire, often under the disguise of self-mockery. Adedeji gives an example of an *Alarinjo efe* (self-mocking poem) which celebrated a tumbler who impregnated a chief's wife and turned himself, trickster-style, into a chameleon, to escape the Alaafin's wrath. Sometimes the satire turned into blatant social criticism of the feudal leaders from commoners' point of view, as Adedeji explains:

> There were cases of troupes who were banned from performing in certain areas on account of unrestrained flair for social criticisms. Sometimes when their sketches were in bad taste, they were stopped in the middle of the act, chased out, and ordered never to return again. [28]

Such incidents go far beyond any 'safety valve' theory of African theatre allowing a society to maintain cultural continuity through licensed criticism. Rather they illustrate a cultural expression of incipient class conflict.

An analysis of *Alarinjo* over a fairly long time scale shows that the theatre form was closely related to the dialectics of pre-colonial society where the political disintegration of the Yoruba confederation was paralleled by increasing secularization, independence and critical attitude on the part of the *Alarinjo* troupes.

The dialectical nature of *Egungun* and *Alarinjo* theatre, where religious cults and entertainments were influenced by class interest and conflicts, serves as a useful reminder that pre-colonial African theatre was not a simple or static activity. It was not merely a useful escape mechanism for repressed emotion, allowing the traditional society to function in an unchanging way. Nor was it a mere repository of spiritual values defining 'the African personality'. It was an arena which reflected economic and social realities, political changes, shifting power relations and ideological struggle.

The class conflicts were usually disguised by kinship systems, age or sex divisions, religious rituals and other institutions binding pre-colonial society. In many cases these divisions themselves, in so far as they involved exploitation by elders over the young or men over women, indicated incipient class divisions.[29] The point is, the conflicts existed, and African popular theatre played a significant part in bringing latent contradictions into people's field of vision.

In this brief survey I have only examined a tiny fraction of African pre-colonial theatre forms. Narrative drama, funerary drama, initiation rites, spirit possession rites, and many others could just as readily furnish material for analysing the relationships between ideology and theatre. In each of these it would be possible to trace the moments where popular movements resisted or were contained by emerging or declining dominant interests. The often fierce cultural resistance to imperialism which pre-colonial African popular theatre forms made when colonialism was imposed in the late nineteenth century can only be explained by the existence of a popular theatre tradition of resistance to dominant ideologies before European imperialism. The transformation of that tradition of resistance in the colonial period is the subject of subsequent chapters.

Notes

1. For some discussion of this see Echeruo (1981), who denies that African pre-colonial rituals were dramatic, and Emekwe, who asserts that they were. Both papers are conveniently reproduced in Ogunbiyi. The same book has a very useful taxonomy of pre-colonial African theatre terms in A. Horn, 'Ritual Drama and the Theatrical: The Case of the Bori Spirit Mediumship'. Other sources which deal with the subject are de Graft (1976), Owomoyela (1985) and chapter one of Schipper (1982). For an example of an African taxonomy of dramatic categories within one geographic culture see Ahmed.
2. For example Finnegan, p. 516.
3. Onoge has called this the Hamitic theory in which the 'image of the cultures of the black people was one of total inertia'. p. 33.
4. Ottenberg, 1975, p. 140.
5. Rugyendo, 1973, p. 1.
6. Francis, p. 25.
7. Brink, 1978, p. 393.
8. Brink, 1978. p. 386.
9. Francis, p. 26.
10. Brink, 1978, pp. 398-9.
11. Brink, 1977, p. 62.
12. Baumann, p. 306.
13. See, for example, d'Azevedo, 'Gala Society: Sources in Gala Artistry' in d'Azevedo.
14. Farris, p. 325.
15. Imperato, p. 15.
16. Quoted in Graham-White, 1974, p. 19.
17. Ottenberg, 1975, p. 96.
18. Ottenberg, 1975, p. 131.
19. Fischer, p. 16.
20. Ben-Amos and Omorogie, p. 66.
21. Poyner.
22. Schiltz.
23. Adedeji, 1969, p. 61.
24. Thompson, p. 201.
25. Adedeji, 1978b, p. 30. For an extensive account of *Apidan.*, see Götrick.
26. Adedeji, 1978b, p. 39.
27. Adedeji,1978a, p. 64.
28. Adedeji, 1978b, p. 37.
29. I am aware that I have concentrated on male-oriented theatre in this chapter. This is largely because I have highlighted masquerades, which are nearly always associated with male secret cults. There are exceptions, however; the *Makisi* masquerade among the Mbunda people of Eastern Angola and North Western Zambia had two divisions. The male cult, Makishi *Makisi Avamara*, was dominant but during the season of the female cult, *Makisi Avampwera*, women were able to get their revenge on men by performing in masks, satirizing men and attacking them with whips if they approached too near. (Information from Kubik.) Another female masquerade cult is the *Sade* society of Sierra Leone. Much research still needs to be done on such cultural forms (and on others like maize-pounding songs and female initiation rites) to redress the male-dominant tradition of research into pre-colonial African performing arts.

2

Colonialism
&
Theatre

In 1497 Vasco da Gama was exploring the coast of Mozambique. He landed at a point he called Angra de S. Brás where he and his men were met by about two hundred Africans with cattle and other gifts. Da Gama recorded in his diary that the Africans 'began to play on four or five flutes, some high-pitched, some low-pitched, and in concert, playing in a very pleasing manner for Negroes, from whom music is not to be expected, and they danced as Negroes do. And the captain-major ordered the trumpets to be sounded, and we in the boats fell a-dancing and the captain-major along with us ...'[1]

The episode contains elements which curiously foreshadow the future attitudes of whites in their contact with African performing arts. Most notable is the admiration of African music, vitiated by condescension and ignorance; less noticeable is the use of African dance as a mechanism of psychic release and vicarious euphoria. But the temporary cooperation of black and white in the dance (albeit separated by the water between vessel and land) is almost poignantly untypical of later developments. The early contact of da Gama serves as a reminder that there was a very long history of interaction between Europe and Africa (which is often called the informal or mercantilist phase of imperialism) before the imposition of formal colonialism in the late nineteenth century.

I shall be mostly concerned in this chapter with the period of formal colonial occupation, particularly late colonialism, as it provided the 'womb' out of which a negating indigenous theatre was born. All the same it is important to realize that during the period of varied and uneven informal imperialism the increasing dominance of European trading companies and concessions was reflected in a deteriorating image in European minds of indigenous African culture. The da Gama incident points to the relative equality of cultural contact in the earliest phases of European exploration. This gradually changed when the economic imperatives of the slave trade helped to create the myth of African cultural inferiority as a spurious moral

F. Horniman's private ethnographic museum, showing Africana in London, 1891. Horniman is second on the left

The Windybrow Theatre, Johannesburg, showing clear architectural nostalgia for Europe

justification for slavery and unequal exchange of commodities.

European reaction to indigenous performing arts was not one of mono-lithic denigration. Some relatively enlightened travellers and ethnographers such as Delafosse (1916)[2] and Labouret (1928)[3] did appreciate the skills of African performing arts, even though the appreciation was usually bound within the parameters of European theatre models (for example, Labouret's comparison of Mandingo theatre with Aristophanes).[4]

More often, European observers treated Africa either as a *tabula rasa* without any theatrical tradition, or as a source of primitive, atavistically obscene rituals, which indicated its inferiority to the supposed rationalism of European culture. Denigration of African culture led to direct attacks by colonialism on indigenous performing arts. Sometimes the attack arose from colonial ignorance of African theatre's function. Kofi Awoonor gives an example of a British District Commissioner in the Gold Coast who banned indigenous village satirical groups called *Halo* on the grounds that songs between conflicting *Halo* groups were a source of dissension and disorder. Awoonor comments that the District Commissioner did not realize that the *Halo* groups helped stabilize village disorders and that by driving the groups underground he was fuelling the fires of conflict and resistance.[5]

A related vandalism of indigenous African cultural artifacts (including those pertaining to ritual theatre) came about. through colonialists capturing valuable artistic treasures as spoils of victory after military campaigns. These treasures now help fill the museums of Paris, London, Brussels and Lisbon. Perhaps the most famous example of this cultural looting is the Benin bust captured by the British in the campaign of 1897, which became a great attrac-tion in the British Museum and was later adopted in independent Nigeria as the emblem of Festac 77.

The most concerted and ideologically articulate attack on African indigenous performing arts came from the proselytizing zeal of European Christian missions. The missionaries justified their attitude on the grounds that they were struggling against what Charles Beart ironically calls 'all traces of indigenous art linked with paganism and sin'.[6]

The fundamental reason why the Christians were so keen to suppress African performing arts was that they realized cultural forms held the symbolic key to the religious and moral bases of indigenous societies. The driving motor of imperialism was leading to the gradual incorporation of indigenous pre-capitalist African economies into a wider capitalist macro-economy directed from Europe and North America. For this to take place it was necessary not only to break down the pre-colonial political and micro-economic systems but also the legal, religious and cultural apparatus which provided their ideological underpinning. Here, despite intermittent apparently divergent policies, there was a rough correlation between the ends of the missionaries and the colonial administrations. Kofi Awoonor refers to the links between colonial church and state aggression:

> At the instigation of missionaries, political and military administrators led raids that destroyed shrines, holy places and religious programs and systems that were drawing a large body of adherents and then presenting intolerable rivalry to the Church of Christ.[7]

Awoonor perhaps oversimplifies the amount of collusion between missionary and administrator; African history is full of disputes between the two types of colonial intruder. All the same, I believe the long view of colonialism's total trajectory supports Awoonor's analysis.

It was particularly in the period before nationalist politics reached the state of organized resistance to colonialism (very roughly, from the 1920s to the early 1940s, though this varied from one part of Africa to another) that the conflict between the Christian missions and forms of indigenous cultural nationalism constituted the arena where more fundamentally economic or political disputes were played out.

A well-documented example of this is the dispute about female circumcision in the Gikuyu area of Kenya from 1928 to 1931.[8] The practice of female circumcision gave ideological support to a social structure dominated by Gikuyu males. However, the attack on circumcision, led by the militant leader of the Church of Scotland Mission, Dr J. Arthur, did little to expose the exploitative nature of the practice, including, as it did, a wholesale condemnation of the indigenous dances associated with female circumcision ceremonies. Arthur's fanaticism met such strong cultural resistance from the Gikuyu people that even the colonial administration became opposed to Arthur's excesses. The whole conflict, far from being merely a narrow religious or cultural dispute, was ultimately related to the alienation of land in the Gikuyu Highlands by the colonial-backed white settlers throughout the 1920s.

In his novel, *The River Between*, Ngugi shows the strong parallel between the growth of Gikuyu resentment over the colonialists' alienation of their land and the growth of Gikuyu cultural resistance to Christianity.[9] Performing arts such as initiation dances played an important part in this cultural 'renaissance'. It was for this reason that missionaries and Christians (such as Livingstone and the convert Joshua in *The River Between*) were so opposed to what they perceived as the diabolic eroticism of the 'pagan' dances, and why their campaign against them was linked to the wider political and economic oppression of colonialism. The clash was not only between two religious cultures but between two world views. That is why what now may seem apparently trivial disputes about clitoridectomy or alleged obscenity of indigenous Kenyan dances were in fact of vital importance and were related to the clash between a colonial work ethic dominated by puritanical standardization and an indigenous moral code where sexual rituals formed an important part of a communalistic ideology. Elsewhere Ngugi comments, 'The European missionary had attacked the primitive rites of our people, had condemned our beautiful African dances, the images of our gods, recoiling from their suggestion of satanic sensuality.'[10] I would add that, by oversimplifying the conflict and reducing it to the level of sexuality, the missionaries masked the ideological and economic basis of the struggle.

The legacy of that conflict has been passed on to the post-independence period where European stereotypes about the eroticism of African dances affect African performing arts and their entry into the more complex and disguised conflicts which arise with neo-colonialism.

So far I have been concerned with colonialism's assault on indigenous performing arts; now I wish to examine the Western media and theatrical forms which were introduced into Africa to support colonial culture. These media can roughly be divided into a) those which were basically transplants from the European metropolitan culture intended to comfort and reassure the colonialists themselves and b) those which were aimed at manipulating or socializing the indigenous population into the requirements of colonialism and capitalism. Examples of the former are literary drama and, to a lesser extent, radio and cinema. Examples of forms aimed at indigenous Africans were school drama, mission drama and performances designed as imperial propaganda. In some ways the latter were intended to fill the cultural void created by the assaults on indigenous theatre which I have already described.

I wish to deal first with the introduction of formal European literary theatre into Africa. In parts of Africa where a European occupation was established early, some kind of literary dramatic tradition sprang up. *Hamlet* and *Richard II* were performed by seamen off Sierra Leone as early as 1607. Portuguese sailors wrecked on the Natal coast staged a comedy to entertain themselves in 1635, and in 1783 the French troops occupying Cape Town staged *The Barber of Seville*.

Such examples, however, were little more than rather freakish and ephemeral transplants from Europe. During the period of informal colonialism up to the end of the nineteenth century, the expatriate bourgeoisie consisted of army officers, missionaries or traders (whether of slaves or nonhuman cargoes), who had little leisure, were culturally disparate and did not require the elaborate homogenizing ritual which regular play attendance provided.

However, by the end of the nineteenth century in South and West Africa, and by the 1920s or 1930s in East and Central Africa, the imperatives of formal colonialism and the closer integration of the colonial economies with those of the European metropoles required a different colonial culture. European enclaves became established in the new colonial cities centred upon the administration: some parts of Africa had large areas expropriated by white settler farmers. This new expatriate bourgeoisie, though still umbilically attached to the European metropoles, needed to localize that dependence by creating cultural and leisure structures such as sports clubs, theatres and multiple media which would allow it to create on African soil an environment in which the whites could define themselves and their Europeanness in contrast to the black African culture by which they were surrounded.

At this stage the expatriate bourgeoisie felt the need for more permanent theatres as symbols of cultural solidity and superiority. This happened very early in some parts of Africa. In 1800 a theatre (inappropriately titled the African Theatre) was built in Cape Town; a measure of this theatre's prestige-bestowing function was that its first performance was Shakespeare's *Henry IV*. The main bulk of theatre building, however, did not take place till much later in the twentieth century and particularly flourished in those areas most settled by whites, such as Kenya, Southern Rhodesia and the Northern Rhodesian Copperbelt; but 'little theatres', often part of a larger sporting complex, turf clubs, gymkhana clubs and so on, were also to be found wherever a sizeable white enclave existed. In Southern Rhodesia theatre was so popular with white settlers by 1910 that one author was led to believe 'the local population must have spent a considerable amount on theatre seats. Fifteen professional companies went on tour that year.'[11]

The function of this expatriate theatre activity was to increase the white community's sense of solidarity and group cohesion. Stephen Chifunyise underlines in strong terms the racist implications of such theatrical activities in Northern Rhodesia:

> From 1950 the Northern Rhodesia Government and Mining Companies spent a lot of money providing sport and other cultural facilities to the white settlers and white expatriates. Many drama clubs were formed in these white areas ... [which] ... grew to become the strongest colonial establishments to propagate white culture and enforce racial segregational laws in the colony.[12]

The racism observed by Chifunyise was an inherent part of the homogenizing function of the theatre clubs. By the early twentieth century the white communities consisted of quite disparate groups, farmers, soldiers, missionaries, civil servants, medical staff, government extension workers, entrepreneurial traders, teachers, and even, in some parts of Africa, a white artisan or proletarian class. For these disparate elements to cooperate with each other in the control and exploitation of the indigenous African population it was essential to find cultural forms which could cement the links between the different sections and ultimately bind them all to the overriding ideology of the colonial administration.

In the colonial administration and civil service the imperial cadres were predominantly drawn from bourgeois families. But this was not the case for other expatriate white groups, many of whom were drawn from a petty-bourgeois, working-class or (in the Portuguese colonies) peasant background. In order for the sense of white solidarity and superiority to be instilled in such lower-class recruits, recreational informal activities played an important socializing rule in instilling a sense of group solidarity. For the lower-class recruits to colonial life, entry to a theatre club and attending dramatic functions provided a *rite de passage* expressing the process of embourgeoisement.

The type of drama performed in the expatriate theatre clubs was significant. Plays at the colonial 'little theatres' were very rarely from the avant-garde or radical European tradition, but were either pretentious productions from the classical canon, or middle-class domestic dramas. particularly of the kind Opubor acidly dismisses as 'the prim and lacy variety of romantic comedies'.[13] These plays helped to reinforce the safely unquestioning bourgeois norms which played so vital a role in homogenizing colonial society.

Although the main function of the theatre clubs was to help the white expatriate bourgeoisie to define itself, there were examples during the colonial period (particularly when the imperatives of comprador capitalism required the recruitment of a local national bourgeoisie) of black Africans being allowed admission to the previously exclusive theatre clubs. This varied enormously depending on the level of white control over the different parts of the economy and according to the racial policies of the colonial powers.

In South Africa where embryonic apartheid discouraged artistic or social integration those non-whites who aspired to white theatrical culture had to create separate clubs in order to imitate it. One such club was the Bantu Dramatic Society, which was formed in 1933 and whose first performance was Goldsmith's *She Stoops to Conquer*.

In Northern Rhodesia and Kenya, pressure from the aspirant black bourgeoisie during the period before independence led to token admission of blacks to some of the previously all-white theatre clubs. John Houghton gives an example from Northern Rhodesia, during the Federal period of the late 1950s:

> When the Lusaka Theatre Club was staging *Lonely Heart*, which had a part for one black man, they invited Elton Muwowo to take the part and made him an honorary member of the club.[14]

In other parts of Africa, however, such as West Africa, the expatriate community was much smaller and less confidently entrenched. There, the indigenous population was able to participate much more actively in the transplanted metropolitan theatre. This was particularly true of the French colonies, where the system of 'la France d'Outre-mer' encouraged the African *évolués* to join the white theatre clubs. In some urban centres such as Dakar and Abidjan, according to one source, 'the African elite ... performed Courteline or the usual boulevard plays, just as you could see in the municipal theatre of the French sub-prefectures'.[15]

Even in parts of Anglophone West Africa there were cases of Africans imitating the colonial forms of theatre. In nineteenth-century Lagos, the 'repatriate' community of ex-slaves from Brazil, West Indies, Liberia and Sierra Leone played a very important role as an 'escalator' for the conveyance of metropolitan bourgeois values between the small white expatriate community and the indigenous Yoruba aspirant entrepreneurs. Among the cultural fields which the Brazilian repatriates opened up was theatre. Michael Echeruo cites a contemporary Lagos newspaper's account of a performance patronized by both blacks and whites – a 'Grand Theatre' concert by the Brazilian Dramatic Company for Queen Victoria's Jubilee on 23 May 1882, which was described as 'humorous, dramatic and other pieces, songs and performances on the violin and guitar'.[16]

Most of the plays performed by the black Lagos elites were in English, and based firmly on colonial models. They were intended to elevate the status of the audiences to the same level as that of the whites. That the African elites absorbed some of these values can be seen by the efforts of the Ibadan Choral Society, which, according to its secretary in 1886, was 'undertaken with the objective of introducing habits of civilization into our midst'.[17]

From a fairly early period, however, a conflict arose between those elites who identified very closely with white colonial 'civilization', and more petty-bourgeois audiences interested in popular and 'vulgar' forms of theatre. Echeruo quotes contemporary critics expressing the need to 'suppress the enthusiasm of this portion of the audience' (the popular rowdy elements), and to 'elevate the moral and intellectual tone of the masses rather than to pander to low and vulgar tastes'.[18]

Such criticism did not daunt those with 'low and vulgar tastes'. According to Obiechina 'less well-educated teachers, clerks and artisans ... who could not share their elite culture [that of the Lagos bourgeoisie] ... even satirized their Victorian standards by setting up anti-theatres like the Lagos "Melo Dramatic Society" which staged such plays as *Don't Use Big Words*'.[19] This was obviously a retaliation against the anti-African snobbery of the elite, some of whose members referred to African language plays as 'low forms of Heathenism' and to national costume as a 'recurrence of primitive quasi-nudity'.[20]

This tension between borrowed colonial culture and indigenous Yoruba language or values was one of the driving forces which later led to the emergence of Yoruba Opera. Such tensions, however, were not restricted to Lagos or the Yoruba elites. The earliest surviving example of an African literary play text, *The Blinkards,* by Ghanaian dramatist, Kobina Sekyi, adopts a populist stance in opposition to cultural imperialism. Written in 1915, *The Blinkards* offers a complex gradation of social levels among the Ghanaian elites, with representatives of different social classes showing attitudes to Western culture which vary from the militant traditionalism of Nana Katawirwa to the absurdly self-conscious (and unsuccessful) attempts to ape the colonialists by Mrs Brofusem. The central irony of the play is that the character who has been most exposed to Western culture, the lawyer, Onyimdzi (who is clearly the mouthpiece for Sekyi himself), has become totally disenchanted with Western culture and identifies himself with the traditionalists. For that reason he bitterly attacks colonial education in Ghana:

> I believe , at school here, I was more anglicized than I became after I had lived six months in England. By the time I finished my course, I found I had become a Fanti man who had studied and thought in England, rather than an anglicized Fanti, or a bleached Negro.[21]

The Blinkards' use of a mixture of English and Fanti was a very progressive technique, which opened the play up to popular audiences, and was an ideal medium for the cross-cultural satire of the play. No fully-fledged African literary drama grew out of Sekyi's experiment: it was to be nearly half a century before some of his ideas were to be pursued by other dramatists. Nevertheless, isolated examples of literary drama were created during the colonial period, particularly where African intellectuals were assimilated into colonial culture.[22]

The extent to which West African anglophone drama at the turn of the century became accessible to protonationalist sentiments shows how difficult the colonialists found it to control the cultural forms they introduced into Africa. The same was true, to a certain extent, of the multiple media of film and radio drama (television being, with a few exceptions, a post-colonial phenomenon). The original purpose in introducing film and radio was to make ideological links between the colonialists and the core metropoles in Europe. It did not prove easy, however, to keep the multiple media as the preserve of the whites.

Cinema reached Africa very early in the medium's history. One of the earliest 'theatograph' projectors was stolen from the London Alhambra Palace in 1896 and found its way to South Africa. Another early model of projector, the Warwick Bioscop, was imported legitimately to South Africa, and to this day South African cinema audiences talk about going to the Bioscop, or 'Bio'. The first films in West Africa were shown in Dakar in 1900, as part of the massive cinematic assault by the French Lumière company.

The dependency relationship between Europe and Africa was particularly blatant in cinema. Africa was either the object of racist films made by European film companies, or was seen as a dumping ground for the most trivial and irrelevant of Hollywood or European films. The colonial regimes made no attempt to set up an independent cinema industry in Africa. The

The Bantu Dramatic Society's performance of Oscar Wilde's *Lady Windermere's Fan*, Johannesburg, 1934

'Darkest Africa'. Advertisement for Hollywood serial film, set in Africa during the 1950s

only exception to this rule was South Africa, where a fairly flourishing cinema industry was established very early in order to project its specific brand of racism. The first full-length feature film in South Africa was a silent film called *Die Voortrekkers* made in 1916 to glorify the Boers' penetration into the Transvaal. This was followed by *Symbol of Sacrifice* about the British defiance of the Zulus at Rorke's Drift. Needless to say, the Africans in both films were depicted as ignorant barbarians who were obstacles to civilization. The pattern was set for a cinema industry based on disseminating domestic imperialism.

Outside of South Africa (and Arab North Africa), no cinema industry was established. But Africa was a very popular setting for displaying what Hannes Kamphausen calls 'the valiant deeds of the white man, bringing civilization, peace and progress to the savage backlands'.[23] Examples of such films were the British *Palaver* (1926), *Trader Horn* (1931), *Sanders of the River* (1935) and *Rhodes of Africa* (1935) or the French *L'Homme du Niger* (1939) and *Les Hommes sans nom* (1937). The 1930s were the heyday of such films, which were mainly intended for consumption in Europe, and offered ideological justification for the imperialists' presence in Africa.

Like the playhouses, cinema halls in Africa were at first intended for cementing expatriate solidarity rather than for African patronage. Cinema auditoria in the British colonies were particularly exclusive. UNESCO statistics show that in British East Africa between 1948 and 1952 every European went on average to the cinema about forty times per annum, while the average for the African population was once every forty or fifty years.[24] Nevertheless, in the larger towns urbanized Africans did start going to the cinema. In the French colonies the assimilated Africans were accepted in the cinema on a relatively equal footing, and some even managed to join cinema clubs where 'quality' art films were shown and discussed, an unheard-of situation in the British colonies. This difference (along with French intellectuals' more serious attitude to cinema as an art form) may have been a contributing factor to the post-independence phenomenon that several francophone African countries developed struggling but dynamic feature film industries, while they have been almost non-existent in the anglophone states.

Another cause of the dismal state of the film industry in the ex-British colonies was the contradiction which arose during the colonial period between the colonialists themselves and the wider dynamic of capitalism. A significant section of urbanized Africans by the late twenties and early thirties were becoming interested in feature films. The Western multinational film distribution companies and their local comprador agents in Africa (who were often Asians) were happy for the free play of market forces to encourage this audience. But many of the colonial administrators were worried about the Western values contained in the films. They developed a paternalistic policy of protecting Africans from the pernicious influence of Western films. This contrasted with the French colonies where a more *laissez-faire* policy was adopted concerning African exposure to Western films.

Sir Hesketh Bell, whose career included the governorship of Uganda and of Northern Nigeria, provides a striking example of British protectionism. Bell thought that the key to British imperial success lay in the amount of respect it could obtain from the subject peoples. and in 1926 he deplored the showing to 'primitive people ... of demoralising films representing criminal and immodest actions by white men and women'.[25] Such attitudes led to demands for strict censorship of imported films, and a resolution to that effect was passed by the Committee of Colonial Governors in 1930. A strict censorship system was imposed in British East and Central Africa modelled on the one already in operation for the 'Bantu' in South Africa.

A more interesting policy in British colonial Africa was the move to find alternative government-sponsored distribution systems whereby approved Western films could be shown. Film units were established in the Information Departments of countries like Nigeria, Northern Rhodesia and Kenya, with mobile film projection vans for showing films in the townships and villages. For example, during the early 1930s W. Sellers used locally-made educational films as part of a primary health care campaign in Nigerian Medical Health Services.

One of the most ambitious schemes for making films within the British colonies was the Bantu Educational Kinema Experiment (BEKE) established at Vugiri in the Usambara mountains of Tanganyika under the direction of Major L. A. Notcutt and G. C. Latham. Although the ideas for the films came from the Kenyan white ruling class, Africans were consulted about cultural content, and some technicians were trained in production and projection skills.

Notcutt and Latham discovered that there was a conflict between those Europeans who wanted a strictly didactic approach and those like themselves who wanted to mix the didacticism with entertainment. The result was that, during the BEKE tour of East and Central Africa from 1935 to 1937, some of the films like *Tea* (about the cultivation and processing of tea) and *Hides* (about correct methods of tanning) were purely didactic instructional documentaries, whereas others used an element of entertainment. Notcutt and Latham found that the films with a story line were much more popular with the African audiences, which is not surprising considering the close relationship between didacticism and entertainment in the indigenous African aesthetics. Examples of the story films were *Tax* (about the social blessings of taxation) and *Post Office Savings Bank*, which used a folk story format of a foolish man who stores his money in the ground (where it is stolen) and a wise man who banks his money. *Post Office Savings Bank* expresses perfectly the avowed aim of the British colonial film-maker to use the cinema 'to help the illiterate African to adjust to the coming of Western capitalist society with its alien social and economic standards'.[26] The emphasis on the themes of taxation and savings shows the importance which the BEKE gave to the need for the African rural economies to be articulated with the machinery of capital.

In their tour of East and Central Africa, Notcutt and Latham were obviously surprised by the relative sophistication with which some Africans were able to adjust to cinema, and the amount of skill they were able to contribute. They noted with astonishment that at Iganga, in Uganda, Chief Kajumbula Nadiope of Kamuli showed his own 16 mm films, so the BEKE's visit was less than pioneering. They also noted the superb acting skills of a Zanzibari professional actor whom they employed, Shabani bin Yusuf, though commented on the aesthetic problems of trying to transpose his essentially participatory acting technique to the more artificial mechanical demands of cinema acting.[27]

Colonial ethnographic film-
making. Jean Rouch making an
anthropological film in Niger

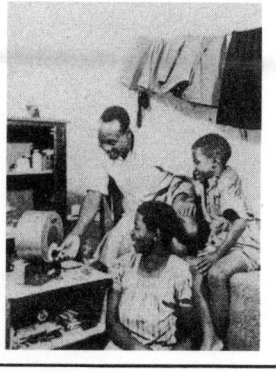

Family listening to Central African Broadcasting
Services on a cheap 'saucepan special' radio

There were other ways in which Africans could participate in the colonial film ventures. One indirect way arose from the method of production and projection. Since the vast majority of popular African cinema audiences did not speak the colonial languages, film-makers carried on making silent movies long after the introduction of sound in European and American cinema. Even when a soundtrack was used it was often simply a musical track with the visuals telling the main story. The idea was that in projection a trained local language 'interpreter' could make a running commentary on the film. Obviously this gave opportunity for considerable creative and sometimes rowdy participation, not only by the interpreter but also by the audiences, to an extent where the intended 'message' of the film was totally transformed. The colonial administrators were fairly oblivious of such 'mis-interpretations', and blithely assumed that their propaganda machinery was effective.

Although the British Colonial Office was keen to expand on the BEKE experiments, the East African governments were either indifferent or positively hostile, mainly because of a profound distaste they felt for any kind of attempt (even of the BEKE's paternalist variety) to integrate the Africans too closely with urbanized art forms.

In general, British colonial film policy suffered from a tendency to link film experiments with the sometimes ephemeral ideological directives arising from changes in the larger dynamic of imperial politics. In 1939, for instance, at a time of colonial insecurity just before the Second World War, the Strand Film Company (London) managed to raise over £4,000 from the Colonial Marketing Board to make *Men of Africa*, a propaganda film praising the benefits of British rule. Smyth comments:

> It was easier to find money for films in defence of the Empire, to counter criticism of British neglect of the colonies, than it was to find money for films as an aid in imperial 'development'.[28]

The opening of hostilities in the Second World War saw a large expansion of film distribution with the formation of the Colonial Film Unit responsible to the Ministry of Information. Its main concern was to explain British war policy to the colonial audiences. Another example of the expediency of British film policy was that the Kenyan government during the height of the Emergency from 1955 to 1956 suddenly increased its number of mobile cinema vans. (Four equipment vans toured the highly sensitive Fort Hall area alone.) The purpose was to use film as a propaganda weapon to win 'the hearts and minds' of the African civilian population. After the Emergency, however, when the cinema vans broke down, they were not replaced. This mixture of paternalism and cynical opportunism was an important factor in the failure of the ex-British colonies to build a viable film industry after independence.

Even in non-British territories, the very nature of colonialism made it difficult for a genuine film culture to emerge among indigenous Africans. As Manthia Diawara says of film-making in the Congo:

> The Belgian officials and missionaries were producing a paternalistic and racist cinema, and in the process they shut out the Zairean as film-maker. Their fetishiza-tion and/or mystification of the technological apparatus prevented them from having a human to human rapport with Zaireans.[29]

As long as Africans were excluded from the technology of film-making they were doomed to be powerless objects of film-making by others – whether liberal or openly racist.

The origins of radio broadcasting in the African colonies were similar to those of film. The primary function was, as Peter Golding summarizes it, to offer 'a service to settler communities, to provide them with news from home, to reaffirm their authority, and to sustain cultural links with the imperial centre'.[30] But, even more than with the playhouses and cinemas, it was not possible to exclude African listeners from tuning into radio programmes. The colonial governments realized the potential of radio as an ideological tool, a fact reflected in the 1937 report to the British Colonial Office by the Plymouth Committee, which envisaged the expansion of broadcasting 'not only as an instrument of entertainment for Europeans ... but also an instrument of advanced administration ... and perhaps not even primarily for the entertainment but rather for the enlightenment and education of the more backward sections of the population'.[31]

The condescending tone of these proposals was close to the Reithian schoolmasterly paternalism which imbued the British Broadcasting Corporation at that time. It is not surprising, therefore, to find that the Colonial Broadcasting Stations which were established in Africa were modelled very closely on the BBC and received almost all their technical staff and recorded material from that source. BBC training schemes for overseas broadcasters (including Africans) started in 1951, thereby exposing African broadcasting cadres to the ideological determinants hidden in the concept of professionalism.

A similar situation existed in the French colonies, except that French broadcasting was even more centralized and tied to the metropolitan Parisian radio company, Société Radiophonique de la France d'Outre-mer, with its training school at Studio-Ecole de Maisons Lafitte.

Like most entertainment programmes during the colonial era, radio drama was imported from the imperial metropoles, though the plays considered fit for Africans were of a restricted type. L. W. Turner and F. A. W. Byron's 1949 Broadcasting Survey of the British West African Colonies concluded that 'The average African's powers of concentration over long periods are limited ... the African likes short plays of the thriller type but not the long drawn-out serial play.'[32] The paternalism which dominated colonial attitudes to Africans as cinema audiences obviously also applied to Africans as radio audiences.

Although the colonial broadcasting cadres had a tight grip on the type of radio programme which was broadcast, there were isolated examples of African broadcasters who wrote or produced radio plays themselves. One of the most interesting examples of these was Andreya Masiye, who was employed as an education officer (and later producer) by the Central African Broadcasting Station (CABS) in Northern Rhodesia. Masiye's motivation to write *Kazembe and the Portuguese* (published as *The Lands of Kazembe*) came from a desire to explore Central African history and explain it in dramatic form to a wide audience. Masiye is one of many examples of authors in the period immediately preceding and following independence who used history plays as a cultural correlative of nationalist sentiments. The play deals with the tribulations of Dr Francis de Lacerda in his attempt to lead a Portuguese trans-Africa expedition in 1798 from the Indian Ocean to the

Atlantic. The source for the play was an English translation of de Lacerda's diary, *Journey to the Lands of Kazembe.*

The irony of having an African author use a white explorer as the main character in a play was matched by the ambiguity of Masiye's attitude to colonial aesthetic and technical influences. On the one hand, Masiye felt he owed a debt to the techniques of BBC radio drama:

> I was greatly aided by the British Broadcasting Corporation's transcripted plays which I quietly studied in the studios of the Central African Broadcasting Station.[33]

On the other hand, Masiye apparently found difficulty in getting local white actors to agree to perform along with black African actors. It was only with the help of a liberal white producer that Masiye eventually managed to assemble his cast. The play caused quite a stir when CABS transmitted it in 1957 both for its mixed cast and for its African authorship; Masiye recalls a Lusaka newspaper headline reading: 'An African Broadcaster Writes a Play!'

The half-heartedness of Masiye's acceptance by colonial broadcasters can be seen from subsequent events. When, in 1962, Masiye made the logical step of defecting from what had become the Federal Broadcasting Service to the United National Independence Party's *Kwacha Ngwee* programme, broadcast from Dar es Salaam, Masiye's scripts in Lusaka (with the merciful exception of *Kazembe and the Portuguese*) were burnt by the Federal authorities. Masiye's experiments with radio drama are a good illustration of the way colonial media and art forms acted as the usually reluctant womb for emergent nationalist dramatic forms.

Another type of radio drama introduced by CABS was the improvised radio play. Michael Kittermaster, the enterprising head of the station in its pre-Federal days, encouraged African artists like Masiye, Alick Nkhata and Edwin Mlungoti to use their oral skills of improvised narrative in the creation of African language plays, mainly on educational topics. One such drama, a Sitonga soap opera called *Malikopo*, was so popular it has been running since the late 1940s, although the actor, Edward Mungoni, who originally created the central character of Malikopo has long since retired. The improvised radio play became a particularly influential form of drama after independence.

Television as a medium was almost unknown in colonial Africa. It was introduced in the period just before independence into those parts of Africa such as Kenya and Northern Rhodesia which were heavily settled by whites. The medium was aimed almost entirely at the white expatriate enclaves and its highly complex technology of transmission helped ensure for the metropolitan countries heavy involvement in the development of television after independence.

The examples I have given of African audiences, and to a lesser extent artists, penetrating those media (theatre, cinema and radio) which were originally aimed at the colonial settlers point to the importance of colonial theatre forms for giving birth to certain types of post-colonial African theatre modes, whether by direct imitation or by dialectical renunciation. For the rest of this chapter I want to concentrate on those theatrical forms which the colonialists aimed consciously at the indigenous population in order to integrate them into imperialist economic or political policies.

One way in which colonialism attempted this integration was by means of rituals designed to dazzle the indigenous populations with demonstrations of imperial pomp such as coronations, jubilees, military parades, boy scout jamborees, or concerts. They were particularly associated with important festivals and anniversaries of great events in the colonial 'mother' country. A comically scathing account of the Empire Day parades held annually in the Gold Coast on 24 May can be found in Kofi Awoonor's novel, *This Earth My Brother*, where he describes Ghanaian schoolchildren enthusiastically singing 'Rule Britannia' and 'The British Grenadiers'.[34] Alfred Opubor describes the function of the Empire Day celebrations as providing 'an occasion set aside by the British government for its colonial subjects to reaffirm their loyalty to the British Crown and rejoice in the knowledge of belonging to that far-flung family, the British Empire'.[35]

A quite different theatrical form produced by a functionally separate component of colonial ideology arose in the field of colonial non-formal education policies. During the period of late colonialism the agricultural sections of imperial administrations embarked on many schemes to involve the indigenous peasantry in cash-crop production of such crops as cocoa, palm-oil, tea, cotton and tobacco. This was part of a much wider imperial thrust to integrate the peasant mode of production more closely with the core economies of the colonial metropoles. The introduction of cash crops effectively made the African peasant economies more dependent on metropolitan capital by means of unequal exchange relations.

The introduction of cash crops was not achieved without considerable resistance from the indigenous peasant productive forces which were quick to notice the increased dependency implicit in the move to 'progressive' farming. The colonial agricultural agencies paid much attention to techniques of communication in order to 'sell' the new ideas. They realized that among a largely illiterate peasantry techniques such as lectures and written explanations had very limited use. Demonstration classes were much more effective. But a few imaginative colonial development officers and extension workers went a stage further by introducing the notion of local-language improvised dramas to reinforce by role play the status and role changes necessary for the transition from subsistence to cash-crop farming. These were colonial embryos of a theatre technique which in the post-independence period was to be called 'theatre for development'.

'Theatre for development' in the colonial period tried to solve a fundamental contradiction in the modes of informal adult education, namely that part of the capitalist dynamic was towards creating a 'modern' or 'progressive' class which could achieve the desired agricultural surplus from cash-crop farming, but another part was to suppress those influences which might create 'cheeky natives' who aspired to equality with whites. This contradiction was particularly strong in British colonial policy, with its non-assimilationist ideology of indirect rule.

To a certain extent, didactic drama helped to gloss over that problem by using elements of pre-colonial performing arts such as dances, songs and narrative motifs to mask the innovative elements in the extension programmes. For example, in Kenya, an agricultural campaign during the 1930s was supported by dramatized versions of indigenous folk-tales. One of the observers, W. H. Taylor, enthused over the way drama could support the work of the Jeans schools by proselytizing for such ideals as 'Better Homes',

'Healthier Children' and 'Better Gardens and Plantations' among 'the pagan population'. Taylor recommended as the most effective medium 'the lecture combined with the propaganda play', which he described as follows:

> The moral or points to be emphasized [in the plays] were always placed in a favourable position by the use of characters personifying animals from native lore. If the object of the play was to teach the value of grainstores, it was the clever Hare who profited by its use and the Hyena who regretted clinging to the old methods; if we were trying to show the value of good management of a village school the poor type of teacher was generally represented by the Monkey or Hyena and the better type by the Hare or the Bee. The acting was burlesque in the extreme and often overdone, but the point or points to be stressed were much discussed afterwards and taken to heart.[36]

Thus the trickster hero, hare, with all his rich mythical resonances from oral culture, was transformed into a progressive farmer. There are complex implications in this use by colonial extension agencies of indigenous performing art techniques. From the agencies' point of view the technique was a kind of 'soft sell' which used an indigenous, didactic aesthetic for functions quite different from those for which it was intended, but which helped to make the alien ideas seem relatively familiar to the recipients. From the African peasant's point of view, his culture was being expropriated by agencies which, however benevolent or well-intentioned were objectively linked to forces of oppression.

The techniques of didactic theatre were not confined to the area of agriculture, but were also applied to other fields of colonial administration such as primary health care, savings and tax collection. In Nyasaland, for example, during the 1930s, a Dr Welch staged plays at Ndirande Welfare Club in Blantyre to back up her primary health care programme, and in 1951 Charles Matinga and the African players staged an inter-racial play, *The False Friend*, encouraging progressive farming methods and use of banks for credit facilities.

Didactic theatre was found particularly useful for breaking down precolonial authority models in African rural areas. The process involved eroding the prestige of traditional authority figures and building up the prestige of civil servants, bureaucrats, teachers or development agents linked to the colonial administration. A. K. Pickering gives an example of this from a 1953 Gold Coast campaign about tax collection, in which a councillor convinces villagers of the usefulness of taxes, finance, health and other development programmes:

> The councillor could tell Kofi on the stage that he was ignorant and reactionary and his influence was a serious hindrance to the development of his village, whereas so to have addressed a village Kofi would have been to court disaster.[37]

The campaign thus used the oblique but powerful ability of dramatic satire to transform the consciousness of an audience by projecting new role models with which they could identify.

In a colonial context, however, this transformation was not one of a radically progressive kind; the relations between the agencies of social change and the African peasantry were vitiated by the exploitative relations inherent in the colonial system. I have commented elsewhere on the manipulative nature of colonial didactic theatre. 'Their messages emerged not from a genuine popular viewpoint, but were imposed by an alien force, one that took from the masses effective instruments of knowledge.'[38] The peasants did not participate in the campaigns, they were the passive objects of a communication system designed to make them conform to strategies pre-planned by remote and manipulative administrators.

Another source for drama during the colonial era was related to the cultural activities of the Christian missions. In those parts of Africa in which Catholic missions were entrenched early there was a tendency for the performance and rituals surrounding religious feasts to take the form of conspicuous consumption, and thereby helped fill the vacuum created by the destruction of those indigenous performances which were also marked by ostentation and display. That was the case in the Portuguese colonies. As early as 1670 there were lavish Festas in Luanda in honour of the Beatification of Francis Xavier. And throughout the eighteenth century there were regular processions and religious plays on the feasts of St Sebastian, Corpus Christi and the Assumption, which proved to be a heavy fiscal burden on the Luanda City Council.[39]

In the French and British colonial systems the missions were closely attached to an ethic of moderation, work and accumulation. Their propaganda was directed at humanizing the myths of Christian religion to make them more accessible to potential African converts and to the already converted. In the Gold Coast they were often associated with annual Thanksgiving services at the end of the rainy season in November. The missionaries thereby showed some subtlety in replacing indigenous rituals which related intimately to the agricultural base of society with Christian rituals of a superficially similar kind.

The favourite topics for dramatization by Gold Coast missionaries were Bible stories such as David, Saul, the Nativity, the Crucifixion, Nebuchadnezzar, the Garden of Eden and the Prodigal Son. In many ways the missionaries seem to have tried to revive the tradition of the medieval European mystery and, to a lesser extent, morality plays. The missions, which maintained a somewhat more intimate contact with the African rural population than the planter and secular colonial cadres, were rather earlier in attempting to indigenize their dramatic efforts. Particularly in West Africa, missionaries saw the psychological advantage of employing converted black African auxiliaries as catechists and ministers to promulgate the Christian faith, and they found them particularly skilful in using dramatic entertainment of a quasi-indigenous kind to sugar the pill of Christian propaganda. These 'mystery' dramas played an important part in the development of the Yoruba Opera.[40]

The most influential medium for the expression of Christian-based theatrical activities, however, was the mission education system This brings me to what is almost certainly the most important state apparatus for the creation of an ideologically motivated theatre in the colonial period, namely the colonial school.

Education in Africa during the colonial period was basically of two kinds, 1) education for the children of the settlers and colonial cadres, which was substantially a transplant of the metropolitan education, with an added dimension of racially conscious elitism, and 2) education for indigenous Africans, which was almost a monopoly of the missions at first, but which the administrations began to cultivate during the period of late colonialism.

In the education for indigenous Africans two apparently contradictory but in fact closely linked educational theories affected the development of school drama. Among the missions, particularly in the French and Portuguese colonies, a theory was early established that a select few 'évolués' or 'assimilados' could be educated up to the level of European children and with syllabuses identical to those found in the 'mother' country; in brief this could be called the 'our-ancestors-the-Gauls' syndrome. The effect on drama was the existence of sometimes ludicrous (but sometimes almost eccentrically brave) attempts to perform pieces from the classical European canon for the annual school play. The tradition of producing Shakespeare in schools was very strong in the British colonies, and its impact on several generations of African intellectuals was considerable. Julius Nyerere has admitted his fascination for the political intrigue found in Shakespeare's Roman plays, and he translated *Julius Caesar* into Swahili. In the French colonies, the schools performed Racine, Corneille and Molière. The comic style of Molière with his satires about the pretentious *nouveaux riches* and their servants was particularly well-suited to a newly emergent indigenous bourgeoisie, and has influenced later generations of francophone African playwrights.

However, a quite different educational theory grew more and more influential during the colonial period, particularly among secular administrators and educationists, by encouraging African pupils to maintain a selective contact with their own culture, and to produce indigenous performances, whether of local dances or original plays.

The earliest dramatic school performances in an indigenous mode were probably initiated less by conscious colonial policy than by a *laissez-faire* attitude of allowing pupils to express their high spirits at end-of-term concerts. There are reports from as early as the 1870s in Lagos of concerts which sounded like a form of vaudeville, with sketches, musical intervals and comic turns, as well as more developed improvised dramas. Michael Echeruo suggests that the school authorities in Lagos even encouraged these highly popular concerts as a way of stimulating enrolment of pupils.[41]

For many schools, concert performances were haphazard, disorganized and rather ephemeral; nonetheless they probably had some impact on the theatrical skills and interests of future African theatre practitioners. In some schools, however, a tradition developed of much more organized and sophisticated African drama, among which should be mentioned Marionhill in South Africa, Achimota in the Gold Coast and, above all, Ecole William Ponty in Senegal.

The colonialists themselves contributed to this strong tradition of indigenous drama under the influence of an educational policy to incorporate traditional pre-colonial cultural forms into extra-curricular and even curricular activities. This was a movement which became particularly strong from the 1920s onwards as a reaction to the increasing number of Westernized educated Africans. The movement pointed to a fundamental contradiction in the development of colonialism. As the productive rural areas of Africa became more closely articulated with the metropolitan core economies a demand grew for semi-educated Africans who could act as clerks, supervisors, teachers, catechists, translators and 'boss-boys', in order to perform the essential task of making the administrative and ideological links between the colonialists and the productive forces. The role of the schools, therefore, was to produce what a French journal described in 1924 as 'reliable auxiliaries in our colonizing work'.[42]

The problem was that many of the semi-educated Africans, once having developed a taste for education, were not content with a mere functional education, but tried to find an advanced education comparable to that achieved by their colonial masters. For such educationally ambitious Africans, those mission schools formed according to the 'our-ancestors-the-Gauls' syndrome provided some kind of answer. It was among this well-educated elite that nationalist sentiments became articulate. The reaction of the colonialists was one of increasing distrust of the newly emergent elite Africans. They felt threatened by the 'cheeky native' with his European suits, his fluency in the colonial language and his apparent airs of cultural equality. Much thought began to be put into an educational policy which would 'keep the native in his place' by retaining his links with the traditional society. The colonialists wanted to create schools which would produce 'the good African', defined by C. T. Loram. a colonial educationist, as 'the native who is proud to be an African, appreciative of the finer elements in his culture, and anxious to accept European culture in so far as it is complementary and supplementary to his own, but quite unwilling to be an imitative or unoriginal white man'.[43]

The impetus towards a practical and more African-oriented education led to the visit of the Phelps Stokes Commission to East Africa in 1923. The practical outcome of the Commission was the establishment of a technical training institute called the Jeans School at Kabete in Kenya, where the pupils were taught technical skills. This became a model for many Jeans schools throughout British-ruled Africa. An important element in the curriculum of the Jeans School was an emphasis on indigenous Kenyan culture as a way of preventing the cultural deracination which the colonialists feared could act as a spur to political ambition. Kenneth King gives an account of a Speech Day programme at the Jeans School, typical of the European and African cultural synthesis; it included a Kikuyu rattle song, a Luo wedding song, praise songs as well as negro spirituals and hymns in Swahili and English. The functional purpose of the performing arts was emphasized by the open-air theatre which was built to stage instructional improvised plays 'as a vehicle of propaganda for health and agricultural improvement'.[44]

It is not at all certain, however, that Phelps-Stokesism was successful. Many of the potential students preferred to go to more elitist mission schools, and even those students who were subjected to the Phelps-Stokes ideology did not become 'good Africans' from the the colonialists' point of view. It is significant that, during the campaign against clitoridectomy by Dr Arthur's Church of Scotland, serious opposition to the campaign came from apprentices from the former Jeans School at Kabete (by that time evolved into the Native Industrial Training Depot). No doubt tho motives of the apprentices were very ambiguous. Their opposition to Dr Arthur's campaign may well have been linked to a male chauvinism which sought compensation for cultural deracination in atavistic aggression towards women's sexuality. All the same, it is interesting to note that the apprentices used their indigenous culture not for conformity to colonial aims, but as a weapon of resistance; the

song which they composed in 1929 (*Muthirigu*) was full of cultural nationalist sentiments and was banned by the Kenyan government in 1930.

The dialectics of colonial cultural policy were equally complicated in the
French colonies. The policy of assimilation created a more identifiably
Europeanized class of African cadres in the French territories than in the
British. In the first part of the twentieth century the policy was seen as a
benevolent aspect of France's 'mission civilisatrice'. This mission was
summarized in Albert Sarraut's book *Grandeur et servitude coloniales* as a duty
'to advance and elevate the primitive peoples to our own standard'.[45]

But by the late 1920s a reaction had set in, and many of the colonial
administrators, like their British counterparts, had become worried about the
deracinating effects of their educational system. A movement similar to
Phelps-Stokesism, but with a Gallic stamp, emerged in the French colonies.
The movement was partly designed to increase the French administrators'
knowledge of their African subjects according to the principle of 'knowing
better, to tame better', but its main function was directed towards the
Africans themselves. In 1933 Governor General Brevié wrote about the need
for African education to have one face 'turned towards France to receive the
light and one towards Africa to capture its energy for action'. The face turned
towards Africa was to prevent too sudden a break with African culture for
the colonized pupils but to allow them 'to approach by degrees this ideal of
a Franco-African culture which shall be the cement of a precise and fertile
relationship'.[46] The difference from the Phelps-Stokes formula was that the
French policy allowed for a gradual evolution towards a semi-European
culture. All the same, in both the French and the British models, the ultimate
aim was the same – to produce efficient auxiliaries in the administration of
their empires.

The new interest in indigenous culture achieved its most famous
apotheosis in the theatrical achievements of the Ecole William Ponty in Gorée
(moved in 1938 to Sebikotane). The William Ponty Theatre has received
lavish documentation in the autobiographical works of its ex-students (Fily
Dabo Sissoko – *La Savane rouge*, 1962, Bernard Dadié – *Climbié*, 1956, and
Boubon Hama – *Katica Nima*, 1968) and critical analysis in, among others,
Bakary Traoré's *Le Théâtre négro-africain*. The Ponty Theatre has a somewhat
disputed paternity. The accepted view is that the theatre was started by an
enlightened French teacher, Charles Beart, in 1933. But Traoré suggests that
Beart only encouraged the drama after witnessing experimental dramatic
improvisations by Dahomean students at the school.[47]

Whatever the origins of Ponty drama, the theatrical performances were
supervised by Beart and other French teachers, and were created within a
colonial ideological matrix. Many of the plays at Ponty were created as part
of ethnographic research into the rural cultures of the students, but they were
encouraged to reproduce a 'folk' culture which was 'the closest to European
taste', thus contributing to that taste for exoticism which was to become so
marked a feature of the relations between African performers and European
audiences.

The Ponty drama achieved such standards of technical polish that it was
sent to the Exposition Coloniale of Paris in 1937 (Traoré drily calls this the
'ultimate consecration' of the Ponty Theatre).[48] At the Théâtre des Champs-
Elysées in Paris, the students performed two plays, a tragedy called *Sokame*

and a comedy, *Les Prétendants rivaux*. The plays were a great success, but inevitably the French critics slotted them into the predetermined aesthetic categories of the grand European literary tradition. They compared *Sokame* to *Iphigenia* by Euripides and *Les Prétendants rivaux* to Molière. More popular with the French audiences, however, were the ethnic dances and sanitized ethnographic folklore samples, which played an influential part in establishing the post-war Parisian taste for exotic 'folklorized' African cabaret performances.

I am not suggesting that the Ponty drama was a completely negative achievement. The fact that skilful playwrights like F. J. Amon, Keita Fodeba and Bernard Dadié received their dramatic apprenticeship there says much for the formulative role played by the Ponty Theatre. What I am suggesting is that at the time the Ponty plays were limited by the colonial ideology within which they were forced to operate. Whether it was due to interference from French teachers (and Traoré testifies that they censored the plays) or to an introjected subservience to colonialism by the pupils, many of the plays served to belittle African history and culture and to glorify the role of the French colonialists. This was particularly noticeable in the history plays. For example, in 1936, Guinean boys at Ponty produced a play called *L'Entrevue de Samory et du Capitaine Péroz*, which was about the resistance of the Guinean leader, Samory, to the French army in the late nineteenth century. The play presents Samory as a childishly impulsive but cruel savage who is forced to sign a peace treaty in 1887 with the French forces under Péroz. At the signing Péroz makes a haughtily magnanimous speech which is blatant propaganda for France's 'mission civilisatrice':

> France certainly wants to reconfirm your authority over the Sofa states which you have grouped together, but she also wants their people to enjoy peace and the fruits of their labour.[49]

In the ethnographic sketches the main thrust of the satire was towards belittling indigenous cultural forms. For example, *Un Mariage au Dahomey* of 1934 satirizes African marriage customs, and in *Triomphe du griot* a progressive intellectual, Justin (culturally akin to the Pontins themselves), morally defeats the stereotypically backward and superstitious 'féticheur'.

It was this kind of client theatre which caused Traoré to complain that the Ponty drama was cut off from the aspirations and struggle of the African masses:

> It should be noted that, paradoxically, the William Ponty theatre often attacks native customs: this type of theatre cannot hope to find a response among the masses ... Thus, a rupture occurs. In fine, the Francophone theatre, by cutting itself off from the masses, becomes merely a class theatre.[50]

Traoré points to the way the Ponty drama conformed to the ideological demands of the French colonial system, which, according to Brevié, the Governor General of Administration d'Outre-mer Français, were to persuade the indigenous Africans 'to link themselves to their place in French life' and to prepare 'the producers and the consumers of tomorrow'.[51] These ideological needs and their impact on several generations of francophone African elites had powerful repercussions on African theatrical cultural forms even after the attainment of independence.

The Ponty Theatre's heyday was in the 1930s, but it continued to exist until in 1948 Ecole William Ponty was upgraded to follow the full French baccalaureate syllabus, with a subsequent demise in ethnographic and cultural pursuits.

In all the different media and dramatic forms which I have examined, the more liberal or far-sighted colonial teachers, radio producers, theatre administrators and extension workers realized the need for encouraging indigenous talent and theatrical forms to satisfy the emergent African cultural nationalism. Though many must have resisted such cultural nationalism, others must have realized the inevitable collapse of strictly political colonialism, and therefore prepared the way for that informal ideological hegemony (often called cultural imperialism) which was to help tie the newly independent African nations to their former colonial masters.

One of the results of the Ponty Theatre's success in Europe was the stimulation of interest in African traditional drama as a source of titillating exoticism for European audiences. Following the Ponty Theatre's 1937 visit to Paris several African folk-dance troupes created by assimilated Africans were established briefly in Paris. Although the Second World War interrupted their activities, they re-emerged after the war and enjoyed considerable popularity.

Christian Valbert describes such performances as 'a tawdry folklore for a public uninformed, yet thirsty for exotic follies after the tension of the war'.[52] This 'negro-guignol' theatre distorted the indigenous African dances to make them conform to European stereotypes of exotic savagery or reified physical grace. Some of the groups tried to avoid stereotyping in an attempt to create a more authentic African drama, the most successful of which was Le Théâtre Africain founded by ex-Ponty dramatist Keita Fodeba. But even Fodeba could not control the misguided enthusiasm of Parisian admirers like Anna Seghers:

> This is the real Africa, the fresh and exquisite spirit of a people wonderfully graceful in gesture and movement, where the body is expressive in its very outline, where all music is rhythm and every word a melody.[53]

Such criticism indicates the ease with which theatrical modes of negritude could be co-opted and depoliticized through a process of exoticization.

Although the vogue for folk-dance troupes faded in Paris, the genre of 'negro-guignol' theatre had a powerful influence on the folklore troupes aimed specifically at European tourists, which were established in many African countries after independence.

What this chapter has tried to show in diverse dramatic media during the colonial period in Africa is the establishment of theatre forms intended to provide ideological ties between the metropolitan cores ('mother countries') and the colonial expatriate bourgeoisies on the African continent. But, as the pre-capitalist modes of production became more closely articulated with the metropolitan international capital and more dependent upon it, the need increasingly arose for educated indigenous administrative and professional cadres, a trained petty bourgeois class and an entrepreneurial group of progressive farmers and petty commodity traders. It was precisely these groups which both provided the leadership for the nationalist movements leading to African independence in the 1960s and which continued after independence to provide the links with international capital. Parallel to these developments, on the cultural level in the two decades leading up to independence the colonialists started to allow and in some cases to encourage indigenous African performing arts within the limits of colonial cultural forms, as part of a general attempt at ideological rather than political control of the nationalist bourgeoisie.

The outcome was the gradual creation of two separate cultures, which Oyin Ogunba calls the 'indigenous' and the 'borrowed'.[54] Theatre was an important contributing force to that cultural split. Bernard Mouralis commented on the contribution the Ponty Theatre made to the creation of two opposing cultures in francophone Africa:

> With the theatre of William Ponty a division appeared, already clearly perceived by the masses – a traditional culture in the villages or 'culture of poverty' in the towns – and a culture which addressed itself to a select group, and which tended to consider itself the only extant culture worthy of the name.[55]

Taking due note of numerous fissures and subdivisions within and between the two cultures, my task in the rest of the book is to chart some of the contradictions in the developments of African theatre as a result of the dialectical relationship between the 'indigenous' and 'borrowed' cultures, and to trace the revitalization of indigenous popular theatre.

Notes

1. Da Gama, pp. 6–7.
2. See Valbert, p. 238.
3. Labouret and Travelé.
4. Cornevin, p. 28.
5. Awoonor, 1972, p. 40.
6. Quoted in Bakary Traoré, 1972, p. 40.
7. Awoonor, 1975, p. 28.
8. Rosberg and Nottingham, chapter four.
9. Ngugi wa Thiong'o, 1977.
10. Ngugi wa Thiong'o, 1972, p. 32.
11. Weare, p. 65.
12. Chifunyise, 1978, p. 39.
13. Opubor, p. 38.
14. Chifunyise, 1978, p. 13.
15. Mouralis, p. 38.
16. Echeruo, 1977, p. 73.
17. Echeruo, 1981, p. 361.
18. Echeruo, 1981, p. 367.
19. Obiechina, p. 11.
20. Echeruo, 1981, p. 367.
21. Sekyi, p. 59.
22. Some highlights of African play-writing during the colonial period are J. E. Dhlomo, *The Girl Who Killed to Save* (South Africa 1935), originally written in Zulu, and two Ghanaian plays from the 1940s, *The Third Woman* by J. B. Danquah and *The Fifth Landing Stage* by E. K. Fiawoo. The other major play-writing school – the drama of Ecole William Ponty – is dealt with later in this chapter. For further information on Dhlomo, see Couzens.
23. Kamphausen, p. 30.
24. Kamphausen, p. 24.
25. Smyth, 1979, p. 438.
26. Smyth, 1979, p. 442.
27. Notcutt and Latham, pp. 75–7.
28. Smyth, 1979, p. 449. For information on post-war cinema in Central Africa see Smyth, 1983, and Kerr, 1993.
29. Quoted in Malkmus and Armes, p. 22.
30. Golding, p. 294.
31. Quoted in Golding, p. 294. For extensive coverage of Western films about Africa, see Cameron.
32. Quoted in Golding, p. 294.
33. *The Lands of Kazembe*, was published by NECZAM, Lusaka, in 1973. This and the subsequent information is from an introduction submitted by the author but not published. I am grateful to the author for permission to quote from it here. For an

interesting account of Masiye's broadcasting career, see his autobiography, *Singing for Freedom* (1977).

34. Awoonor, 1972, p. 39.
35. Opubor, p. 9.
36. Quoted in Kamlongera, 1986, pp. 37–8.
37. Quoted in Graham-White, 1976, p. 65.
38. Kerr, 1981, p. 150.
39. Boxer, p. 137. For information on another kind of drama introduced by Portuguese missionaries, the semi-literary, *autos* (one-act Catholic mystery plays) in São Tomé Principe and Angola, see Moser.
40. See Chapter Five.
41. Echeruo, 1977, p. 54.
42. Quoted in Warner, p. 105.
43. Quoted in King, p. 157.
44. King, p. 157.
45. Quoted in Warner, p. 105.
46. Quoted in Warner, p. 107.
47. For the two views, see Bakary Traoré, 1971, and Sabatier.
48. Traoré, 1971, p. 49.
49. Quoted in Warner, p. 109.
50. Traoré, 1972, pp. 72–3.
51. Mouralis, p. 33.
52. Valbert, p. 39.
53. Quoted in Traoré, 1972, p. 38.
54. Ogunba, p. xiv.
55. Mouralis, p. 36.

3

The Reaction of Indigenous African Theatre to Colonialism

A widely accepted model of cultural imperialism in Africa is one which suggests that colonialism had a totally deracinating effect on indigenous culture with the result that forms of pre-colonial theatre were suppressed. Traoré makes that assertion: 'With colonization African theatre is cut off from its ancestral source.'[1] Most existing books on African theatre tend to reinforce this image. In Traoré's *Le Théâtre négro-africain*, Graham-White's *The Drama of Black Africa*,[2] Banham's *African Theatre Today*[3] and Cornevin's *Le Théâtre en Afrique noire*[4] there exists one chapter on pre-colonial theatre, and in Graham-White's meticulously researched book that chapter (on what he calls traditional drama) is particularly rich in aesthetic insights. But even with Graham-White, and certainly with the others, an almost teleological perspective is applied to the impact of colonialism, so that it seems part of an inevitable evolution towards major modern post-colonial forms of literary theatre. The assumption is that pre-colonial theatre somehow withered away after the introduction of Western theatre forms. Graham-White and Banham do devote considerable space to popular syncretic forms of theatre like Concert Party and Yoruba Opera, but even there a tendency exists to deal with them more for their influence on literary drama than as vital dramatic forms in their own right.

I believe there are dangers in an evolutionary perspective of African theatre which sees pre-colonial and syncretic forms of theatre logically progressing into the more 'developed' forms of literary drama. This misconception is a kind of aesthetic version of modernization theory in political economy, which links African development to Westernization and modernization. I would not go so far as to stretch the analogy by asserting that literary drama has 'underdeveloped' indigenous forms of theatre (though there might be some truth in such a model). Rather, I would suggest that a popular non-literary theatre consisting partly of adapted pre-colonial paradramatic forms and partly of more innovative syncretic dramas has asserted itself fairly independently of literary theatre and the multiple media.

In a paper on Zambian culture I borrowed Raymond Williams' terms of 'dominant' and 'residual' cultures to describe the opposition between an indigenous African aesthetic and the imposed (or borrowed) neo-colonial culture.[5] Although the contrast is useful, I now feel that 'residual' contains unfortunately passive overtones, reminiscent of economic 'dualism theory', with its rather depressing image of an African culture (like its economy) abjectly dependent on the skills of capital and neo-colonial culture. There are, it is true, examples of peasants' and workers' theatre showing an apparently passive dependence on colonial or capitalist culture, but, as I hope to show, there are other examples of an emergent resistance to it.

It is rather ironic that the notion of pre-colonial theatre's annihilation should exist in theories of African drama, when one of the methodological problems of investigating pre-colonial theatre is precisely the need to extrapolate an 'authentic' model for indigenous theatre free from the extant distorted or impure versions tainted by colonialism and urbanization.

One reason why pre-colonial theatre may seem to have withered away is that many of the scholars who write about it do so with an understandable elegiac tone of regret for the passing of richly complex artistic forms. This regret appears in official post-independence cultural policies. For example, the Intergovernmental Conference on Cultural Policies in Africa, which met in Accra, Ghana, in 1975, passed resolutions aimed at preserving African performing arts, because it viewed 'with alarm the rapidity with which many of the finest forms of African music and dance are disappearing from everyday life as a result of social transformation.'[6]

The elegiac chord is also struck by academic researchers. A good example is P. André Vrydagh's article on the *Makisi* masquerade theatre among the Mbunda of North Western Zambia.[7] Vrydagh notes the ritual function of *Makisi* as an ancestral masquerade performed during a boys' initiation ceremony known as *Mukanda*. Vrydagh observes the devastating effects of the modern cash economy on *Makisi*; modernization causes difficulty in finding experienced initiators and corresponding truncation of the time required for the *Mukanda* ceremonies. The decline of *Mukanda* has aesthetic implications. Vrydagh comments that the elaborate and beautifully decorated costumes of the *Makisi* are no longer made out of the authentic sisal and dyed with pigmentations from the *munyumbe* and *munjongolo* trees, but are made from cotton and decorated with artificial dyes. Moreover, fewer masks are made and the manufacturing skills are declining. Vrydagh says the costumes 'are knitted so loosely and are so badly joined that the dancer's skin is easily visible, violating the concept that the *Makisi* are the ancestors'.[8] He concludes, 'In 1969 the *Makisi* of the Old Mbunda were in an advanced state of disintegration'.[9]

Similar regret for the decline of masquerade theatre is expressed by Ottenberg in his study of the Nigerian Afikpo masquerades[10] and by Adedeji for the Yoruba *Alarinjo* theatre.[11] For expatriate academics like Ottenberg and Vrydagh, the motivation to lament the decline of pre-colonial African theatre may sometimes be related to a psychological escapism, a quest for a romantic unobtainably pristine 'pre-industrial culture' (the 'back-to-the-womb' syndrome which Mphalele refers to). For an African academic like Adedeji, the elegiac stance is very understandable. There is enormous poignancy at witnessing one's own vital, complex and rich culture being destroyed in a few generations.

Makisi masquerade of the Mbunda people, with toes showing through the sisal costume

But there is another temptation for African academics – that of 'Golden Ageism' (Adedeji refers in one article to 'the Golden Age of the Oyo empire'.)[12] The danger is that in emphasizing the achievements of pre-colonial theatre it is easy to underestimate the achievement of indigenous African theatre after its 'contamination' by colonialism. Adedeji's case is particularly interesting, because he notes that one reason for the decline of the *Alarinjo* theatre is the ascent of a more popular urbanized syncretic theatre, the Yoruba Opera, and that many of the skills and techniques of *Alarinjo* have contributed to the Yoruba Opera.

I could suggest (at the risk of sounding presumptuous) that the re-channelling of aesthetic energy noted by Adedeji into forms of popular theatre which have been modified to suit the changing world is worthy of support and intellectual enquiry rather than indulging in hopeless hand-wringing about lost dramatic treasures. Vrydagh, for example, notes that although the aesthetic quality of *Makisi* has declined (applying the ritualistic criteria inherent in *Mukanda*), nevertheless the theatre itself is fairly flourishing as a semi-commercial entertainment. 'Old Mbunda men dance *Makisi* only at social occasions held by wealthy persons and are paid for their performance.'[13] It would be possible, I believe, to make a study of modern *Makisi* (particularly outside the Mbunda region), using modified aesthetic criteria, which would show the theatre's transformation into a vehicle portraying class formation, the Mbunda people's contact with the neighbouring dominant Lozi people, and ultimately its articulation with the wider cash economy of Zambia.

The note of regret for lost skills struck by the cultural spokesmen of independent African governments and by Africanist scholars is similar to the elegiac tone found in much African literature on the subject of disappearing African dance. The poetry of Leopold S. Senghor is, of course, a celebrated example, with its use of rhythm as a category powerfully demarking an inherent black genius and with its nostalgia for dances observed in his childhood, expressive of an almost prelapsarian innocence.

> I remember the dance of the girls who are ready
> for marriage. The choruses at the wrestling ...
> Oh! the young men in the final dance bodies.[14]

The convergence of Senghor's poetic iconology of African dance with the views of academic researchers and apologists for government cultural policies points to what I feel is a fundamental weakness in the elegiac attitude to African pre-colonial theatre forms. Frantz Fanon, in a vigorous and very valuable section of *Wretched of the Earth* points to Negritude's inability to reflect the changes in conciousness which take place during the struggle against colonialism. Fanon is particularly acute in showing the danger of reifying and romanticizing the concept of 'tradition':

> When a people undertakes an armed struggle or even a political struggle against a relentless colonialism. the significance of tradition changes ... during the period of struggle traditions are fundamentally unstable.[15]

Fanon goes on to give a timely warning that intellectuals are often for this reason out of date, having been unable to keep up with the changing culture of the masses. I believe that Fanon's perspective on tradition applies very much to study of pre-colonial theatre forms. Some performing arts appear to have changed very little, whereas others have change considerably under the impact of colonialism and it is the duty of the researcher into African theatre to chart those changes (even where they seem accompanied by aesthetic decline) rather than, as Taban Lo Liyong bluntly puts it 'crying over spilt milk'.

One of the pre-colonial performing arts which was able to adapt very easily to the new social roles demanded by colonialism was the spirit possession dance. In the pre-colonial era spirit possession dances were a form of physical and/or mental therapy by which a spirit medium attempted to cure his/her patient by means of extended dancing in the course of which both patient and doctor were possessed by powerful spirits. These spirits might be ancestral forces, indigenous to the community, or what I. M. Lewis calls peripheral spirits, belonging to ethnically alien groups.[16]

It was particularly the alien spirits which allowed possessed persons to use their psychological affliction as a means of protesting against injustice. For example, in both pre-colonial and post-colonial Africa it has been common for women to become possessed at times of marital crisis (such as upon being widowed, or when a husband takes a second wife) as a way of focusing attention on the causes of the affliction. Such possession became a socially permitted form of sexual protest.

It was not difficult for the inbuilt elements of protest and responsivness to innovation to interact with the forces unleashed by colonialism and modernization. This was especially true of peripheral possession, where the patient was temporarily absorbed by an alien spirit. Duerden comments:

> Possession by the spirit of a successful foreigner thus indicates that the profits of societal changes realised by intrusive foreign innovations may be placed at the disposal of the society's members.[17]

During the early contact between the European colonizers and the rural peoples of Africa, it was fairly natural for spirit mediums to include Europeans as powerful foreign spirits to be absorbed by patients. Thus, among the Chopi of Southern Mozambique, spirit possession, before heavy colonial contact, was usually by alien African spirits such as the Ngoni or Ndau, but by the 1920s they also included such eclectic powers as Indian merchants, Jewish storekeepers, Portuguese farmers and Roman Catholic priests.

Much research needs to be done on the way in which capitalist values penetrated the psyche of African rural peoples., to transpose them into peasants. I would suggest that acceptance of European status symbols in paradramatic rituals marked a significant stage in the psychology of 'peasantization'. Elizabeth Colson gives an example of European status symbols aspired to in the *masabe* spirit possession dances of the Tonga from Southern Zambia and Northern Zimbabwe. She notes that 'the desires of the *masabe* include dress, food, special luxury goods, status symbols and ceremonious forms of dress'.[18] She also gives the example of *mangelo* dances performed during *masabe* rituals in which the performers' songs bragged about the high quality of skirts manufactured in Britain. Such performances performed a dual function: from the point of view of the existing Tonga culture they acted as ways of absorbing or psychologically controlling the alien cash economy with which the Tonga were becoming articulated, but from capital's point of view the performances acted as rituals of immersion by Tonga peasants into consumer mentality.

A similar example is given by John Beattie of spirit possession among the Bunyoro of Western Uganda:

> Through the cult ... Bunyoro can cope in ritual and dramatic if not in 'practical' terms with the new and alarming forces of social change ... Europeanness could be manifested in the familiar idiom of the traditional culture, and so could be accommodated and come to terms with. [19]

Beattie's example makes clear the limitations of this dramatic mimicry of colonial power. The spirit medium who invokes European spirits is far from being a revolutionary artist; rather we should see such mimicry as an initial and rudimentary technique of psychic adjustments which was capable of being transcended by more complex and combative forms of African popular theatre as Africans became more class-conscious.[20]

Not all spirit possession affected by colonialism dealt with the absorption of 'Europeanness'. Sherilynn Young notes that among the Chopi, spirit possession was closely related to the economic situation of women who had become the main agricultural workforce, owing to the absence of men as migrant labourers in the South African sub-metropole. In this distorted economy 'the cults extended to feature dramatizations of the sins committed by men at the mines, sometimes naming the men, and they dramatized the roles of the housewife, the chief, the gold-miner and the pedlar'.[21] The Chopi example, much more than those of the Tonga and Bunyoro, shows an indigenous dramatic form adapting to the quite new role models thrown up by the distortions introduced into African economies and societies by colonialism and capitalism. Of particular interest is that the female possession cults abrogated traditional male chiefly fertility rituals, but adapted them to a context of capital/labour relations, reflecting the increased responsibility which female commoners had achieved in Southern Mozambique.

Spirit possession dances, therefore, as with many other pre-colonial performing arts. seem to express an ambiguous attitude to modernity and the cash nexus. Some examples, like the Tonga and Bunyoro, may have the spirit medium invoking European or modern spirits as a symbol of power, while in others, like the Chopi, there may be a critique of the changes brought about by modernity. Ottenberg gives an example in masquerade theatre of rejection of modernity. He describes an all-male Afikpo play which is almost the inverse of the Chopi example just cited. The Afikpo play satirizes a woman who in real life was a midwife and who had started a club for 'progressive' women, much involved in trade and the cash sector. The play shows obvious signs of insecurity on the part of the male performers, who caricatured the woman as a Europeanized anti-traditionalist. In the play she breaks a taboo of secrecy about male initiation ceremonies, the revelation of which leads to the purging of her 'humour', expressed though a tearful repentance. The women's hubris relates mainly to male/female conflicts, particularly male resentment of the combined women's attempt to obtain maximum material advantage from the festival. However, it is also possible to see elements of an incipient conflict between a communalistic ethos and a vigorous, commercial materialism.[22]

Many adaptations of pre-colonial art forms in a colonial context display resistance by peasants to capital's penetration into a pre-capitalist economy. One form of indirect resistance was for peasants to pour aesthetic energy into

Odwira festival, Ghana

Satirical *Apidan* masks of European District Officer and his wife

festival drama, that is, theatre performances associated with local celebrations, especially for commemorating historically significant events like the crossing of a river, the inauguration of a town, or divine blessings bestowed on a lineage. The conspicuous consumption displayed by peasant participants in festival drama frequently puzzled and irritated colonial authorities, who were trying to instil a puritan ethic of cash saving and capital accumulation. Oyin Ogunba gives a good example of festival drama serving to consume surplus wealth. He describes how in the Yoruba festival at Ondo in honour of the god Ogun:

> A middle-aged chief who wants to draw attention to himself, or a young rascal-about-town who has some money to spare may decide to do something spectacular during the festival like building a fantastic costume for himself and marching about like a prima donna.[23]

This was not a simple case of festival participants indulging in the pleasure principle rather than the work ethic. To some extent the ostentation may relate to existing pre-colonial traditions of conspicuous consumption among the Yoruba aristocracy. There may have been additional motives, however, in that the festival revellers were probably willing to work hard for their own food needs but were unwilling to create a surplus, most of which would be extracted from them by the machinery of unequal exchange relations.

The rationale of ostentatious surplus-consuming drama is related to the social needs of the community. Capital's penetration into Africa often preserved the pre-capitalist economic and social formations but attempted to extract its surplus wealth by a complex system of articulations with the colonialist economy (including hut tax, forced labour and patronage). According to Arrighi and Saul:

> Peasants still largely involved in a pre-capitalist mode of production are likely to have a strong preference for present consumption and often for unproductive accumulation. which by maintaining or strengthening social cohesion, preserves the security offered by the traditional system.[24]

This helps to explain the African peasant's notorious reluctance to become involved in capitalist ventures; it was a form of indirect resistance to exploitation and to the destruction of indigenous social cohesion. Popular festival theatre played a role in resisting the penetration of capital and its alienating social values.

Despite the potential for resistance in dramatic forms like festival drama and spirit possession dances it was of a rather spontaneous kind lacking in self-consciousness. It is not easy to find examples of pre-colonial theatre forms articulating strong self-awareness at the penetration of mercantile capital into African economies. This is because that penetration was usually disguised by colonialism's exploitation of existing economic, social and cultural forms. Cultural resistance in drama requires easily identified roles for denunciation, parody or satire.

One colonial apparatus which provided easily identified roles was that of the Christian missions. The clerical garments, distinctive religious language, the alien Christian ethics and iconology, and most of all the close contact which proselytizing missions had with even remote African communities made them convenient butts for stereotyping and satire. I have already referred to the way Chopi women from Mozambique caricatured Catholic priests; similar examples of dramatic parody of missionaries are found in masquerade theatre among the Igbo, Akan and Yoruba. Ottenberg gives an example of an Afikpo skit about a white Ibibio mask being used to represent a Catholic priest 'holding a prayer book and mumbling in English'.[25] The satire is pointed by the suggestion that the Catholic father is greedy and hypocritical.

What I would like to do is deal with one particular example of anti-Christian satire at length – the *Gule wa Mkulu* male masquerade of the *Nyau*, found among the Chewa from Malawi, Eastern Zambia and bordering areas of Mozambique. According to Matthew Schoffeleers the *Nyau* cult can be traced back to a Stone Age hunting and gathering economy in the first millennium AD.[26] The *Gule wa Mkulu* dance associated with it is divided into daytime performances and nocturnal dances. The nocturnal performances were full of ritual significance. Zoomorphic figures such as elephant, antelope and lion danced with ancestral spirits in a symbolic re-enactment of a creation myth, dealing with a prelapsarian harmony between animals, man and God, before it was destroyed by man's original sin in inventing fire. At the political level the cult also expressed an anarchic ideology of fissure by commoners from the centralized authority of chiefs, particularly during July/August after the harvest. At the kinship level *Nyau* expressed ritualized male revolt against the matrilineal Chewa marriage customs. Although *Gule wa Mkulu* had very serious ritual features during its performances at chiefs' funerals and girls' initiation ceremonies, it also developed (like Yoruba *Egungun* performances) considerable comic elements through the presentation of masquerade stereotypes such as the old man, the syphilitic and the drunkard. The stereotypes were extended to outsiders such as the Arabs, who were satirized in the *Gule wa Mkulu* performance among the Mang'anja, a group which had considerable contact with Arab slave-traders.

It was this element of stereotyping which became dramatically powerful in *Nyau*'s resistance to Christian missions. Linden and Schoffeleers explain how the Christian missions in Nyasaland, particularly the Roman Catholic (which had their own iconographically vivid rituals), were vehemently opposed to *Nyau*.[27] The reason for Christian opposition was partly one of prurience, an objection to male *Nyau* performers dancing naked at night in front of women, and partly a political hunch that *Nyau* societies formed centres of resistance to colonial rule.

An important element in *Nyau*'s resistance to Catholic missions was the parodying of Catholic religious iconography in the *Gule wa Mkulu* performances. Linden and Schoffeleers give the following description of anti-Christian *Nyau* satires:

> In order to reduce the mystique of the Catholic cult costumes were invented for key Christian figures such as the Virgin Mary, Joseph and St Peter. 'Maliya' portrayed a white woman with pronounced breasts, made of 'magwebe' [fruit of a type of palm] an animal tail for hair and red complexion, carrying a baby. The figures 'Josephe' and 'Simon' also imitated Europeans with red faces.[28]

These Christian stereotypes were mocked through obscenely sexual or scato-logical songs. One irony of these parodies was that the very charge of impropriety which the Christians made of the *Gule wa Mkulu* theatre was

Nyau 'Simon' mask, in action during a Gule wa Mkulu performance at Tembuna village, near Chipata, Zambia, July 1975

The British Prince of Wales inspecting an animal mask from the Gold Coast in 1925

turned back upon the missionaries themselves. For the Chewa, the apparent obscenity of the naked *Nyau* dancers was in fact not obscene within its ritual context, but the behaviour of European couples in kissing or publicly holding hands was considered obscene. The satire of 'Maliya' and 'Josephe' incorporated this absurdly improper European behaviour. A Zambian researcher, Mapopa Mtonga, comments:

> Yosefe may at one stage stand up and try to touch her [Maliya's] 'breasts' at which phase Maliya will simulate annoyance or pretend to be as docile as the girl who has just graduated from *chinamwali*. When the dance is over the two lovers once more walk hand in hand.[29]

The impact of these satires was not merely at the ideological level; they were backed up by more direct opposition to the missions. In Nyasaland the *Nyau* leaders' decision to change the cult rules by allowing initiation of pre-pubertal boys into the society had a devastating effect in the late 1920s on the enrolment of boys into Catholic mission schools. In parts of Northern Rhodesia *Nyau* societies reinforced the boycott of Christian schools by, as Mtonga puts it, 'banning of such items as books, papers or pencils which were considered as symbols of Christianity and Colonialism'.[30]

The interest of the cultural counter-offensive by the *Nyau* cult lies not only in its material success in hindering mission proselytization, but also in its use of drama to 'conscientize' the audience members about the alien nature of colonialism.

Missionaries were not the only colonial agents, however, to be represented in indigenous African satires. The European's very whiteness made him an unusual and therefore mockable subject for inclusion in the masquerade system of stereotypes, whether the European was explorer, missionary, soldier, policeman, nurse or extension officer.

A measure of the speed with which African satirists were able to create stereotypes of the white man can be seen in the visit of the explorer, Clapperton, to the Yoruba King Mansola of Oyo in 1825. Mansola arranged a command performance of *Egungun*. Clapperton's celebrated account is as follows:

> The third act consisted of the white devil. The actors having retired to some distance in the background, one of them was left in the centre, whose sack falling gradually down, exposed a white head, at which the crowd gave a shout that rent the air, they appeared indeed to enjoy this sight and the perfection of the actor's art: The whole body was at last cleared of the incumbrance of the sack, when it exhibited the appearance of a human figure cast in white wax, of the middle size, miserably thin, and starved with cold. It frequently went through the motion of taking snuff and rubbing its hands; when it walked, it was with the most awkward gait, treading as the most tender-footed white man would do in walking bare-footed for the first time over frozen ground. The spectators often appealed to us, as to the excellence of the performance, and entreated I would look and be attentive to what was going on. I pretended to be fully as much pleased with this caricature of a white man as they could be, and certainly the actor burlesqued the part to admiration.[31]

Despite Clapperton's lack of genuine amusement it is very unlikely that this satire had any malicious intention towards an honoured guest in the audience.

That respect rapidly disappeared when whites became unwelcome guests in African communities. It was particularly the officially uniformed European

A reconstruction (based on a drawing by Harry Johnston) of the *Egungun* performance (including satirical mask of a white man) for Clapperton at King Mansola's court

agents who were most easily parodied and transformed into stereotypes of oppression. John C. Messenger cites examples of forceful anticolonial *Ekoe* satires among the Anang of Calabar in Nigeria, witnessed by D.W. Jeffreys in 1930.[32] These included skits about the colonial government for introducing taxation, hypocrisy of Christian converts and corruption among native court officials. Oyin Ogunba gives another more recent Yoruba example. At the Ogun Festival at Ondo in Nigeria the stock characters at the processions include 'the police officer marching about the arena, officious, cruel and insincere; the foreigner, usually white, authoritarian, his pointed nose high up in the sky'.[33] Ogunba goes on to record that another masked character plays the bishop, 'sometimes with his choir boys and girls, usually with an exaggerated appearance of holiness'.[34]

These literal examples of 'black skins, white masks' are very different from Fanon's metaphor. Fanon talks about the way status-seeking black men and women introject the values of colonialists by adopting a white mask (in the sociological sense of role). The psychology of the indigenous masquerade theatre is the precise opposite – it is a popular form of 'extrojection' or exorcism of alien roles by means of exaggeration and mockery.

The juxtaposition of authoritarian white man and religious caricature is an indication of the identification between the religious and secular wings of colonialism in popular African iconography. This combination can also be observed in the *Gule wa Mkulu* masquerades. Alongside the parodies of Catholic ritual which I have already described, other *Nyau* masks depicted more secular and sometimes political stereotypes. One of the favourite masks in the eastern parts of Zambia was *mzungu* (white man), alternatively called *bwana*. Mtonga's description of this mask is very revealing:

> He appears wearing a coat, a hat and smoking a pipe. Sometimes he may be in a car of wood or bamboo pushed by another *nyau* mask representing an African servant.[35]

It is hardly necessary to point out the political consciousness represented in this type of polemical paradrama. Mtonga goes on to explain that '*mzungu* is asked, through song, why he likes eggs too much yet he does not rear any fowls himself!' The context is humorous but relates to quite serious legitimate resentments felt by the African peasantry, and displays sensitivity about the exploitative mechanics of production and consumption under colonialism.

The *Nyau* masqueraders were bold enough to include overtly political stereotypes in their masquerades, such as the tax collector or District Commissioner. That the colonial administrators were sensitive to the mockery of such satires can be gauged by the concern felt during the 1920s in Nyasaland that *Nyau* centres could be foci of resistance to the government, and a Provincial Commissioner in Lilongwe attempted to blunt the edge of *Gule wa Mkulu*'s satire by banning the dramatic depiction of human beings. 'Effigies may only be made to represent animals, not men,' he proclaimed'.[36]

One of the favourite masks in Northern Rhodesia was *Sajeni* (a corruption of 'sergeant'). *Sajeni* was a very tall mask (an aesthetic effect achieved by stilts and extended head pieces). He carried a whip and acted the role of a cruel white policeman in Salisbury's Harare township. When he entered the arena he tried to whip women with his sjambok, and they scattered from him making the circle wider. Although *Sajeni*'s sjambok-wielding ferocity and tallness depicted the most fearful, cruel aspects of white colonialism, this was neutralized by the mask's ineffectiveness with the whip. Mtonga explains that his height seemed 'quite unnatural ... he's above life itself' but at the same time 'because he's so tall [he] cannot even bend and beat somebody who is sitting down ... and they ridicule him'.[37] There was perhaps an element of compensatory wish-fulfilment about this caricature. Nevertheless, it is likely that the compensatory elements were mingled with genuine audience emotions of collective cultural resistance to colonialism's armed might.

The existence of such satires suggests ways in which indigenous culture, under the impact of colonialism, transformed itself into an instrument for self-awareness and emergent political or class-consciousness, which culminated at a more advanced level in the struggle for independence. Basil Davidson has noted the surprise which settlers in Northern Rhodesia felt when confronted by articulation of anticolonial feelings among the African workers and peasants. He says that the politics of national liberation 'went on quietly beneath the surface, exploding only now and then, so that when the Congress movement finally did appear, late in the forties, it surprised both the settlers and the colonial authorities by the strength of its appeal to natives not previously believed ... to be capable of discussing together "any matter of importance at all" '.[38] I would suggest that performing arts like *Gule wa Mkulu* contributed to the raising of political consciousness which made such articulation possible.

Another paradramatic entertainment which was easy to transpose into a politicized medium was the work song. The work song is capable of acquiring dramatic elements through the technique of singing to another character, whether real or imaginary. In the *Maghabugu* song from Mozambique, for example, about a miner going to 'Joni' (Johannesburg) as a migrant worker, the song was structured so that provision was given for members of the chorus to improvise lines expressing their individual points of view, as in this domestic scene:

Miner: Drive carefully we are going to Joni.
        Drive carefully otherwise our provisions will spill off.
Wife: Father, please buy your son a pair of trousers.
Miner: You must take care of my field – cultivate it properly and plant every crop.
Wife: You must write letters, father.
Miner: I will send money for hut tax, I shall send the money.
Wife: Please don't forget me at home.[39]

The song centres around domestic issues of a fairly low-key kind. In other situations, however, it was possible for a work song to articulate protest against oppression by singing to an imaginary adversary (or even to a real overseer who did not understand the song's language or code). Alan Merriam gives such an example from the Boshi people in the eastern part of Belgian Congo during the early 1950s. Merriam recorded young female plantation labourers complaining that the plantation owner had taken away their oil ration. In the work song they threatened to leave the plantation to work at the Catholic mission.

So we are waiting now to see whether Bwana X will give us oil. Be careful! If we don't get oil we won't work here![40]

As with the *Sajeni* example there are elements of compensatory bravado about the song as well as genuine protest. At the aesthetic level, although the work song morphology may be based on a typically pre-colonial lineage-based call-and-response cultural form, the economism of the protest suggests that the song had transformed itself in ways which place it more comfortably within a semi-proletarianized aesthetic.

A very well-documented diachronic study of a satirical work song's development through its contact with a colonial plantation economy has been made by Leroy Vail and Landeg White. The authors achieve a thorough analysis of a call-and-response work song called 'Paiva', which was collected in many different versions on the Sena Sugar Estates between 1975 and 1976; they trace the history of the song from its putative origins as a canoe song in the mid-nineteenth century through its crystallization as a work song protesting about labour conditions on the sugar estate throughout the twentieth century, leading to a final version celebrating the overthrow of Portuguese colonialism by Frelimo in 1974. In all the many variants recorded there is one fundamental refrain, 'Paiva ndampera dinyero ache, Nsondo wache,' which translated from chiSena means, 'Paiva I've killed his money for him. His penis.'[41] The authors note that the all-pervasive sexuality of the song is part of an aesthetic of sexual insult to express outrage against the injustice perpetrated by international capitalism; they sum it up as 'a satire on the disproportion between wages and profits'.[42]

Vail and White meticulously trace the relationships between the development of capitalism on the Sena Sugar Estates and the aesthetic developments of the song. In its crystallized form the song was first associated with José de Paiva Raposo, who in 1889 was appointed administrator of the Prazo Maganja Aquem Chire in Mopeia. Later the song was transferred to other individual members of the Paiva family, but was also extended to refer more widely to the Estates as an employing agency and more widely still to the system of forced labour, referred to by the authors as 'a capitalist monopoly built on racial violence'.[43] At first the songs were performed by both men and women, though their complaints were rather different; the women tended to denounce ill-treatment, the men poor pay and long work hours. From about the 1940s the song became almost exclusively associated with women, owing to the Sena Sugar Estates' monopolization of cotton concessions and their increasing exploitation of enforced female labour.

It was particularly as a female song that 'Paiva' developed strong dramatic qualities. The female contract workers used it not only as a work song but also for entertainment accompanied by dances in which performers caricatured specific white overseers. The authors give an example of a caricature called 'chibeket' referring to the ugly, notoriously promiscuous and cruel Alberto Paiva, employed by the Sena Sugar Estates in 1940. Such caricatures developed into improvised dramas which satirized the follies or cruelties of key colonial officials like a policeman, cotton *capitao*, a *chef do posto* or a state-appointed headman. According to Vail and White, the audience

> screamed with laughter at the caricatures of rapes and bribes and beatings. The themes vary – the administrator drunk in his machila, police brutality during a kachasu raid, panic in the village over the arrival of the rice concession holder, the cotton overseer ill-treating the women under his charge.[44]

Although this might seem like a form of agit-prop highly politicized drama,

Vail and White take pains to caution that 'Paiva', particularly in its work song version, did not in fact incite the labourers to rebel against the *prazo* system. When the overseer heard the obscenities sung about him he 'just smiled', confident that the songs kept the women's work norms high. Nevertheless, the authors specifically reject a 'safety valve' theory for 'Paiva' and assert instead that the performances served to define 'a tiny area in which the labourers and their families have a separate identity'.[45]

'Paiva', like most work songs, provides what Cohen calls a 'Dialectic between "resistance" and "adaption" ... seen most clearly in the case of a work culture, which can act either as an insulative force or a set of symbols to mobilize the grievances of workers.'[46]

Despite its evident qualities as committed popular theatre 'Paiva' had some aesthetic limitations. Its strengths were humour and vividness of caricature; its weakness was narrative thinness and characterization which was somewhat divorced from complexity or mythic resonance.

One pre-colonial art form which had a different aesthetic emphasis in its attempts to mediate the experience of colonialism was the oral narrative. Oral narratives adapted very easily to the external trappings of the modern world without altering the basic moral framework or morphological features. For example, animal trickster heroes like Ananse the spider from Ghana incorporated cars, radios, bicycles and planes quite naturally into their scheming plots.

Some narratives, however, were able to penetrate much more deeply into the basic structural relations between capital and the newly forming peasantry. A fascinating example is 'The Story of Kaswa' collected among the Fipa people of Southern Tanzania. The story tells of a prophecy by a wise diviner which he conveys to a village gathering. The audience is divided into commoners and elders, the latter seeming to have attitudes of superiority. The diviner concentrates on the commoners as he prophesies the disruption of Fipa communalistic society at the hands of strangers from the East. The strangers are described as 'monstrous inventors'; among their inventions are to be monsters with 'protruding eyes' (headlamps) and anuses which exude smoke (exhaust pipes). Of course, these descriptions have mainly the wisdom of hindsight, but other prophecies by the diviner display authentic insights into the impact of capitalism on communalistic Fipa values. At one stage the diviner says, 'Everything becomes currency [*ifyuuma*] – grass and the very earth itself.'[47] This is a pithy but eloquent synopsis of the transition which takes place under capitalism from usufruct land cultivation to individual land tenure. The whole narrative draws upon shared values and symbolic systems to highlight the destructive and reifying tendencies of capitalism.

However, this kind of complex critique is comparatively rare in pre-colonial theatre forms. Although indigenous African theatre undoubtedly survived the encounter with colonialism, adapted to it in an innovative way, and sometimes even reacted vigorously against it, a need also arose (particularly in the new colonial cities) for a theatrical form which combined the humour, vivid conflicts and spectacular display of indigenous dance drama, with the narrative drive and thematic clarity achieved by dramatic mimesis in a plot conceived to comment on specific social and historical events. It was this nexus of needs which stimulated the birth of a radically different but still indigenous African drama which I refer to as syncretic popular theatre.

Notes

1. Traoré, 1972, p. 84. Traoré's original phrase, 'source populaire' (popular source), is actually less ambiguous than Adelugba's 'ancestral source'.
2. Graham-White, 1974.
3. Banham.
4. Cornevin.
5. Kerr, 1979.
6. Quoted in UNESCO, p. 2.
7. Vrydagh.
8. Vrydagh, p. 15.
9. Vrydagh, p. 19.
10. Ottenberg, 1975.
11. Adedeji, 1978b.
12. Adedeji, 1969, p. 60.
13. Vrydagh, p. 18.
14. Senghor, p. 106.
15. Fanon, p. 180.
16. Lewis.
17. Duerden, p. 111.
18. Colson, p. 85.
19. Beattie, p. 168.
20. The possibility of ancestral spirit possession being linked to self-conscious forms of African nationalism is examined in Chapter Eleven.
21. Young, pp. 77–8.
22. Ottenberg, 1975, p. 124.
23. Ogunba, p. 21.
24. Arrighi and Saul.
25. Ottenberg, 1975, pp. 125–6.
26. Schoffeleers.
27. Linden and Schoffeleers, p. 267.
28. Linden and Schoffeleers, p. 261.
29. Mtonga, 1980, p. 90. (*Chinamwali* = girl's initiation ceremony)
30. Mtonga, 1980, p. 112.
31. Clapperton, p. 55.
32. Messenger.
33. Ogunba, p. 21.
34. Ogunba, p. 23.
35. Mtonga, 1980, p. 90.
36. Quoted in Linden and Schoffeleers, p. 264.
37. Mtonga, 1977, p. 2–3.
38. Davidson, p. 231.
39. Quoted in Johnson and Bernstein, p. 104.
40. Quoted in Merriam, pp. 51–2.
41. Quoted in Vail and White, 1978, p. 2.
42. Vail and White, 1978, p. 6.
43. Vail and White, 1978, p. 20.
44. Vail and White, 1978, pp. 14–15.
45. Vail and White, 1978, p. 25.
46. Cohen, p. 253.
47. Willis, p. 254.

4

Syncretic Popular Theatre: ~ Militaristic Mime

Sadla Beni formed in 1938 ... was a break-away youth movement from the two prominent bands, Kingi and Scotchi. Since it was mainly composed of young people, Sadla always won during competitions ... Sadla is a corruption of Settler. This Beni called itself after the Settlers and sometimes its uncouth behaviour was like that of the Settlers. They imitated the rough type of living of the Settler community of Kenya, and fashioned their uniforms according to the Khaki shirts and trousers and wide hats, just like those worn by the Settlers.[1]

Superficially, this description by George Mkangi of the *Beni* dance in Mombasa seems to belong to a similar level of consciousness to the popular theatre forms like spirit possession dances, ancestral masquerades and song drama examined in the last chapter. But I would like to suggest that the organized use of costumes and mime by the Sadla dancers to parody the white settlers of the Kenyan Highlands was rather different from the incorporation of white or colonial stereotypes (missionary, military or administrative) into already existing pre-colonial popular theatre forms.

The examples in Chapter Three showed the capacity of pre-colonial theatre forms to adapt to the impact of colonialism. All the same, these forms were mostly restricted to the perceptions of specifically rural or peasant consciousness. The rapid urbanization which took place in the early twentieth century in such cities as Lagos, Accra, Mombasa, Nairobi and Johannesburg created a need, as I explained in Chapter Two, for a bourgeois theatre and cinema which could link the expatriate and emergent comprador bourgeoisies to the metropolitan culture of Europe. But another, less easily identified need arose among the newly created African petty bourgeois and proletarian classes of the cities and administrative centres – a popular theatre which could mediate the experiences of modernization, urbanization and class formation.

In East, West and Southern Africa, strikingly similar popular theatre forms emerged, fairly independently of each other, combining elements of pre-colonial indigenous African dramaturgy with features borrowed or parodied from colonial cultural forms like military bands, church choirs and vaudeville. I use the term syncretic popular theatre as a catch-all phrase to describe such forms. In two separate chapters I want to examine three varieties of syncretic popular theatre; in this chapter the militaristic mimes, and in Chapter Five West African Concert Party and Yoruba Opera, although other syncretic forms will be referred to in later chapters.

The militaristic mimes of *Beni*, *Mbeni*, *Kalela*, *Muganda* and *Malipenga* constitute a halfway stage between the 'modified' form of pre-colonial African theatre and fully developed syncretic urban theatre. The mimes were syncretic in so far as they combined' elements of colonial spectacle (particularly the military parade) with indigenous *ngoma* dance forms, but unlike Concert Party or Yoruba Opera, they did not develop a fully narrative form or spoken dialogue, and their staging remained within the indigenous theatre-in-the-round aesthetic rather than the proscenium arch stage. The mimes also differed from the other two forms in that, although urban in origin, they proved capable of reabsorption into the peasant culture of the rural areas, and acted as a cultural vehicle for the penetration of urban and modernizing values into the rural areas. Concert Party and Yoruba Opera, on the other hand, tended much more to maintain their urban identity.

Militaristic mimes developed in several areas of Africa. In West Africa, for instance, dances such as *Soja* (from 'soldier'), *Goge* (the music of which incorporated army bugle motifs) and *Goumbe* acted as an important transition between pre-colonial and modern dance forms among the Muslim youths in Nigeria and the Ivory Coast.[2] But the militaristic mimes were far more widely developed (and far more extensively researched) in East Africa, and this chapter deals almost exclusively with that region.

The most thorough account of militaristic dance mime is found in Terence Ranger's study of *Beni, Dance and Society in East Africa*.[3] *Beni* was an entertainment dance in which the participants dressed in smart, often military uniforms, and danced in regular columns with sticks, imitating guns or batons. There was a hierarchy of roles including a king, officers and subordinate ranks. This parody of stratification with its dance aesthetic involving the music of bugles, flutes and side-drums, ordered ranks, neat uniforms and regular marching-like steps suggests a heavy influence of colonial military bands. However, Ranger is at pains to explain that *Beni* had pre-colonial precedents on the Swahili coast of Kenya and Tanganyika. He cites the *Chama* dance, an adaptation of the Arab *Razha* war dance, using swift, synchronized movements with sticks, in imitation of Arab sword combat.[4] Moreover, the sponsors and controllers of *Beni*, at least initially, were not the Christianized, mentally colonized freed slaves, but the traditional Swahili aristocracy, which, in the 1890s, still retained some hegemony in the coastal cities. The result was a hybrid or syncretic form of paradrama combining Swahili, colonial British and indigenous African *Vinyago* masking traditions.

From the outset, *Beni*, like the aggressive Swahili coastal dances it replaced, was associated with already existing binary moieties in the towns of Mombasa, Lamu and Dar es Salaam. In Lamu, for example, *Beni* competitions were organized between the well-established Mkomani and Mtambweni factions. Throughout the 1890s the rivalry was expressed by competitive and very expensive carnivals in the streets, in which the crowds awarded victory to the most opulent floats and most impressive, best drilled dancing troupes. In Mombasa, the competition was between the Kingi group (vaguely associated with King Edward of England) and the Kilungu band; in Malindi it was between Kingi and Sultani. Around the turn of the century, the rivalries in all the coastal cities had crystallized into those between Kingi and Scotchi. Despite the aggression it displayed, this 'locational factionalism' was an integration device for breaking down potential tribalism into the values of urban life. Factionalism was to continue playing an important role in the development of *Beni*.

Some time in the first decade of the twentieth century in Tanga, Pangani and Dar es Salaam, the rivalries between Kingi and Scotchi transformed into different groupings: Marini and Arinoti. This division reflected important changes in the social development of the cities; it was not a rivalry within the Swahili aristocracy, but represented a rivalry between the status-conscious Westernized Swahili, who supported Marini and whose performing image, as its name suggests, was modelled on the smartness of the British navy, and the Arinoti, whose name meant the 'unclean ones', and whose support came mainly from the lower-class up-country labour migrants. An example of this competitive, aesthetic pride linked to the forces of colonial modernization is the following Marini song:

> We Marini are favoured by God
> To be able to speak and read the language of Europe
> The gates of Heaven are opened for us
> Let us tighten the fetters on these Arinoti.[5]

It was this element of class-consciousness and conflict, even though mediated in a symbolic dramatic rather than consciously articulate way, that enabled *Beni* to become a genuinely popular form of theatre, which was capable of being transplanted in inland towns and villages away from the Swahili coast. Its incipient class-consciousness appealed to the inhabitants of inland Tanganyika towns like Ujiji and Tabora when the theatre form was introduced by the somewhat deracinated civil servant class, who acted as cultural 'carriers' for the modern values embodied by *Beni* in the period just preceding the First World War.

During the First World War itself, the heavy military activity in East Africa between German and British armies and the extreme mobility of African soldiers and prisoners-of-war also helped spread the popularity of *Beni*, as far afield as Nairobi, Nyasaland, the Northern Rhodesia Copperbelt and Katanga in the Belgian Congo. Not surprisingly, *Beni* assumed an even more militaristic image at this time. Ranger quotes sources describing military ranks 'from General to Private' and with female roles for nursing sisters, badges to identify ranks, and with junior ranks saluting senior.[6] Even more remarkable were the elaborate 'war games' which were presented by some *Beni* troupes, particularly in Dar es Salaam. Ranger describes these theatrical extravaganzas as partly a recreation of traditional Swahili war games, and partly re-enactments of German colonial war exercises.[7]

After the First World War *Beni* underwent considerable change. On the coast the Swahili elites' status and political prestige was being undermined, and they could no longer afford to act as patrons of the extravagant parades.

The *Beni* groups became professionals for hire as entertainers, usually for the new 'labour elites' of clerks and government employees.

In the up-country rural administrative centres and provincial towns powerful offshoots of *Beni* emerged, namely *Mbeni, Muganda* and *Kalela* in Northern Rhodesia, and *Mganda* and *Malipenga* in Nyasaland. Compared with coastal *Beni*, these were much closer to indigenous village entertainment dances. For example, in the villages of Nyasaland, if Westernized brass-band instruments such as trumpets (*malipenga*) were unavailable, then improvised trumpets (*zigubu*) were made out of gourds, with a spiders' web membrane over the mouthpiece.[8]

Some of these up-country dances became very vigorous during and after the Second World War, at the same time that *Beni* itself was declining. *Beni* found itself becoming dated because its professional exponents, who had entered the entertainment business, were outflanked by more modish musical fashions, such as Congolese rumba and South African township jazz. Moreover, organizational power, which made *Beni*'s independence of colonial bureaucratic structures seem progressive to the clerical elites during the 1930s, seemed far less attractive to them in the 1950s, when more openly nationalistic political movements replaced forms of cultural nationalism. By the time of independence in East Africa, *Beni* had become a rather archaic dance remembered by the older generation in the coastal towns, and only performed by a few migrant labourers.[9]

In the up-country areas, however, the militaristic mimes retained their vigour up to and even after independence. One of the aesthetic advantages which the militaristic mimes had in the rural areas over most pre-colonial dance forms was that the steps and movements were not rigidly bound by 'tradition', but were capable of innovation, mimetic experiment and adaption to the changing social milieu. For instance, as recently as 1981, I witnessed primary school boys in Mzimba district of Malawi using a *Mganda* dance to mime the process of mothers feeding babies with porridge – a theme far removed from the warlike origins of *Mganda* but perhaps relevant to post-independence welfare campaigns about nutrition. I observed an even more interesting example in 1993 during a Malawian United Democratic Front rally at a village in Machinga, where a *Beni* band expressed solidarity with the democratic struggle against one-party dictatorship.

After this cursory chronology of militaristic mime I would like to turn to its function; Ranger describes the mimes' function as 'a series of brass-band responses by people in a transitional period from pre-industrial to industrial society'.[10] As my brief historical synopsis has tried to indicate, the details of the East African people's responses to transition depended on their developing consciousness of the economic, social and political changes into which their lives were inserted. When *Beni* originated on the East African coast in the 1890s, the societies acted as 'a way of recasting the network of relationships within a moiety or quarter; they were an expression of most of the existing values of Swahili urban society and they were also mechanisms of innovation'.[11]

The function of social cohesion was particularly important during the early phase when *Beni* acted as an outlet for 'locational factionalism', but traces of that function remained even after the dispersion of militaristic mime to the up-country areas. In Nairobi, Ujiji, Tabora, and most particularly

Chigubu, or gourd trumpet, used in *Malipenga* as a substitute for Western commercial trumpet

Uniformed musicians using marching steps and simultaneously playing the drum in *Muganda*

Beni group performing at a democracy rally at Ntaja in Malawi, June 1993

the new mining towns of the Northern Rhodesia Copperbelt and Elizabeth-ville in Congo, *Mbeni, Muganda* and *Kalela* were important instruments in the self-control of ethnic tensions by the emergent African proletariat and petty bourgeoisie. For instance, in the Copperbelt in the 1940s, *Beni* came to be associated with the Bemba, *Kalela* with the Bisa and *Mganda* with the Nyasas. This did not represent a simple case of tribalism. For example, *Mganda* was performed by Nyasa groups with different ethnic origins (Tonga, Henga, Likoma Island, Tumbuka), and in this sense expressed regional rather than strictly ethnic consciousness. Nor should the apparently 'tribal' (to use Clyde Mitchell's term) nature of the militaristic mimes obscure the fundamental integrative function of the dances. They should be seen, alongside other social devices like joking relationships, as very successful popular tech-niques for solving the problems of ethnic diversity at a time of rapid industrialization and urbanization.

The ability of militaristic mimes to mediate a regional rather than merely village or tribal consciousness applied even to the rural areas. In Nyasaland, for example, the organization of *Malipenga* and *Mganda* in the 1950s demanded a considerable amount of hospitality and interaction between different villages and districts in order to hold the competition festivals.

However, of the two functions referred to by Ranger, integration and innovation, it was the element of innovation which came to dominate militaristic mime. According to Ranger, *Beni* was patronized at an early stage by young, fashionable men who were interested in adopting certain 'progressive' or Western life styles and values, 'to show that whatever was powerful in the way of life of their conquerors could be absorbed and mastered and displayed by themselves'.[12] There are resemblances here to the symbolism I noted in Chapter Three by which indigenous African spirit possession dances appropriated elements of colonial iconography.

At a later stage, when the up-country rural migrants adopted militaristic mime, the element of modernity was still important; the dances provided a medium through which the dance participants could assert 'a familiarity with the modern world as a result of labour migration, or of some schooling'.[13] Villagers from Northern Nyasaland, for example, travelled as far as South Africa, Southern Rhodesia, Mozambique and Northern Rhodesia in order to look for work. According to Malawian researcher, Koma-Koma, the search for the paraphernalia of *Mganda* was one of the incentives for travel. 'Some went looking for clothes, some looked for European drums, others for side drums.'[14] The elision of economic and aesthetic motives is perhaps over-simplified here, but the aesthetic incentive should not be underestimated.

The militaristic mimes also allowed returned labour migrants to display their modernity in the village through a knowledge of English and of Western culture. For instance, the *Mganda* dance organizations (*bomas*) often had Europeanized names like 'Landani', 'Amereka' and 'Koleji'. The dances were accompanied by parodies of English military commands such as:

Tensheni! Sitanditi Hizi! ... Kwiki Machi!
Silopu Amusi! Wani! Tuu! Goo![15]

Kerr and Nambote explain how in recent Malawian *Malipenga* a split has developed between *Mganda Ukulu* (the big *Mganda*), which retains the militaristic iconography of the original *Mganda*, and *Chigaruka*, a variant which appeals mostly to young migrant workers recently returned from Johannesburg.

> Songs and choreography of *Chigaruka* show cultural influences from the urban centres where the labour migrants have worked on contract. For example, the songs sometimes contain words of Afrikaans or Bemba, and the dance steps often imitate the popular township dances of Johannesburg or Harare. In *Waya Boma*, for instance, one of the favourite choreographic routines is called 'Sibongile step', an imitation of the popular South African township dance, *Smanje Manje*. By means of such artistic forms *Chigaruka* provides a medium through which returned labour migrants can assert their adventurous spirit, sophistication and familiarity with Western life.[16]

Thus *Malipenga* has not remained fixed at the militaristic phase, but has evolved to allow dancers to become 'cultural carriers' for Western values even in remote rural areas.

A particularly important controversy which has arisen over the modernizing function of *Beni* concerns whether the dance signified a reactionary apeing of colonial and Western mannerisms, or whether it opened up cultural channels for socially progressive and modern self-esteem. The main proponent of the idea that the militaristic mimes were basically an abject imitation by Africans of the trappings of colonial power has been made by Clyde Mitchell in his study of the *Kalela* dance on the Northern Rhodesia Copperbelt. Mitchell called *Mbeni, Kalela* and other militaristic mimes 'a sort of pantomime of the social structure of the local European community'.[17]

Mitchell's analysis takes a broadly functionalist approach in which he places the psychology of the militaristic mimes within an exclusion/compensation paradigm, so that the rigidly hierarchial structure of *Kalela*, with its Governor, officers, nurses and privates, and the emphasis on smartness, 'the well-pressed grey slacks, neat singlets and well-polished shoes', the neat handkerchiefs and carefully combed and parted hair, provided a psychological escape from the oppression of colonialism by imitating the rigid hierarchies of that system.[18] There is certainly no lack of evidence that the organizers of militaristic mimes stressed uniformity and smart appearance. Koma-Koma refers to different *bomas* of *Mganda* distinguishing themselves through uniforms (different permutations of shorts/trousers, black/khaki and so on) and emphasizes the importance of European clothing such as jackets, ties and long stockings.[19]

For Mitchell the wearing of European clothes in *Mbeni* and *Kalela* was a symptom of the colonized's psychological dependence on the colonialists:

> The appeal of the *Mbeni* dance, therefore, seems to have been the vicarious participation of the Africans in social relationships, from which they were normally excluded. Striking evidence to show that this was not just a local reaction comes from Goodall, who says that earlier *Mbeni* dancers in Tanganyika actually whitened their faces.[20]

I would suggest that the question of white face make-up is more complicated than Mitchell seems to think, but I shall postpone my remarks on the implications of white face make-up until my discussion of West African Concert Party theatre in Chapter Five.

Mitchell goes on to assert that the lack of hostile satire against colonialism proves the compensatory impulse behind *Mbeni* and *Kalela*. Thus, for Mitchell, the militaristic mimes of the thirties and forties were manifestations of an introjection by colonial Africans of the rigid social structuring inherent in colonial values. As a theatrical form, therefore, it could be catalogued as a kind of popular version of colonial theatre, equivalent perhaps to literary imitations of European 'high' theatre by authors like H. E. Dhlomo and J. B. Danquah.

That such apparent 'apeing' of colonial culture and life styles existed at different levels in Africa during the 1930s and 1940s cannot be denied, it has received considerable historical analysis in the concept of 'the new men', and magnificent satirical representation in Okot p'Bitek's *The Song of Ocol*.[21] All the same, I believe such an analysis is potentially misleading; it tends to ignore the sudden changes which can take place in the relationship between historical events and cultural attitudes. At certain points in the historical development of imperialism. a reaction of imitation by the oppressed of their oppressors might, in a rather devious way, be an example of progressive economic aspirations or self-definition, rather then mere callow apeing. For instance, it is easy to smile at the apparently pretentious system of *bomas* which *Mganda* and *Malipenga* dancers set up in Nyasaland as an imitation of the colonial provincial administrative centres, and at the rather elaborate, formal invitations which the 'adjutants' of various *bomas* sent to each other to prepare for dance competitions.[22] But it should be remembered that imitation of European bureaucratic habits provided useful practice for Africans in organizational skills, independent of any European supervision, a process which was a necessary stage in building a protonationalist consciousness.

An interesting example of the care with which it is necessary to treat popular theatre forms is the history of *Muganda* in the Katete district of Northern Rhodesia during the period leading up to Zambian independence (1964). Between 1951 and 1966, the Katete mode of *Muganda* appears to have gone through three different phases: *Simati* ('smart') from about 1951 to 1956, in which the steps and uniforms imitated those of the occupying army, the King's African Rifles, *Chibeza* from about 1956 to 1961, an anarchic, less disciplined stage, which gave much scope for disgruntled criticism of the colonial master through the words of the songs, followed by *Kandele* from about 1961 to 1966, in which the steps returned to a quasi-military precision, but of an anti-colonial nature, in which the songs were highly political, expressing solidarity with UNIP's struggle for the independence of Zambia.[23] If *Muganda* of Katete district had been analysed synchronically during its *Simati* period, it could easily have been interpreted as an almost reactionary dance expressing a colonized mentality. Only a diachronic study could do justice to its progressive role in mediating a political consciousness among the rural population around Katete.

A similar diachronic view is necessary in looking at Malipenga on Likoma Island on Lake Malawi. Most of the early 'kings' of the Likoma *bomas* during the 1920s were white missionaries or colonial administrators, as testified by an old informant, Mr Katandula:

> At first London Boma used to be called Tabora. but the name was changed by Bwana Beckan, then the Headmaster of St Michael's College, who renamed it after his British Government. There were other European kings: for example, Bwana Snodding, the Chauncy Maples engineer, was king for Bwaila Boma, Bwana

Audrey, King for Dar es Salaam Boma; Captain Heywood was king for England Boma, and Reverend Glossop was king for America Boma ... These Europeans were quite helpful to *Mganda*. They would often donate money for guest Bomas which were holding a *Mganda* festival and they gave provisions like cattle, rice and salt.[24]

Imposing themselves on the *bomas* was the colonialists' way of controlling the dynamic and potential danger of modernization. But by the 1940s the 'kingship' of the *bomas* had passed on to Africans, who were respected in the community for their organizational ability and knowledge of *Malipenga* lore. In that way *Malipenga* became independent enough to support the anti-colonial struggle during the late fifties and early sixties.

Ranger rejects any form of compensatory thesis about popular militaristic mime. Some of the examples he cites might seem to fall neatly into such an interpretation. For instance, the *Sadla* mode of *Beni* from Mombasa, formed in 1938, was a corruption of the word 'settler'. According to Ranger's inform-ant, George Mkangi, the young dancers 'imitated the rough type of living of the Settler community of Kenya, and fashioned their uniforms according to the Khaki shirts and trousers and wide hats, just like those worn by the Settlers'.[25]

But, elsewhere, Ranger emphasizes the potential in the dance for assertion by the newly urbanized African workers and migrants within a colonial context. For example, he quotes with approval R. J. B. Moore's analysis that *Muganda* and *Kalela* on the Northern Rhodesia Copperbelt during the 1930s were progressive dances in which the imitation of European clothes was not a sign of psychological dependence but 'were affirmations of the right to live conveniently and with dignity in the "different" world of the towns'.[26]

One good way of assessing whether the militaristic mimes were pro-gressive or reactionary is by examining the reaction to them by the colonial authorities. As I have shown, in some places, like Northern Nyasaland, colonial authorities, after some initial resistance, patronized the *Malipenga bomas* as a way of controlling them. But, in most areas of Southern and Eastern Africa, the colonial administrators and the missionaries seemed to have been virulently hostile to the mimes, an indication that the dances appeared to signify a cultural threat to colonialism.

The earliest colonial condemnations of *Beni* were for the waste involved in the competitive carnivals, a complaint which continued well after the First World War. This was a refrain found all over the continent during the colonial period – the spirit of capital accumulation outraged by pre-capitalist techniques of surplus consumption. For instance, in 1924, the District Commissioner of Malindi complained that the coastal Africans 'will spend their savings of a hard year's toil on the useless ngoma competitions'.[27]

Another more trivial complaint was that of noise. *The Mombasa Times* of 1931 declared that 'it was high time something was done to prevent professional native bandsmen from creating such a lot of noise in the middle of the night'.[28] The objection to the noise of indigenous nocturnal dances is an almost tediously common theme in colonial reactions to African theatre.

A more substantial objection by the colonialists to the militaristic mimes was the complaint that *Beni*'s use of uniforms and pseudo-military ranks caused confusion. An army officer in Nyasaland, Major Stephens, thought *beni* 'would be an incentive to the theft of parts of uniform and equipment'.[29]

By analogy I would conclude that the East African militaristic mimes were certainly not in themselves revolutionary or even overtly nationalistic for the most part, but they did serve to provide a popular 'rehearsal' for the organized nationalism of the 1950s and early 1960s.

Where the militaristic mime survived into the post-colonial period (and *Kalela*, *Mganda* and *Beni* are still very vigorous art forms in Zambia and Malawi), it has mainly been as a form of cultural solidarity. Kerr and Nambote summarize these functions with respect to Likoma Island:

> In *Malipenga* the inhabitants of Likoma Island have synthesized indigenous African and alien Western traditions to create an artistic form capable of acting as a lens to focus the community's economic and social preoccupations within a rapidly changing historical context. The mime has given the islanders the ability to respond creatively to the complex pressures associated with the penetration of Western values. It provides a cultural matrix within which the poles of stratification, individualism and bureaucratic discipline on the one hand and communal integration and solidarity on the other can be explored and controlled. *Malipenga* also provides cultural tools which a fairly remote and peripheral people are able to use to negotiate their psychological dependence on metropolitan values and pressures.[41]

In transformed ways, the militaristic mimes since independence have restored some of the functions of their nineteenth-century origins in the use of competitive theatre for community solidarity.

For more direct expression of sustained anticolonial sentiments, overt nationalism or class-consciousness, it is necessary to examine other examples of syncretic popular theatre, ones which relied not only on parody, mime and symbolic self-assertion, but on dialogue, role conflict and a narrative framework.

Notes

1. Quoted in Ranger, 1975, p. 89.
2. For *Soja* and *Goge* see Ames. For *Goumbe* see Halas.
3. Ranger, 1975.
4. Ranger, 1975, p. 20.
5. Quoted in Mapanje and White, p. 65.
6. Ranger, 1975, p. 52.
7. Ranger, 1975, p. 52.
8. Kerr and Nambote, pp. 12–13.
9. *Beni* has survived in Malawi as a dance associated with the Muslim lakeshore districts of Nkhotakota and Mangochi, in contrast to the Christianized areas to the North and West, where *Mganda/Malipenga* is the dominant militaristic dance. See Kamlongera, 1987.
10. Ranger, 1975, p. 6.
11. Ranger, 1975, p. 20.
12. Ranger, 1975, p. 31.
13. Ranger, 1975, p. 108.
14. Koma-Koma, p. 19.
15. Koma-Koma, p. 15.
16. Kerr and Nambote, p. 15–16.
17. Mitchell, p.11.
18. Mitchell, p. 2.
19. Koma-Koma, pp. 15–17.
20. Mitchell, p. 12.
21. p'Bitek, 1970.
22. Koma-Koma, p. 25.
23. For the information about *Muganda* in Katete I am indebted to Chirwa, 1979.
24. Quoted in Kerr and Nambote, p. 5.
25. Quoted in Ranger, 1975, p. 89.
26. Quoted in Ranger, 1975, p. 136.
27. Quoted in Ranger, 1975, p. 82.
28. Quoted in Ranger, 1975, p. 88.

29. Quoted in Kamlongera, 1987, p. 8.
30. Ranger, 1975, p. 92.
31. Quoted in Ranger, 1975, p. 64.
32. Quoted in Ranger, 1975, p. 80.
33. Quoted in Ranger, 1975, p. 44.
34. *Bajas* in Zambia, or *zigubu* in Malawi.
35. I have tended to neglect the aesthetic appeal of militaristic mime in order to emphasize its historical or social significance. It is important to remember that the mimes had a powerful aesthetic impact and clearly defined forms. In Malawian *Malipenga*, for example, according to Kerr and Nambote (pp. 11–13), the dance was normally divided into three phases: first, *Matchowa*, a prologue in which selected dancers purified the arena, second, *Chilomo*, in which the most military steps took place, and third, *Chitawala*, in which opportunity was given for individual virtuosity and mime. It was particularly the *Chitawala* stage which allowed dancers to make mimetic comment of a satirical and sometimes subversive nature on any innovations brought about by modernization.
36. Kamlongera, 1987, p. 10.
37. Quoted in Ranger, 1975, p. 129.
38. Quoted in Ranger, 1975, p. 138.
39. Quoted in Mwale, p. 17.
40. Boal, p. 141.
41. Kerr and Nambote, p. 17.

5

Syncretic Popular Theatre: Concert Party & Yoruba Opera

During roughly the period when *Beni* and the militaristic mimes became popular in East Africa, two rather different kinds of syncretic African theatre developed in West Africa: Concert Party and Yoruba Opera.

As with *Beni*, Concert Party was based on an indigenous performing aesthetic, but transformed by the impact of colonialism to respond to social developments in the modern world. Two Ghanaian authors who have made separate studies of Concert Party, Efua Sutherland and K. N. Bame,[1] both identify indigenous and European influences, though Bame feels the indigenous tradition predominates: 'Despite the acculturative influences they [Concert Party] reflect, they are African in content and features'.[2]

The main indigenous source appeared to have been the pre-colonial Akan/ Fanti tradition of oral narratives. Oral narratives had theatrical potential all over Africa, through their technique of audience response and of vocal characterization. Among the Akan and Fanti peoples the narratives took on further theatrical possibilities through the use of mimes interpreting the dramatic elements of the narrative. This was particularly true of the narrative form known as *Anansesem*, stories about Ananse, the spider trickster hero.

The *Anansesem* developed a complex performing organization. The performing group (*Anansesemkuo*) was often professional and had specific roles such as chief of the group (*Anansesenhene*), chief of the women (*Kuwwura*), spokesperson (*Okyeame*), narrator (*Anansemwura* or *Mafo*), drummers (*Akyerema*) and mime artists (*Anansegoro mma*). The staging of the stories and the relationship of narrator to audience allowed scope for visual interpretation. The constant interruption of the *Anansesem* narrative for musical interludes (*mboguo*) provided the structure for such improvised interpretive mimes.[3]

It is not surprising, therefore, that it was within this culture that a form of syncretic popular drama arose, and that many aesthetic elements of *Anansesem* contributed to Concert Party. Nor is it surprising to learn that Ishmael Johnson (better known by his stage name Bob Johnson), who was the

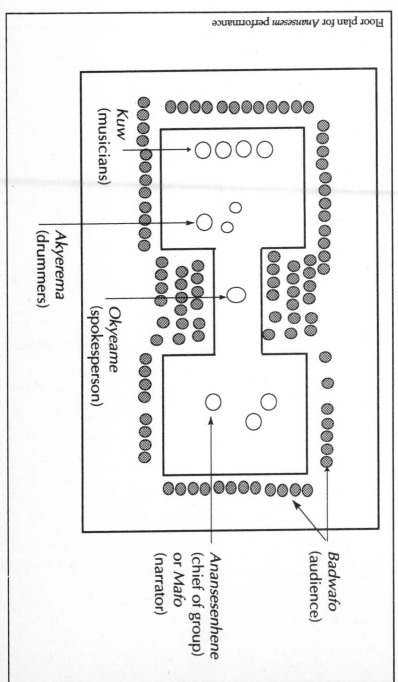

Floor plan for *Ananseem* performance

Kuw
(musicians)

Akyerema
(drummers)

Okyeame
(spokesperson)

Anansesenhene
(chief of group)
or *Mafo*
(narrator)

Badwafo
(audience)

most famous and influential Concert Party performer, was heavily influenced by *Anansesem* performances he saw as a child in Saltpond, particularly the use of female impersonation in the mime.[4]

Although pre-colonial narrative performances provided the aesthetic core of Concert Party, its development was also heavily influenced by syncretisms derived from colonial culture. First was the influence of concerts performed on Empire Day and at the end of term in schools (this seems to be the origin of the name 'Concert Party'). The school concerts and Empire Day parades often provided only stuffily propagandistic spectacles in praise of the British Empire, but there was also scope for more popular song and vaudeville performance.

One of the earliest records of Ghanaian vaudeville performances within the structure of colonial schools was that of Master Yalley, who started performing at Sekondi Elementary School in 1918. His performances were one-man shows using song, mime, and a variety of props, make-up and costumes. The make-up and costumes were sometimes inherited from Ghanaian pre-colonial tradition, such as the raffia skirt, *asafuwa*, worn by priests and priestesses, and sometimes imitations of Western culture, such as theatrical false wigs or moustaches, and 'black-face' minstrel-type make-up. Master Yalley was a sort of proto-Concert Party performer whose innovations and technique of quick-change costumes were later adopted by artists like Bob Johnson for use in a dramatic context involving three or more characters.

Other influences on Yalley were:

1) the sea-shanty tradition of Liberian sailors, and such black American vaudeville genres as tap-dancing, ragtime song and stand-up comic patter;
2) the tradition of plays, hymns and cantatas performed at the Christian missions, which provided a model for the mixture of music and drama;
3) Hollywood movies of the 1920s and 1930s. Bob Johnson specifically acknowledges Charlie Chaplin, whose famous walk Johnson transformed into a comic dance mime. Johnson was also influenced by the musical films of Al Jolson, particularly the latter's use of 'black-face', which reinforced the influence of Master Yalley.

The irony of a black African imitating a white American imitating a black American points to the complexity of syncretic theatre. It is tempting to see the minstrel influence as a sign that Concert Party was inherently derivative and locked into a psychological inferiority complex. However, that would be a dangerously over-simple interpretation. As with some early examples of militaristic mime, a psychological need for newly urbanized migrants to mimic Europeans was not abnormal. It provided a kind of aesthetic legitimization for the newly transformed personality. This white 'mask' could be sloughed off at a later stage of cultural development when syncretic African theatre artists were more confident of their role in the urban capitalist milieu.

A diachronic approach is particularly necessary for analysing the ideological viewpoint embedded in Concert Party. The proto-Concert Party of Master Yalley was specifically aimed at an elite audience (such as the Optimism Club Accra) of 'lawyers and other professional men of social standing'.[5]

Bob Johnson in 'black-face' make-up, during an early Concert Party stand-up comedy routine

Yalley himself, as an elementary school teacher, was petty bourgeois, rather than a strictly 'professional' man. His 'black-face' performances in the early 1920s were geared to the rather small bourgeois sectors which were not so absorbed in colonial culture as to participate with absolute ease in colonial theatre (as the assimilated elites tended to do in francophone and lusophone Africa) but needed a theatre form different from the 'bush' culture of pre-colonial dances and narratives. Concert Party provided these elites with a theatre form which could mediate the problems, conflicts and psychological pressures arising from the process of rapid urbanization and embourgeoisement in a colonial context. For such audiences, Concert Party played a role of 'filling in the emotional vacuum for the newly urbanized'.[6]

The appeal of Concert Party to economic improvement remained an important feature of Concert Party throughout its development. Even after Concert Party became more open to subaltern audiences from about 1935 onwards, it retained some snob appeal. K. N. Bame quotes a Concert Party advertisement from the 1960s for Bob Cohen and Princess Trio, with the outrageously (perhaps tongue-in-cheek) snobbish boast: 'It's Gentleman Smart, the ladies man, who spends NC20,000 a day.'[7] Moreover, by that time, Concert Party had widened its popularity enormously, and the appeal was not so much direct snobbery as a kind of compensatory fantasy for glamorous costumes – a common ingredient in popular urban theatre all over the world.

The career of Bob Johnson provides an interesting case study of Concert Party's shifting class base. Bob Johnson was the son of a skilled artisan in a colonial shipping and trading company (Swanzy) at Saltpond and Cape Coast. As with the East Coast syncretic theatre of militaristic mime, which started in the coastal cities of Mombasa and Lamu, so with Ghanaian Concert Party, it was the belt of modern coastal cities, Sekondi, Cape Coast, Saltpond and Accra, which provided the innovative 'womb' for its development.

The organizational base of Bob Johnson's group was that of a typical small-scale entrepreneurial enterprise. In 1930 Ishmael Johnson teamed up with two former school friends after they had completed standard six. They started making satirical sketches modelled on schoolmaster Yalley's technique. Initially they had almost no capital or other resources. They borrowed musical instruments from schools, until they had accumulated enough capital to buy their own instruments.

The entrepreneurial nature of Bob Johnson's group was reflected in its financial insecurity. The group had to keep constantly on the move in order to remain profitable. It was a dispute over finances which caused Bob Johnson to split from his first two partners, J. B. Ansah and Charles Hutton, in 1935, and to form a new group, the Axim Trio, with Charlie Turpin and E. K. Dadson. The Axim Trio made a very successful tour of the whole of Nigeria in 1935. This trip helped give them the incentive to tour regularly outside the Akan/Fanti-speaking area within the Gold Coast. They also made tours during the 1940s to Ivory Coast, Liberia and Sierra Leone. This thrusting initiative of Bob Johnson's theatre company parallels the growth, in the wake of the cocoa boom, of the West African entrepreneurial marketing class, travelling the coast selling textiles and other petty commodities.

Despite their humble origins, the early appeal of the Two Bobs and the Carolina Girl was fairly 'up-market'. They performed in schools, at the High

The Axim Trio during the early 1930s. Bob Johnson is on the left

Court, Cape Coast, and in night clubs, including the Optimism Club, frequented by American sailors and members of the emergent Gold Coast bourgeoisie. A contemporary photograph of the Axim Trio shows them all wearing three-piece suits like prosperous businessmen – perhaps a piece of posed photographic wishful thinking, but presumably indicative of the group's upwardly mobile aspirations.

The political consciousness of Bob Johnson's groups in the 1930s seems to have been quite acquiescent to colonialism. The Two Bobs and the Carolina Girl were happy to play to the exclusively white European Club at Abussa Mine. And, in 1930, the Axim Trio created a rather spectacular play glorifying the coronation of King George VI, with characters such as the Archbishop, the Admiral, the Altar Server and the King.

However, with the broadening of the groups' popular bases through wide-ranging tours and performances in church halls, villages, town squares, barns and converted warehouses, the Axim Trio was able to keep pace to a certain extent with the growth of popular nationalism and class-consciousness By 1950 when Kwame Nkrumah was imprisoned by the British for his militant leadership of the Congress People's Party, the Axim Trio did two plays on the subject, *Nkrumah is a Mighty Man* and *Nkrumah is Greater than Before*. The proceeds of the latter play were donated to the CPP, and the theme song, 'Kwame Nkrumah will never die', became an enormously popular expression of anticolonial sentiment.

By means of parables and ambiguously allusive metaphorical lyrics, the Highlife songs were able to comment upon tension in Ghanaian politics. For example, by the mid-1960s, when Kwame Nkrumah's regime had become unpopular, the Concert Party comedian, Bob Cole, attacked the oppressive system of detentions and police surveillance with his dramatized song, Aban Kaban ('The Government's in Chains').

> When you and I were there,
> and you saw a policeman following me,
> did you not know that there was
> a government chain in my hands?[8]

Kofi Awoonor comments, 'Bob Cole got away with it because nobody really in the political set-up at that time actually felt that Bob Cole was taking a jibe at the whole Nkrumah structure.'[9] Awoonor suggests that Concert Party's freedom to make oblique criticism of the government was an extension of the system of licence allowed to pre-colonial satirical dance groups called *Halo*. With both *Halo* and Concert Party, popular discontents and feuds found artistic expression normally denied to overtly political channels of communication.

However, where *Halo*'s topicality was normally restricted to village life. Concert Party was capable of responding to more modern national or even international events. During the Second World War a troupe called Bob Vans and the Burma Jokers travelled to India to entertain Ghanaian soldiers on duty there.

Other popular trios in the forties and fifties were Bob Cole and the Happy Trio, the Dix Covian Jokers and the West End Trio. In 1952 E. K. Nyame, who led a troupe called the Akan Trio, introduced Highlife music, and this proved a powerful factor in the increasing popularity of Concert Party. By 1970 there were estimated to be over fifty troupes operating in Ghana, mostly along the coastal belt.

Another reason for Concert Party's rapid popularization among the subaltern classes was its ability to deal (if only at a fantasy level) with themes vitally affecting the daily lives of ordinary Ghanaians. E. J. Collins lists five major themes as characteristic of Concert Party:

1) problems [such as crime] arising from urban migration;
2) problems associated with cash crops [such as inheritance disputes];
3) changing sexual mores [especially the emancipation of women];
4) inter-generational conflicts;
5) social stratification and class conflict.

Naturally plays often displayed more than one theme, where connections were made, for instance, between emergent social stratification and other sexual or generational conflicts. *So Is the World* by Kojo Brake's Band, for example, offered a quite complex analysis of the strained relationship between the new capitalist cocoa-farming elite and the ethical standards surviving from pre-colonial rural kinship systems.[10]

It was not only the themes of the plays which appealed to the subaltern classes, but also the increased willingness of the Trios to seek out such audiences. Efua Sutherland cites an example of a Concert Party troupe in 1967 performing in a cheap cinema in a shabby shanty town called Tema outside Accra to an audience of 500 workers who each paid 1 cedi admission.[11] Concert Party could achieve success in such unlikely places largely because of the performers' energetic courting of popular audiences.

Owing to Concert Party's mobile nature, its influence reached beyond the borders of Ghana. In the 1950s Concert Party had a very strong influence on Nigerian popular theatre. The genre also spread to Togo and the Ivory Coast. In a fascinating study of a Togolese group, The Happy Stars of Lomé, Alain Ricard has shown how Concert Party spread from Ghana to Togo, and he cites the example of a guitarist in the Lomé group who had originally played for the similar-sounding Happy Stars of Accra.[12]

Ricard's study provides particularly useful insights into the performing conditions of Concert Party and the relationship of the troupe to urban communities in Lomé. The troupe had a fairly tight hierarchy (somewhat reminiscent of *Beni*) which included a President, a Director and a Vice-President. The troupe consisted of a core of professionals, earning a very moderate salary (the President earned only US$12 a month in the late 1960s), plus a more marginal group of interested amateurs.

The Happy Stars of Lomé performed in bars and nightclubs in the working-class areas of Kodjoviokope or Lam Nava and their plays were sandwiched between extensive Highlife popular music performances. Most of the stages were open thrust arenas, but some were like the Happy Stars' favourite stage at Tonyeviadji Bar, which had a raised platform thrust stage with a miniature box set.

Ricard gives an example of a typical play plot by the Happy Stars. *Francis the Parisian* is a satire mocking pretentious Africans who imitate European mannerisms. It deals with a train-driver, John, who has two wives, the faithful Elise and the fickle Marie. While Elise nurses John through his convalescence from an accident, Marie runs off with a grotesquely

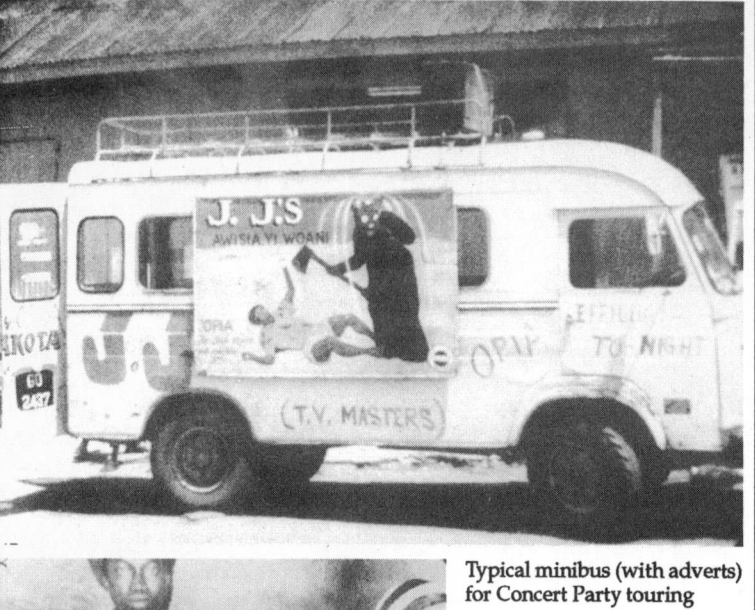

Typical minibus (with adverts) for Concert Party touring

Some Concert Party stereotyped roles

Europeanized playboy, Francis. Eventually, in a climactic role reversal, Francis is reduced to poverty after the collapse of his debt cycle, and he receives the come-uppance the audience longs for. The meekly chastened Francis and Marie return to John's household as domestic servants.[13]

Though the play's interest in class-consciousness is more typical of post-independence Concert Party, the central concern with domestic issues from a male viewpoint in an urban setting is at the heart of Concert Party from its inception. Such preoccupations can be found in much earlier plays, such as *Afei Menu Moho* (Had I Known), a popular play by Bob Johnson in the 1940s. The play tells of a thoughtless man, Kwamena, who loves his wife Georgina, but neglects her for a younger, more sophisticated girl who tries to take all his money. In the climactic encounter between Georgina and the other woman, Kwamena nearly loses both, but finally succeeds in persuading Georgina to stay with him.[14]

The moral obsession with the acquisitive young marriage-breaking woman might seem to indicate a very modern male insecurity in the face of female economic emancipation in urban Africa, but the actual didactic tone and plot structure is very close to an older pre-colonial didactic tradition.

At this point, it is useful to summarize some of the theatrical features of Concert Party, showing the influence of an indigenous dramatic tradition and its adaptation to an urban setting. The stereotyped characters in *Afei Menu Moho* (faithful wife, gullible husband, gold-digging girlfriend) are typical of Concert Party. Other common caricatures include the poor farmer, the corrupt policeman, the prostitute, the smooth-talking swindler and the wily old man. The costumes backed up the stereotyping by including some element of stylization or exaggeration. Specific examples of costume carica-ture are threadbare rags for a farmer, excessive powder for a prostitute, a false belly for a greedy businessman, long trousers and a hat for a bureau-cratic clerk, dark glasses and a cigarette for a playboy.

Another reinforcement of stereotyping was the identification which certain actors developed for specific roles. For example, in the Two Bobs and the Carolina Girl, J. B. Ansah usually played a gentleman, Charles Hutton a money-grubbing girl-about-town, and Bob Johnson a comic servant. In the Happy Stars of Lomé, the Vice-President usually played the role of a playboy swindler, Alex an old man, Cyprian a prostitute, Teobald an unfaithful crafty wife, and Ben's speciality was 'Nago', an exaggeratedly brutal Yoruba brewery worker. The use of ethnic stereotypes was not very common, but did exist; another example found in some plays from the 1940s was that of a Liberian stevedore.

The whole technique of caricature is almost certainly derived from the stereotyping found in pre-colonial West African theatre forms such as *Anansesem*, *Halo* and comic masquerades. The use of male actors to play female roles is another pre-colonial survival. Although the use of caricature makes complex characterization difficult, it is appropriate to the stylized semi-musical theatre form of Concert Party and its didactic function of social commentary.

There were several other features of Concert Party which show a strong residue from the indigenous theatre tradition. One was the organizational base of the troupes. Although the original trios were entrepreneurial groups held together by a strong-minded individual, more cooperative traditions reasserted themselves with some of the later groups. In the Jaguar Jokers, for example, studied by Collins in 1976, there were 23 members of the troupe, consisting of 13 actors, nine musicians and a promoter.[15] As in the pre-colonial performance troupes, there was a cooperative system of helping members at times of sickness or funerals, and stage discipline (for example, fines for drunkenness on stage) were enforced on a collective basis.

For publicity Concert Party sometimes employed Western techniques like posters and radio announcements, but often used direct means such as bell-ringers, clowns and drummers. The formulaic plots (Ricard (1977) calls Concert Party 'a theatre of cliché') were required by the oral technique of improvisation the actors employed. These rambling, episodic plots, the repetitive motifs, the apparently gratuitous use of catch-phrases, comic business, songs and dances related less to a European literary/dramatic aesthetic (where stage business is normally subordinated to overall plot design by a system of theatrical decorum) than to indigenous popular narrative and dance techniques designed to comment on the plot or to stimulate audience participation.

The Concert Party performing area was normally a thrust stage without curtains. Stage lights consisted of tilly lamps or simple electric bulbs rather than an elaborate panoply of formal stage lights and dimmer boards. Rapport with the audience was far more important than creating a realistic illusion. Concert Party encouraged active audience participation, as Bame explains, 'Spectators laugh, applaud and show sympathetic feelings according to what happens in the plays.'[16] More active and specifically indigenous forms of audience participation included offering money to actors in mid-performance and women waving handkerchiefs over a star actor's head after a particularly eloquent song or speech. Similarly if the audience disagreed with some statement or action it heckled the offending actor.

This summary of Concert Party's basic theatrical features shows the way the dramatic form was able to provide a popular medium of entertainment and instruction which was sufficiently indigenous to appeal to audience needs for an African aesthetic, but with enough urban sophistication and relevance to help it interpret the fast-changing mores of modern capitalist Ghana.

Concert Party's Euro-African mixed parenthood was similar to another syncretic theatre form in West Africa, Yoruba Opera. The dramatic elements of Yoruba Opera were derived from both the pre-colonial Yoruba masquerades, *Egungun*, and the tradition of Christian cantatas introduced by European missionaries. These origins are related in a particularly complex way to the history of interaction between indigenous and colonial cultures and to the growth of class formation in Nigeria.

The mission ancestry of Yoruba Opera is the easiest to trace because of the documentation which exists on the transition from Christian cantatas to secular operas. In Chapter Two I referred to the brief flowering of elitist theatre in Lagos during the 1870s and 1880s. That theatre, focused on the school halls, catered not only for the colonial administrators, traders and missionaries, but also for the Christianized and Westernized Yoruba elites. In the 1890s, however, a cultural split grew between the Europeans and the African elites, caused, according to Oyekan Owomoyela, by the increasing

Obra Ye Ko (Life is War): a scene from a 1965 production by the Ghana Brigade Group in the Concert Party style

A scene from Ogunde's *Bread and Bullet* (1950)

racism of the Europeans after the imposition of formal colonialism in 1888.[17] As a result. the Westernized Yoruba elites started to develop proto-nationalist sentiments.

The expression of these sentiments in the Christian community took the form of breakaway African churches, such as the Apostolic church and the Cherubim and Seraphim. The African churches gradually created syncretic rituals based on indigenous cultural forms as well as those of Western Christianity, an aesthetic related to the submerged nationalist sentiments of religious millennialism. The secessionist churches also had guilds which created a type of religious theatre called 'New Dramas'. These were popular with the Lagos elites, and were performed in the recently built public halls, such as Glover Memorial Hall, Lisabi Hall and Ebute Metta. Sometimes the 'New Drama' groups incorporated secular European traditions such as vaudeville entertainments, but there was heavy reliance on Yoruba cultural forms as well. For example, one late nineteenth-century group entitled the Lagos Glee Singers performed European operettas by such composers as Gilbert and Sullivan, but also introduced an 'opening glee' similar to the introductory *ijuba* of the pre-colonial *Egungun* masquerades.[18]

Another manifestation of the reaction against colonialism was a surge of intellectual Yoruba cultural nationalism among the African Lagos elites; it took the form of a selective interest in Yoruba religion, history, philosophy, language, music and art. The effects of such a sensibility were felt in the 'New Drama' where attempts were made to introduce Yoruba music into nativity plays and other Christian entertainments. The pattern was established of a tension among the Yoruba emergent bourgeoisie between, on the one hand, an elitist culture which could reinforce their status as an educated class different from the 'up-country natives' (by making links with the colonial culture imported from the European metropoles), and forms of cultural nationalism, on the other hand, which could employ elements of indigenous culture as weapons in the struggle for independence. That conflict was bequeathed to Yoruba Opera at a later stage.

Despite the excitement of cultural nationalist movements in Western Nigeria from about 1890 to the end of the First World War, the theatre form of the Christian cantata did not develop much during what Owomoyela (1976: 31) calls the 'dormant period' of the 1920s and 1930s. New energy did not create fresh dramatic forms until a process of democratization and secularization helped produce the Yoruba Opera proper in the 1940s. The biggest aesthetic impact of the early 'Native Air Operas' was to break with an indigenous in-the-round stagecraft and replace it with a shallow picture-frame stage. Jeyifo says this 'makes an epochal shift in the spatial aesthetics of the African performance'.[19] No matter how much revival of pre-colonial art forms took place in later Yoruba Opera developments, the picture-frame stage remained a stable constraint.

I can best show the transition from Yoruba Christian cantatas to secular Yoruba Operas, and the extent to which an indigenous aesthetic contributed to the new dramatic form, by examining the career of Hubert Ogunde. Fortunately, Ebun Clark has written a well-documented account of Ogunde's theatrical career; she details Ogunde's development from a Christian choir-master to a thoroughly professional, secular theatre artist, and I rely heavily on her research.[20]

The cultural tradition which Ogunde found in the African churches was that of the 'Native Air Opera', under the direction of choir-masters like S. Onimole, A. A. Layeni and A. B. David. These operas were more like cantatas than fully dramatized operas. The production 'usually had members of the cast standing on the stage swaying from side to side and singing continuously to the accompaniment of drums or the organ rather as in the eighteenth-century English oratorio'.[21]

Ogunde's first operas shared with the 'Native Air Operas' very Christian plots, as a list of some titles will suggest: *Garden of Eden* and *The Throne of God* (1944), *Africa and God* (1944), *Israel in Egypt* (1945), *Nebuchadnezzar's Reign and Belshazzar's Feast* (1945) and *King Solomon* (1945). Their message too, often gave praise to a Christian God, as in this quotation from an 'opening glee' in *Journey to Heaven* (1947):

O come! mankind, for us to sing a song
glory to the Lord.[22]

What differentiated them from the earliest cantatas was the amount of dramatization, choreography and movement in the plays, and the increasing use of realistic situations and dialogue. Another significant feature of Ogunde's operas, even in the early 'Christian' phase, was the incorporation of Yoruba cultural forms. These included Yoruba music, songs and chants, though the main body of the early operas was in English; they also included the portrayal of scenes from a rural pre-colonial Yoruba setting. For example, most of *Africa and God* is set in a pre-colonial period, showing the way of life of the Yoruba before the arrival of Christianity.

The strong traces of indigenous culture in Ogunde's early Christian plays are not surprising. The cultural tradition of the separatist churches was already a syncretic one. Moreover, although Ogunde was brought up as a Christian, he was never cut off from the pre-colonial tradition of popular *Egungun* theatre. He has suggested that the desire to start a professional modern theatre came from the example of the professional *Egungun* groups:

I was playing drums with the masqueraders in my home town when I was young and these *Egungun* people gave me the urge inside me to start a company of actors.[23]

The sense of Ogunde's self-conscious search for a Yoruba theatre aesthetic is implicit in the first title for his theatre group, the African Music Research Party. Even Ogunde's theatre organization bears a resemblance to *Egungun* as much as to a typical European drama troupe. In December 1945, after failing to attract with an advertisement young girls as actresses for the African Music Research Party, Ogunde expediently married potentially skilled performers, and used his wives as the basis for his dancers, singers and actresses. This solution of making the troupe into a family business was similar to the lineage-based professionalism of the pre-colonial *Alarinjo* masqueraders. The influence of the indigenous tradition on Ogunde's theatre organization affected many aesthetic features of Yoruba Opera, as I shall try briefly to explain later in the chapter.

The interplay between the Western and Yoruba sources of Ogunde's theatre relates both to his position in the class formation of Nigerian society and to the dialectic of different phases through which his theatre styles progressed. Clark divides Ogunde's career into three broad phases: the Opera (1944-9), the Concert Party (1950-64) and the Contemporary (1964-78, the time of publication of Clark's book). Allowing for the simplification inevitable with all historicist phasing of artistic works, I believe this is a useful division and illuminates not only Ogunde's artistic progress, but also, in a rough-and-ready way, three important phases of Nigerian history:

1) cultural nationalism and economic protests against colonialism;
2) the rise of nationalist party politics;
3) post-independence adjustments to neo-colonialism and modern urban social problems.

In the Opera phase of his career Ogunde tried to resolve some of the problems created by his petty-bourgeois, slightly Westernized background. From 1933 to 1940 Ogunde had worked as a primary school teacher and church organist, and from 1941 to 1944 he was a police constable in Enugu, Ibadan and, finally, Lagos. In 1944 Ogunde resigned from the police to take up professional theatre.

The Opera phase of Ogunde's theatre can roughly be subdivided into Christian and the social, proto-nationalist phases. During his Christian period, Ogunde tried to reconcile the Christian Europhile sentiments which had provided the context of his colonial acculturation, with the proto-nationalist attitudes towards which his petty-bourgeois class position in post-war Nigeria spurred him.

Africa and God is a good example of those conflicts. A synopsis of the plot places the opera firmly in a tradition of colonized client drama offering an apology for Christianity and colonialism. *Africa and God* deals with a pre-colonial Yoruba tyrant, Oba Labode, who oppressed his people and kept them ignorant. A contemporary review in the *Daily Comet* summed up the regime in a brief sentence: 'Oba Labode and his people worshipped the gods of Egungun, Smallpox, Agemo and all other gods that came into their fancies.'[24] This rule of 'darkness' is redeemed by the intervention of the colonialists when the British Consul declares war on and defeats Labode. Ogunde claimed that *Africa and God* followed the events of the British military campaign against Ijebu. The conclusion of the play shows the triumph of Christianity over superstition. The negative image of pre-colonial feudal African rule is akin to that represented by the assimilationist plays of Ecole William Ponty in the 1930s. The main difference is that, with Ogunde, a more fruitful tension manifested itself between the text of the play and its subtext. The vivid re-enactment of pre-colonial Yoruba cultural forms, such as chants, dances and divination rites, provided a subtext to *Africa and God* that was very appealing to the emerging second wave of cultural nationalism, and was at odds with the Christian/colonialist message of the play. The radicalization of Yoruba Opera followed a pattern similar to Concert Party.

The contradiction at the heart of *Africa and God* was closely tied to conflicts arising from Ogunde's class position. As a petty-bourgeois former colonial employee he was in the front line of the clash between imperial interventionist capital and more indigenous entrepreneurial capitalism which fuelled the nationalist movements of West Africa. As such, he was in a somewhat marginal position during the 1940s, identified neither with the rural peasant class of cultivators with their roots in pre-colonial cultural forms, nor with the metropolitan colonial culture of the Lagos elites. Ogunde's intermediate position helped him use Yoruba Opera performances to analyse and redefine some of the cultural contradictions felt by the emergent petty-bourgeois and proletarian classes.

In his relations with pre-colonial culture Ogunde lost status considerably when he gave up his job as a colonial policeman in 1944 to become a professional theatre entrepreneur. According to Yoruba concepts of prestige and ethics his abandonment of a steady job to join a theatre group put him on the same social rank as the very low-status performers of the *Alarinjo Egungun* theatre. It was only among the urban communities that Ogunde slowly earned respect. Ogunde's ambiguously syncretic operas combining Christian messages with a Yoruba aesthetic appealed to the mood of refined ethnicism which characterized urban Yoruba sentiments during the immediate post-war period.

Ogunde's later Christian plays were far less overtly colonial than the earlier ones, and marked a transition to the secular nationalist plays. The image of pre-colonial African society in *Journey to Heaven* and *The Black Forest* (both 1945) was much less negative than that of *Africa and God*. Ogunde's co-director at that time, G. B. Kuyinu said:

> We would not like to portray ourself as backward, which was the belief of the colonial masters in those days. That's why we tried hard to study our culture very well: to study many things about our country, and then to bring it out in a polished way.[25]

Kuyinu captures very precisely the attitude of Christianized urban communities in Western Nigeria during the period of cultural nationalism. They would not deign to participate full-bloodedly in a pre-colonial 'bush' theatre form like *Egungun,* but did appreciate some refined or 'polished' dramatization of Yoruba culture which could compete with the 'high' culture of colonialism. In following popular will, the Ogunde company was obeying what Jeyifo called 'the cardinal rule' of the Yoruba Opera 'that ultimately the company must defer to the wishes of the audience'.[26]

Ogunde's economic base was another indication of his class position and reflected the historical development of Nigerian capitalism. The post-war period saw the flourishing of petty-bourgeois entrepreneurial capitalism in textiles and food marketing. This involved the expansion of transport between the rapidly growing urban centres of West Africa. Along with this expansion, there was a growth of urban tension and a competitive spirit fuelled by a cash economy. Ogunde's African Music Research Party (changed in 1947 to the more individualistic sounding Ogunde Theatre Party) was in many ways a cultural homology of that economic development. His theatre company was entrepreneurial in that it was financed and organized by Ogunde and his family. In 1945 he organized house-to-house appeals for an African theatre 'scholarship fund', and this provided the capital for him to go professional.

As with other entrepreneurial companies Ogunde soon found himself in competition with rivals. For example, a correspondent of the *Daily Service,* who noted in 1946 that hooligans had tried to disrupt one of Ogunde's performances at the Glover Hall, commented, 'It is understood that some of these hooligans are members of a rival musical party.'[27]

As with Bob Johnson in Ghana, Ogunde found that the only way his professional theatre group could remain solvent was by travelling, in order to find new paying audiences. His earliest Christian operas were all first performed at the Glover Hall in Lagos, but were later shown in other Yoruba towns such as Ibadan, Oyo, Owo, Ilesha, Osogbo and Ife. Some were shown even outside the Yoruba-speaking area. In 1946, for example, the Ogunde Theatre Party travelled with a more secular repertoire to Jos, Zaria, Kano, Kaduna and Minna.

The audiences for Ogunde's operas were mainly petty bourgeois and urban working-class. It was these groups which provided the cutting edge of resistance to colonialism. It is not surprising, therefore, to find that Ogunde quickly responded to his audience's allegiance to the struggle for national independence. Some measure of Ogunde's close relationship with national-ist politicians can be seen from the fact that the nationalist leader Nnamdi Azikiwe was the chairman of one of Ogunde's early anticolonial plays, *Worse than Crime* (1945). A poster advertising the show stated, 'Slavery in any shape or form is WORSE THAN CRIME.'[28] The audiences of the time found no difficulty in substituting the word 'colonialism' in their minds for 'slavery'. Owing to the political implications of the play, Ogunde and G. B. Kuyinu were detained by the colonial police for two days.

Other examples of Ogunde's explicitly anticolonial plays were *Herbert Macaulay* and *Human Parasites* (both 1946), but the most controversial plays were *Strike and Hunger* and *Bread and Bullet*. *Strike and Hunger* was first performed in October 1945 in Lagos. It was a topical story dramatizing the Nigerian general strike which had occurred only a few months earlier (June/July). Although *Strike and Hunger* focused on political issues, it did not completely abandon the Christian perspective of the earlier operas. The salute in the opening glee included a Christian validation of the nationalist message:

> God almighty who owns the earth
> Says we should eat and drink
> That we may never suffer hunger till night or lament.[29]

The colonial government did not react to the performances in Lagos (where expressions of anti-British patriotism were not uncommon anyway). But the play received much official opposition when it was taken on a tour of Northern Nigeria. The most critical incident occurred in Jos, where the colonial police raided the theatre, scattered the audience and arrested Ogunde and some of his troupe. Ogunde was eventually released, but not allowed to perform his play.

The Assistant Superintendent of police in Jos accused Ogunde of importing metropolitan seditious values into the more conservative Hausa regions, proclaiming, 'Your business is to educate the Northerner in your Lagos politics.'[30] This gives an interesting perspective on the way colonial authorities perceived Yoruba Opera as a carrier for urban political and social values.

No doubt much of the sensitivity about *Strike and Hunger* was based on the clear identification which the play made between African poverty and racial oppression. In the following series of antitheses, for example, Yejide represents the white man:

> Yejide eats butter
> The blackman eats leather from animals

Yejide eats bread
The blackman eats beniseed
Yejide eats sugar
The blackman drinks peppery water.[31]

Coming so soon after the general strike, such lines might well have seemed inflammatory.

In 1950 Ogunde created another controversial play, *Bread and Bullet*, dramatizing the events of a different disturbance. Again the events were very recent – the Enugu Colliery strike of 1949, in which eighteen miners were shot dead by police during demonstrations. And again it was the attempt to take the play to the North (where the British system of indirect rule was more effective than in the South) which caused problems. The play was banned by the police in Kano on the grounds that it was seditious and Ogunde was fined £6 for putting up posters. The play was also banned in Kaduna and Makurdi.

Clark makes the important point that Ogunde's anticolonial plays were not opposed to whites in general or even colonial culture. It was the political machinery of colonial authority which Ogunde perceived as the main agent of oppression. Loyal to his roots in missionary culture, Ogunde always respected the whites who were involved in proselytizing Christianity.

Bread and Bullet was the last major play by Ogunde which made an uncompromising stand against colonial power. During the 1950s in what Clark calls the Concert Party phase, Ogunde turned to themes reflecting problems caused by urbanization. The more domestic nature of these plays is suggested by the titles: *My Darling Fatima* (1951), *Portmanteau* (1952), *Beggar's Love* (1952), *Highway Eagle* (1953), *Princess Jaja* (1953), *Village Hospital* (1957) and *Delicate Millionaire* (1958). The roots of this transition derive from the impact of Ghanaian Concert Party on Ogunde after he toured the Gold Coast in 1948.

In the Gold Coast Ogunde had to adapt his theatre technique to the much more Westernized commercial style made popular by the Concert Party theatre trios. It is often the case in cultural history that cultural imports from another country can provide the impetus for modernization and innovation. When Ogunde returned to Nigeria he embarked on a new type of theatre, the Concert Party style, and eventually changed the title of his troupe to Ogunde Concert Party.

During this phase Ogunde introduced Western musical instruments like guitars and saxophones. The dance choreography used a chorus girl line-up and there was a strong influence of American jazz and Highlife in the music. In this Ogunde was also influenced by a rival Nigerian group, Bobby Benson's Modern Theatrical Troupe. Bobby Benson and his American wife, Cassandra, enjoyed a brief popularity in the late 1940s in Lagos with shows imitating New York Harlem musicals, and employing titles like Bobby and Cassandra in *Coochi Coochi and Fantango Dance* or *Congo-Samba Tojass*. Ogunde followed suit with Concert Party shows such as *Swing the Jazz* or *Gold Coast Melodies*, although Ogunde maintained a much more Yoruba flavour than Bobby Benson. An important innovation copied from Concert Party was the use of improvisation for creating dialogue, but with songs and the opening glee remaining learned and fully rehearsed.

Ulli Beier feels that the Concert Party phase was a regression. He suggests that it caused Ogunde to distinguish between two different types of opera, the 'cultural play' (such as *The Black Forest*), which was close to Ogunde's own Yoruba aesthetic but was not commercially popular, and 'jeun-jeun' – the more debased Concert Party genre which Ogunde reluctantly espoused.[32] This analysis, however, might be coloured by Beier's known preference for 'authenticity'. The influence of black American and Ghanaian culture should not be seen simply as a distracting form of urban escapism. Those entertainments served a purpose at the time of providing a modern, Westernized innovatory form of entertainment which the audiences could enjoy without feeling they were succumbing to the cultural milieu of the British colonizing power.

The extensive use of English which Ogunde employed during the Concert Party period helped him create a theatre medium intelligible outside the Yoruba area, a necessity for a theatre form reflecting the currents of trans-ethnic nationalism.

One possible reason for recent academic disdain for the Concert Party performances is that nationalist sentiments were much less obvious than in the late opera phase of 1946–50. It was perhaps surprising that, during the period which coincided with the final struggle for Nigerian independence, Ogunde should have been more concerned with the social issues (marriage, crime, sorcery, prostitution) that characterized Concert Party plays than with explicitly nationalist politics. I believe the explanation is that, during the 1950s, the nationalist struggle tended to move away from the fairly violent common front and trade union conflicts which had provided fertile themes for Ogunde up to 1950. Instead, nationalist politics tended to be diverted into the complex manoeuvrings and machinations of party politics – an area much less amenable to theatrical representation.

All the same, Ogunde's long-standing commitment to the cause of nationalism was rewarded at Nigeria's independence by the commissioning of a special play, *The Song of Unity*, to celebrate the event in October 1960. The play marked the beginning of another phase of Ogunde's development, the post-independence 'play' phase. In the post-independence period Ogunde moved away from the Westernized Concert Party vaudeville style. In its place was an increased use of pre-colonial Yoruba theatre techniques – *Bata* drums instead of saxophones, and an increased use of play motifs based on history and folklore. The semi-literary operas of Ogunmola and Ladipo might have provided some impetus for the change. A measure of the 'indigenization' of Ogunde's post-independence operas is that from *Yoruba Ronu* onwards (1964) Ogunde used Yoruba titles for almost all his operas. The aesthetic innovations in the third phase were a response (as well as a contribution) to the post-independence sentiments of pride in indigenous African culture, and in a sense marked a return to some of the political pre-occupations of the late 1940s.

The play phase marked the culmination of Ogunde's financial success. From the humble beginnings, when Ogunde had been despised and had had to struggle with rival Lagos theatre troupes, to the early 1960s he had built up a flourishing entrepreneurial capitalist enterprise. His prominence in Nigerian theatre was recognized by other artists., who elected him chairman of ATPN, the Association of Theatre Practitioners of Nigeria. One of the secrets of his success was his incredibly productive output (51 plays between 1943 and 1977). This meant that audiences kept coming back for the latest

Ogunde performance. In Lagos the nature of theatre-going does not allow for a constant migrant audience (as in London or New York where tourists and visitors can keep a show on stage for years). As Clark explains, 'on the contrary, the repertoire of the Yoruba theatre companies has to be extensive and constantly changing in order to draw the public and maintain a sizeable box-office intake'.[33] The popular theatre impresario, therefore, not only has to have a large repertoire of plays, but must also be willing to travel to the people – rather than expecting them to travel to the performance. Ogunde's indefatigable willingness to travel was another contribution to his financial success. Some indication of the hazards of his barnstorming tours is given by the number of entries for 'lorry breakdown' which were logged in Ogunde's itineraries.

Yet another reason for Ogunde's financial success was his business acumen and willingness to diversify. In addition to the theatre company he also founded two subsidiary companies, the Ogunde Record Company (1967), the main function of which was to market the songs and records made popular by the operas, and the Ogunde Dance Company (1966), geared to creating ethnic 'folk-dance' shows for overseas tours .

Several critics have commented on the difference between the organiza- tion of Yoruba Opera and that of the skill specialization found in Western professional theatre. Robert Armstrong noted that another opera artist, Duro Ladipo, 'is at once author, composer. stage director, business manager and chief actor of his company'.[34] To these, for both Ogunde and Ladipo, could be added choreographer and set designer. Martin Banham has noted the creative tension achieved in Yoruba Opera by having the 'dynamism that comes from the very strong leadership of the actor/manager/playwright' linked to the collective creativity owing to the 'close community that the company forms, living together, often married or inter-related, creating their work's music and story as one process'.[35]

I would suggest that the artistic vigour which Banham notes is closely related to the economic enterprise of the theatrical mode of production. Ogunde's various entrepreneurial and artistic skills, for example, must be seen in the context of the expansion of small-scale petty-capitalist ventures during the 1950s and 1960s. Although Ogunde's class position can by no means provide a reductively total explanation of the social and political features of his theatre aesthetic, I would like to suggest in the ensuing analysis of the play phase that there have been important links.

One way of highlighting some of Ogunde's ideological attitudes is to compare his career with that of a very different Nigerian theatre artist, the academic literary playwright, Wole Soyinka. In 1960, while Ogunde was receiving triumphant official plaudits for *The Song of Unity*, Soyinka's play, *The Dance of the Forests*, which had won a Nigerian independence competi- tion, was unofficially dropped from the celebrations.[36] The celebration organizers objected to the sceptical attitude Soyinka's play showed to the glories of the pre-colonial African past. The play was an early, perhaps premature, example of a reaction away from negritude and those kinds of cultural nationalism which stress the merits of pre-colonial African history, at the expense of analysing post-colonial discontents. Far more than Ogunde, Soyinka was able to foresee the dangers in an over-complacent cultural nationalism.

The comparison, of course, is not really fair; Ogunde was working within the rather rigid conventions of an established genre, whereas Soyinka was able to experiment with new dramatic forms. All the same, the comparison between the two artists raises important issues concerning the relationship between varieties of popular and literary theatre towards the shifting pattern of social and political change. A popular, commercial artist like Ogunde tends to keep abreast of the political tide and to reflect the ideological interests of the petty bourgeoisie and the urban subaltern classes. In exceptional cases a literary radical playwright like Wole Soyinka is able to anticipate the problems which might affect future generations. As Soyinka put it, 'I can smell the reactionary sperm years before the rape of the nation takes place.'[37]

The comparison between the two theatre workers is worth continuing into the subsequent phase of Nigerian history – the collapse of democracy, the military coups and the civil war over Biafra.

After independence, the next major play by Ogunde was *Yoruba Ronu* (Yorubas Think) in 1963. On the surface the play had a historical theme, analysing a nineteenth-century defection by Field Marshal Afonja of Ilorin from the authority of the Alafin of Oyo, Oba Fiwajoye. Afonja allies himself with the invading Fulani, but is eventually killed by the people of Ilorin. Oba Fiwajoye is reinstated on the throne, the Fulani are expelled and the Oba brings in a renewed era of prosperity. Although the play was based on real historical incidents, the contemporary audiences were quick to take up the play's modern relevance. The plot was accepted as a thinly disguised allegory about post-independence politics in Nigeria's Western Region. Oba Fiwajoye was identified with Chief Awolowo, the leader of the Western Region Action Group. The defection of his deputy was paralleled by the creation in 1962 of a splinter party, the Nigerian National Democratic Party, led by Chief Akintola, away from the Action Group and in alliance with the Northern and Federal politicians.

Yoruba Ronu was banned by the Western Region government in 1964. This led to disturbances in Ibadan, a bloody riot in Ilesha, and vehement protests in that section of the press which supported the Action Group. In addition to banning the play, Chief Akintola also banned Ogunde's very popular musical records.

In 1966, after the first military coup, Lieutenant-Colonel F. A. Fajuyi, Military Governor of the Western Region, lifted the ban on Ogunde's records and on *Yoruba Ronu*. Ogunde was allowed to produce the play again, with Chief Awolowo as a prominent guest. The play was enormously popular, both for its political content and for its spectacular use of indigenous Yoruba theatre techniques. Nevertheless, there was a latent ethnicism in the message, which with hindsight of the ensuing war seems rather ominous.

Wole Soyinka was also disgusted by the corruption and political chicanery of Chief Akintola and wrote a play which satirized that type of post-independence African politics. The play, *Kongi's Harvest* (1965), attacked corruption, the empty rhetoric of political sloganeering, and the manipulation of mass media to legitimatize dictatorship and the cult of personality.[38] Contemporary audiences saw allusions to Chief Akintola, but also to other African leaders such as Kamuzu Banda and Kwame Nkrumah. Where *Yoruba Ronu* was an entirely topical play pointing to a specific event in Western

Nigeria, *Kongi's Harvest* was far more eclectic and applicable to different African situations both within and outside Nigeria. *Yoruba Ronu* was more popular at the time, stirring strong feelings with mass audiences and perhaps having a direct impact on political events; *Kongi's Harvest* has proved more durable, enjoying many performances throughout Africa and also in Europe and the USA, not only in the mid-sixties but in the seventies and beyond.

The reactions of Ogunde and Soyinka to the Nigerian Civil War are also worth comparing. Although the title of Ogunde's play, *Keep Nigeria One* (1968), sounds like an impartial plea for unity, the play, a satire about the major Nigerian ethnic groups, Hausa/Fulani, Ibo and Yoruba, was so savagely anti-Ibo that even the *Nigeria Daily Times,* which normally supported the Federal Government, felt obliged to protest. *Keep Nigeria One* was one of the plays which the Federal Government allowed Ogunde to take on his 1968–9 trip to London. Presumably the government saw the play as part of its public relations exercise during the civil war. The other plays performed in London were Yoruba dance dramas, created by the Ogunde Dance Company and geared to European tastes for exotic spectacle. The titles of the shows were *Mama Eko, Oba'nta* and *Ogun Pari*, plus a dance drama whose title, *Oh Ogunde!*, was presumably a facetious allusion to the London sex review, *Oh Calcutta!*, which was enjoying success in 1969. These apparently innocuous musicals actually constituted a form of propaganda counterbalancing the bad publicity the Federal Government received in Europe over its conduct of the civil war.

Ogunde's compliance with the government (when its policies coincided with his own Yoruba affiliations) contrasts with the attitude of Soyinka, who, while far from supporting the Biafran cause, had sufficient sympathy for the Ibos to protest against the war and the policies of the Federal Government. His critical attitude earned his detention for over two years, much of it in solitary confinement. Soyinka's disgust with both the imbecilities of war and the political ineptness and corruption which led to it found theatrical expression in the absurdist play *Madmen and Specialists* and the allegorical farce *Jero's Metamorphosis*.[39] These plays reflected the complexity and horror of life in Nigeria in the late 1960s far better than the slick commercial dance dramas Ogunde took to Britain.

I am not suggesting that a literary playwright like Soyinka is inevitably superior to a popular professional artist like Ogunde, but that the popular artist sometimes finds difficulty in maintaining the flexibility needed to adjust to a rapidly shifting national political scene.

For a petty-bourgeois artist like Ogunde, dependent on his creativity for economic survival, and without the institutional security offered to academic artists, the most fruitful dramatic field tends not to be politics as much as social analysis. Many of Ogunde's most successful plays have dealt with themes such as crime, marriage, corruption, prostitution and the world of business.

A fairly typical example of Ogunde's social plays in the post-independence period is *Onimoto*. The story is about two men who are sacked from their jobs as lorry drivers, and who go to Lagos in search of success. Balelayo does succeed by dint of hard work at a small car hire business. Ilumo is also initially successful by means of sorcery after he joins a secret cult, but his opulent hedonistic life style (including drugs) causes him to go insane. The strong moral contrast between the two friends, backed up by the very melodramatic plot is typical of Ogunde's social satires. The petty-bourgeois ethic of the play is also typical, endorsing qualities of hard work in order to achieve wealth.

As is often the case in popular theatre, however, there was sometimes a tension between the avowed didactic aim of Ogunde's plays and the performance subtext. For example, one of Ogunde's most popular shows, *K'ehin Sokun*, a 1971 remake of the 1953 Concert Party-style show, *Highway Eagle*, had a different effect on the audience from the one intended. The original story of *Highway Eagle* told of a duel between a clever female police officer, Detective Sergeant Awero, and Awodi Oke, a ruthless murderer and armed robber. After a convoluted plot involving deceptions and a takeover of the prison by Awode Oke, the outlaw is eventually hanged. The moral, of course, is that crime does not pay. In the revival, *K'ehin Sokun*, Ogunde added a lot of contemporary material, including having Awodi Oke shot at the Bar Beach (instead of hanged in private). The 1971 audience identified Awodi with Dr Oyenusi, a notorious armed robber who had terrorized the public and defied the police. The Lagos public made an anti-hero out of Oyenusi, finding in his defiance of the law a compensatory fantasy for their own inability to succeed in the capitalist jungle of post-civil-war Nigeria. The crime-does-not-pay moral, therefore, did not fully come across to the 1971 audience. As Clark puts it, 'Ogunde was appalled by the audience's admiration for the actor who played the part of Oyenusi. They cheered his every utterance, and made the militant sign of power.'[40]

K'ehin Sokun is a good example of the way the overt moral of a popular play can be modified or even subverted by its unintentional appeal to group emotions, often indicating inarticulate but deep-rooted fears, fantasies and allegiances. This type of almost instinctive 'feel' for the theatre techniques, forms and motifs that appeal to popular audiences is related to the collective improvised creativity which Ogunde taps in his performances, and ultimately to the whole aesthetic of Yoruba Opera.

Much of Ogunde's popularity, like that of Ghanaian Concert Party performers, was due to his skill at maintaining and adapting those elements derived from an indigenous aesthetic which appealed to modern urban audiences. Examples of pre-colonial theatre techniques which Ogunde inherited from the *Alarinjo* and other pre-colonial theatre traditions were: the use of stereotyped characterization, costumes and props, improvised dialogue, didactically formulaic plot sequences, and the synaesthesia of music, dialogue and mime.

A good example of a specific technique is the structural device of the opening glee. Adedeji explains that the technique was adapted from the pre-colonial professional *Alarinjo* theatre and served two important functions. First, the author sought divine blessing to absolve himself from blame for his social criticism, and, secondly, the author instructed the audience about the play's moral purpose by 'informing and exposing certain deviant behaviours in society in an entertaining way … to regulate the norms of society.'[41] Ogunde's ability to adapt this aesthetic heritage (for instance, by transforming the opening glee into a 'curtain-raiser' during the Concert Party phase) is based on the flexible scriptless technique of improvisation which he employed and on his theatrical instinct for audience demands.

However, another approach to theatre has developed within Yoruba Opera, which is somewhat more calculated, and closer to literary drama. One theatre artist who became associated with such a modified form of Yoruba Opera was Kola Ogunmola. Like Ogunde, Ogunmola, who was a teacher in an Anglican primary school, started off with mainly Christian-oriented operas in the late 1940s, such as *Reign of the Mighty* (1948). But later, especially after the establishment of the Kola Ogunmola Travelling Theatre Company, he extended his work to social satires and dramatizations of literary works (but not to overt political commentary).

One important early difference between Ogunmola and Ogunde was that Ogunmola was content to take parts other than the hero or king. This broke with the custom started by Ogunde and followed by several other Yoruba Opera groups that the troupe leader played the king or hero and 'radiates the other members around his star role relative to their standing in the hierarchical structure of the group'.[42]

Ogunmola's satirical didactic plays were close to the social comment genre of Ogunde's operas. A good example of this style is *The Love of Money*, a play using a common West African formula about polygamy. The story centres on a foolish man, Adeleke, taking a second wife, Mopelola, who is beautiful but avaricious. Adeleka not only loses Mopelola and his money, but also his first wife, Morolayo, and their two children. The moral warning concerning the dangers of gold-digging town women was a formula in many Concert Party and Yoruba Opera plays.

> The girls of nowadays are bad, you know
> The girls of now are hard.
> They merely come to eat you clean.[43]

Ogunmola moved more quickly and firmly than Ogunde from the Concert Party style which had dominated Yoruba Opera during the 1950s. Ogunmola's interest in pre-colonial Yoruba theatre forms won the interest of influential European critics like Ulli Beier, who felt that Ogunmola's theatre was more authentic than that of Ogunde.

> Ogunmola cut out the music hall element from Ogunde's plays: the horseplay, the sex appeal, the saxophones; and he tried to substitute all these by serious acting. His music is more purely Yoruba than Ogunde's.[44]

Beier was impressed by what he perceived as the purer traditionalism of Ogunmola's performances, and their sense of stylization. 'Ogunmola's plays did not present a mirror image of Yoruba life: they gave a sharpened, heightened, concentrated image.'[45] Two other European expatriates, Martin Banham and Geoffrey Axworthy, were instrumental in associating the Ogunmola Travelling Theatre with the School of Drama at the University of Ibadan. The climax and main fruit of this association was the theatrical adaptation in 1962 by Ogunmola, Demas Nwoko (a theatre designer) and Geoffrey Axworthy (director of the School of Drama) of Amos Tutuola's novel, *The Palm-wine Drinkard*. The production was noted for its constant use of music, either instrumental or choral, throughout the play, and for the very careful integration of indigenous mime with the play's plot and theme.

The cross-cultural interchange which created the final stage version of Ogunmola's *The Palm-wine Drinkard* was extremely complex. Most of the original plot motifs were derived from pre-colonial Yoruba oral narratives. Owomoyela has described the opera as 'essentially folklore in a dress more compatible with a new milieu'.[46] The original Yoruba oral narratives were transposed by the novelist Amos Tutuola into a unique, fantasy world described in idiosyncratic English. Axworthy then created an English language libretto from the novel, which Ogunmola then translated back into Yoruba. In the process, the rather stark conclusion of Tutuola's novel was given a happy ending. The whole transposition was an interesting restructuring of pre-colonial culture for post-colonial audiences and was an important step in the creation of a semi-literary genre of Yoruba Opera.

The main innovation in the transformed Yoruba Operas like *The Palm-wine Drinkard* was the transposition of text onto tape or paper, a process which Ogunde and similar improvisatory artists had never been very interested in. A significant agent in the process of transposing operas into text form was Robert Armstrong, a researcher at Ibadan University's Institute of African Studies, who recorded performances not only by Ogunmola but also by Duro Ladipo.

Ladipo's background was similar to that of other syncretic theatre artists like Johnson, Ogunde and Ogunmola. He was an untrained primary school teacher and catechist in an Anglican Mission school in Osogbo, and his first theatre experiments were within a Christian framework. Like Ogunde, however, Ladipo has testified to an interest in indigenous performing arts:

> From my childhood I showed a keen interest in traditional Yoruba culture and customs as amplified by the fact that I followed closely the activities of different masquerades and cultists.[47]

He was introduced to some Yoruba Opera techniques by a mission teacher, Alex Peters, and he started dramatizing Bible stories for end-of-term school concerts during the 1950s. After a teaching spell in Kaduna, Ladipo returned to Osogbo in 1961 and used his talents as a choir-master to create a Christmas cantata at All Saints Church, which was recorded and became nationally famous. The following Easter, Ladipo wanted to incorporate Yoruba drumming into an Easter cantata. At that time the Anglican Church did not allow traditional drumming in church, so Ladipo performed the cantata in schools and town halls. This marked the beginning of a process Ogunde had already gone through in the 1940s, a secularization of the opera, and its transformation into a theatrical mode.

At about this time Ladipo caught the attention of influential Afrophile European artists, critics and academics, including Beier, Armstrong, Axworthy and Suzanne Wenger. It was partly through their support that Ladipo opened the multi-purpose arts centre Mbari Mbayo in Osogbo in 1961. Despite the backing from Western intellectuals, Ladipo was keen on making Mbari Mbayo a genuinely popular arts centre. The name tells some of the story. It derives from the Mbari Club at the University of Ibadan, a literary/artistic/cultural club founded by Soyinka, Christopher Okigbo, John Pepper Clark and Ezekiel Mphalele. The name Mbari came from an Ibo word meaning 'creation', a consciously pan-ethnic touch in the Yoruba heartland of Ibadan. Mbari Mbayo in Osogbo was a name coined by market women who were not familiar with the Ibo word 'mbari'. In Yoruba the phrase 'mbari mbayo' means 'when I see it I shall be happy'.

The participation of the common people in bestowing the name Mbari Mbayo is indicative of the links Ladipo tried to maintain between artists and popular audiences. The centre itself was in an industrial site, made out of a rather ramshackle yard in Ladipo's father's house. There was a deliberate policy of avoiding an excessive display of academic patronage even though it was given much moral support by intellectuals. A black American visitor at a festival there noted with relief that there were 'no pledges, no salutes, no academic palaver'.[48] Where the Mbari Club was a little exclusive, Mbari Mbayo was open to a much wider public, 'market women with their trays on their heads, hunters ... chiefs and kings in full regalia and preceded by their drummers, schoolteachers, children, farmers, politicians, hooligans'.[49]

The play which was presented at the opening of Mbari Mbayo was Ladipo's *Oba Moro*. The eclectic creativity of the centre, including music, art, sculpture, architecture, creative writing, dance and theatre, continued to feed Ladipo's talents and helped him create a characteristic style based on indigenous Yoruba traditions. For a few years in the 1960s, the relative absence of rigid class distinctions at Mbari Mbayo gave rise to an artistically productive atmosphere to which Ladipo was well tuned.

A measure of Ladipo's closeness to the Osogbo community is that he remained in that small market town long after he had received international fame. The first performance of *Moremi* was to the Ife chiefs who had served as his consultants when writing the play. However, Ladipo was in no way parochial; in the same *Moremi* he introduced Agbor dancers from the Ibo region of Nigeria, far from the Yoruba heartland.

The sensibility of both the Ibadan School of Drama and Mbari Mbayo at that time was one which encouraged an exploration of the pre-colonial artistic heritage and a reinterpretation of Nigerian myth and history from an African point of view. This emphasis, aptly termed 'reformed negritude' by Oyin Ogunba, was as common among the Afrophile Europeans as the Africans themselves.[50] Ulli Beier, in fact, carried the process of 'authenticization' of Yoruba Opera even further than Ladipo, in the literary operas which he wrote in conjunction with Obotunde Ijimere.[51] Their plays paid particularly close scrutiny to Yoruba mythology, proverbs and pre-colonial ritual verse. The slightly romantic ruralism of Beier's aesthetics is perhaps betrayed by the term 'Folk Opera' which he gave to Yoruba Opera, a term rejected by most Nigerian critics.[52]

Ladipo joined whole-heartedly in this authenticist sensibility. He moved away from Christian themes towards an exploration of Yoruba myth and history. His reading of nineteenth-century religious and historical sources, such as A. C. Hethersett and Reverend S. Johnson, provided him with the background for his major mythological and historical dramas, *Oba Koso, Oba Moro, Oba Waja* and *Moremi*.[53]

Although Ladipo allowed scripts of his operas to be published, he did not completely cut his links to an improvisation tradition. Martin Banham shows how adaptable Ladipo's performances were by quoting two quite different versions of the opening of *Oba Koso*. The two versions differ because they derive from two different performances, one recorded by Armstrong, the other by Beier.[54] Beier himself notes that Ladipo would 'alter or adapt a play in order to make use of new actors' talent that he discovers'.[55]

In general, while encouraging the transposition of Ladipo's operas to the printed page, European critics were sensitive to the inadequacies of English translation from Yoruba. The following from *Oba Koso* is a good example:

> You think the worm is dancing
> – but that is merely the way it walks.
> You think Sango is fighting you
> – but that is merely the way he is.[56]

Beier explains how the lines refer to a multi-layered context of allusive wisdom and a technique of proverbial montage which is almost untranslatable into English.[57] Critics like Beier, Banham and Armstrong would agree with Olajubu that with Ladipo's work 'printed words of the play [are] mere shadows of the real thing'.[58]

What distinguished Ladipo's operas from Ogunde's was not simply the fact that Ladipo's were transcribed and published; there was a rather different attitude to the audience with Ladipo's performances. Away from his popular base of Mbari Mbayo, Ladipo tended to appeal to a somewhat more sophisticated audience than Ogunde. Ladipo's plays had a seriousness and self-consciousness which won the respect of Nigerian academics. Olajubu, for example, speculates that Ladipo's history cycle might have been influenced by Shakespeare's history plays (with Hethersett's *Iwe Kika Ekerin li Ede Yoruba* acting as a kind of Nigerian Holinshed).[59] This 'high seriousness' was justified by the academics because it related to tragic elements in indigenous Yoruba masquerades and because it gave the operas more respectability in the pantheon of world literatures. The mood is captured in the following rationale offered by the publishers of an early edition of Ladipo's plays:

> To put on permanent record the history and ways of life of the Yoruba for the present and future generations ... To remind the people of the existence of traditional songs, dance, and drum beats and to demonstrate the beauty and melody that abound in the specially selected words of the various genres of Yoruba traditional poetry.[60]

The political atmosphere just after independence was ripe for such cultural pride. With the additional help of influential friends, Ladipo quickly became famous. In the early 1960s he had a contract with Western Nigerian Broadcasting Services to perform one opera a month on television. His play, *Oba Koso*, was performed at the 1963 independence celebrations and was shown with enormous success in Berlin (1964) and at the 1965 Commonwealth Festival in London.

Oba Koso (The King Does Not Hang) became a particularly celebrated example of literary Yoruba Opera and provides a convenient touchstone of the whole genre. The plot provides an explanation for the deification of the god, Sango. King Sango rules by encouraging enmity between his two chief rivals, Timi and Gbonka, in the hope that they will eliminate each other. When Gbonka captures Timi, Sango orders a second contest. This time Gbonka kills Timi and cuts off his head. Gbonka, swollen with pride, insults Sango and encourages other Oyo citizens to do the same. Sango, becoming angry, tries to burn Gbonka to death, but Gbonka emerges laughing from the flames, upon which all Sango's subjects defect to Gbonka. Sango hangs himself in remorse and shame at his defeat. The *magbas*, followers of Sango, tell the terrified people of Oyo that Sango is not really dead (hence the play's title) but has been transformed into a god.

The play won much praise not only because of its treatment of a fundamental Yoruba religious myth, but also because of its very effective adaptation of pre-colonial Yoruba theatre techniques. In order to achieve authenticity Ladipo was initiated into the cult of the Sango priests as part of his research into the background of the play. Some of the indigenous sources of *Oba Koso*, traced by Olajubu, are: *Egungun* masquerades, *ijala* (hunters' poetry), *Sango pipe* (praise poems of Sango), *ofo* or *ogede* (incantations) and *rara* (poetry of professional praise singers). Moreover, many of the performers were familiar with indigenous Yoruba performing traditions. For example, Ademola Onibon-Okuta, who acted Gbonka from 1963 to 1965, used to sing *ofo* from his own repertoire of incantations in Acts 4 and 6, and the words of Agba Aje, the senior witch, were contributed by the actress, Abiodun Ladipo. The *bata* drummers in the orchestra required very little coaching because they were already skilled in the necessary traditional techniques.

The total effect of the production was one in which there was a complete balance between all the different choreographic elements, a point particularly noted by European critics. For example, a review in the British weekly, *The Spectator*, of 1965, said, 'here was something Europe cannot do', and praised the synaesthetic effect of singing, drumming, 'brilliant mime, comic face-play, cut and thrust dialogue and sharp bursts of stylized dancing'.[61]

Soyinka used different, almost neo-Aristotelian criteria to celebrate *Oba Koso*. He praised the play's presentation of a cathartic conflict which 'drains off the evil energies of excess' and provides 'an integrated matrix of cultural forces'.[62] Soyinka felt that Ladipo's use of stage space to suggest a supernatural cosmology controlling human destiny helped the play depict a fundamental and universal tragic conflict, and that this was why *Oba Koso* was so well received in Europe. Beier, too, felt that '*Oba Koso* has the feeling of Greek tragedy.'[63]

What is perhaps not clear is whether the critics' euphoria about *Oba Koso* was because of its tragic essence, or because it offered an exotic theatre spectacle which was still amenable to European aesthetic criteria. Robert Armstrong has commented, 'It may be Beier's influence that gives the opera its tightly paced and carefully timed shape that makes it readily performable in Berlin, London and New York as well as the University of Ibadan.'[64]

There is something a little ironic in the suggestion that, despite its closeness to pre-colonial African theatre sources, *Oba Koso* also relied on a European dramaturgic discipline to achieve its effects. That view, however, is supported by Clark, who feels that Ladipo's plays of the 1960s, though traditional in content and some techniques, were in other ways too strongly influenced by a European academic theatrecraft to be truly popular. She gives the example of curtain calls. Ogunde's plays concluded with a closing glee (as in the pre-colonial *Alarinjo* theatre) whereas Ladipo closed with a European-style curtain call, by which time 'the auditorium is half empty and the ovation sparse'.[65] Clark feels that Ladipo's 'authenticized' operas were in fact 'popular only in the minority theatre of the university circuit, particularly among expatriate intellectuals'.[66]

The implication of Clark's analysis is that there is a distinction between the ersatz and romantic popularizing of an opera style which attempted to re-create a long-vanished pre-colonial heritage and a much more urban, 'rough' theatre. For her Ladipo only became popular with broad-based non-elite audiences in the 1970s after he changed his style to something looser and more geared to contemporary urban problems, a trend which Clark says 'alarmed some of his university mentors who felt that in order to gain appeal he had become too commercial'.[67]

The split which appeared to develop in the 1960s between a popular, commercial variant of Yoruba Opera and one closer to a literary tradition is in fact an artificial one (as Ladipo's return to a popular tradition probably illustrates). Jeyifo asserts that the emergent split between 'commercial' and 'art' troupes 'did not fossilize ... all troupes continued to ultimately measure their worth and impact against the standards generated by their dynamic interaction with a constituted popular patronage'.[68]

A good example of the easy interplay between literary and popular variants of Yoruba Opera is the work of Isola Ogunsola. The Abeokuta-based Ogunsola gained his theatre apprenticeship with Akin Ogunbe's group in the early 1960s. But, since starting his own group in 1968, Ogunsola has played the typically entrepreneurial role of dominant leader:

> In my group I am the director, producer and master drummer. I also supervise the other operations like booking a hall and publicity and production.[69]

On the other hand, Ogunsola was more amenable to a literary tradition than other artists. He adapted a novel for television (Oladejo Okediji's *Aja lo l'eru*) and adapted several Nigerian secondary school literature set books for the stage. He respected the literary tradition of Soyinka and Rotimi, and occasionally created tragic plays specifically for intellectual audiences at schools and universities. At the same time he retained close links with popular audiences and techniques, for example, by using improvisation, even for those plays which were already scripted, and by an innovative selection of venues. The audience of 14,000 which crammed Liberty Stadium in Oke Ado to see his play *Efunsetan Aniwura* is probably one of the largest ever recorded for any twentieth-century dramatic performance.

Ogunsola illustrates the inclusiveness of Yoruba Opera and the vigour with which the popular tradition is able to reassert itself, a tradition that Jeyifo describes as 'neither pristine nor congealed but ... rather manifoldly eclectic, permissive and democratic'.[70] Some idea of the eclecticism of recent Yoruba Opera can be seen from the specializations of the following list of modern Nigerian theatre artists: Oyin Adejobi, who used *juju* bands as accompanying entertainment, Akin Ogunbe, who attracted customers with fire-eating acts, Ola Balogun and Ade Afolayan, who favoured historical dramas, and Funmilayo Ranko, who specialized in female dance troupes, opening glees and didactic play structures. Altogether, Jeyifo lists a total of 115 documented popular theatre troupes, offering a staggering variety of styles.

A dominant recent tradition is exemplified by the theatre of Moses Olaiya, whose troupe proved phenomenally successful in the 1970s and 1980s. Olaiya achieved his popularity by constantly introducing innovatory entertainment such as magic shows, or, even more spectacularly, inserted film clips, where the costuming and story line of the play matched the film excerpts.

Olaiya has maintained a grip over audiences through the peddling of a stock character, Baba Sala, described as 'a braggart, a coward, a liar, a cheat, a glutton and quite often a dangerous idiot [who is] given solely and single-mindedly to the gratification of his inordinate lusts for money, food, sex and influence'.[71] One interesting feature of this character noted by Michael Etherton is that Baba Sala's social status rose as Olaiya the actor also got richer. Olaiya marketed Baba Sala's popularity through complementary media – records, videos and photo-journals. While the audience is waiting for the plays, Olaiya's records are played, and vendors move around selling them on the spot.

Olaiya represents an extreme example of the commercialization of Yoruba Opera, as Etherton comments:

> Anything which is likely to be popular with audiences is brought into the performances. The autocratic nature of Moses Olaiya's rule over the members of his company allows him to determine everything from touring schedules to the content and style of the plays to the detailed conduct of each performance.[72]

One of the side-effects of the commercialization epitomized by Olaiya has been the emergence of a hierarchical status system within Yoruba Opera. The rates charged in the mid-1980s by 'super-groups' like Olaiya and Ogunde, backed up by mass-media publicity hype, were as much as 10 naira, four or five times higher than those by new groups, struggling without proper transport or logistical back up. This meant that some venues (like the National Theatre in Lagos, which charged 1,600 naira in advance to book the hall) could only be used by the super-groups, whereas a hall like Oduduwa in Ife had a much more reasonable rate, not requiring any advance deposit, and was therefore accessible to less established groups.

The strongly entrepreneurial nature of Yoruba Opera, where each group was dominated by a somewhat dictatorial artist/manager, was in contrast with Concert Party, where, in its later phases (after independence), a more democratic collective organizational base developed. At this stage it is worth looking at some other points of comparison between Concert Party and Yoruba Opera. There were several obvious differences between the two important forms of West African popular theatre, especially types of music, play structure, venues, and, not least, the fact that female parts were played by women in Yoruba Opera, but by men in Concert Party; and that Concert Party was usually restricted to comic treatment of contemporary life, whereas Yoruba Opera was sometimes capable of historical themes and serious treatment.

At the more fundamental level of ideology and function, however, there were strong similarities between the two forms. Ideologically, both forms were capable of populist resistance to colonialism and to some of the more easily targeted evils of the post-independence West African states (corruption, nepotism, violent robbery). Nevertheless, both forms shared an ideological ambiguity, particularly over the acquisition of wealth.

In an analysis of plays by two lesser-known Yoruba Opera companies (*Ono Ola* by Oyin Adejobi Theatre and *Gbangba d'Ekun* by Lere Paimo Theatre), Karin Barber comments on the escapist ideology of the plays, whereby a radical analysis of capitalism in Nigeria is avoided, to be replaced by a compensatory wish-fulfilment for wealth achieved through hard work, combined with a condemnation of ill-gotten gains. She says that for the makers of these plays:

> It is impossible to acknowledge that in modern Nigerian society all great wealth is baseless and unearned, acquired by more or less dubious means. Instead, the criticism of the baseless fortune is displaced sideways onto armed robbery and magical money, which are the bi-products (the one real, the other imaginary) of the petro-naira economy.[73]

In a similar analysis of the plays of Olaiya, Jeyifo suggests the plays 'function as a sublimation of the prevailing social order and its underlying ideological self-justifications'.[74] Much the same could be said of Ghanaian Concert Party's unwillingness to condemn capitalism, and its reliance instead on implausible happy endings, bestowing wealth on its reformed or hard-working characters.

Despite this ideological narrowness, Yoruba Opera and Concert Party also share some of the positive features of syncretic popular theatre, particularly in the way they manage to be very eclectic in adapting modern media and urban forms of entertainment, and in seeking out popular audiences through travel. In an assessment of the impact of Concert Party, Collins emphasizes that the audiences were 'newly urbanized and polyglot'; he asserts that Concert Party provided 'a humorous lingua franca [which could] educate the audience to the complex multiple roles met in modern Ghanaian society'.[75]

Despite the modern content of most Concert Party and Yoruba Opera performance, the forms still retain strong links with pre-colonial African cultural traditions. In the face of colonial attempts to devalue African culture, Yoruba Opera and Concert Party have played a very important part in reasserting the cultural value of the performing arts.

Some of Jeyifo's enthusiastic observations about Yoruba Opera could epitomize these qualities for West African syncretic popular theatre in general. He asserts that such theatre reflects a 'spontaneous reconstruction of experience and reality in the popular consciousness'.[76] Travelling theatre performance has become a 'repository and a medium for the revitalization of the traditional performing arts'.[77] Jeyifo goes so far as to suggest that popular theatre can almost be equated with religion as a carrier of cultural unity and catharsis:

> In all the performances of the Travelling Theatre troupes ever attended by this writer, a suffusing gregariousness, a feeling of being at a public rite, at a communal festivity has always been so palpable an emotional and spiritual ambience that one could almost feel and touch and taste it … They provide for their audiences a potent vehicle for secular rites of social entropy and spiritual solidarity.[78]

In a continent attacked by the most subtle and potent weapons of cultural imperialism, such strongly revalorizing forms of indigenous culture are a considerable achievement. What West African syncretic theatre has lacked in ideological analysis it has compensated for in the ability to foster cultural loyalty and solidarity. Its eclecticism and ability to mediate fairly complex modern social issues for popular audiences have allowed it to interact with more intellectually elitist forms of art theatre without losing its own identity.

In the process it has issued a challenge to the art theatre by maintaining far closer links to the texture of the people's daily lives than the art theatre has been able to do. The acceptance of the challenge by well-educated theatre practitioners, and their attempt to come to terms with popular performance traditions, is the subject of the next chapter.

Notes

1. Sutherland, 1970; Bame, 1968.
2. Bame, 1968, p. 30
3. For the information on *Anansesem* I am indebted to Mapopa Mtonga of the University of Zambia.
4. Sutherland, 1970, p. 12.
5. Sutherland. 1970, p. 6.
6. Ricard, 1977, p. 26.
7. Bame, 1968, p. 30.
8. Quoted in Duerden and Pieterse, p. 39.
9. Duerden and Pieterse, p. 39.
10. Bame, 1968, p. 34.
11. Duerden and Pieterse, p. 192.
12. Ricard, 1977. For another francophone account (concentrating on the subject of stereotyping), see Apedo-Amah.
13. Ricard, 1977, p. 25.
14. Sutherland, 1970, pp. 13–14.
15. Collins, p. 55.
16. Bame, 1968, p. 34.
17. Owomoyela, 1976, p. 31.
18. Adedeji, 1976, p. 47.
19. Jeyifo, p. 17.
20. Ebun Clark.
21. Ebun Clark, p. 7.
22. Quoted in Adedeji, 1976, p. 50.
23. Adedeji, 1978b, p. 49.
24. Quoted in Ebun Clark, p. 112.
25. Quoted in Ebun Clark, p. 21. For an over-view of Yoruba cultural nationalism in this period see Peel.
26. Jeyifo, p. 4.
27. Quoted in Ebun Clark, p. 32.
28. Quoted in Ebun Clark, p. 11.
29. Quoted in Ebun Clark, p. 101.
30. Quoted in Ebun Clark, p. 37.
31. Quoted in Ebun Clark, p. 89.
32. Beier, 1967a, p. 246.
33. Ebun Clark. p. 141.
34. Armstrong, p. 362.
35. Banham, p. 14.
36. Soyinka, 1973. For much of the information in the comparison between Ogunde and Soyinka I am indebted to James Gibbs (oral testimony 13/8/93).
37. Quoted in Gibbs, 1981, p. 71.
38. Soyinka, 1974.
39. Soyinka, 1975. See also the accounts of his prison experiences in Soyinka, 1971 and 1972.
40. Ebun Clark, p. 31.
41. Adedeji. 1976, p. 54.
42. Jeyifo, p. 24.
43. Quoted in Beier, 1967b, p. 248.
44. Beier, 1967b, p. 247.
45. Beier, 1981, p. 323.
46. Owomoyela, 1976, p. 39.
47. Owomoyela, 1976, p. 39.
48. Kennedy, 1968, p. 14.
49. Beier, 1968, p. 102.
50. Ogunba, p. x.
51. Ijimere. It has been suggested that Ijimere is a pseudonym for Beier.
52. The terminology for describing what I call 'Yoruba Opera' is not very precise. Most Africanists have discarded 'Folk Opera', but Jeyifo also dismisses 'Yoruba Opera', preferring the wider term 'Yoruba Popular Travelling Theatre'. I decided not to use Jeyifo's term, partly out of brevity, but partly also because I thought it could be confused with other forms of popular travelling theatre, such as the pre-colonial *Alarinjo* or the post-colonial university travelling theatre.
53. See Beier, 1967a, and Ladipo.
54. Banham, pp. 19–21.
55. Introduction to Ladipo, p. 74.
56. Ladipo, p. 8.
57. Beier in Ladipo, p. 74.
58. Olajubu, p. 360.
59. Olajubu, pp. 336-50.
60. Quoted in Olajubu, p. 336.
61. Quoted in Olajubu, p. 330.
62. Soyinka, 1979, pp. 187–8.
63. Beier, 1967b, p. 251.
64. Armstrong, p. 363.
65. Clark, 1979, p. 140.
66. Clark, 1979, p. 140.
67. Clark, 1979, p. 144.

68. Jeyifo, p. 59.
69. Interviewed in Jeyifo, p. 150.
70. Jeyifo, p. 61.
71. Jeyifo, p. 109.
72. Etherton, 1982, p. 51.
73. Barber, 1982, p. 448.

74. Jeyifo, p. 109.
75. Collins, p. 54.
76. Jeyifo, p. 4.
77. Jeyifo, p. 15.
78. Jeyifo, p. 123.

6

Literary Drama
&
Popular Theatre

It would be fairly easy to avoid all consideration of literary and art theatre, to abandon it as unmitigatedly elitist drama lying outside the parameters of this book. That would be a very harsh exclusion. I am not interested in elitist or coterie drama, but, owing to drama's fluid and open nature, it is still possible for even literary theatre to reach popular audiences. What I want to do, therefore, is not to give a thorough analysis of post-independence literary African drama, but to give a brief survey of the structure and performing conditions which provide the context for art theatre's contrasting elitist and popular tendencies.

As I explained in Chapter Two, art theatre in Africa had its roots in the colonial theatre of school drama and the elitist theatre clubs. Much of the history of the art theatre in post-independence Africa concerns African attempts at decolonizing the theatre through the search for alternative indigenous structures and dramatic forms. That search provides a major focus of this chapter

The vigour of colonial 'expatriate' theatre clubs after independence was related to the survival of white enclaves in the African metropoles. These enclaves often, in fact, became larger after independence, swollen by the incursion of contracted expatriate 'experts'.

Christian Valbert describes the cultural milieu of Abidjan's white enclave in these scathing terms:

> A closed world where a white crowd circulates, driving itself silly with money, snobbery, the obsessive reconstruction of 'home', feelings of technical and cultural superiority, and with a whole panoply of air-conditioners, sports cars, food, films, in an overwhelming negation and scandalous provocation of Africa.[1]

Abidjan's plateau 'haut culture' is perhaps an extreme example of an expatriocracy; in many parts of Africa, liberal or, more rarely, radical whites were attracted to contracted posts. But there were enough examples of the elitist enclaves to have a deleterious effect on African culture, by becoming 'carriers' for metropolitan neo-colonial values.

The indigenous national elites acted as 'renegades' from their own culture, using the local whites as a reference group for reinforcing their own bourgeois values. The Kenyan, Hilary Ng'weno, identified this attitude.

Talk of anything indigenous here and most likely it is an African intellectual who will be the first to tell you that indigenous is synonymous with primitive. 'We must maintain standards' you often hear from African civil servants. What standards you'll never be told though it is obvious what they mean.[2]

Many of the former colonial theatre clubs took on a new lease of life after independence, swollen not only by the fresh wave of contracted expatriates, but also by the status-seeking local elites. This bourgeoisie tended to co-opt pressure for cultural decolonization. Kenya provides a striking example. The Donovan Maule Theatre, founded in 1948, was the focus for white expatriate drama, offering skilfully produced versions of West End London hits, intermingled with a judicious selection of such European classics as Shakespeare, Goldsmith, Wilde and Gilbert and Sullivan.

Soon after independence, however, more progressive elements in the Kenyan intelligentsia began to demand a national Kenyan theatre. These demands culminated in the building in 1969 of the Kenyan Cultural Centre (which was to be the centre of a variety of indigenous cultural activities) and a more conventional stage – the Kenyan National Theatre. A Kenyan, Seth Adelaga, was appointed as the first artistic director, with a mandate to create a theatre which would reflect the national aspirations of post-independence Kenya.

The high hopes proved difficult to realize. Adelaga found his creativity constrained by the machinations of a neo-colonial bureaucracy. The National Theatre Governing Council consisted of nine people: six Africans, three Europeans and two Asians. Of these, three were government representatives (two Europeans and an Asian) who were very committed to attending meetings. Most of the African appointments were more interested in the prestige of the post than in the running of the theatre. Since the Council only needed a quorum of three, the non-African committee members dominated the Council meetings, and there was little pressure to indigenize the theatre policies. Nearly all the plays in the early years of the Kenyan National Theatre were staged by the confident and active white theatre groups. As Hilary Ng'weno put it: 'The National Theatre ... is not national in any sense of the word. It is merely a building which provides facilities to expatriate amateur groups to stage plays and musicals from time to time.'[3]

The proposed training scheme for black Kenyan actors and actresses made little progress; plans to tour Swahili plays around the countryside were dropped. The entry charges to the theatre were too high for the majority of Kenyans, and the theatre was sited discouragingly far from the high-density areas of Nairobi. It was not until the mid-1970s that the expatriate hegemony of the Kenyan National Theatre was challenged by a new wave of decolonization, spearheaded by Ngugi wa Thiong'o.

There were other techniques by which neo-colonial agencies attempted to maintain control over post-independence African theatre. One of the most important was the way the former colonial powers used educational aid to help mould the ideological formations of post-colonial African cultural policy.

Kenyan National Theatre, Nairobi

A scene from *Carrefour*, Dakar

In francophone Africa, for example, the system of drama competitions set up in 1953 by the Governor General of the French West African Federation continued after independence. The French Cultural Centres in the major African sub-metropoles (with the exception of Conakry, Guinea) established a network of drama competitions by which French aesthetic criteria were imposed on West African drama. This system of play-offs, culminating in finals in Dakar, was highly bureaucratic and ensured the administrative survival of French ideological interests. The plays which reached the finals (usually in the pseudo-traditionalist vein of the Ponty school) received the ultimate seal of neo-colonial approval, selection to represent Africa at the 'Théâtre des Nations' in Paris. The rules of the competition were fairly rigid. The plays had to be short with no more than 25 actors, written in French (apart from songs) and assessed by an elite (usually French) jury. The very rules of the competition debarred any popular, innovative African language theatre geared to an indigenous aesthetic.

France also used the Cultural Centres extensively as a way of sending French professional theatre productions as models for the former colonies. This was organized by the Bureau des Exchanges Artistiques et Culturels under the arm of the Ministry of Cooperation (after 1956 the Ministry of External Affairs). Somewhat more progressive was the Bureau's attempts to encourage African theatre organization by sending celebrated French theatre directors to help set up professional African theatre groups. For instance, in 1965 they sent Raymond Hermantine to Senegal, where he produced a Senegalese play, Amadou Cissé Dia's *Les Derniers Jours de Lat Dior N'Gone*, and helped in the foundation of the Senegalese National Theatre, Le Théâtre Daniel Sorano. Later, Hermantine visited Congo (Brazzaville), Gabon and Cameroon. Similarly, Le Chevalier helped set up the Dahomey National Theatre and the Institut de Recherches Appliqués du Dahomey. Jean Favoral was associated with the foundation of a professional troupe in the Ivory Coast and a parallel actor-training school, Ecole Nationale d'Art Dramatique.

These contributions were by no means necessarily negative. It was partly by such transfer of technology and skills that francophone Africa was able to achieve a much more professional theatre and cinema than anglophone Africa. On the other hand, the early installation of theatre media catering so professionally for the assimilated Africans and for the white enclaves made it difficult for francophone African theatre workers to attempt making theatrical links with popular, non-elite audiences.

In the newly independent ex-British colonies, the British Council was much less creative than the Bureau des Echanges Artistiques et Culturels in feeding African theatre with professional British theatre skills. One of the British Council's main functions has been to organize trips by troupes like the London Shakespeare Company to display professional productions of Shakespeare texts (normally those studied by secondary school pupils for 'O' level). Such tours, no matter how well-intentioned, tended to reinforce the impression that European high culture is something remote and glamorous, beyond the reach of non-literate African masses.

Like the French Cultural Centres, the British Council has been very active in promoting drama competitions. These have usually been at school level, and associated with national organizations for the teaching of English, with restrictive regulations similar to the French, aimed at moulding a theatre

dependent not only on the English language, but also on a European dramatic tradition. These competitions were invariably held in an atmosphere of
fierce rivalry. Unlike the rivalry of indigenous theatre forms, however (such
as the East African *ngomas* and mimes), the competitions did not promote
social community interaction and solidarity, but factional bitterness and
envy.

The most objectionable feature of the British-sponsored drama competitions has been the use of British theatre 'experts' as adjudicators, a practice
which has created fierce resentment among African theatre workers. In a
very comprehensive attack Peter Nazareth complains that British adjudicators have been obsessed with Western theatrical criteria of 'diction, delivery,
timing, pauses, clumsiness'.[4] In this way 'the aspiring East African dramatist
was forced by the educational process to abandon his indigenous cultural
forms only to face dramatic ideals which were totally alien and not the best
and most relevant that Europe had to offer'.[5] Consciously or unconsciously,
the British adjudicator used Western criticism 'as a sledgehammer to beat
down any attempts by East Africans to be innovative, creative and relevant
to East Africa'.[6] The effect of this critical indoctrination was 'to reinforce the
colonially-induced inferiority complex; to undermine from the very beginning any attempts to experiment with language and dramatic forms'.[7]

Indigenous theatre workers often made the expatriate outside adjudicator
the focal point of their resistance to neo-colonial control of dramatic media.
A good example is the debate which developed over alien white adjudicators
for drama competitions in Zambia.

In the years immediately following Zambian independence, whites (both
Zambian and expatriate) continued organizational and aesthetic domination
of Zambian theatre. The administration of the national theatre organization,
called the Theatre Association of Zambia (TAZ), was almost entirely in the
hands of whites and was little more than a continuation of the colonial
Northern Rhodesia Drama Association. Each year TAZ organized a national
drama festival open to all drama clubs. ranging from secondary school
drama clubs to the almost exclusively white theatre clubs in Lusaka and the
Zambian Copperbelt The plays were assessed by an adjudicator, often flown
out from Britain at the expense of TAZ.

The continuation of European dramatic criteria imposed on post-
independence Zambian theatre was challenged by staff and students from
the University of Zambia theatre group, UNZADRAMS. The first sign of
antagonism came in 1969 when the adjudicator, David Pownall, rated the
UNZADRAMS entry one of the poorest in the festival. The UNZADRAMS
play was a tragicomic melodrama *The Fools Marry* by Kabwe Kasoma. The
dialogue accurately captured the argot of the Copperbelt mining com-
pounds, and the play was enormously popular with Zambian audiences,
attracting over 700 people a night at Chikwakwa open-air theatre.

In his introduction to the published text Kasoma explains why he believes
Pownall misunderstood the play:

> He could not make up his mind whether the play was a tragedy or a comedy. It just
> did not measure up to the rules of comedy or tragedy as he knew them in Western
> theatre's cultural tradition. The adjudicator was both angered and puzzled when
> the black Zambian part of the audience burst out in laughter at a certain line which,
> in the adjudicator's estimation, did not constitute a joke.[8]

Kasoma goes on to explain how the line, an apparently innocent reference to men going to the moon, was actually a slightly risqué pun (referring to menstruation) for those members of the audience understanding Zambian languages. For the Zambians in the audience, the joke worked as a concise reference to the moral confusion brought about by rapid urbanization, a point totally missed by the adjudicator.

The problem was not that the white adjudicators and the administration of TAZ were completely unsympathetic to the development of African theatre. Pownall considered himself an advocate of Zambian theatre, in fact, and went on to write novels with an African setting and fairly sympathetic to an African viewpoint. The problem was that white adjudicators and theatre promoters did not understand popular Zambian theatre forms, and thought that Zambian drama would have to develop on European traditions.

The conflict between TAZ and UNZADRAMS came to a head in 1973, and again the clash arose over an English 'expert' (Arthur Hodgson) adjudicating an UNZADRAMS play (Soyinka's *The Strong Breed*). In the end, UNZA-DRAMS withdrew from the festival. Throughout August 1973, as an aftermath of the festival, a debate raged between UNZADRAMS and the white administrators of TAZ, in the national newspaper, *The Daily Mail*.[9]

UNZADRAMS asserted that Arthur Hodgson 'confessed later after the performance that a) he did not understand the play b) the performance was excellent, however c) he did not understand why Zambians laughed at scenes which in the West roused tears and d) he would re-read the play and try to recapture the scenes as performed at Chikwakwa in order to have an inkling about it'.[10]

What angered the UNZADRAMS theatre people was not that the white theatre had survived independence, but that it wanted to dictate the pace and direction of the fledgling Zambian art theatre. The patronizing tone of the white theatre administrators is caught in this TAZ statement condemning the UNZADRAMS pull-out: 'What they [UNZADRAMS] appear not to appreciate is that before being able to act or write plays one must study the theatre, the form of a production, the limitations as well as the possibilities.'[11] The article went on to praise those Zambians who stayed within the organizational and aesthetic guidance of TAZ, in contrast to UNZADRAMS which pulled out. Fay Chung, the artistic director of the University Chikwakwa Theatre, was quick to point out that it was paternalistic for Europeans to assume they held the keys for the future of Zambian theatre.

Whilst Zambians have bent over backwards to learn as much as possible from expats, many expats have assumed that they have nothing to learn from traditional Zambian dramatic forms or from the ideas and the highly imaginative approach of the Zambian theatre people.[12]

The dissatisfaction of UNZADRAMS led in 1975 to the establishment of an alternative national theatre organization run by black Zambians, the Zambian National Theatre Arts Association (ZANTAA). It held workshops and theatre festivals, but of a non-competitive nature. It was much less centralized than TAZ and was able to attract most of the school drama clubs and the indigenous theatre groups. TAZ did not entirely wither away, but bent to the inevitability of Zambianization; by 1980 most of the previously exclusive theatre clubs had been taken over by Zambians. The distinction between TAZ and ZANTAA had become not one between white and black but between drama geared to a fairly ambitious literary art theatre and one with a more popular orientation. In 1986, after continuous and rather scandalous public wrangling, the two factions were forcibly merged by the Minister of General Education and Culture, Kebby Musokotwane, into the National Theatre Arts Association of Zambia (NATAAZ).[13]

A struggle for organizational control of theatre buildings and administrative structures was fought by progressive intellectuals in many African countries. A similar process took place in francophone Africa. In Upper Volta the struggle focused on the independence celebrations of 1956. Two theatre groups were rivalling for attention in that year, one led by a Malian, Boubacar Dicko, whose productions were closely associated with the French Cultural Centre in Ouagadougou (and with a French dramatic tradition), and one led by Felix Boyaru, whose productions reflected a much more nationalist viewpoint and an African aesthetic. Just before independence Boyaru's group successfully lobbied the incoming Upper Voltan government to perform for the celebrations Moussa Sauadogo's *La Fille du Volta,* a nationalistic play about the historic patriot, Princess Nyennego. The thrust towards a decolonized nationalist theatre was given an organizational base in 1966 with the formation of Cercle d'Activités Littéraires et Artistiques de Haute-Volta (CALAU).

Although the creation of nationalist theatre groups like ZANTAA and CALAU was a necessary stage of decolonization, they did not of themselves guarantee a commitment to theatre for the African masses.

The new organization often reflected the mixed ambitions and interests of the more progressive segments within the national bourgeoisie. The struggle to create a theatrical organization committed to the popular drama of the subaltern classes required a much more radical approach, a subject I shall examine in the last chapter.

Naturally, these different waves of decolonization sometimes found a specific theatre structure as an arena of struggle. As I have tried to show, the Kenyan National Theatre, which neo-colonial interests had co-opted through a subtle use of tokenism, provided one such focus.

A somewhat similar, but less protracted struggle grew around the National Theatre in Kampala. The structural links between the Uganda National Theatre and the former colonial power were quite blatant, in that the British Council offices after independence were incorporated into the National Theatre building. This potential conflict of interests came to a head when Okot p'Bitek was appointed Director of the National Theatre. P'Bitek had a history of artistic opposition to colonialism. As a secondary schoolboy at Budo Mission he was so incensed by the experience of being forced to sing in Mozart's *Magic Flute* that he wrote his own opera called *Acan.* His mature poem, *The Song of Lawino,* is a celebrated dramatic monologue attacking neo-colonial values. Okot p'Bitek found a simple device for 'evicting' the British Council staff.

> One of the ways we chased the fellows out was to get thirty drums and start drumming from 8 o'clock until lunch time. And the fellows in the offices upstairs could not do any work. And then we'd start again at two until four. And we had meetings with them. The issue was that the thing should be National.[14]

There is an irony in p'Bitek's trick in the light of the long colonial opposition to the noise of African indigenous theatre.

The humour of p'Bitek's account suggests that the 'eviction' of the British Council was a relatively painless operation. With the exception of a few countries like Kenya and Ivory Coast, where white enclaves were very vigorous, the creation of indigenous theatre groups and organizations to counterbalance neo-colonial influence did not prove too difficult. Once confronted, representatives of the former colonial powers (like the Kampala British Council staff) were only too willing to make diplomatic concessions in order to avoid alienating the emerging national theatrical cadres.

Neo-colonial ideological penetration of African theatre, however, was not confined to structural controls. Far more pervasive was the aesthetic legacy which colonialism had bequeathed to African literary theatre. As I suggested in Chapter Two, the theatre tradition of the settlers and the white enclaves was inherently conservative. It attempted to preserve links with an idealized metropolitan culture by ossifying the late nineteenth-century theatre aesthetics of the naturalistic *pièce bien faite* performed on a proscenium arch stage. Ugandan playwright Robert Serumaga explains how that legacy was one which bore no relationship to pre-colonial African theatre forms:

> The saddest thing about theatrical development in Africa has been the fact that the theatre of Europe came to Africa and established itself in complete ignorance of and indifference to [indigenous] traditions. It did not even try to superimpose itself onto the traditions, but rather led an isolated existence related only to the needs of the few who fell within its ambit.[15]

Those European dramatic conventions continued with remarkably few modifications in the expatriate enclaves after independence. Anthony Graham-White has commented on the irony that 'at the very time that Europe was freeing itself from the restrictive dramatic conventions of the well-made play on the well-made proscenium arch stage, Europeans in Africa were unconsciously using such standards to judge African culture as wanting in drama'.[16]

This nineteenth-century European dramatic tradition proved a most unsuitable aesthetic model for African playwrights. What was perhaps worse, the proscenium arch stages which had been built in the schools, public halls and theatre clubs throughout Africa constituted an architectural strait-jacket stifling the emergence of an indigenous modern theatrical tradition.

I am not trying to make a very mechanistic identification of *la pièce bien faite* with neo-colonialism; the relationship between the theatrical mode of production and ideology is far too complex for that. For example, there have been interesting and in modest ways quite progressive African plays written within a naturalistic setting for a proscenium arch stage. Examples of these are *The New Patriots* by Sarif Easmon (Sierra Leone), *Trois prétendants, un mari* by Guillaume Oyono-Mbia (Cameroon) and *Sons and Daughters* by Joe de Graft (Ghana).

The question is not whether African playwrights are capable of handling naturalistic stage conventions, but whether the conventions can provide the dramaturgic womb for an African theatre capable of speaking to broadly varied audiences. The problem with the European naturalistic legacy is that it is far too restrictive for a popular African theatre. One major disadvantage is that the proscenium arch stage tends to encourage the creation of plays with a bourgeois setting. This is partly because of the bourgeois aesthetic legacy of naturalism in Europe. Another reason is associated with the practicalities of theatre production for a proscenium arch stage. In order to avoid frequent scene changes (with the associated tedium of frequent and protracted curtain breaks), naturalistic plays often have long scenes with a fixed indoor *mise en scène*. In an African context it is far easier to design sets for the interior of a spacious bourgeois home than for a cramped village hut or shanty town hovel.

Even more restrictive has been the relationship between actors and audience. Where most pre-colonial indigenous theatre forms allowed intimate contact between performers and audience, the proscenium arch stage created a gulf between them. With very few exceptions, African critics and theatre workers have condemned the proscenium arch's stultifying effect. Lewis Nkosi, for example, complains about the relationship between performers and audience in the bourgeois art theatre, where the audience is considered hostile or indifferent, and which must be 'wheedled', persuaded, and if necessary 'coerced into approbation'.[17] In a similar vein, Mukotani Rugyendo contrasts indigenous popular audiences with those attending the bourgeois art theatre:

> The active participator at theatrical performances now passively allowed his unchallenged sources of aesthetic satisfaction to be invalidated for fear of being called uncultured or through having a lame view of what theatre essentially is.[18]

Rugyendo's comments capture the strong feeling shared by many African theatre workers that African theatre needed to reject Western theatre traditions and explore the indigenous heritage.

One direct outcome of these convictions was the movement to build alternative stages more attuned to an African theatrical tradition. I have already referred to the importance of the Mbari Mbayo Centre in Osogbo, Nigeria. This was a thrust stage without curtains, flats or cyclorama, and proved a very influential model for a decolonized theatre. Mbari Mbayo owed much of its popularity to the unpretentious atmosphere and to its ease of access for ordinary Osogbo residents. 'The building itself', one witness describes, 'was rough, almost crude and stood shoulder-height in Siamese twin proximity to shops that queued the long street.'[19] As a spin-off from Mbari Mbayo. other Mbari theatres were constructed in Nigeria, most notably in Ife, where the Ori Olokun theatre drew upon the historical associations of Ife as a centre for ritual cults. Elsewhere in the book I refer to interesting experimental open-air stages in Accra, Lusaka and Kamiriithu (Kenya).

So far, however, there have been surprisingly few architectural attempts to break out of the proscenium arch strait-jacket. The bulk of African theatre groups have to perform on the type of stage the South African critic, Kavanagh, complains about:

> The church halls, predictably, have proscenium arches, impossibly designed cyclo-ramas in some cases, raised stages that aren't raked and oblong auditoriums without ranked seating.[20]

The major innovations in African art theatre have not been so much in architecture as in the form and content of the plays and in the stagecraft of their performance. The strong psychological need of progressive African intellectuals after independence to reject colonialism led to an interest in pre-colonial theatre forms.

Dialectically, this represented a desire to 'negate the negation' of colonialism. Of course, African intellectuals did not intend to switch back the historical clock to a pre-colonial period, but to search for those ingredients in pre-colonial culture which could be reassembled as a way of constituting a validly authentic post-independence African culture.

At the ideological level the movement towards African authenticity was given expression in philosophical doctrines like Sekou Touré's communo-cracy, Nkrumah's conscientism, Kaunda's humanism and Nyerere's Ujamaa. The cultural interest in pre-colonial art forms was homologous to those ideological movements. It strongly influenced the African Studies insti-tutions which were established to research folklore, oral culture and pre-colonial art forms. An impressive number of African dramatists did some kind of research into pre-colonial theatre forms; these include Keita Fodeba, J. P. Clark, Wole Soyinka, Ola Rotimi, Efua Sutherland and Credo Mutwa. The research led to experimentation with African theatre forms and to the creation of dramatic genres which could be very loosely termed neo-traditional drama.

The interest of African dramatists in creating neo-traditional drama based on selected pre-colonial theatre forms is not necessarily identical with a desire to create a theatre for popular audiences. The dynamics which inter-connect the ideological attitudes of African dramatists, their preferred interests in pre-colonial theatre and their disposition towards audiences are extremely complex. Many authors have been torn between the polarities of an academic elitism and the desire to forge creative links with popular audiences.

The plays of Nigerian author John Pepper Clark illustrate the dilemma of neo-traditional dramatists. Clark is a poet, critic and dramatist who became very interested in researching the theatrical forms of his native Ijaw people, and gained a scholarship to do that research at Ibadan University. The celebrated results of his research were the collection and translation of an oral text, *Ozidi*, a still-performed epic, which Clark refers to as a dramatic ritual. Subsequently, Clark transformed the epic into a play text, also called *Ozidi*, the seven days of the original cut down and streamlined for presentation on a Western stage. Many readers feel, however, that the pre-colonial mythic elements in *Ozidi* (and this is even more true of the earlier plays, *Song of A Goat* and *Masquerade*) are at cross-purposes with the neo-Shakespearean language of the plays and with their structural motifs reminiscent of Greek tragedy.[21]

The reason for this uneasy synthesis lies in the attitude of the author towards myth. The thrust of neo-traditional drama was often not towards a rebuilding of the bridges to popular theatre forms. Myth was seen as a reservoir of traditional, proto-dramatic elements which could feed a healthy literary drama.

African academics have been fond of comparing the relationship between an ideal African literary theatre and pre-colonial rituals with the relationship in ancient Greek theatre between classical literary drama and such proto-dramatic rituals as the Dionysian mysteries. Michael Echeruo, for example, compares Ibo festival theatre with Sumerian purification rituals, and feels that a formalizing of those rituals is needed to achieve genuine drama:

> The Igbo should do what the Greeks did, expand rituals into life and give that life a secular base. That way, we may be able to interpret and reinterpret that serious view of life which is now only so dimly manifested in our festivals.[22]

As I have suggested in Chapters Three to Five, Echeruo may be neglecting the 'serious view of life' which is latent within already existing indigenous and syncretic African theatre forms. Nevertheless, his desire for African drama to emulate classical Greek theatre is not necessarily a symptom of psychological dependence on Europe. Part of the motivation may be to 'improve' indigenous African theatre, but there is also the assertion of a link between African literary drama and its primary ritual sources at a time when European theatre has become cut off from its nutritive ritual origins.

Another reason why African academics are interested in exploring myth and history is as a way of legitimating African nationalism. There has been an awareness among intellectuals that European nationalism often found cultural expression in drama based on national mythology and history.[23] As with some of the plays by nineteenth-century European dramatists, African playwrights' dramatization of pre-colonial myth and history is meant to nourish the psychic roots of national pride.

The exploitation of national myth is closely linked to dramatization of history. Nearly every independent African nation's cultural cadres have attempted to create a major epic-size history play as a way of asserting an identity (ravaged by colonialism) through the re-creation of a 'usable past'. It would be possible to monitor the fluctuation in nationalist sentiments by examining the ambitions, strengths, doubts and weaknesses in a series of African historical figures, as seen through the eyes of literary dramatists.

Prominent among such heroes would be the Zulu leader, Shaka, the Dahomean kings, Samory and Gbehanzin, Oba Ngbaisi from Benin, the Congolese heroine, Dona Béatrice, the Tanzanian seer, Kinjeketile, and the Kenyan freedom fighter, Dedan Kimathi.

I do not have the space to make such an analysis of these heroes here, but I believe that one conclusion to be drawn from a close examination of African literary plays with a historical setting is that, with a few exceptions (notably Dedan Kimathi in the plays about him by K. Watene and by Ngugi wa Thiong'o and Micere Mugo), the bulk of these heroes are from the ruling classes. They are kings, chiefs, obas, high priests or generals. Colin Granderson has calculated that more than 50 per cent of francophone African plays (of all kinds, not just history plays) have a chief as a central character.[24] If a content analysis were made purely of history plays, I suspect that this would be nearer 90 per cent. African literary dramatists have found little interest in presenting heroes representing the sufferings or aspirations of the subaltern classes. Consciously or unconsciously they have re-created ruling-class heroes who would embody qualities of leadership, as a way of dramatizing the problems of unity and consensus in the post-independence nation-state.

This function of providing role models or unifying tendencies is explained by Mudimbe-Boyi Mbulumwanza, a Zairean critic. 'The heroes provide a mythic allure and become a symbol for their people.'[25] The technique of

A production of the Nigerian play *Shaihu Umar* by Umaru Ladun and Dexter Lyndersay, showing the prominent role played by chiefs in African literary drama with a historical setting

A scene from Ola Rotimi's *Ovanramven Nogbaisi*

symbolization allows literary dramatists to invest historical heroes with modern relevance. Post-independence popular audiences are rarely content simply to observe ancient heroes and customs out of antiquarian sentiments. As Bakary Traoré explains:

> Historical plays can still engender enthusiasm and awake interest on condition that they express present day aspirations The present day has scant sympathy for forgotten themes. We must seek to go beyond history and myth to readjust our models to fit the needs of our own times.[26]

One common technique for making history plays relevant to modern audiences is that of allowing the historical plots to act as loose allegories for modern situations. Seydou Badian's *La Mort de Chaka*, for example, is often thought to reflect the power struggles in Nkrumah's Ghana, and Dadié's condemnation of the megalomaniac pre-colonial king, Nahoubou I, in *Les Voix dans le vent* offers a lesson for many a post-colonial African despot.

A similar technique for achieving relevance is by allowing historical characters to have a prophetic vision of the future (made accurate of course by the hindsight of the author). In Cheik Aliou Ndao's *L'Exil d'Albouri*, the hero, Albouri, recognizes the danger of the European invasion to the whole of Africa. 'My mind is not confined to our small kingdom; it goes right into the future.'[27] Less obliquely, Dona Béatrice in Dadié's *Béatrice du Congo*, before she is burned at the stake by the Portuguese, appeals to her country-men. 'I say to my brothers and sisters of Zaire that the alien structures – that iron girdle attentively guarded by specialists – must be overturned.'[28] It is not difficult for the modern African audiences to realize that the appeal is also addressed to them.

In an anglophone example, Ola Rotimi's recasting of Sophocles' *King Oedipus* in a pre-colonial Yoruba setting creates a central character, Odewale, whose tragic flaw is a misguided ethnic pride, a fault which comments directly on the Biafran war which was raging at the time when *The Gods Are Not to Blame* was first performed.

The problem with such methods of making plays relevant is that the theatrical allusions demand techniques of decoding which tend to be far more accessible to educated elites than to popular audiences. One way in which dramatists have attempted to broaden the appeal of history plays beyond the narrow constituency of intellectuals is by experimenting with African theatre forms. Several playwrights have attempted to cast their history plays within neo-traditional dramatic forms. For example, Cameroonian Jean-Baptiste Obama used a traditional West African griot as a framing device for his radio play *Assimilados.* Credo Mutwa's South African play, *uNosilemela*, produced in Soweto, 1974, was based on pre-colonial Zulu dramaturgy; it used an in-the-round staging and a technique of simul-taneous action to achieve 'a constant stream of acting, dancing, singing and dramatic appearances literally from all sides and at any time'.[29]

Ola Rotimi's history plays like *Kurunmi*, *The Gods Are Not to Blame* and *Ovanramven Nogbaisi* relied heavily on pre-colonial theatre techniques to make the intellectual content of the plays accessible to non-literary audiences. Among the formal elements (or 'viable ingredients' as the author puts it) which Rotimi relied on to achieve popularity were proverbs, dance mime and crowd scenes.[30] He says his use of proverbs has been influenced by watching audience reaction to proverbs in Yoruba Opera performances, and that of mime by 'ritual drama' such as *Egungun*. He justifies the use of large casts and crowds on the grounds that 'most African celebrations involve some amount of communal participation and the use of crowds in a play is one way of establishing some definition of an African theatre'.[31] *The Gods Are Not to Blame* has proved to be particularly popular. The 1970 revival, tempered by the experience of performing to non-academic audiences, relied far more on mime, songs and traditional dirges than the original 1968 production. Massive crowds attended 1970 performances at the Ori Olokun Mbari theatre in Ife (so massive that a stand collapsed during one performance).

The advantage of heavy reliance on mime and songs in African languages is that they allow those members of the audiences not able to follow the intricacies of the English dialogue to absorb the main contours of the play. The interest in formal experimentation as a technique for literary dramatists to reach non-elite audiences has by no means been restricted to history plays. Several African authors have been aware of the need to make their plays more popular by introducing elements borrowed from pre-colonial or syncretic popular theatre.

At a simple level, that awareness is expressed as a guilty feeling that the author is cut off from the vital currents of popular theatre. The Ghanaian dramatist, Ama Ata Aidoo, famous for her sensitive but sometimes rather academic explorations of the roots of bourgeois morality in Africa, admits, when contemplating Concert Party performances, 'I think it is the most valid thing going. I feel almost guilty myself writing the type of thing I write really.'[32]

Ghana, with its rich pre-colonial culture and its lively Concert Party tradition, is a country where sensitivity by literary dramatists to the merits of popular theatre is almost inevitable. One Ghanaian writer who has been very concerned with bridging the gap between popular and art theatre is Efua Sutherland. After 1958, when she founded the Ghana Experimental Theatre programme, Efua Sutherland became very active in trying to build a sophisticated and skilled art theatre on the basis of Ghanaian popular performing traditions. In addition to typically literary pursuits such as organizing Arts Council activities (drama clubs and a writers' workshop), editing a literary magazine, *Okyeame*, and helping build a University School of Drama at Legon, Sutherland attempted to stimulate influence in bilingual (Twi and English) popular drama for children at Atwia village and did research into Concert Party theatre. Her enthusiasm for blending the vigour of indigenous performing skills with an academic art theatre bore fruit in the building of an experimental open-air playhouse in Accra. This theatre, the Drama Studio, discarded a Western proscenium arch design, and borrowed heavily from Ashanti courtyard theatre with its tradition of close contact between audience and performer. The Drama Studio was situated next to a lorry-park in an unfashionable area of downtown Accra and attracted very mixed audiences. Sutherland's ambition was to create an art theatre that would be as proficient and popular as Concert Party.

Of Sutherland's published plays, her preoccupation with popular theatre is most obvious in *The Marriage of Anansewa*. The play is an attempt to build on the Akan tradition of *Anansesem* narrative drama (which I discussed briefly in Chapter Four). In a preface to the published text Sutherland distinguishes between the domestic amateur *Anansesem* and the much more polished *Anansegoro* with its professional players and musicians. *The Marriage of Anansewa* is described as a literary *Anansegoro*, employing many devices derived from the pre-colonial form. The most obvious devices are the use of a narrator to link the players and the audiences, the on-stage property man who distributes props whenever they are needed, the organization of actors and actresses into an on-stage pool of players, and the musical accompaniment (drum and guitar instead of the authentic drum, clappers, gongs and castanets) provided by the chorus, *Mboguo*.

The overall effect is to create a fluid stylized mode of theatre with close contact between audience and performers as in the indigenous *Anansesem*. Sutherland's stage instructions are very insistent on the style of presentation. 'All performers in the play, grouped together in a unified pool of music-makers, dancers, actors *and as a participating audience.*'[33] Some idea of how close narrative relationship between performers and audience is maintained in practice can be seen in this extract:

Storyteller: So then, Ananse didn't toil in vain?
Players: No.
Storyteller: Still, isn't this the first sign of trouble?
Players: We shall see.[34]

The idea is for the players to recreate the querulous participatory attitudes of a village audience in the pre-colonial *Anansesem*. The problem is that the participation of the on-stage 'audience' in a performance of *The Marriage of Anansewa* is somewhat contrived, in that it is a calculatedly rehearsed effect: the real audience, unlike in pre-colonial narrative dramas, cannot intervene for improvements or embellishments to the story.

Michael Etherton suggests that the dazzling theatrical form of *The Marriage of Anansewa* diverts attention from a content which is fundamentally irrelevant to the preoccupations of the Ghanaian masses.[35] The plot of the play concerns the trickster hero, Ananse, betrothing his beautiful daughter, Anansewa, to three different rich suitors to obtain their wealth. Though the setting is contemporary (with Anansewa worried about fees for the secretarial school she attends), and though Sutherland asserts that Ananse is a 'medium for society to criticize itself',[36] there is some doubt whether the traditional plot motifs of Ananse's tricks adequately analyse the problems of contemporary Ghanaian society. The dénouement of the play, a happy-ever-after wedding between Anansewa and the rich, handsome chief-who-is-chief smacks of escapism, though it might well be argued that escapism is indeed characteristic of some variants of Concert Party popular theatre.

The problems of a literary dramatist attempting to explore indigenous theatre forms and claim a popular constituency are illustrated in an even more complex way by the career of Wole Soyinka. One image of Soyinka is that he is an intellectual mandarin, concerned more with expressing his own individual fertile creativity than with achieving popular contact with audiences. That reputation is earned not only by the opaque density of his poems and novels, but also by eruditely allusive plays like *Dance of the Forests, The Road, Madmen and Specialists* and *The Bacchae*.

In an interview with Lewis Nkosi, however, Soyinka has shown concern

Storyteller and Ananse in Efua Sutherland's *The Marriage of Anansewa*

A scene from Saka Acquaye's *The Lost Fishermen*

with reaching popular audiences. Of his difficult epic, *Dance of the Forests*, he says, 'What I found personally gratifying and what I considered the validity of my work, was that the so-called illiterate group of the community, the stewards, the drivers – the really uneducated non-academic world – they were coming to see the show every night.'[37]

Soyinka's interest in communicating to popular audiences probably explains why he draws considerably from African traditions of satirical farce and trickster narratives in his very accessible comedies, *The Lion and the Jewel*, *The Trials of Brother Jero* and *Jero's Metamorphosis*. The Ghanaian critic K. E. Senanu feels that *The Lion and the Jewel*, with its extensive use of dance and mime is a model for a play capable of communicating to non-elite audiences. He says he reached that conviction 'as I observed the "Zongo" audience clamour for a repetition of the seduction scene between the Bale and Sidi'.[38] Throughout his career Soyinka has kept contact in a dialectical fashion with the comic roots of his art, even while experimenting with avant-garde and Western techniques. His little-known satirical sketches such as *Before the Blackout* (1965) were in a topical agit-prop popular theatre tradition. He is also a strong admirer of Yoruba Opera, and acknowledges the influence of Ogunmola and Ladipo. The plot of *Death and the King's Horseman* is based on Duro Ladipo's opera *Oba Waja*, and the play's reliance on contrasting dances to express the core themes owes much to the influence of Yoruba Opera. Although Soyinka's *Opera Wanyosi* is based on Brecht's *Threepenny Opera*, the relationship between songs and dialogue and the play's ferocious topicality is close to the Yoruba Opera tradition.

It is in the themes of Soyinka's plays, however, that most controversy has arisen concerning his identification with the African subaltern classes. Soyinka's drama often has a strong feeling for history and dialectical conflict. In *Death and the King's Horseman*, for example, the Elesin, while primarily a tragic figure, is also representative of a traditional African culture which has wilted under the assault of colonialism (represented in the play by Pilkings and the mentally colonized Sergeant Amusa). The reaction against colonialism is achieved through an intellectual adherence to indigenous culture, associated with a younger generation of educated Nigerians; Olunde depicts that generation. A similar, but historically later, dialectic is found in *Kongi's Harvest*, where Danlola represents the thesis of pre-colonial power structures, Kongi the antithesis of modern post-colonial despotism, and Daodu the synthesis of a younger, radical generation attuned to grievances of the masses. This schematic analysis does not do justice to Soyinka's sense of three-dimensional characterization, but does throw useful light on the play's submerged ideology.

One remarkable feature of the subaltern characters in Soyinka's plays is that most of them are from the lumpenproletariat. This is not surprising in satires about the criminal class (as in *Jero's Metamorphosis*). But, even in plays such as *The Road* and *Kongi's Harvest*, many of the characters (the professor, Samson, Kotonu, Say Tokyo Kid and Segi) are either marginal or positively deviant. The prostitute, Segi, is a particularly interesting character. She seems to be almost an allegorical figure, representing the people of the imaginary state of Isma. Although there are references in *Kongi's Harvest* to Daodu's progressive farming community, the main focus of socialist/democratic opposition to Kongi's dictatorship emanates from Segi's notorious nightclub.

A scene from *Kongi's Harvest* by Wole Soyinka

In characters like Segi (*Kongi's Harvest*), the professor (*The Road*) and the old man (*Madmen and Specialists*) Soyinka goes well beyond depiction of class allegiances; he uses marginal characters to focus on apparently broader themes such as creativity, heroism and the inextricable polarity between vital energy and the death-wish. It is precisely on the issue of absence of class-conscious themes that Soyinka has been criticized by a younger generation of Nigerian critics and dramatists. Olu Obafemi, for example, has called for drama of 'conscious ideological commitment' instead of 'the universal verities and metaphysical profundities of Soyinka and J. P. Clark'.[39]

It is partly in response to this kind of attack that Soyinka addressed the following remarks on committed popular theatre:

> The creative ideal in revolutionary theatre is not a self-conscious pandering to a proletarian illusion ... And it is not the immediately definable or tangible but the inherent potential of a society – technological, political, artistic etc. – that constitutes the totality of a people's culture.[40]

The 'self-conscious pandering to a proletarian illusion' probably refers to European leftist dramatists (such as Arnold Wesker), but could also be applied to the work of a school of younger Nigerian playwrights such as Femi Osofisan, Bode Sowande and Kole Omotoso. Where Soyinka sees popular theatre as deriving from a mystical sense of a people's cultural essence, the younger radical authors base their theory of popular theatre on a materialist interpretation of African society. They are committed to revolutionary change by Nigerian peasants and workers and feel the need, as Osofisan puts it, 'to create an alternative tradition ... from a materialist perpective. We look at literature as a social force, an ideological weapon.'[41]

Nevertheless, the differences between the radical school and the older generation of Soyinka and Clark are not as great as they might appear; in particular, there are strong formal similarities. The radical school, for example, has a tendency to construct theatrical parables, one of the best examples of which is Kole Omotoso's *The Curse*. The absurd situation of this play – two servants locked in cages while their master is on an extended holiday away from the house – is a parable commenting on the way the Nigerian bourgeoisie is able to survive by pitting different factions of the subaltern classes against each other. However, it is only the savage focusing on class conflict which distinguishes the play from some slightly earlier parables like *The Raft* by J. P. Clark and Soyinka's *Madmen and Specialists*.

Femi Osofisan is a particularly interesting example of the radical dramatists. Despite his participation in a movement 'to create an alternative tradition', Osofisan has put on record his admiration for and debt to Wole Soyinka. The debts are not hard to recognize. In *Once Upon Four Robbers* Osofisan takes up the topic of armed robbery and the Bar Beach executions, a favourite theme of Soyinka. Where *Jero's Metamorphosis* uses the Bar Beach as a parable about militarism during the Gowon regime, the allegory in Osofisan's play is about class conflict. Similarly, Osofisan's *The Chattering and the Song* adds an element of revolutionary class-consciousness to the notion of the radical farmers' group, introduced in Soyinka's play, *Kongi's Harvest*. In Soyinka's play the emphasis is on individual heroism (particularly of Segi and the intellectual, Daodu); in *The Chattering and the Song*, by contrast, Osofisan stresses the solidarity of the masses, where individuals are 'mere threads in the loom of the state'.⁴² Nevertheless, Osofisan's play does not centre upon the peasant farmers themselves, but on a class much more familiar to the author, a group of young intellectuals committed to the farmers' cause.

A similar observation can be made of Bode Sowande's plays, *The Night Before* and *Farewell to Babylon*, which the author explains, in a brief preface, arose from his experiences of student campus politics at Ife in 1971. Much material seems to have come from the 'Palm-wine Drinking Club', a gathering which Sowande says always took place 'between the running of the rag-underground press, moods of rebellion, and downright disillusionment'.⁴³

The oblique approach of Osofisan and Sowande – discussing peasant issues through the filter of a radical intelligentsia – raises a serious problem for the radical school of Nigerian dramatists: how to avoid preaching to the converted. Many of their dramatic techniques, particularly the use of the 'play within a play' as in Osofisan's *The Chattering and the Song* and Sowande's *Farewell to Babylon*, seem aimed at a sophisticated audience of young radical students and intellectuals rather than at the peasants and workers whose mobilization would seem to be a prerequisite of revolutionary change.

A major cause of the gap between radical popular aims and prestigiously complex formal technique centres on the conditions of art theatre production. Michael Etherton gives a succinct summary of that contradiction:

> The means of production of the new dramatic art, which can be summarized as university or government patronage for shows in expensive theatres with elaborately technical stages, and resulting in international publication of play texts and internationally toured productions of successful plays, is generally accepted and remains largely unchallenged. This theatre and even its 'revolutionary' drama, remains inaccessible to the mass of people.⁴⁴

What challenges have been made by African literary authors are precisely in the area of making radical plays 'accessible to the mass of people'.

The dilemmas of young radical literary authors attempting to widen their artistic constituency from a position of relative cultural privilege has been faced outside of Nigeria. Some East African playwrights have made interesting attempts to create a literary popular theatre based on the potential of indigenous popular theatre forms.

In his short parable, *The Contest*, Mukotani Rugyendo has tried to create a play appealing to peasant audiences by yoking a pre-colonial theatre form with a very class-conscious radical stance. Rugyendo admits in the introduction to the published text that the pre-colonial form of the play belongs to a pastoral East African society with a communalistic economic base. In origin the form was not overtly political or class-conscious; 'it deals with heroic feats of adventure in war, cattle-raiding, hunting etc.'⁴⁵ But Rugyendo feels that the heroic recitation contains a coherence and radical potential since 'it is the expression of the spirit of the collective; the embodiment of their struggle for survival in a hostile environment'.⁴⁶ Rugyendo has recharged the original rather oblique communalistic ideology of the heroic recitation, with a more dialectical and tendentious set of themes concerning the struggle between capitalism and labour.

The two heroes in *The Contest*, who are vying for the hand of the beautiful Maendeleo, are allegorical figures representing conflicting class viewpoints. The boasts of Hero 1 of the Kungwe people are suffused with neo-colonial capitalist attitudes which do not gain the village's approval:

Hero 1: We built and developed,
        Stood on the mountains and surveyed the land,
        And the masters of knowledge from across the sea
        Helped the sons of the Mungwes.
All: Hm![47]

Hero 2 of the Nkozi people articulates a radical socialist stance:

Hero 2: Most of the wealth is produced by those who work on the land
        In the big plantations and the small fields,
        And those who have run to the towns only see it being taken by lorries
        and trains for sale. So those who do the work must get its rewards!
Voices: Yees! Yees! You, the Nkozis understand things.[48]

The contest of course is won by Hero 2.

There is no attempt to make the two heroes plausible at a naturalistic level – they are clearly allegorical types. One of the main attractions about *The Contest* is that the indigenous elements are not simply ingredients (song, dance and so on) added to a fundamentally Western drama form (such as tragedy), but inform the whole concept of the play as a heroic recitation. What is not clear from an examination of the published text (which is in English, but which is presumably intended for translation back into an African language) is whether the indigenous form is capable of withstanding its transplantation into the abstraction of a debate about political economy and the class struggle.

A somewhat similar but more ambitious attempt to harness the African peasantry's 'spirit of the collective' is *The Trial of Dedan Kimathi*, the historical epic by Ngugi wa Thiong'o and Micere Mugo. The play is about the 'Mau Mau' military campaign of resistance to British colonialism in Kenya in the early 1950s. The authors relied heavily on *Mau Mau from Within* by Donald Burnet and Karari Njama for source material, but in an introduction to the published text they explain how they also used oral sources gathered by primary research among old peasants in Kimathi's own village. During the research the villagers revealed that Dedan Kimathi 'was clearly their beloved son, their respected leader and they talked of him as still being alive'.[49]

This notion of Kimathi 'still being alive' provided the central shaping metaphor for *The Trial of Dedan Kimathi*. The play works on two different levels. The audience realizes that, in the 'reality' recorded by history books, Dedan Kimathi was executed after being condemned to death at the sham trial in Nyeri. Ngugi and Micere are not interested in that level of reality: they create a Dedan Kimathi charged with mythical strength, a hero who escapes death at the hands of the colonialists through a kind of spiritual meta-morphosis into revolutionary symbol. Michael Etherton has convincingly shown how the subtext of the play echoes the trial and passion of Christ, and in fact the whole play structure is akin to the temptations in a medieval Christian morality play, even though the thematic content is vehemently anti-Christian.[50] The temptations offered by various characters, the colonial soldier, Shaw Henderson (first, in a liberal guise, later as a fascist torturer), and capitalist stereotypes (European banker, Asian trader, African entrepreneur) fail to divert Kimathi from his commitment to the total liberation of the Kenyan masses.

The trajectory of the play is from heroic gathering of that power and commitment in Dedan Kimathi's character to its transfer in the form of spiritual/political solidarity to the Kenyan masses (represented by the Woman, the Boy and the Girl). This power of Dedan Kimathi's spirit (the sense in which he is still alive) is meant to transfer to the audience as a way of igniting them in their struggle against neo-colonialism with the same flame which served in the struggle against overt imperialism.

It is interesting to note that the audience which saw *The Trial of Dedan Kimathi* in 1975 was almost entirely African, and it was staged at the National Theatre. By that date the expatriate interests (as in Zambia and Uganda) had relaxed control of the theatre to a certain extent, bending to the pressure from progressive Kenyan intellectuals. However, the fact that the play was first performed in the prestigious environment of the National Theatre in the Kenyan capital points to a contradiction between the purpose of the play and its dramatic technique.

Michael Etherton remarks on that contradiction:

> The play's complicated theatricality (which makes any performance dependent upon the technical resources of stage lighting, amplified sound levels and effects) suggests that its intended audiences are not so much the Kenyan masses, as African intellectuals.[51]

Etherton is perhaps rather harsh in that it is possible to produce *The Trial of Dedan Kimathi* in a more modest way than the text suggests (for instance, by using a natural voice for the spirit of Dedan Kimathi rather than the elaborate sound system recommended by the stage directions).

The original obstacle to a very popular appreciation of *The Trial of Dedan Kimathi* is the fact that it is in English. Ngugi was particularly sensitive to the point of language and in the next development of his theatrical career (which I will look at in Chapter Twelve) he turned to theatre in African languages. In 1980, the University of Nairobi-based Tamaduni Players corrected the language contradiction by performing a Swahili version of Ngugi and Micere Mugo's play called *Mzalendo Kimathi* (Patriot Kimathi), which was shown in Nairobi and in Kimathi's birthplace, Nyeri. The purpose of Kimani Gecau's production of *Mzalendo Kimathi* was 'to take the message of Dedan Kimathi … to as wide a national non-English speaking audience as possible'.[52]

In fact the move from performing plays in the colonial language to performing in African languages is probably the most crucial change in tilting literary drama towards popular theatre expression. Partly this is an aesthetic question – African language drama seems more natural and authentic than African drama in English or French, a point made by Abiola Irele:

> In drama the use of a European language has the effect of making it difficult for an audience, either African or European, to suspend its disbelief sufficiently to make for the deepest kind of response to the dramatic situation. The cleavage between the African 'content' and the European 'form' appears at every stage of African drama of European expression, underpinning unduly the artifice of drama.[53]

Though the aesthetic problem of authenticity and dramatic decorum referred to by Irele is very important, I would suggest that the language question goes beyond mere aesthetics. The use of an African language is not of itself a sole determinant of theatrical popularity and relevance. As we saw in Chapter Two, colonial educators sometimes encouraged a vernacular drama that was basically manipulative, paternalistic and supportive of colonial ideology.

The main criterion for creating a genuinely popular literary theatre is not simply the use of an African language, but the casting of the plays within an ideological framework that reflects the class interests of the African masses and within a dramaturgy which is based on a local indigenous aesthetic.

The two elements, ideological and aesthetic, do not necessarily coincide. There is often a very complex relationship between theatre forms, language and conscious and unconscious ideological content. A common pattern after independence in many African countries was the creation of two theatre traditions, one an amateur but prestigious art theatre in the colonial language, with a university as patron, and the other a more popular, often professional African language theatre. Uganda provides a good example.

At independence in 1962 an incipient literary art theatre was gestating in the Ugandan schools and at Makerere University. But far more vigorous were the Luganda plays of Wycliffe Kiyingi, who had started a school drama festival in 1958. He created many Luganda plays and serials for the stage, radio and television, and he initiated a travelling theatre group which toured different parts of Buganda.

The two tendencies were by no means mutually exclusive. Kiyingi's popular African language plays were influential on the Makerere Free Travelling Theatre movement of the mid-sixties. Moreover, representatives from the two groups cooperated with each other. For example, the talented and seminal drama group, Theatre Ltd, founded in 1970, included literary academic drama workers like Rose Mbowa, David Rubadiri and Robert Serumaga, and popular artists like Kiyingi and Byron Kawadwa.

After Idi Amin's coup in 1971, the creative cross-fertilization between the two traditions was cut down; many art theatre workers like John Ruganda, David Rubadiri and Okot p'Bitek went into exile in Kenya.

Robert Serumaga, who stayed and founded the famous Abafamu Players, tended towards a stylized theatre without dialogue based on mime and music, a kind of traditionalism filtered through Artaud, Brooke and Grotowski.

Uganda theatre, however, gained a revival of interest. There were very small, unpolished but lively groups such as the Kampala Shining Star Association, the Kayaayu Film Players, the Kintu Players and the Baganda Cultural and Dramatic Society. By far the most prominent Luganda group was the Kampala City Players. This was a troupe formed by Byron Kawadwa in 1964 and, according to Andrew Horn, 'drawn mainly from the ranks of the middle levels of the Civil Service'.[54] Kawadwa was a disciple of Kiyingi and like him drew most of his popularity from his own Baganda people. His semi-operatic plays, such as *St Charles Lwanga* and *Oluyimba Lwa Wankoko* (The Son of Wankoko) played to packed houses at the National Theatre in Kampala.

Despite Kawadwa's links with art theatre, there are strong parallels between the career of Kawadwa and that of Hubert Ogunde. Like Ogunde, Kawadwa was a professional who derived most of his support from urban petty-bourgeois and proletarian elements of a particular ethnic group (the Kampala Baganda). Kawadwa shared Ogunde's strengths (the ability to create vivid topical theatre based on an indigenous performing tradition) and his weaknesses (the tendency to restrict audience appeal to a specific ethnic constituency). As with Ogunde's post-independence operas, Kawadwa's plays seemed often to explore cultural nationalism rather than overtly contemporary politics, but, as with Ogunde, the close contact between artist and audience helped create topicality and relevance through a technique of allegory. For example, in the very popular *Oluyimba Lwa Wankoko*, the main plot, a conventional love story about Prince Suuni and Princess Barungi, seemed to be historically rather remote, but the sub-plot was much more relevant to contemporary issues. It dealt with Wankoko, a labourer in the Kabaka's palace who 'tries to organize a trade union amongst the workers, who have never before considered their numerical power at the bottom of the feudal scale'.[55]

However, the contemporary relevance of Kawadwa's plays had far more tragic results than the prison terms, bannings and harassment suffered by Ogunde. Like Ogunde, Kawadwa was detained for his political allegiance. This happened in 1966 under Obote, during the time of the Kabaka's return to Uganda. Kawadwa's appeal to Baganda 'nationalism' was considered dangerous at a time when there seemed to be a chance of Uganda lapsing into civil war. But in retrospect this seemed to be a mere anticipation of the much greater martyrdom which was to occur under Amin.

The fate of Kawadwa at the hands of Amin's agents was not without its tragic irony. Several Baganda theatre artists welcomed Amin's coup, at first. Popular theatre artists like Kiyingi and Kawadwa, and literary dramatists like Serumaga, thought Amin would reinstate the Kabaka (who had been deposed from his traditional kingship by Obote). Although the Kabaka was not reinstalled, in the early years of Amin's regime, Kawadwa's productions did seem to spearhead a Baganda renaissance.

Eventually, however, Amin's paranoia took offence at one of Kawadwa's most popular plays. *St Charles Lwanga*, first produced in 1970, was a play about the nineteenth-century Baganda Christians who were martyred by Kabaka Mwange. Kawadwa decided to revive the play in 1976, and, owing to its Christian content, sought and received approval for the performance from Muslim Amin's presidential office.

In 1977, the year of the performance, Amin's notorious Bureau of State Security outraged Ugandan and world opinion by murdering the Anglican Archbishop, Jenani Luwum. Suddenly Kawadwa's play was transformed from a relatively innocuous exploration of nineteenth-century Ugandan history into a politically sensitive allegory on contemporary state terrorism. Soon afterwards, Byron Kawadwa and several members of his theatre company were picked up by the Bureau of State Security, and their burnt bodies were discovered in the bush 33 km outside Kampala.

Kawadwa's fate seems all the more pathetic because he was not an oppositional author of a consciously ideological stamp (unlike Sowande, Osofisan, Ngugi or Rugyendo); it was just that his ability to create theatrical forms with a wide popular appeal outside Amin's permitted propaganda machinery eventually seemed a threat to the state. The political manoeuvrings of a despotic regime like Amin's are often not concerned with basic economic issues of imperialism and dependence, but with overtly superstructural questions such as religion or cultural habits. For such tyrannies apparently innocent plays can seem a direct threat. It is within relatively liberal and stable regimes that popular African language plays dealing with fundamental issues of imperialism have been possible. Such examples, however, have been very rare: the example of *Ngaahika Ndeenda* (to be examined in Chapter Twelve) shows the extent to which the surface liberalism of a regime can rigidify into oppression when its fundamental ideology is challenged.

One fairly early example of a committed African language literary play is *Kinjeketile* by Tanzanian author, Ebrahim Hussein. Although the play now exists in an English published version, it was originally written and performed in Swahili in 1967. The play concerns the Maji Maji rebellion against German colonialism in 1905–7. Swahili was a particularly appropriate language for the play because the rebellion 'drew its support' as M. H. Abdulaziz puts it, 'from different mother tongue speakers who already possessed a rallying force in Swahili'.[56]

The nationalist theme of sinking ethnic differences in a common struggle against colonialism is fundamental to the play. The story deals with the way a religious leader, Kinjeketile, forges a united force by offering a revival of indigenous religious beliefs to counter German imperialism. Kinjeketile is a fascinating figure, torn between his allegiance to a traditional ancestral past and to a modern ideology of resistance to colonialism. Unlike the Dedan Kimathi of Ngugi and Mugo's play, he is by no means an idealized totally heroic figure. Towards the end of the play, he is plagued by self-doubts after he has witnessed the death of African peasants, mistakenly thinking that the sacred water provided by Kinjeketile would protect them from German bullets.

> A man gives birth to a ... word. And the word ... grows ... it grows bigger and bigger. Finally it becomes bigger than the man who gave it birth.[57]

With the increasing self-doubt experienced by Kinjeketile, the leadership of the Maji Maji movement passes from Kinjeketile's ideological control to the military pragmatism of Kitunde. This transition seems to be a fairly accurate dramatization of the historical events.

The historical source for the play was a programme of extensive research done among peasant communities by Hussein for G. C. K. Gwassa, a junior historian at the University of Dar es Salaam at the time when Hussein was a student there. The songs, dances and even some snatches of dialogue were drawn from the music and memorates of African peasants who remembered the historical events. The play's popularity therefore derived from its analysis of the relationship between pan-ethnic unity, different modes of leadership and historical determinants, portrayed in an accessible theatre form with roots in popular memory and culture.

The student drama group which first produced *Kinjeketile* (under the author's guidance) went out of its way to perform to peasant and proletarian audiences rather than to elites. This was particularly noticeable when they took the play to Nairobi. They avoided playing in the prestigious National

Theatre in the city centre, choosing instead to perform in a tawdry community hall in a high-density area to a wildly excited and very non-elite audience.

Swahili is, of course, a rather privileged language in that it is the lingua franca over much of East Africa, and is therefore ideal for trans-ethnic popular theatre. In other parts of Africa there have been greater problems in trying to present African language plays. In Nigeria several languages provided material for literary drama. Yoruba authors have been particularly prolific – not all of them seeing their plays performed. Significant titles are *Basorun Gaa* and *Won Ro Pe Were Ni* by Adebayo Faleti, *Rere Run* by Oladejo Okediji and Efunsetan Aniwura, *Koseegbe* and *Aye Ye Won Tan* by Akinwumi Isola. In some parts of West Africa, theatre artists have preferred to use pidgin variants of the colonial language to make plays appeal to audiences outside a specific ethnic group. When this happens (as in a play like *Big Berrin* by Sierra Leonean author Pat Maddy) the pidgin is in fact no longer a colonial but an African language adapted to African needs and thought structures.

Ghanaian drama worker, Saka Acquaye, gives a vivid account of an attempt to achieve a popular theatre in the creation of what he calls a 'modern Folk Opera' entitled *The Lost Fishermen*. He explains how, when the play was created in 1960, the performers changed from a Ga presentation to English.

> Initially the dialogue was in the vernacular Ga; we discovered that strong tribal prejudices existing in the country prevented its acceptance in other tribal areas.[58]

Acquaye admits that the gains in wider acceptance were offset by aesthetic losses. 'The choice of the English language meant sacrificing some of the valued expressions best communicated in the vernacular in order to reach that varied audience.'[59]

In many ways *The Lost Fishermen* typifies some of the problems faced by intellectuals attempting to break out of the bourgeois art theatre's confines in order to reach popular audiences. It was not only the question of finding a suitable linguistic medium, but also of reorienting the relatively urban and bourgeois performers towards identifying with peasant roles and audiences. As Acquaye comments:

> At first the girls felt uneasy when asked to play the roles of fisherwomen.[60]

There was a problem with getting 'the more sophisticated cosmopolitan members of the group to place themselves even nominally at the village level'.[61]

Acquaye's experience with bourgeois performers highlights one of the major problems of art theatre pitched at peasant and proletarian audiences – how to achieve rapport between performers and audience without resorting to artistic 'slumming'. This is a crucial problem in the analysis of the Travelling Theatre and Theatre for Development movements to be examined in subsequent chapters.

One way of trying to avoid the dilemma is for an art theatre director to attempt to work not with students, intellectuals or trained actors, but with performers who are themselves peasants or workers. Ghana provides another interesting example of that. Felix Morriseau-Leroy, a Haitian, was chief drama adviser for the Institute of Art and Culture in the early 1960s. In addition to producing versions of European classics, such as *Antigone* by Sophocles and Strindberg's *Miss Julie*, and his own plays, like *Owo Ye*, he also gave production advice to amateur groups.

Alfred Opubor re-creates Morriseau-Leroy's experience with one amateur troupe:

> A group of Accra fisherment, called the Good Samaritans auditioned their own eight-act play in Ga, the language of the Accra area. In the original, each act was an hour long. Morriseau-Leroy spent days trimming the play to two hours, then sponsored it in a city auditorium. When the Samaritans got going on opening night, they skipped the reduction and played from 7.30 until 3.00 am. The audience kept coming and going![62]

This description captures very well the problem of trying to impose a Western concept of structure and dramaturgy on an indigenous aesthetic tradition.

In fact, attempts of this kind to create a popular theatre within a peasant or working-class group have been comparatively rare until the late 1970s. The building of popular drama which crosses class boundaries demands structural transformations between authors, directors, performers and audience of a kind which are almost impossible within the Western tradition of art theatre which has nourished African literary drama.

I believe that the examples in this chapter illustrate a continuing tension in African art theatre since independence. This is expressed as a growing desire within some theatre groups and artists to break away from neo-colonial bureaucratic control over theatre administration and from certain aspects of Western dramaturgy. The result is that literary drama in Africa displays a spectrum from the most elitist (with strong institutional and aesthetic links to a neo-colonial 'expatriocracy') to those genuinely attempting, either by neo-traditional experimentation, by political radicalism or by use of African language, to reach much more popular audiences. Some of these experiments have involved a reorganization of the relationship between performer and audience. I examine important developments arising out of that rethinking in the next chapter.

Notes

1. Valbert, p. 242.
2. Ng'weno, p. 68.
3. Ng'weno, p. 68.
4. Nazareth, p. 93.
5. Nazareth, p. 93.
6. Nazareth, p. 93.
7. Nazareth, p. 94.
8. Kasoma, p. iv.
9. These letters have been conveniently assembled in the TAZ house magazine, *Stage*. See Batsford, Chung and UNZADRAMS. For an overview of the events leading to the establishment of ZANTAA, see Mwansa, 1983a.
10. UNZADRAMS, p. 15.
11. Batsford, p. 12.
12. Chung, p. 13.
13. See Anonymous, 1986.
14. p'Bitek, 1982, p. 33.
15. Serumaga, p. 52.
16. Graham-White, 1974, p. 15.
17. Nkosi, 1982, p. 177.
18. Rugyendo, 1973, p. 3.
19. Kennedy, 1968, p. 10.
20. Kavanagh, 1977, p. 66.
21. Clark, J. P., 1964.
22. Echeruo, 1976, p. 84.
23. Examples are Ibsen's early plays based

largely on Norwegian myth and history, and the Cuchulain cycle of plays by Irish author, W. B. Yeats.

24. Granderson, p. 74.
25. Mbulumwanza, p. 19.
26. Bakary Traoré, 1972, pp. 107–8.
27. Quoted in Granderson, p. 76.
28. Dadié, 1970b, p. 145.
29. Kavanagh, 1981, p. 4.
30. Quoted in Johnson, Alex C., p. 137.
31. Rotimi, 1973, p. 6.
32. Aidoo, p. 21.
33. Sutherland, 1975, p. ix, emphasis Sutherland's.
34. Sutherland, 1975, p. 21.
35. Etherton, 1982, pp. 215–17.
36. Sutherland, 1975, p. v.
37. Soyinka, 1970, p. 177.
38. Senanu, p. 74.
39. Obafemi, 1982a, pp. 118–19.
40. Soyinka, 1971a, p. 79.
41. Osofisan, quoted in Obafemi, 1982a, p. 120. For his views on theatre see Osofisan, 1985.
42. Osofisan, 1977, p. 54.
43. Sowande, p. 7. Sowande does not find any contradiction between radical drama and indigenous metaphysics. 'Socialist realism is an inevitable outgrowth of materialism, which in the Yoruba cosmos is an extension of the metaphysical reality.' (Quoted in Obafemi, 1982b, p. 236.)
44. Etherton, 1982, p. 318.
45. Rugyendo, 1977, p. 37.
46. Rugyendo, 1977. p. 37.
47. Rugyendo, 1977, p. 53.
48. Rugyendo, 1977, p. 53.
49. Mugo and Ngugi wa Thiong'o, p. 2.
50. Etherton, 1982, pp. 175–6.
51. Etherton, 1982, pp. 178.
52. Alot, p. 128.
53. Irele, p. 51.
54. Horn, p. 25. For a fuller account of the theatre of Kiyingi and Kawadwa see chapters 4 and 5 of Kasule.
55. Horn, p. 55.
56. Abdulaziz, p. 157
57. Hussein, 1970, p. 36.
58. Acquaye, p. 62.
59. Acquaye, p. 62.
60. Acquaye, p. 62.
61. Acquaye, p. 62.
62. Opubor, p. 28.

7

The
Travelling Theatre
Movement

The crucial problem facing African literary drama workers attempting to create popular theatre is the relationship between performers and audience. The art theatre companies are invariably in urban centres, normally sponsored by government or university official patronage, and appealing to sophisticated urban audiences. In order to break out of that narrow constituency, several university-based drama companies have resorted to a pattern of theatre organization commonly found in pre-colonial and syncretic African popular performance traditions – the travelling theatre.

The University of Ibadan in Nigeria provides a good example of the emergence of the travelling theatre movement. Much of the initial energy for theatre productions at University College came from informal theatre activities by the students themselves, which were brought into focus by the arrival in 1956 of two imaginative and enthusiastic expatriates, Martin Banham and Geoffrey Axworthy. They helped break with the University Dramatic Society's tradition of showing London West End hits and classic European plays such as Shakespeare's *The Merchant of Venice* and Obey's *Noah* (not to mention the even more arcane productions in Latin and Greek by the Classics Club, Hoi Phrontistai). In 1958 they were instrumental in staging two of Soyinka's early plays, *The Swamp Dwellers* and *The Lion and the Jewel*. In 1962 a School of Drama and Arts Theatre was set up with the assistance of a US $200,000 grant from the Rockefeller Foundation.

At about this time, in the first flush of post-independence cultural enthusiasm, the University College of Ibadan Dramatic Society (UCIDS) attempted to broaden its audience appeal beyond the university community. The initiative for this came from the students themselves. In 1960 when the Arts theatre was unavailable owing to construction work, student drama groups had to find other venues for performance. They hit on the idea of touring one-act plays around the student halls of residence. Two of the plays were adaptations: *The Gossip of Ewa* from a play by Lady Gregory, and

Munchi Charm, adapted by Frank Aig-Imoukhouede from W. W. Jacobs' *The Monkey's Paw*. The third play was an original creation by Yetunde Esan, *Don't Say It in Writing*. Alfred Opubor, one of the student activists in UCIDS, describes the impact of these productions:

> The plays were enthusiastically received by the undergraduate audience before whom they played. But what is most interesting about the production is the casualness of the staging and the atmosphere of impromptuness generated. All the emphasis was placed on good acting and simplicity of the stage set and lighting facilities, since this was mobile theatre. The experience gained from this production showed that a permanent and well-equipped theatre building was not really a pre-requisite to the creation of high quality dramatic entertainment. The production also provided early evidence of the comic potential of pidgin English in a dramatic situation. Yetunde Esan's play had a number of characters who spoke in Pidgin and who brought the house down each time they opened their mouths.[1]

No doubt the explosive laughter over pidgin was partly due to the insecurity felt specifically by undergraduates experiencing the intense acculturation of a university education. But much of the theatrical experimentation with simple mobile staging in 1960 served to create a dramatic style which UCIDS could draw upon for more popular audiences.

Out of these experiments three undergraduates, Opubor, Dapo Adelugba and Brownson Dede, assisted by Axworthy and Ernest Ekon, created a full-length pidgin play, *That Scoundrel Suberu*, adapted from Molière's *Les Fourberies de Scapin*. Molly Mahood, a respected English critic, felt that the adaptation was an improvement on the original.[2] The production was important partly because of its collective technique of creation, breaking with a Euro-American tradition of individual authorship, and partly because of its adaptability for travelling purposes. The play was enormously successful, not only in Ibadan but also in many other places. It was toured as far as Calabar and the staging was simple enough to fit almost any conditions. Axworthy comments, 'The stage for Suberu was variously a Town Hall, a Law Court, an open-air cinema, the table tops of a school dining hall, or the studios of EHTV in Enugu.'[3]

That Scoundrel Suberu marked the beginning of the UCIDS travelling theatre. Its mode of operation was directly influenced by the touring techniques of the Yoruba Opera. It is significant that Kola Ogunmola was attached to the University of Ibadan's School of Drama in 1961. In Chapter Five I described the influence of the University on Ogunmola's opera, *The Palm-wine Drinkard*. But, in his turn, Ogunmola also contributed much to the spirit and organizational skills of the University Travelling Theatre. Axworthy describes Ogunmola's mobile theatre, which became a common sight on campus and influenced the student production techniques: 'His gaily painted Mammy Wagon was equipped with a large generator, control boards, and lights to carry some basic scenery as well as the whole company.'[4] The most important lesson which UCIDS learned was that of adaptability, to which Axworthy testifies:

> All our Travelling Shows were evolved in … a method now common-place but still valid. The object was to arrive at an entertainment perfectly adapted to the audience and the conditions of performance. We were often playing in areas never visited by a theatre group and where social custom was very different from that assumed by the author.[5]

In a continent as culturally heterogeneous as Africa, the lesson of adapt-ability is essential for any travelling theatre movement.

The travelling theatre programme at Ibadan lasted from 1961 to 1967. In 1967 Axworthy left to take up a post in London. His place was taken by Wole Soyinka, but almost immediately Soyinka was imprisoned over the Biafra secession issue. Dexter Lyndersay was appointed director, and his interests lay in training schemes for actors rather than in the Travelling Theatre. This question of personnel raises an important problem with the travelling theatre movement – the fact that university popular theatre practitioners are often transitory; the enthusiasm of a few individuals may not necessarily strike deep roots in the people's own organizational structures.

The Ibadan Travelling Theatre set an example which several other African universities were to follow. One of the most highly organized experiments was the Makerere Free Travelling Theatre in Uganda, which made its first tour in 1965. Just as Ibadan had the *Alarinjo* pre-colonial theatre and the Yoruba Opera syncretic theatre as models, so the Makerere Free Travelling Theatre was influenced by the popular Uganda theatre of Wycliffe Kiyingi.

As with Ibadan, the Makerere travelling theatre had its organizational base in a university and was backed by outside sponsors. The Makerere Free Travelling Theatre was initiated by two expatriates, David Cook and Betty Baker. Support for the theatre came from the university itself (with the extra-mural departments in the provincial areas being particularly useful), the Ministry of Planning and Community Development and British Council (both of which lent Land-rovers), Esso, which provided some petrol, and from a few well-established art theatre groups like the Uganda Theatre Guild, the Makerere Players and the Makerere Dramatic Society (which lent costumes).

The aim of the Makerere Free Travelling Theatre 'was to pioneer popular drama amongst the general public.'[6] The almost missionary idealism behind the movement was linked from the outset with a more general pedagogic enthusiasm for disseminating education among the broad section of the public outside Kampala; there was a loose structural connection between the Travelling Theatre and the university extramural department.

The Makerere Free Travelling Theatre was backed up by a quite formidable logistical infrastructure and administrative preparations. There was a fleet of government and British Council Land-rovers, a large multi-coloured splash-dyed backdrop, stands, trunk and three boxes for props and costumes, a folding screen for girls' dressing-room, a tape recorder and transformer. Although there were obvious concessions to a notion of a flexible mobile theatre. there was a feeling that the fairly elaborate resources (for example, the more than 50 custom-designed costumes) were intended to give the rural areas a feeling of polished urban art theatre. This is borne out by the rehearsals, which lasted for five weeks, including language laboratory work for those learning or improving an East African language. The plays were performed entirely by students at Makerere University, and the relatively long preparation and rehearsal period was partly geared towards welding the individual performers into a cohesive team motivated for travel.

Because the Makerere Free Travelling Theatre toured a very wide area (even touching towns within border areas of Kenya), the plays chosen were very varied in language, cultural background and complexity; the idea was to have a wide repertoire which could fit almost any performance situation.

The plays on the first 1965 tour included four in African languages and seven in English. These ranged from classics like Chekhov's *The Bear* and Julius Nyerere's Swahili translation of Shakespeare's *Julius Ceasar*, to serious English-language plays by local authors, such as Tom Omara's *The Exodus*, based on Luo mythology, to satires like Elvania Zirimu's *Keeping Up with the Mukasas* and farcical sketches like Sadru-Kassem's *Bones* (Swahili) and Joseph Mukasa-Balikuddembe's *The Mirror* and *The Famine*, which were performed in Luganda and Runyoro/Rutoro. The plays were nearly all based on literary texts, but two sketches, *The Mirror* and *The Famine*, relied on the improvisatory skills of the 'author', Joseph Mukasa-Balikuddembe. Cook and Miles Lee explain that 'he took each of the leading parts himself, and would ad lib at will from the basic script, adapting various allusions to whatever town he happened to be in, rather after the manner of the Commedia dell'Arte in Renaissance Italy'.[7] A more proximate comparison is with the popular, semi-improvised Luganda theatre of Wycliffe Kiyingi.

The variety of plays on the tour was partly determined by the variety of performance areas. Some African language plays (such as those in Luganda and Runyoro/Rutoro) were obviously restricted to a particular linguistic group. But apart from the question of language the plays had to be flexible enough to adapt to a great variety of venues. Cook gives a list of some of these performing areas:

> We acted in such various places as a boxing ring, a bandstand, the façade of one of the Uganda Hotels (where a splendidly varied audience assembled), a modest wooden social centre, a community hall of a housing estate where the 'stage' consisted of a series of shallow steps, the social halls of the Kilembe mines and Tororo Cement Factory, the vast social centre in Kisimu, and the tiny intimate Garrison theatre in the same town.[8]

Cook comments on the skill with which the performance adapted to the unorthodox demands not only of the different performing areas but also of the different audiences. These differences included the cultural distinction between the Bantu speaking audiences of Southern Uganda and the Nilotic audiences of Northern Uganda.

This adaptability was an indication of the Makerere Free Travelling Theatre's main achievement – its ability to communicate with a variety of popular audiences. At the beginning the Travelling Theatre was extremely eclectic, and was prepared to cater for all kinds of audience from elitist expatriate to rural peasant. However, an experience in the very early stage of performances made the organizers realize that the urban expatriate and bourgeois audiences were not attracted to the Travelling Theatre. At the beginning of the campaign the Travelling Theatre put on some shows at the Kampala Theatre aimed at raising funds by attracting the normally responsive bourgeois audiences. Despite a massive publicity campaign both in town and on the campus, the attendance was pitifully small. The attitude was confirmed when the tours outside of Kampala got under way. Cook refers to the voluntary donations given by audience members.

> I was struck by how much, relatively, the less wealthy of our audience gave – hundreds of people to whom ten cents was a lot of money proffered it eagerly; and how relatively little the professional, substantial spectators (including Europeans) contributed.[9]

Inevitably the Travelling Theatre members responded to the warm reception given them by the popular audiences. The success in attracting large audiences was partly due to an effective advertising campaign, which relied very little on conventional techniques of radio, press or poster advertisements, but used the more direct approach of cruising through town with loud-hailers announcing the shows just before they took place, a technique backed up by processions of performers decked out in variegated costumes. The unorthodox publicity systems worked; Cook estimates that the total 1965 audience attendance was at least 17,000. Often the audience was so big it strained the resources of the hall.

> They squeezed round doors and through windows, hung from projections, clung even to backstage windows when every other spot was crammed. We even saw people standing on each other's shoulders throughout whole plays.[10]

The type of popular audience encountered meant that the University players had to adapt the bourgeois technique of keeping a distance between players and audience to that of a more participatory active audience.

> Most of the actors had thoroughly Westernized expectations of their audiences, and were shocked at first to hear the non-stop burble of talk throughout the performance. But they soon got used to it when they realized that the chatter was about the play being performed, and was an expression of positive, indeed, dynamic reaction and participation.[11]

Cook goes on to explain that the somewhat rowdily participatory reaction is normal in the perspective of world theatre history, and it is the decorum of late nineteenth- and twentieth-century bourgeois theatre which is historically deviant. He suggests that the East African audiences for Nyerere's version of *Julius Caesar* were much closer to the original Shakespearean audience than the subdued polite audiences of modern English performances.[12]

Despite players' initial disconcertion at the rowdy response, they grew to respect the reactions of popular audiences. 'To our surprise it was not always the more educated audience who responded best to moderately sophisticated points in, for instance, *The Bear* and *Third Party Insurance*.'[13] Cook gives a specific example of a proletarian audience of miners at Kilembe mine where the noise was so great that the performance seemed like 'a kind of mime before a football final crowd' and the audience blew whistles and promenaded with transistor radios playing. 'When it was over we were quite taken aback and even humbled to realize how enthralled the audience had in fact been.'[14]

An issue related to that of noise is that of laughter. Western observers have constantly commented on the way African popular audiences laugh at tragic scenes. The Makerere players, used to Western theatre conventions, were similarly alarmed by the unexpected laughter evoked by their plays. Cook rationalizes this:

> We all know that a comic fulfilment causes us to laugh even when we foresee what is going to happen; but an expected tragic fulfilment may also demand a release which comes out as 'laughter'.[15]

He goes on to warn future popular theatre performers to distinguish between different types of laughter – 'delighted, raucous, awed and self-protective'.

The ability of the Free Makerere Travelling Theatre to lose many of its early Western preconceptions and to adapt to the participatory enthusiasm and intensity of popular audiences points to its main strength. The Travelling Theatre genuinely sought to break out of the strait-jacket of the art theatre – both as a theatre plant (especially the proscenium arch stage) and as a staidly exclusive social institution. In the process, the Travelling Theatre, like the Ibadan Travelling Theatre before it, made important organizational and aesthetic transformations designed to improve the relationship between performers and popular audiences.

There were some features of the Makerere Free Travelling Theatre, however, which prevented it from achieving a totally popular theatre campaign amongst East African subaltern classes. The main problem was that the impressively elaborate logistics of the tours (fleets of Land-rovers, lengthy rehearsals in Kampala, copious costumes and so on) tended to prevent a completely fluid interaction between performers and community. In these conditions the incipient elitism of urban intellectuals entertaining provincial masses is difficult to avoid. Some flavour of it comes out in Cook's observation concerning the need for Travelling Theatre members to provide their own food on the grounds 'that ordinary school diet is neither palatable nor adequate to a mixed group of East Africans under considerable physical and nervous strain'.[16]

Such special treatment, however understandable, reinforces the feeling that the university players are gifted elites, generously bestowing their talents on popular audiences. Peter Nazareth makes a similar complaint. 'Once a year theatre descends upon the people instead of growing out of them, and then disappears.'[17] The criticism is important and influential. It is also fairly typical of the continuous evaluation and self-criticism which have done much to shape the evolution of the travelling theatre movement. That tradition of reflective analysis has influenced the structure and motivation of travelling theatre outside Uganda.

In neighbouring Kenya, the University of Nairobi initiated its own free travelling theatre in the early 1970s. As with Makerere, at first it concentrated on literary plays in English and sometimes in Swahili. It was associated with fairly established authors such as John Ruganda, Kenneth Wanene and Francis Imbuga. In the mid-1970s, however, under the direction of Kimani Gecau, it embarked on a more radical policy of touring politically committed plays, such as the Swahili version of Ngugi and Mugo's *The Trial of Dedan Kimathi*. The policy was a powerful influence on the emergence of a popular theatre which was not based on a university campus but within a community of peasants and workers at Kamiriithu. This is a development I shall examine in Chapter Twelve.

In Ghana there was a short-lived travelling theatre movement called the Legon Road Theatre, based at the University of Legon near Accra. The Legon Road Theatre was quite heavily influenced by the Ghanaian Concert Party tradition, and as with the trios was associated with a star performer/playwright who had a particular knack for communicating to popular audiences. This driving force behind the Legon Road Theatre was Mohammed ben Abdullah, who joined the university in 1969 as a Masters student, and who had had experience of producing Shakespeare in secondary schools in the late 1960s. His first productions were of such ambitious literary works as

Brecht's *Trial of Lucullus* and *The Caucasian Chalk Circle*. The Legon Road Theatre really started to live up to its name in 1970 when Ijimere's *The Fall*, along with four other productions, was toured to Accra, Winneba, Cape Coast and Kumasi. According to James Gibbs, the appeal of Abdullah's production of *The Fall* (an Africanized, rather comic version of Genesis) was the Ghanaian audiences' delight 'in the Nigerian pronunciation of English and the crisp cultural twists which have been added to a familiar story'.[18] As with the Ibadan and Makerere travelling theatres, Abdullah found he had to solve the material problems of transporting a production. His solution was to use simple props and an attractive, portable, non-illusionistic, multi-purpose set consisting of light wooden frames and tie-dye cloth. According to Gibbs the audience for the Legon Road Theatre was normally 'varied and invigorating'[19] and was comprised of both bourgeois and subaltern elements.

James Gibbs himself is a good example of the way ideas concerning travelling theatre have spread around different parts of Africa. His experience with the Legon Road Theatre contributed much to the injection of energy he gave to the University of Malawi Travelling Theatre, which had been started in 1970, and which Gibbs took control of in 1971. Two of Gibbs' earliest productions in Malawi were former 'hits' from the Legon Road Theatre. The University of Malawi Travelling Theatre illustrates very well the way shifting personnel in African universities have contributed to the dispersal of popular theatre techniques. Apart from the inputs provided by Gibbs, other contributions have been made by Mupa Shumba and the author, who had experience of the Makerere Free Travelling Theatre and the University of Zambian Chikwakwa Theatre respectively.

The university travelling theatre movement has been mainly an anglophone development. The reasons for this are probably, first, that theatre training schools have been established in francophone Africa, with close organizational links to France, so that theatrical energy has tended to run in the direction of the literary art theatre, and, secondly, that the French colonial tradition of assimilation has meant that university students in francophone countries have tended to be linguistically and culturally more deracinated than their anglophone equivalents, and consequently less able to make theatrical communication with subaltern audiences.

Nonetheless, there have been some attempts to create popular theatre movements at francophone universities. B. Kotchy has noted that francophone theatre practitioners 'pleaded more and more vigorously the merits of a permanent dialogue between the university and the countryside'.[20] Amadou Koné, a young lecturer at the University of Abidjan, attempted to put such theories into practice in the early 1970s with plays which have been shown to peasant rural audiences as well as to the university community. Koné feels that an authentic African drama must be based on indigenous pre-colonial theatre forms such as the Bobo troupes of Ivory Coast, 'which toured the Bobo provinces, and criticized society with plays that resembled medieval farces'.[21]

Koné wanted to create a university-based theatre which would use open-air touring performances to present plays to peasant audiences in villages and which would contain a critical analysis of capitalism and its impact on Ivorian society. The nearest he got to such a theatre was his production of his own play *Le Respect des morts*. The play was about the need for an

A scene from an UNZADRAMS production of *The Trial of Zwangendaba*
by David Kerr and Solomon Mbuzi, at Chikwakwa Theatre, Lusaka, 1976

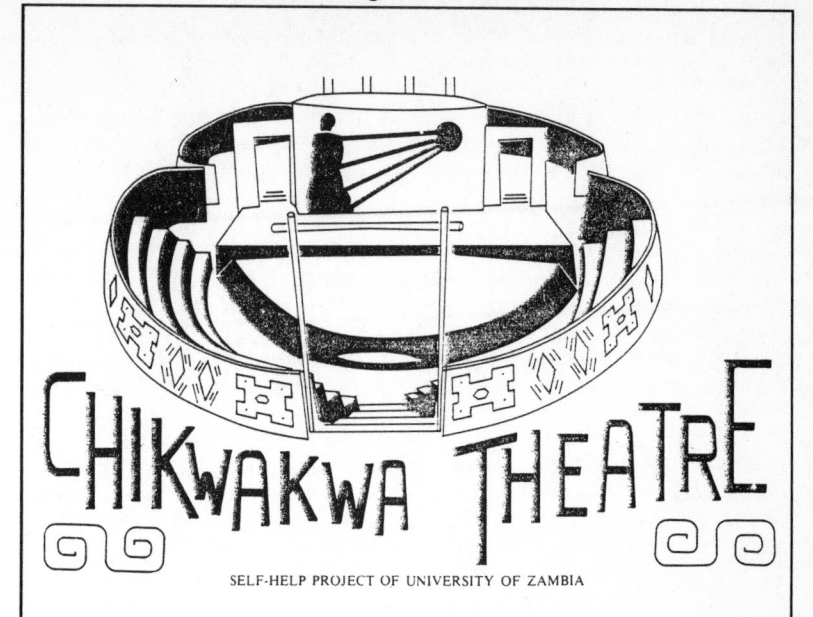

CHIKWAKWA THEATRE

SELF-HELP PROJECT OF UNIVERSITY OF ZAMBIA

THIS IS A MULTI-PURPOSE THEATRE ARTS CENTRE TO SERVE THE WHOLE LUSAKA COMMUNITY IN GENERAL. AND THE MUNALI AREA IN PARTICULAR WHICH IS DEVELOPING INTO THE ONE ALL-CLASSES AREA IN THE CAPITAL. IT IS DESIGNED TO PROVIDE POPULAR AND PROFESSIONAL ENTERTAINMENT AND TO FOSTER CREATIVITY IN ALL ASPECTS OF THE PERFORMING ARTS INCLUDING RADIO AND FILM.

THE PROJECT OPERATES BY GRANTS, DONATIONS AND SUBSCRIPTIONS
CONTRIBUTORS SO FAR HAVE BEEN
  ROADS AND PAVING
    (Mr. NICHOLSON)
  WILLYKIT
    (Mr. SHAMWANA)
  CULTURAL SERVICES
    (Mr. L. NYIRENDA)
AND MANY OTHER INDIVIDUALS WHO HAVE GENEROUSLY GIVEN MONEY.

**PLEASE JOIN THEM SEND YOUR
DONATION TO THE MUD THEATRE FUND
c/o BURSAR, UNIVERSITY OF ZAMBIA**

PUBLISHED BY THE UNIVERSITY OF ZAMBIA, P.O. BOX 2379, LUSAKA.

A fund-raising appeal for Chikwakwa Theatre, Lusaka

141

industrialization policy which avoided an excessive economic and cultural exploitation of the rural peasants. It was shown in Abidjan to bourgeois audiences at the prestigious Théâtre de la Cité, but also in an African language to peasant village communities. Koné felt that the peasants of Ayame village appreciated *Le Respect des morts* more than the Abidjan audiences. Popular theatre ventures of this kind, however, have been comparatively rare in francophone Africa.

With the possible exception of the University of Nairobi's Free Travelling Theatre the examples I have given have suffered from the complaint which I have already quoted by Nazareth that the popularity of the travelling theatres was rather synthetic, imposed on the people rather than rooted in their own culture. Some of Nazareth's desire for a popular theatre with a closer relationship to people's culture and communities is reflected in one of the most interesting and sustained travelling theatre movements – Zambia's Chikwakwa Theatre.

Like the Makerere Free Travelling Theatre, Chikwakwa Theatre was based at the national university, and was initiated mainly by expatriates (particularly Michael Etherton and Andrew Horn), and involved student performers from a campus drama group, UNZADRAMS. From the outset, however, Chikwakwa embodied a conscious attempt to minimize elitist tendencies in the theatre movement.

The movement had a dual thrust, one geared to domestic programmes in Lusaka, and one to travelling theatre projects, though in both theory and practice the domestic and travelling programmes fed into each other. The theatre activities at the university attempted to provide a focus for popular theatre by building in 1969 an open-air mud and thatch theatre with a thrust stage, and incorporating the painted wall of a disused tobacco barn as a backdrop. The theatre design, thatching techniques and art work on the dried-mud seats were based on African architectural and artistic motifs. Funds and materials were raised from private donations, but much of the labour was provided on a self-help basis by the staff and students themselves. Some feeling of the grass-roots self-reliant energy which went into the project comes from the title, 'Chikwakwa', a Nyanja word for grass-slasher.

The choice of site for the theatre was very significant. Chikwakwa was built in a bush setting about 5 km from the campus, close to a high-density 'site and service' compound, Kaunda Square. The idea was to break down the class barriers between the student audiences and the general public by placing the theatre close to a working-class compound. At the same time, the rural atmosphere provided by both the surrounding bush and the neo-traditional architecture was intended to open bridges between the university and the rural peasantry. As Etherton puts it:

> The theatre was meant to develop a style of drama that used the dances, songs and music of the rural areas and the urban townships, the masks and the fabulous costumes, the artefacts, the fires and the lamps of traditional story telling.[22]

That vision was backed up by research into indigenous Zambian performing arts of dance and narrative, which fed into the university drama teaching and the Chikwakwa productions as part of a quest for a basic, popular Zambian theatre aesthetic.

The aesthetic return to cultural roots was linked to the humanist ideology of anti-capitalist self-reliance which was given voice by the ruling United National Independence Party (UNIP) in the years following the Mulungushi declaration of 1967. There was in fact a brief honeymoon period between the Zambian government and Chikwakwa Theatre, climaxed by the performance of Mario Fratti's *Che Guevara* in 1970, which was witnessed by the Zambian president and other heads of state attending the Commonwealth Conference in Lusaka. By 1971 the honeymoon was over, after the deportation of Horn and Etherton, following student demonstrations against French sales of arms to South Africa. From that period on, as the anti-capitalist rhetoric of UNIP appeared increasingly hollow, the relationship between Chikwakwa Theatre and the government tended to remain distant and very cool.

The founding aim of Chikwakwa Theatre to bridge the gap between student and local subaltern audiences only achieved partial success. There certainly were mixed audiences, but the members who came from Kaunda Square tended to be children and teenagers rather than adults. For that reason, the Chikwakwa organizers made several attempts to build a theatre movement for local children, using the Chikwakwa plant and equipment. In various reincarnations this group was called The Slaves of Music, Black Moses and, most successfully and recently, Tafika Theatre, a loose coalition of school-children and teenagers who had not managed to find a place in secondary school or in regular employment.

The popular theatre achievements of Chikwakwa were probably more successful in the travelling than in the domestic programme. The first Chikwakwa Travelling Theatre was in 1970. In many ways it was similar to the Ibadan and Makerere precedents, but there were important differences. Instead of attempting to tour the whole nation over an extended period of time, it was decided to concentrate on one province for a short period of about two weeks; this meant that it was possible to use one Zambian language, Chinyanja, the lingua franca of Eastern Province (though some of the songs were in other Eastern Province languages like Chitumbuka and Chinsenga). The organizers of the 1970 Eastern Province tour also tried to avoid the problem referred to by Nazareth in his critique of the Makerere Free Travelling Theatre. As well as showing plays already prepared in Lusaka, the students and lecturers also held a drama workshop in Chipata, the provincial capital, in order to attempt a transfer of drama skills and ideas into the province.

The performances themselves were held for urban audiences in Chipata and Katete on a football field and in community halls, and for rural audiences in villages. The total attendance for the tour was estimated at 7,000. Despite logistical problems caused by the shortage of rehearsal time and the top-heavy administrative machinery, the tour aroused enormous enthusiasm and set the pattern for future provincial tours. Every year throughout the 1970s Chikwakwa Theatre went to at least one of the rural provinces with workshops and/or toured plays. The tours were marked by the increased mastery of dramatic resources by skilled Zambians like Kabwe Kasoma, Mumba Kapumpa, Youngson Simukoko and Mapopa Mtonga.

As the tours progressed there was an increasing reliance on plays which were created for and geared to local audiences. In the first 1970 tour to

Eastern Province, all the plays were based on literary texts, *Spreading the News* by Lady Gregory, *Return of Nsato* by Ezekiel Mphalele and *Homecoming* by Zambian author Musisimi Fwanyanga. In the 1972 tour to Southern Province, some of the plays were adaptions of literary scripts – Oyono-Mbia's *Three Suitors One Husband*, *Cheelo Ca Madaala* from Plautus's *O Mostelleria*, and *Unity* from Odets's *Waiting for Lefty*. But two of the plays, *Kalyabantu*, devised by Obi Nazombe, and *Mucaala*, devised by Patrick Hamujompa, were adapted not from literary texts, but from local Tonga oral narratives. Not surprisingly, these plays proved particularly popular in the villages.

By the 1973 Chikwakwa tour to Northern Province, all the plays performed, *Drown in a Drink* by Whitney Lukuku, *The District Governor Visits a Village* by Stephen Chifunyise and *The Poisoned Cultural Meat* by Kabwe Kasoma, were derived from Zambian scripts. Another important change was that the Unzadrams students on the 1973 tour took complete charge of the trip, without any accompanying staff, and used public transport, rather than a university vehicle, for much of the journey. This was a measure not only of the students' confidence and initiative, but of their increasing mastery of 'appropriate' material modes of theatre production. The 1970–2 trips had been bedevilled by inconveniences caused by an over-elaborate administration (stolen money and accommodation problems in Eastern Province, broken-down transport and missing props in Southern Province). By the 1973 tour the performers relied on much more modest administrative and material resources and on adapting plays to a local situation rather than on elaborate advance planning in Lusaka.

Probably one of the most successful features of the Chikwakwa Travelling Theatre was the incorporation of drama workshops into the play creation process. The purpose of the workshops (which were held in schools or teacher training colleges) was to establish popular theatre traditions in the rural areas, organized by local teaching cadres, so as to avoid a patronizing policy of simply 'taking theatre to the people'. Another important function of the workshops was to ensure that the languages, customs and culture of the areas being visited provided the main medium for the plays.

The 1975 Travelling Theatre to Western Province illustrates the emergence of that emphasis. Unzadrams found themselves unable to recruit student performers for the tour who could speak Silozi, the lingua franca of Western Province. Moreover, the leaders of the tour, Rabson Chileshe and David Kerr, felt themselves incapable of creating plays in Lusaka fully in tune with the cultural values of the Western Province 650 km away. The solution was to hold a drama workshop at Senanga Secondary School in the heart of Western Province, during the course of which the plays were created by a process of improvisation. Two of the plays, *Mabusisi* and *Blood*, were based on scripts by Stephen Chifunyise (though the final version of *Mabusisi* bore little relation to the original English-language script). The other plays, *Mulimi ya Butali*, *Likumuca* and *Kwa Kuta*, were entirely improvised. Two of the plays were based on Lozi oral narratives; local dance and musical interludes were incorporated into the plays. This technique of play creation, along with the use of performers who had a thorough knowledge of Silozi language and culture, helped make the plays acceptable to Western Province audiences.

Another feature of the Western Province tour was that the logistics of transporting a fairly large cast over a long distance by minibus on appalling roads meant that few props and costumes could be carried. A minimalist, in-the-round dramaturgy, relying heavily on mime rather than elaborate props, costumes or decor, became necessary and very effective. A great advantage of these 'rough theatre' techniques was that the artists were able to adapt their performances very easily to the appropriate conditions.[23] Audiences varied enormously and an adaptable theatre technique meant performers could adjust their responses accordingly. Some flavour of that comes out in this account of *Kwa Kuta*, a play about a traditional court trying the case of a schoolboy who had impregnated a co-pupil:

> In the villages the play was very popular because the situation was so familiar, and because tradition is triumphant in the end. In several villages, the headman praised this particular play for its didactic content (the warning to youths to avoid immorality and disrespect). When we performed in town, the audience found other attractions in the play. The school audiences tended to laugh at the pedantry of the court officials and to identify with the young characters.[24]

Sometimes the performers only needed to make slight changes of emphasis to catch the mood of the audience, in other cases a system of radical trans-formation or even self-censorship took place, to the extent that at Chief Sisii's village the whole ending of *Mabusisi* was altered to avoid offending the very autocratic, semi-feudal chieftainship.

One of the features of the Chikwakwa Travelling Theatre tours was the praise villagers gave to the performers for the educational value of the plays. One reason for rural audiences emphasizing the educational value of the plays was that the indigenous theatrical traditions of narrative and dance drama had a strong didactic content. Chikwakwa Theatre did not, in fact, have any conscious policy of educational drama, except in so far as local arrangements for the tours were often made through the resident tutors in the university's extramural department. However, the scripted plays which were popular with rural audiences did have strong didactic elements; these included *Drown in a Drink* (about the evils of excessive drinking), *The Poisoned Cultural Meat* (about a hypocritical self-proclaimed 'humanist'), *Blood* (about prejudices against blood donation) and *The District Governor Visits a Village* (about conflicts between local government bureaucracy and rural peasant values). The leaders of the 1976 Northern Province Travelling Theatre (Mapopa Mtonga and Youngson Simukoko) became conscious of the didactic possibilities of drama and decided that two of the plays performed (*Blood* and *Kamsakala*), which carried messages about health problems, should help focus the tour on primary health care. *Kamsakala* was particularly interesting in that it used an almost dialogue-free technique of dance, mime and singing, based on Zambian music, to convey a message about the importance of smallpox inoculations. The fact that the two lecturers who led the group were very proficient drummers and were able to teach those and other drama skills at the preliminary drama workshop at Kasama Teacher Training College helped forge links between the artistic traditions of the Chikwakwa performers and the Northern Province audiences.

The general drift of the Chikwakwa Travelling Theatre towards some kind of socially committed development-oriented popular theatre was given even more focus by its contact with the theories developed by the *Laedza*

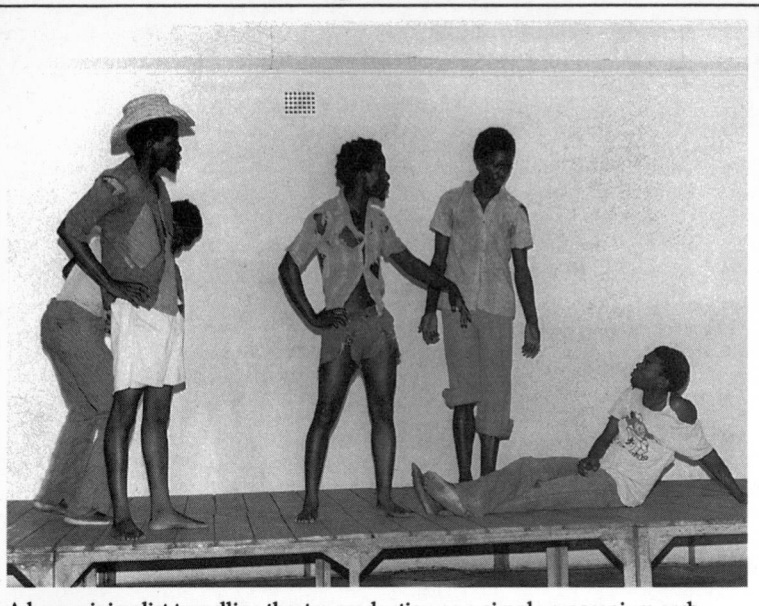

A bare minimalist travelling theatre production on a simple proscenium arch stage in Changalume community hall, Malawi, 1984

An in-the-round open-air travelling theatre production in Silele village, Zambia, 1975

Batanani popular theatre workers from Botswana.[25] On the 1977 Chikwakwa trip to Luapula Province two Batswana veterans from the *Laedza Batanani* experience, Jeppe Kelepile and Kutlwano Matenge joined David Kerr and Garikayi Shoniwa in leading the drama workshop and travelling theatre.

This proved a useful way of exchanging ideas and practical experiences about theatre. Some attempts were made to introduce the *Laedza Batanani* ideas about researching local problems. The research led to the creation of (among others) a play called *The Funeral* about a typically Luapula problem of widows' rights of succession. The play caused much animated discussion, particularly when performed to a peasant audience in Kashiba village, though the discussion was not structured to any further action. With another play, *Credit Union*, about agricultural credit, leaflets (regrettably in English, not Bemba) prepared by CUSA, the Credit Union association in Zambia, were given to those audience members who could read them, but no CUSA member was available to answer detailed technical questions. The audiences tended to respond to the folk-narrative structure of the story (concerning fratricide) rather than to the didactic elements concerning agricultural credit.

The pattern of the Northern and Luapula travelling theatres was followed by the tours in 1979 to Southern Province and 1980 to Eastern Province. The research into the problems of Southern Province resulted in the creation of several Tonga plays, including one about bride-price and another about peasant cattle sales to the Cold Storage Board. That of Eastern Province produced plays in Chinyanja about tensions in the extended family, venereal disease, conflicts between peasant farmers and the bureaucracy of the local marketing board, and a dance drama with the self-explanatory title, *The Hazards of Poor Sanitation*.

In the long run the idea of turning the Chikwakwa Travelling Theatre into a tool of development-oriented conscientization did not really work; this was largely due to the lack of integration between the university drama animateurs and locally-based development agents in the various provincial centres. The main achievement of the tours was a very vigorous policy of drama workshops stimulating local culture and local-language theatre skills. Chikwakwa contributed much towards a Zambian dramaturgy which was opposed to the urban, neo-colonial theatre dominated by expatriates. In contrast to the typical Western form of drama (the naturalistic *pièce bien faite* with a unilinear plot, elaborate props and decor played on a proscenium arch stage with an emphasis on dialogue in English and with a politely observant audience) the Chikwakwa enthusiasts helped build an indigenous Zambian dramaturgy using mime, dance, Zambian languages, simple symbolic props and decor, episodic plots, a thrust or in-the-round stage and a participatory audience.

In 1981, after the arrival of a new Ghanaian Artistic Director of Chikwakwa Theatre, the emphasis on rural-based popular theatre was changed towards a different theatrical policy – the production of more prestigious and spectacular English language plays, such as Césaire's *A Season in the Congo* (1981) and J. Tamakloe's *Jogolo* (1982), which were shown in the 'line of rail' towns of Lusaka, Kabwe and the Copperbelt.

As with the University College of Ibadan Travelling Theatre, Chikwakwa displays an important weakness of the university as a source of popular theatre – its reliance on specific enthusiastic individuals, who do not necessarily have a permanent theatre base. In the case of Chikwakwa, however, the emphasis on training workshops seems to have paid off in that many of the cadres trained either at the university itself or in the provincial workshops continued popular theatre activities outside university institutions.

The example of Chikwakwa Theatre (and also of Kenya's Free Travelling Theatre) illustrates a pattern in the travelling theatre movement whereby the main impetus for popular theatre moves away from the university into the specific communities in the form of popular workshops, cultural societies or community theatres. Of themselves, university-based travelling theatres suffer serious impediments in that their theatre cadres are transient (obviously the students, and usually the staff too). Although this is advantageous for the spreading of ideas, it requires a demanding policy of constantly recruiting fresh, committed personnel.

Even more problematic is the class position of university students, who form the bulk of travelling theatre workers. By origin, many students are from working-class or peasant backgrounds, but in their aspirations and training they are impelled towards a bourgeois life style. This class limbo often makes the students somewhat marginal to their society and capable of wild vacillations of ideology. The radical ambitions of student performers, linked to an ultimately petty-bourgeois world-view, often produce theatrical policies which waver between unacknowledged elitism and a romantically immature ultra-leftism.[26]

The difficulties of matching the idealistic fervour of university intellectuals with the day-to-day lived constraints of the rural masses have pushed many activists in the travelling theatre movements towards other forms of popular theatre in which it is possible to create a theatre context closer to a peasant or working-class community and far more attuned to its needs than is possible in occasional popular tours.

Notes

1. Opubor, p. 20.
2. Cited in Opubor, p.23.
3. Axworthy, p. 18.
4. Axworthy, p. 17.
5. Axworthy, p. 18. For an alternative view of the UICDS see Adelugba.
6. Cook, 1965, p. 2.
7. Cook and Lee, p. ix.
8. Cook, 1965, p. 7.
9. Cook, 1965, p. 11.
10. Cook, 1965, p. 13.
11. Cook, 1965, p. 15.
12. Cook, 1965, p. 16.
13. Cook, 1965, p. 16.
14. Cook, 1965, p. 15.
15. Cook, 1965, p. 16.
16. Cook, 1965, p. 10.
17. Nazareth, p. 27.
18. Gibbs, 1972, p. 34.
19. Gibbs, 1972, p. 34.
20. Kotchy, p. 12.
21. Koné, p. 83. For other articles on francophone African interest in popular travelling theatre see Meillassoux, 1964, and Ndumbe. 1986.
22. Etherton, 1973, pp.19–20.
23. For a theatrical analysis of the concept 'rough theatre' see Shank.
24. Kerr, 1975. Detailed information about Chikwakwa Travelling Theatre's performances and workshops can be found in the yearly reports of the Chikwakwa Review from 1971 to 1980. See also Idoye, Mwansa, 1983a, and Chifunyise and Kerr.
25. *Laedza Batanani*'s role in the Theatre for Development movement is examined in Chapter Eight.
26. See Chifunyise and Kerr, pp. 79–80.

8

Theatre
for
Development

A frequent aspiration of the university travelling theatre movement has been to interact with non-academic theatre campaigns aimed at community renewal, particularly in the rural areas of Africa. This wider mode of drama is commonly referred to as 'Theatre for Development'.

There have been two major sources of Theatre for Development: the colonial tradition of theatre as propaganda, and another more radical tradition of community theatre.

The colonial heritage set a pattern which has had a continuing deleterious impact on post-independence popular theatre, establishing a pattern whereby 'control and goal-setting are kept out of the hands of those for whom the programme is run'.[1] Several African governments, such as Nigeria, Ghana and Sierra Leone, carried on with the colonial tradition of didactic theatre and cinema after independence, as part of developmental media 'packages' on topics such as health, agriculture and birth control, discharged from centralized information sources. With such packages theatre was looked on as another 'mass' media like radio or cinema, capable of reaching remote 'target' audiences.

An element of respectability was given to the package theatre programmes by aid donated from such prestigious agencies as UNESCO (which described Third World Theatre for Development as 'folk media'[2]).

Many adult educators, however, felt dissatisfied by the centralized use of folk media packages. To use the fashionable jargon of adult education, there was a desire to displace the domesticating 'top–down' approach to communication with a more participatory 'bottom–up' approach. The participatory method derived some of its impetus from the ideas of the Brazilian educator Paulo Freire, and, though he has not been overtly concerned with theatre, he has remained a powerful influence on the debates about how to achieve a genuinely participatory popular theatre.[3]

A seminal experiment in Theatre for Development took place during the mid-1970s in Botswana. The campaign was called *Laedza Batanani* and had its

Puppet theatre show with developmental message as part of a packaged programme on nutrition in Zambia

A page from a 'How-to' manual on Theatre for Development, published for the *Laedza Batanani* campaign

origins not in a literary/art theatre movement as the university travelling theatre had, but in a desire by adult educators to find an appropriate medium for communication with peasant communities.

Much of the early theorizing and practical organization for *Laedza Batanani* came from a group of adult educators (including Ross Kidd, Martin Byram, Frank Youngman and Adrian Kohler) associated with the University of Lesotho, Swaziland and Botswana (later University of Botswana). They felt dissatisfied with the kinds of adult education extension programmes offered to the rural population. There was an excessive reliance on traditional extension media such as posters, written instructional pamphlets, demonstrations and chalkboard lectures/seminars.

Other faults identified with unimaginative communication strategies were: the lack of coordination between different development agencies (such as health, agriculture, literacy and community services), a lack of focus in attempting to concretize the constraints to rural development, and a tendency to a moralizing exhortatory approach on the part of extension workers. The last defect was particularly important because it was symptomatic of a general cultural gap between adult educators and the people, whereby experts were perceived as 'purveyors of alien and borrowed ideas'.[4]

Popular theatre seemed to be a technique which could resolve the apathy created by poor methods of communication. Those aspirations are contained in the following definition of popular theatre which was contained in a manual on organizing the *Laedza Batanani* campaigns:

> Popular theatre includes performances of drama, puppetry, singing, and dancing. These performances are called 'popular' because they are aimed at the whole community, not just those who are educated.
>
> They are performed in local languages and deal with local problems so everyone can understand them and find them useful ... This new type of theatre in Botswana builds on local ability and interest in story-telling, singing, poetry, and dancing.[5]

The definition covers some of the most important advantages which communicators saw in theatre – its ability to reach subaltern audiences, thus overcoming the barriers of illiteracy, its use of local languages and locally accepted cultural values/artistic forms, and its innate attraction because of performance's entertainment value. The element of entertainment was meant to be less a sugaring of the didactic pill than a galvanizing break in routine which could stimulate community cooperation. The mood of progressive activism is captured by the slogan, 'Laedza Batanani', which in Setswana means 'The sun is up, let us go and work together.'

An important feature of *Laedza Batanani* was its use of popular theatre to make concrete the practical constraints impeding development in the rural areas. Kidd and Byram call the process 'constraint analysis', a process which they describe as 'listing people's knowledge, attitudes and practice with respect to each problem; identifying from this list the key constraints (e.g. misbeliefs, lack of resources); and deciding which of these constraints might be successfully challenged and which current practices should be built on and supported'.[6] The constraint analysis interpreted through popular drama was meant to provide a kind of coding similar to the generative words which Freire made the key to literacy dialogue in the Third World.

I don't want to give the impression that the *Laedza Batanani* experience was a mere theoretical or uncreatively bureaucratic extrapolation from Freirian premises. The organizers tried to ensure that the productions were entertaining and aesthetically close to the Botswana performing traditions. This was partly achieved through absorbing indigenous artistic skills such as songs, proverbs and dance (like the Kalanga dancer who was incorporated into the 1976 performances). Another interesting adaptation of a traditional form was the way *Laedza Batanani* campaigns made use of the *Kgotla*, or village meeting place. The theatre performances aimed not only to revive the tradition of community village debate, but also to use the architectural tradition of the *Kgotla* stockade as a backdrop for theatrical performances.

At a deeper level there was a sense that the didacticism of the plots and the use of stock character types were a revival of indigenous didactic forms of narrative drama, similar to syncretic theatre. Elsewhere, I have suggested that such plays could be described as 'induced' popular theatre in that they have often been created in cultures like that of Botswana or Zambia where the migrant labour system or rapid urbanization has eroded most 'organic' forms of indigenous popular theatre, creating a vacuum which popular theatre 'induced' by intellectuals has been able to fill.[7] As I shall suggest later, however, the artificial nature of this collective play creation leads to some fundamental problems.

The artistic and organizational form of *Laedza Batanani* emerged through the practice of the popular theatre activists. For that reason it would be helpful to synopsize the campaign process from 1974 onwards. The first performances grew out of a conference on communication techniques for adult educators at Tutume Community College in 1974. Videotapes made in some villages aroused interest at the conference, and it was suggested that they should be shown back in the villages along with relevant plays. This was done and *Laedza Batanani* was born. In later years the videotapes (as a somewhat inappropriate medium for village performances) were dropped, and the plays continued alone.

The 1974 *Laedza Batanani* experience set the basic pattern for future years. The format consisted of a one-week campaign, usually during September or October before the ploughing season, in the Bokalaka region, near what was then the Rhodesian border. The campaign brought together extension workers, community leaders, performers, teachers from Tutume College and university adult educators. Through participatory research, drama, workshops, performances and community discussions the team integrated the skills of theatre and community planning.

The first campaign focused on problems concerning migrant labour, cattle theft, village development, domestic conflicts and youth problems. In later years, themes adopted were: stray cattle, youth unemployment, tuberculosis, and government land reform proposals (1975); nutrition, venereal disease and sanitation (1976). In the later campaigns the organizers learnt from the mistakes of the 1974 performance. They felt that in 1974 some of the themes (such as village development, or youth problems) were too vague to give rise to concrete proposals for remedial action. In later years this was rectified; from 1975 the organizers tried to ensure that plays and post-performance discussions could lead to direct comments and action, for example, digging latrines, avoiding spitting (health), using contraceptives (venereal disease) or growing vegetables (nutrition).

A very significant finding was that during the research process it was the most articulate members of the community who monopolized discussions; and they often had dominant class values. For example, the 1974 play about cattle theft reflected a problem faced by fairly wealthy cattle-owners – not the poorer peasants. In later years more care was taken to research the viewpoints of the subaltern classes in the Bokalaka.

The *Laedza Batanani* committee and workshops had a considerable impact on the community and attracted wide interest, including from the Botswana government, which found that the emphasis on local community development fitted in with the official government slogan of *Boipolego* (self-reliance).

Funds were found in 1976 to set up a National Committee. This helped not only to ensure the healthy continuity of *Laedza Batanani*, but also to stimulate similar Theatre for Development projects in other parts of Botswana. The most prominent spin-off was the *Bosele Tshwaraganang* campaign in Mochudi in December 1976, but there were smaller popular theatre workshops for family welfare educators organized by the Ministry of Health (1977), puppet show at agricultural shows and at the Rural Industries Innovation Centre in Kanye (1977), drama shows to advertise the Botswana Extension College's literacy campaigns (1977), and an anti-bilharzia popular theatre campaign in Kgatleng District (1978). In these campaigns the resources and organizational skills increasingly passed to indigenous Batswana such as Jeppe Kelepile, Sports Koitsiwe, Martha Maplanka and Kutlwano Matenge.

An even more ambitious project, and one which was to have a strong impact outside of Botswana, was the National Popular Theatre Workshop held at Kgari Sechele Secondary School, Molepolole, Kwenang District in May 1978. This brought together some of the veterans of the *Laedza Batanani* and *Bosele Tshwaraganang* campaigns, as well as outside resource persons such as Michael Etherton (Nigeria) and Godwin Kaduma (Tanzania). The National Workshop allowed the ideas of the preceding four years to be critically analysed by experienced theatre workers in the context of a real popular theatre campaign around Molepolole. From that experience emerged the following very influential model for a popular theatre workshop:

- a general introduction to popular theatre for the whole group;
- intensive work by the participants on one of the four performance skills (drama, dance, song, puppetry);
- information gathering in the villages;
- preparation and rehearsal of the village performances;
- performing in the village;
- evaluation and preparation for follow-up programme.[8]

With minor variations this format was adopted by many other theatre workers in the course of a remarkable dispersal process during the years following 1978.

In Zambia the theatre workers found the Botswana Theatre for Development ideas very attractive. In fact, there had already been examples of plays in Zambia before 1978 which used a didactic technique to highlight social problems. For example, the Lusaka Housing Unit used drama in the mid-1970s for demonstration of techniques of building low-cost houses in the 'site and service' schemes. One such play, *Chawama! Chawama!*, mixed drama with slide shows (with electricity run from a grocery or bar) and songs from a popular township group called the Buntungwa Star Band.

Probably more typical were some of the plays by authors such as Steve Chifunyise and Kabwe Kasoma (referred to in the last chapter) which dealt with social problems in Zambia. The theatre workers at the university had built up strong links with the *Laedza Batanani* movement through correspondence and exchange visits, and it was mainly from the university that a Theatre for Development movement began. After the 1978 Botswana National Workshop, some of the organizers, who had links with the main funding agency for the workshop, the Canadian University Service Overseas (CUSO), suggested the idea of a regional popular theatre workshop in Zambia. That idea was enthusiastically taken up by the Zambian theatre workers.

In order to obtain financial aid for the workshop and to provide an organization which could plan and administer it, an International Theatre Institute (ITI) Centre was set up in Zambia. The ITI (Zambia) Centre managed to raise funds, mainly from the Gulbenkian Foundation and CUSO) for the considerable expense of the regional workshop. International resource persons came from Botswana, Tanzania, Lesotho, Canada and USA. There was also a strong resource contingent of workers or extension officers from different agencies within Zambia.

The regional workshop was held at Chalimbana Training Centre about 40 km east of Lusaka in August 1979. It followed closely the Botswana format of research in villages, problem analysis, play creation (at the centre), performance in the villages, discussion with the villagers, and evaluation and planning for follow-up activities.[9]

One crucial difference between the Zambian regional workshop and the Botswana national workshop was that, despite the attempts at participatory research, there was a larger gap between the workshop participants and the villagers. Partly this was a result of having so many non-Zambians in the research and performance teams. Probably even more significant was the language question, which made even many of the Zambians outsiders. Chalimbana is located in an area inhabited by one of the less populous ethnic groups in Zambia, the Soli. Although many of the Zambian participants could communicate with the villagers in Nyanja, which is a lingua franca in Lusaka, very few could speak the local Soli language. (In Botswana there is a widely accepted national language, Setswana, which made communication a lot easier at Molepolole). It was significant, for example, 'that one of the plays at Chalimbana about a literacy class was completely transformed when a talented Soli-speaking primary school teacher joined the cast. There was much closer rapport with the audiences when he was performing.

Another different emphasis at Chalimbana was the greater attention paid to performing skills. Particularly impressive was the way the dance team, which contained two very skilled drummers and choreographers, Mapopa Mtonga and Stephen Chifunyise, created a didactic play without dialogue. The performance by the dance group illustrates some of the basic contradictions in the aesthetics of Theatre for Development. In five movements the play highlighted the theme of poor water supply, which the participatory research revealed to be a major problem. The story dealt with a man suffering from a gastric complaint caused by dirty water. After rejecting a false, mercenary *sing'anga* (spirit medium), the man goes to a clinic from where he is transferred to the main hospital in Lusaka. He returns triumphantly cured; the villagers dig a clean well and celebrate.

The plot sounds crude, but the play actually had considerable impact, both on the audience and on the other participants at the workshop. Each movement of the play was associated with a dominating dance motif; these ranged from Lozi *Siyomboka* rhythm, Tonga *Chingande*, Tumbuka *Fwemba* to West African Highlife and Afro-rock; the whole was choreographed to produce a unified ballet performed in the round near the primary school at Chilyabele village.

Such polished performances were quite different from most of the *Laedza Batanani* sketches where the resource persons often had advanced skills in social mobilization rather than in performing arts. The different emphasis led to a debate about the role of aesthetics. In Botswana there was a tendency to avoid a display of intimidatingly sophisticated theatre skills. The idea was that a fairly simple set of skills which were nevertheless close to indigenous performing traditions could be an appropriate communication and con-scientization tool for villagers to adopt. Doubts existed, however, whether such a 'rough' theatre might not in fact be a euphemism for a second-rate theatre, especially bearing in mind that the pre-colonial traditions of popular theatre were certainly not 'rough' in the sense of de-emphasizing skills.

Performance of a play like the untitled water-borne diseases mime described above at Chalimbana was meant partly as a giving back of pre-colonial performance arts to the people. Unfortunately, in the context of a two-week workshop like that of Chalimbana there was no time for the villagers to genuinely participate in and learn (or relearn) such performing skills. This meant the villagers were dazzled with the spectacular perfor-mance at Chilyabele, but it remained a metropolitan performance with little impact on their cultural life once the workshop was over.

The lack of follow-up applied not only to the cultural/aesthetic impact of the Chalimbana workshop, but to the developmental issues to which the workshop addressed itself. After the dust had settled down from the last performances the people around Chalimbana were still plagued by illiteracy, poor roads, inadequate water supply and lack of health facilities. In the absence of a dynamic group within the community mobilizing for develop-ment, the half-hearted schemes which the ITI organizing committee made for follow-up programmes were doomed to failure.

Where the Chalimbana workshop did succeed was in disseminating the concept of popular Theatre for Development among theatre workers and extension workers. Within Zambia a whole network of smaller popular theatre organizations sprang up, each setting up their own modest work-shops. Since these extension officers and artists were much closer to the communities than at Chalimbana, some of them were more successful in encouraging follow-up programmes. An example of a dynamic Theatre for Development project was the 1980 campaign associated with a group of community workers called BAM (Brotherhood of Man), based in Chief Chungu's area, Luwingu District, Northern Province. In the rural areas of the Copperbelt at Mufucheni a theatre programme was set up, which, according to a principal catalyst, university adult educator, Dickson Mwansa, 'led to renewed community solidarity with greater potential for initiating local projects'.[10]

Many of the Zambian government and non-government organizations were attracted to the communication possibilities of popular theatre. The Ministry of Health organized a theatre workshop on primary health care in Kalingalinga and other high-density Lusaka suburbs in August 1980. Tapiwa Muchenje of the university's Institute of African Studies led a participatory research and theatre team to Mwacisompola in Central Province, to analyse the 'community response to alcohol-related problems' in September 1981. And, in June 1983, a theatre group known as Target 200 researched the experiences of patients at Chainama Hills Mental Hospital in Lusaka to create a play entitled, *The Plight of the Mentally Ill Person*, to coincide with the Mental Health Association regional meeting for Southern Africa. The play dealt with the way the stigma of mental sickness prevents the main character, Sokisi, from integrating into society, and won considerable praise from Zambian government leaders.

The proliferation of Theatre for Development was not restricted to Zambia. Experimental popular theatre workshops took place in many other countries, particularly in Southern and Eastern Africa.

In October 1981 there was a large theatre workshop at Nhlangano Farmer Training Centre in Swaziland, with plays toured around the communities of Kontjingile, Manzini and Nsingizini.[11] Veterans from the Botswana and Zambian movements, Martin Byram, Mapopa Mtonga and Stephen Chifunyise, were available as organizers or resource persons. Community Health extension workers eagerly took up the use of theatre for their communication work in later years.

The Travelling Theatre of the University of Malawi, under the leadership of Chris Kamlongera and the author, held a small-scale, two-week drama workshop in 1981, with community theatre performances at and around Mbalachanda Rural Growth Centre in a remote part of the Northern Region.[12] This project did not lead to any wide theatre work among the extension officers at Mbalachanda after the workshop, but it had a powerful impact on urban popular theatre in Blantyre, Zomba and Lilongwe, when the Travelling Theatre used its techniques there for improvised Chichewa drama, concerning urban problems.

In Sierra Leone the National African Popular Theatre and the Sierra Magnamex Theatre were set up in 1983 to undertake popular theatre using the *Laedza Batanani* model. The theatre work was linked to existing community activities such as sports, film shows and dances.[13]

The Ford Foundation helped fund an ambitious Theatre for Development project near the Roma campus of the University of Lesotho in 1982. Out of this a popular company of university students was created under the leadership of Andrew Horn, who had experience with Chikwakwa Theatre in Zambia. Later, leadership passed to Zakes Mda, a South African exile, who was author of many accomplished plays on the problems of Southern Africa.[14] The university team set a pattern of travelling during the long vacation around the scattered villages of the Lesotho mountains, with plays on themes such as sanitation, migrant labour, the rehabilitation of ex-prisoners, and the setting up of village producer cooperatives.[15] One interesting feature

Villagers preparing an impromptu theatre for a developmental drama production in Mulangali, Malawi, 1988

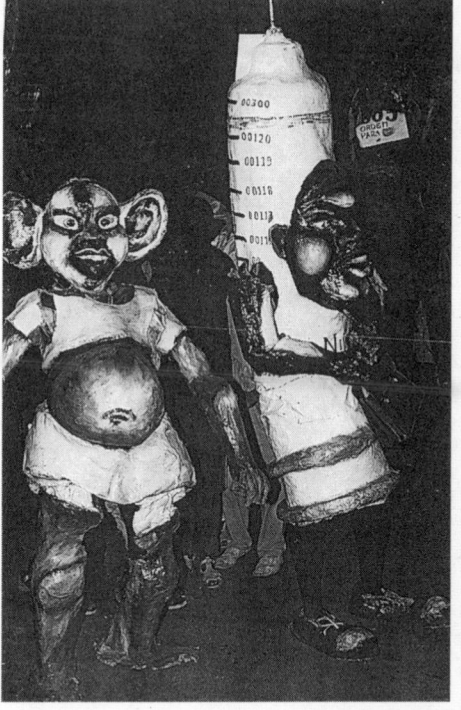

Masquerade figure of a hyperdermic needle in a carnival on the theme of Vaccination for Health, Guinea Bissau, 1987

of the Lesotho popular theatre was the extensive use of media such as radio drama, cartoon comics and even video performances, either to supplement the live performances or to replace them in the most inaccessible village.

Although the original Botswana model was a strong influence on popular drama projects, many of the workers who had been involved in Theatre for Development began to question the whole idea of a workshop which uses a rural community as a sort of test-tube for experimenting with popular theatre techniques. The shortness of the two-week stay among the peasant 'guinea-pigs' was felt to provide particular problems.

In Tanzania a team of diligent theatre workers from the university, prominent among whom were Penina Mlama, Eberhard Chambulikazi and Amandina Luhamba, attempted to create a theatre campaign which was capable of more sustained community participation and deeper analysis. The Oxfam-funded campaign, entitled Theatre for Social Development, was centred on Malya, a large Ujamaa village in Mwanza Region.[16]

Malya was chosen because it had a quite large mixed peasant and proletarian population of about 5,000, it had an alert 25-person Ujamaa executive committee led by a village chairman and secretary, and finally because it had a vigorous performing tradition which had already found some dramatic expression under the guidance of the village cultural sub-committee.

The most obvious differences between the Malya experience and some of the earlier Theatre for Development projects was the length of the campaign. Over a period of about eighteen months in 1982–3, the theatre team from the University of Dar es Salaam made five visits, some short of two weeks, others longer visits of over a month. The advantage of the extended and frequent visits was that the university team was able to build a closer relationship with the core team in Malya, and could enter into the social dynamism of Malya political life. For example, the first play which was performed was about older men impregnating young girls; this precipitated a crisis in the village leadership (because the story cut so close to the bone), leading to the dismissal of the chairman and secretary of the Malya drama core group. The new chairman and secretary were able to mobilize within a much freer and cooperative atmosphere. The incident contrasts with the Mbalachanda Theatre for Development campaign in Malawi, where a similarly obstructive scandal was only revealed to the catalyst group on the last day of the workshop.

The catalyst group in Malya became so well-accepted that they were able to influence a Malya Christian sect, the African Inland Church to stop its hostility to drama performances. In general, the campaign led to a revitalization of cultural life, and paved the way for economic projects to alleviate problems such as unemployment and vagrancy.

At the aesthetic level experiments were made in incorporating local songs and miming traditions into drama performances. Particularly successful was the integration of local Sukuma dances such as *Bugobogobo*, *Wigashe* and *Bunungule* into the structure of the dramas. The close mesh of formal drama skills from the university Theatre Department lecturers with the local popular dance skills contrasts with the rather exhibitionist quality of the dance drama creations at Chalimbana.

The advantages of the Malya project in fact were not just the more intensive contact and larger time-scale, but the fact that the university animateurs, rather than having to galvanize and unify separate agencies, were able to work closely and on reasonably equal terms with an already integrated, vigorous community and cultural organization.

The direction of the Malya experiment ran parallel to the theoretical shifts in the thinking about popular theatre of those who had been involved in earlier popular theatre experiments. Ross Kidd and Martin Byram provide a striking example of this shift. Their 1981 paper, 'Demystifying Pseudo-Freirian Non-Formal Education', constituted a major critique of the *Laedza Batanani* experience, which they themselves had been instrumental in establishing.[17] I have drawn extensively from that critique in my analysis of Theatre for Development's limitations. With compelling honesty, Kidd and Byram acknowledge that the Freirian emphasis on conscientization and participation in *Laedza Batanani* (and, by implication, most other Theatre for Development campaigns) was, in practice, a smokescreen for domestication.

Kidd and Byram see a dual potential for popular theatre: 'authentic popular expression and raising critical class-consciousness on the one hand and disseminating dominant class ideas inducing acceptance of the status quo on the other'.[18] Despite the attempts at a participatory pedagogy they concluded that *Laedza Batanani* tended more to the second than to the first direction.

The major disadvantage of Theatre for Development workshops has been that they have not been truly popular. In *Laedza Batanani*, 'the whole process is controlled by the more powerful members of the community leaders'.[19] For example, the 1976 campaign about VD, nutrition and sanitation was strongly influenced by the large contingent of government health staff in the *Laedza Batanani* organizing committee.

One reason why Theatre for Development projects tended to be dominated by the powerful was that they usually had very close links with government ministries or semi-government institutions. The workshops were often opened by government dignitaries. For example, the 1978 Molepolole workshop was opened by the Honourable K. P. Morake, Minister of Education; the Chalimbana workshop by the Honourable K. E. H. K. Mudenda, chairman of the Social and Cultural Committee of the Central Committee; the Nhlangano workshop was opened by the Honourable D. A. G. Nhlabatsi, Deputy Minister for Industry, Mines and Tourism, and closed by the Permanent Secretary in the Ministry of Health and the Under-Secretary for Agriculture. The function of this official involvement was to legitimatize the government's position in relation to popular theatre. For example, in Zambia and Botswana there was a suggestion that the aims of popular theatre were in accordance with the respective national ideologies of humanism and *Boipolego*.

The participation of government officials pointed to a crucial ambiguity in the Theatre for Development programmes. The jargon used by popular theatre workers to describe Theatre for Development ('participatory', 'bottom–up', 'conscientization', 'liberation' and so on) derived from the combative Freirian language of popular resistance. But the actual practice had to conform to the paternalistic (or, in some cases, repressive) realities of government hegemony. Most of the nations in which the workshops took place had a history of collaboration between political and economic elites. As long as the government was closely monitoring these theatre experiments there was no likelihood of drama being used for creating genuine solidarity of peasants and workers against oppression. Instead, theatre was used to legitimate existing power structures by providing a semblance of government participation in grass-roots cultural movements.

The close relationship between the ruling elites and the organizational infrastructures of the Theatre for Development workshops accounts for the ideology of domination and manipulation which permeated the basic tenets of the drama campaigns. One such ideological factor, pinpointed by Kidd, is that of 'scapegoating the poor', that is, 'a deprivation view of disadvantage: that poverty is self-inflicted, that the poor are poor because they have certain deficiencies or inadequacies'.[20] This results in a development strategy based on changing the poor rather than the system of oppression which makes them poor.

'Scapegoating the poor' is seen most clearly in the dramatic use of stereotyped characters. The rationale for creating characters based on stereotypes seemed unobjectionable. According to Paul Hurley the *Laedza Batanani* performers used 'core set types' (such as miner, village drunkard and juvenile delinquent) to focus on specific problems which were obstacles in the development process.[21] Superficially, such stereotyping conformed to indigenous traditions of pre-colonial and syncretic popular theatre, but a closer analysis shows that there were important differences:

> Within the apparent stereotyping of indigenous African theatrical arts ambiguity is possible. For instance, villains such as animal tricksters in oral narratives or figures like the hoodlum or prostitute in syncretic dramas, can sometimes appeal to seams of anarchic sympathy in the audiences, despite their outrageously amoral behaviour. The thin figures of didactic theatre, such as the obscurantist witch doctor, the rapacious land-owner or the heroically hard-working peasant, are too often presented without the countervailing irony or shading of an alternative viewpoint.[22]

What made the stereotyping in Theatre for Development especially patronizing was the way it tended to reflect a crude Manicheism between traditional characters (bad) and modern (good). Since the class elements which identified most closely with Theatre for Development were pettybourgeois professional extension officers – precisely a group trained in the ideology of modernization – they tended to create traditional characters such as the illiterate peasant, the superstitious patient, the greedy herbalist, who were sunk in ignorance or apathy, from which they could only be rescued by the dynamism of the modernizing characters (doctors, extension workers, teachers, community officers). The contrast was a mere extension of the old Mr Wise and Mr Foolish formula inherited from the colonial didactic theatre, and served to substitute an elitist analysis of the modernization process for a more relevant class-conscious analysis of exploitation.

Another defect of Theatre for Development, arising from the ideology of modernization and economic dualism, has been the tendency towards issue-oriented, problem-solving campaigns. The research element in the *Laedza Batanani* methodology stressed the identification of disparate problems – and the theatre campaigns were judged a success to the extent that problems had been 'solved' – that is, cabbages planted, VD cases reported to the clinic, or latrines dug. There was no attempt to see the problems within the historical context of imperialism and underdevelopment. For example, many of the problems which were identified in the *Laedza Batanani* campaigns could only be understood within the context of Botswana's dependence upon the Southern African migrant labour system, and the social anomie and marginalization deriving from it. By concentrating on disparate constraints divorced from the underlying structural causes of underdevelopment Theatre for Development often obscured issues for the rural poor rather than clarifying them.

The limitations of Theatre for Development did not go unnoticed by drama practitioners. The good communications between popular theatre workers in different parts of Africa meant that experiences were shared and a critical attitude developed, which helped the animateurs create improved Theatre for Development practices. One group which undertook a sustained critical reappraisal of the Theatre for Development process was the ABU Collective at the University of Ahmadu Bello in Zaria, Northern Nigeria. From 1977 onward the ABU Collective embarked on a series of projects, each of which attempted to make a more radical adjustment than the previous one to the needs of the people.

The ABU Collective was established by experienced expatriate lecturers, Michael Etherton and Brian Crow, and by such committed young Nigerian theatre workers as Salihu Bappa, O. Abah and Tunde Lakoju. Conceptually they felt it important to turn their backs on the various strong Nigerian theatre traditions – whether that of the elitist literary drama, or the politically co-opted theatre of indigenous dance festivals, or the commercial urban popular travelling theatre. Instead, they determined to make their theatre skills available to the peasants and workers of the Zaria region in their struggle against oppression.

The Collective was heavily influenced by the concept of 'rehearsal theatre', developed by Latin American drama worker and theorist, Augusto Boal.[23] Boal emphasized 'theatre as discourse', where, instead of a polished performance presented to popular audiences by an elite cadre of artists, the theatre team actually collaborated with the audiences in the creation of drama. Boal's ideas provided a solution to a persistent problem in Theatre for Development: how to encourage audiences to join in discussions. As Kidd puts it:

> If people are left out of the action and dialogue in the play it's difficult to turn them on like a tap when it's all over.[24]

On the other hand, when people participate in the creation of a play, theoretical analysis of the issues is an integral and inevitable part of scenario-making. For Boal and those whom he has influenced the various 'rehearsals' *are* the performance and are scarcely distinguishable from the audiences' analysis. Kidd comments:

> It is the drama-which-is-never-finished, constantly being restructured to extend the insights of the participants. Nothing is presented as a final statement: each new scene is questioned, challenged and probed for deeper meaning.[25]

In other words, there is a shift of emphasis from theatre as a finished 'product' to theatre as a continuous and alterable 'process'.

The first ABU popular theatre project was that of *Wasan Manoma* (Hausa for 'Plays for Farmers'), held in March 1977 in Soba, a rural market centre about an hour's drive from Zaria. The workshop was partly intended to research and dramatize the attitudes of farmers to OFN (Operation Feed the Nation), which had recently been launched by the government throughout Nigeria. From the start the organizers were anxious not to reflect official government positions on agricultural development; they wanted to avoid being 'mercenaries at the behest of any government or development agency'.[26]

Apart from its relative independence from official development agencies, the Soba workshop was fairly similar in technique and format to the *Laedza Batanani* model. At the end the team created four plays on the themes of corruption, profiteering and migration to the towns. There was no attempt at follow-up or linking of the plays to popular organizations.

However, the cultural differences between Northern Nigeria and Southern Africa created performance conditions which demanded different theatrical approaches. For one, the predominance of Islam in the towns and villages around Zaria gave rise to a problem about the extent to which religion played a liberating or conservative role in society. The emphasis which was at the heart of popular theatre of preserving and building upon indigenous cultural forms had to be tempered by the knowledge that some cultural forms (such as the practice of accepting dowry for pubescent girls) had degenerated under the influence of the cash nexus into an excuse for customs little better than prostitution.

Another difference was that class formation was more advanced in the rural areas of Northern Nigeria than in those of Southern Africa. As Etherton comments on the *Wasan Manoma* shown in Shalabari village:

> The division in the village was essentially between the wealthier farmers, who enjoyed some measures of organization, and the poorer farmers, who seemed to have no organization at all to protect and further their interests.[27]

In such villages it was much less easy than in Zambia, Swaziland or Botswana to suppress theatrical class analysis under the cloak of slogans such as 'humanism' or 'self-reliance'.

The rather confusing conjuncture of religious and class-based ideologies emerged clearly from the next popular theatre workshop, *Wasan Maska*, held in January 1979 at Maska and its satellite village of Lasanawa, about 50 km from Zaria. *Wasan Maska* consisted of three improvised plays in Hausa, one about hygiene, one about corruption in the distribution of fertilizer, and one about the conflict between illiterate poor farmers and the *Alhajis* (technically those who had made the journey to Mecca). The group met considerable resistance from the privileged section within Maska and Lasanawa. For example, the chief refused to allow women to see the play about hygiene, even though the issues were specifically directed to women.

More troublesome than such direct resistance were the innumerable indirect obstacles put in the way of a radical theatrical critique of Maska society. Salihu Bappa, a leader of the *Wasan Maska* project, highlights those obstacles:

> Adult educators should keep a wary eye on ... the possibility of allowing a popular theatre programme to be manipulated by the exploiting class in rural communities so that the villagers are brought in only to be entertained and sent back to their respective homes happy, subservient and contented.[28]

Bappa cites an example of an attempted co-option by village elites of a play's radical message. The chief of Maska did not convey to the community the date of the performances in his village. When the team moved to Lasanawa an agent of the chief went round to 'educate' the villagers about the plays' theme, saying that it was to 'respect their leaders and to stop causing trouble'. From this, Bappa concludes, 'one could see that the ruling class would use anything in its way to further intimidate and confuse the villagers'.[29]

In rural Africa, traditional elites such as chiefs promote a kind of 'indirect rule', not of colonialism, as in the days of British autonomy, but of neo-colonialism – distracting attention from the way metropolitan elites extract surplus labour from rural peasants through a series of articulations with the capitalist economy. Bappa testifies to popular theatre's role in illuminating the process.

> The audiences were quick to view the root cause of the problem along class lines ... Once the class issue was established the villagers were able to have an insight into the deeper meaning of their problems. They were able to see the link between their illiteracy and their deprivation, between the scarcity of fertilizer and the business activities of the *alhajis*.[30]

For such critical class analysis to be effective it was important for the ABU team to avoid the appearance of clumsy iconoclasm; they had to respect those traditional values or mores which were not obviously exploitative. For example, the research into local problems were undertaken in the *Zaure* or traditional Hausa parlour for receiving and entertaining male guests. The delicate social skills which contributed to *Wasan Maska* were necessitated by the presence of advanced class formation in Northern Nigeria, somewhat disguised behind the social cement of powerful religious traditions.

These complex social conditions were rather similar to those in many parts of Asia. It was not surprising, therefore, that the ABU Collective, in addition to the inspiration of Latin American popular drama, was also influenced by theories developed by Asian popular theatre workers in India, Sri Lanka, Bangladesh and the Philippines. A combination of the Asian and Latin American theatrical influences, and the analysis arising from the theatrical praxis, led the ABU Collective to question the achievements of the workshops in Soba and Maska. There was a desire to achieve a closer creative working relationship with the audience/community and to conceive a coherent follow-up programme which could grow naturally from the performance, but without lapsing into the problem-solving tokenism of the *Laedza Batanani* and Chalimbana workshops.

In 1980 the ABU Collective initiated two theatre projects which attempted to put into practice the more radical thrust of this analysis. In April they undertook a theatre workshop at Bomo, a village fairly close to the university. That workshop was an advance on the earlier two workshops in several ways. It brought together drama students and literary officers, and there was a much closer rapport between the theatre team and the villagers.

A particularly impressive feature of the *Wasan Bomo* was that the improvisations were created not only by the theatre team but also by some of the villagers. Etherton explains the process with respect to improvisations about farmers losing their land:

> In examining the increasing appropriation of their land by outside agencies, the

Theatre for Development play about Primary Health Care in Malawi, 1988

farmers 'role-played' various ways they could question and resist these practices. After each 'rehearsal' the farmers analysed their action – its limitations and potential obstacles – and then redramatized their course of action.[31]

Thus the emphasls was not on a finished performance, but on a continuous process of scenario creation and modification by which the farmers strategized the possible methods of resisting exploitation.

By having actors among the oppressed community of landless farmers and petty marketeers acting out more privileged roles, such as that of the Sarkhin Masawa (chief of the market) or a police inspector, the actors were able to think their way into the strategies and practices of the dominant class. In that way the participants in the workshop 'began to realize that high-blown rhetoric was quickly contradicted by reality'.[32] The elimination of over-optimistic or idealized methods of resistance is an essential step in the process of achieving solidarity among the subaltern classes.

Eventually the *Wasan Bomo* were put together as a performance in Bomo village, but Etherton felt that those performances were less significant and valuable than the earlier rehearsals.

A somewhat different attempt at popular theatre was the annual drama workshop called *Wasan Samaru*, which the ABU Collective initiated in 1980 in the town of Samaru and the overspill squatter compound of Hayin Dogo. Samaru and Hayin Dogo are squalid, high-density townships which provide cheap labour and other services for the relatively privileged lecturers and students at Ahmadu Bello University. The workshops gave the opportunity for first-year drama students to research and analyse social problems in the local community, and to create, under the supervision of the drama tutors, improvised plays about those problems, to be shown to the community. In the process of the play creation the tutors tried to emphasize to the students that 'scenario-making involved particularization and characterization, conflict, irony, and a sequence of events that brings out the problems in such a way as to show their interrelatedness'.[33]

The plays were in Hausa or pidgin (or a mixture of both) and were performed in the streets. The group blocked off a quiet road with access to a small square, set up a tarpaulin backdrop and allowed the audience (with their backs to the setting sun) to create a semi-circle in the dust of the road. At first performances tended to attract mainly children, but when the seriousness of the plays' themes was established adults attended in large numbers.

A synopsis of scenario plots performed for the *Wasan Samaru* in 1980 and 1981 illustrates the type of problem which emerged from the research process. In 1980 there was a play about illiteracy, one about the break-up of a family under the social pressures of urban slum life, one about prostitution, and, most successful with audiences, a play about an aspirant clerk being forced by corruption to take a menial job as an exploited labourer. The 1981 plays all focused on health topics, and received help from the Ahmadu Bello University Teaching Hospital. One play was about contaminated water, another about post-natal amnesia, and another about complications in child-birth caused by traditional medical practices.

The Samaru plays did not achieve the full participation which had been realized in the 1980 *Wasan Bomo*, but they did provide a very useful shock for the privileged drama students, by forcing them to confront in theatrical terms the problems and living conditions of the local urban poor.

The achievements and techniques of the ABU Collective were taken out-side the Zaria region in 1982, when they were invited to organize a large-scale theatre workshop (the Kitsina-Ala project) at Makurdi by the Benue State Arts Council. Whereas most Nigerian State Arts Councils spent their funds on prestigious dance troupes geared to tourists, Benue State was keen to channel some of its funds to grass-roots drama in the villages. The idea was to have a theatre workshop combining drama practitioners and extension workers, and including outside resource persons from selected international agencies. In fact, most of the extension workers turned out to be from media such as radio and journalism, and consequently received an even greater shock than most extension workers in having to engage with the rural subaltern classes.

Although the format of an intensive workshop involving research, play creation and performance was superficially similar to the *Laedza Batanani* model, the organizers were determined to draw upon the advances made by the ABU Collective. One major advantage enjoyed by the Benue Workshop which did not apply to most earlier Theatre for Development workshops was the existence among the local Tiv community of a very rich indigenous popular theatre tradition which had its own self-reliant organizational base. In that sense, the Benue State Arts Council workshop was not 'inducing' popular theatre, but attempting to build upon, and possibly reorient, an existing tradition.

The theatre form which was already very popular among the Tiv of Benue was *Kwagh-hir*, a syncretic theatre described by Kees Epskamp as 'a mixture of traditional ritual elements and modern theatrical effects, a kind of whirling, "vaudeville" programme with a narrator, acrobats, dancers, a puppet-show, whims and fancies'.[34] This richly stylized and complex form of 'total theatre' emerged in the 1960s at the time of the Tiv riots. It was a syncretic drama using elements of pre-colonial masquerades. Its function was to honour the ancestors as a way of purifying the people from the contamination of rapid modernization and generation conflict. Huge raffia masks provided ritual dancing which was intended to placate the ancestors; but there was also much modern satire in the puppet shows, the clowning of the 'light-man', and in the narrator's comments, which often referred directly to members of the audience.

In the Benue area there were several *Kwagh-hir* companies, each with about 30 to 40 men and women, based on a village community. At the inter-village competitions there were huge audiences which participated vocally in the performances. The Benue State Arts Council decided to make the Theatre for Development workshop coincide with a large *Kwagh-hir* festival, which was attended by over 10,000 people, and which provided a constant reminder to the organizers that the Tiv had their own vital tradition of popular theatre.

The 'constraint analysis' arising from the Benue Workshop research find-ings revealed that major problems in the eyes of the chief and other village men were the desertion of husbands by wives, and the difficulty faced by the village cooperative in obtaining fertilizer from the government store. The organizers were determined not to allow the dramatization of these prob-lems to get stuck at the superficial level of problem-solving; they were also determined not to impose an artificially neat theatrical (and moral) solution to the improvised scenarios.

The approach taken was to create unfinished scenarios in the workshop and take them to the villagers for discussion and collective development. The fertilizer play had a trader buying all the government fertilizer and reselling it at four times the government rate. The angry meeting provoked by the trader's action formed the starting-point for the farmers' improvisations and collective discussions. The villagers strategized with the drama team about possible steps to resist the corruption of traders and the collusion of government officials. The important factor was that the choices in the play were not merely related to the fantasy world of the play, but to the real choices available to the community in their everyday lives. The improvisation led to an actual visit by the drama team to the government cooperative office in the nearby town of Gboko, in which the team tried with some success to argue the farmers' viewpoints.

The play about wife desertion was linked to that of the fertilizer problem in that the fictional wife in the play runs away from her husband owing to the beatings she receives from him, but also owing to poverty exacerbated by the lack of fertilizer. The drama team felt that the play-creation process and discussions, which had been dominated by male villagers, illustrated a mentality of 'scapegoating the women'. They therefore obtained permission from the chief to hold separate 'performances' and discussions with the village women. This led to an interpretation of wife desertion from the women's point of view, one in which the double oppression of women, economic and sexual, was the major problem. From this analysis emerged a more complex scenario which was less dependent on moralizing and stereotypes and which went much further in demystifying the sexual nature of women's desertion of their husbands.

The public performances of the 'finished' plays at the end of the workshop were very successful. They attracted huge audiences, which felt at home with the plays just as if they were *Kwagh-hir* performances. Epskamp describes the crowd reaction at one performance:

> The audience that is either sitting or standing walk off at times, come back, fetch something to eat ... The bar owners and female peddlers take their booze and their goodies and go into the audience. When there are shouts for beer on the other side of the stage, the merchant is not afraid of walking across the stage right through the scene.[35]

Such incorporation of Theatre for Development performances into traditional popular theatre audience conventions is a fairly sure sign that they were accepted into the cultural practice of the Tiv people.

There were other significant achievements. The villagers obtained more confidence in dealing with government officials such as the cooperative officer in Gboko, and they also started their own drama groups in the hope of continuing popular theatre activities after the team left.

For the theatre workers who participated in the Benue experience the whole process provided an important education in the roots of rural exploitation. As one observer puts it:

> The workshop confirmed ... that the main obstacle to development is not the villagers' ignorance or apathy or bad habits but the policies and structures which limit the villagers' access to resources, information and power ... The workshop challenged the conventional stereotype of farmer conservatism and showed that it

is the traders and bureaucrats who are far more resistant to change, especially a change which disturbs the status quo.[36]

Despite these successes, the organizers were not entirely happy about the workshop. Although the catalyst group achieved a much closer integration with the village community than is normal with Theatre for Development campaigns, there was some dissatisfaction with the shortness of the workshop. Crow and Etherton, for example, two members of the ABU Collective, who were resource persons at Benue, felt that it was 'only over a period of time that focal members of the target audience can be fully introduced to [the] idea of community play making and be imbued with enough acting skills and performance procedures to initiate it on their own when the catalyst group eventually does move on'.[37]

Nevertheless, the experiments of the ABU Collective were sufficiently challenging to initiate a search among popular theatre workers for finding ways of involving more participation in the organization of plays and for creating more permanent structures within the communities to support the theatre process.

In Zimbabwe the International Theatre Institute and UNESCO organized a month-long Popular Theatre workshop at Morewa in August 1983. The animateurs found their job was made a lot easier at Morewa because there already existed a vigorous indigenous popular theatre form, the *Pungwe*, in which night-long songs, dances and satiric sketches mobilized people against the Smith regime durlng Zimbabwe's struggle for independence. Kidd comments on the importance of the *Pungwe*'s self-reliant origins:

> The peasants not only perform in it but also organize it. It is their initiative, not something externally induced.[38]

The hope of the workshop was that self-reliant popular control over the mobilization process would continue after independence in the battle against poverty, ill-health and economic oppression. It did not take long, however, before a conflict arose within the Theatre for Development movement in Zimbabwe between those cadres who wanted to revitalize the self-reliant peasant initiative of the *Pungwe* and those representing a new breed of Zimbabwean bureaucrats who preferred a much more centralized, manipulative form of didactic theatre.

The ITI and UNESCO sponsored another international theatre workshop in Cameroon in December 1984, with theatre work based on three large villages, Keke II, Konye and Kurume. In the early stages the workshop followed the *Laedza Batanani* model. but the actual performances incorporated the participatory techniques introduced by the ABU Collective. At Kurume, for example, a play was created in which a series of interlocking cases involving problems of witchcraft, village brawling, unemployment and illiteracy were brought to a traditional village council. The play as 'play' was stopped at that point, and the audiences asked to take over the role of the village council. According to Eyoh, at the discussion:

> Some elderly people tried to defend traditional customs; others admitted that the youth had some reason. The debate went on and on, with the villagers challenging each other's perceptions.[39]

After some time the play was resumed with one of the main characters,

Margaret, miscarrying, since her illiteracy caused her to misread drug instructions. The discussion resumed at that point among the 'Village Council' (the audience), and carried on till the early hours of the morning. As a comment on the whole process the (real) chief councillor said:

> It was worthwhile for me to have gone through this experience before I die. Never has the village been offered such an opportunity for detailed self-analysis and been provided with so much entertainment.[40]

In the evaluation of the workshop, however, Eyoh (like Crow and Etherton with the Benue Workshop) had reservations about the role of some of the student participants, who 'seem to have abrogated to themselves leadership roles which they saw being challenged by the methodology'.[41] Eyoh is suggesting that many of the problems revealed by the popular theatre process lay not with the people being mobilized but with the bureaucrats who were supposed to be helping them.

A rather different Theatre for Development process was initiated in Malawi in 1985 when a team from the university joined forces with the Primary Health Care Unit of a rural development agency in Liwonde. After the rather abortive experience of Mbalachanda the theatre team was determined to make a longer-lasting impact with these health-oriented dramas. It was decided to avoid the workshop project format altogether and to link the theatre work in as unobtrusive a way as possible with the on-going education/mobilization work of the Primary Health Care Unit. Under the supervision of a dynamic Malawian community nurse and a West German doctor, the university team did research in several rural communities where there were serious health problems, in a process termed 'community diagnosis'. The team kept going back to the villages for performances, follow-up visits and evaluations. In the end it became very difficult to distinguish between research, performance and evaluation, since the evaluatory/research process was deepened by the repeated performances.

At Mwima Trading Centre, for example, several plays were performed in 1986 as part of a mobilization process in setting up Village Health Committees for self-help primary health care. This did much to improve the health of the community (such as by drastically cutting down the rate of cholera infection). However, the establishment of the Village Health Committees precipitated different problems, particularly of role conflict with political or economic leaders in society. A whole new cycle of plays was created in 1987 to address the new problems, in which it was necessary for the villagers to start examining the ideological and structural problems which led to difficulties in the distribution of medicines and cement. The form of the drama process began to take on the fluidity of life itself. For such plays 'the temporary abeyance of normality ... exists in a situation where the gaps between reality and illusion are constantly being blurred, corresponding to the flux and potential transformation taking place in society'.[42]

One radical methodology which the Malawi Primary Health theatre borrowed from the Boal/ABU Collective model was that of incorporating the audiences into the structuring of the play. The participation was achieved by creating dilemmas or arguments as 'cut-off points' in the scenario where the debate was opened up by the actors through direct address to the audience. The Mwima community used this 'decision-making through theatre' to agree on issues like cementing the surrounds of wells, electing Village Health Committees and confronting the Area Health Committee about misappropriated or badly administered medicine. I have described that theatrical dialogue as follows:

> Whenever a debate over moral or ideological issues broke out the audience actively joined in the debate and urged the actors towards collectively projected choices ... [This] gives the popular will a chance to counteract some of the power exercised by influential individuals.[43]

The debates were able to mobilize people because the Liwonde Primary Health Theatre was not part of a prestigious international workshop or a short-term experimental project, but a long process by catalysts who had become fairly well accepted within the community through frequent visits.

The whole issue of the relationship between the catalyst group and the community became a crucial one. Some Theatre for Development workers felt that it was necessary for the catalyst groups to keep a distance between themselves and the community. One anonymous spokesperson at a Popular Theatre conference in Lesotho put it very graphically:

> A doctor doesn't have to have gonorrhoea to cure the disease. I don't think you have to be poor to help the poor.[44]

While animateurs may not need to be poor most Theatre for Development workers have found difficulty in attempting to use theatre as a radical tool of conscientization as long as some of the catalyst's analysis remained outside the community. For example, there were contradictions in having the ABU Collective's activities written into the formal university training programme at Ahmadu Bello. There was a distinct advantage in forcing otherwise pettybourgeois students to face the problems of creating drama for and with popular audiences; but it also led to the serious contradiction that the students' ultimate motive was less that of linking themselves with the people's struggle, than that of ensuring they obtained good grades in Popular Theatre units. There was a tendency for the catalysts to try to make short cuts in conscientizing the audiences.

Freire, one of the original inspirations for Theatre for Development, puts the dilemma succinctly:

> I cannot think for others ... Even if the people's thinking is superstitious or naive, it is only as they rethink their assumptions in action that they can change.[45]

The rethinking process requires the continuous dialectic of day-to-day dialogue and creativity, not just the excitement of two- or three-week workshops from energetic catalyst groups – however sympathetic and committed they might be.

Even in favourable conditions there are severe limits to the amount of support which catalyst groups attached to government or other official institutions (such as universities) can give to people's movements, struggling against traders, corrupt bureaucrats, comprador capitalists and political manipulators. The ideological links which exist between institutions in post-independence Africa tend to blunt the sharpness of class-conscious theatre.

These links are made even stronger when backed up by overseas aid. At the Maseru conference on Theatre for Development, an anonymous delegate commented on the aid backing which supports most theatre projects in Africa:

No strings attached just mean invisible strings – and they entangle you the most.[46]

One of the follies arising from aided projects is that, in the glossy brochures which are usually produced after the theatre projects, there has been a tendency to paint a glowingly optimistic picture of the projects, so that the donors would continue to give funds in the future. This kind of developmental jingoism not only masks the real problems facing the rural poor, but also works against the self-reliant attitude which the projects are intended to encourage.

Theatre for Development has made some remarkable achievements in breaking down barriers between performers and audiences in Africa, but, as with the university travelling theatre movements, the biggest obstacle lies with the organizational structure monitoring the campaign and with the ambiguous class position of the animateurs.

The achievements of movements like the ABU Collective probably represent the limits of what can be done within projects linked to formal institutions. The way towards a liberated drama (which will be examined in the last chapter) lies precisely in the building of cultural movements independent of state-backed or aid-oriented bureaucracies.

Notes

1. Kidd, 1979, p. 4.
2. See, for example, Ranganath.
3. That Freire was aware of the potential of mime and drama in African popular education emerges from an illuminating footnote to one of his letters to literacy workers in Guinea Bissau. See Freire, 1978, p. 91.
4. Dall, p. 186.
5. Popular Theatre Committee, p. 4.
6. Kidd and Byram, p. 6.
7. Kerr, 1981, p. 150.
8. Adapted from Mackenzie.
9. See Chifunyise, Dall and Kerr.
10. Mwansa, 1983b, p. 7. See also Mwansa, 1982.
11. Byram, Moitse and Boeren.
12. Kamlongera, 1982 and Kerr, 1982.
13. Sharkah.
14. Mda, 1981.
15. Mda, 1986.
16. Chambulikazi, and Mlama, 1983.
17. Kidd and Byram.
18. Kidd and Byram, p. 1.
19. Kidd and Byram, p. 12.
20. Kidd, 1979, p. 5.
21. Hurley.
22. Kerr, 1981. p. 154.
23. Boal.

24. Kidd, 1979, p. 5.
25. Kidd, 1984b, p. 13.
26. Etherton, 1978, p. 12. See also ABU Collective.
27. Etherton, 1978, p. 21.
28. Bappa, 1983, p. 34.
29. Bappa, 1979, p. 19.
30. Bappa, 1979, p. 16.
31. ABU Collective, p. 15.
32. Abah and Balewa, quoted in Etherton, 1982, p. 352.
33. Abah and Etherton, p. 226.
34. Epskamp, 1982, p. 2. See also Eyoh, 1986.
35. Epskamp, 1982, p. 7.
36. Kidd, 1982, p. 53.
37. Crow and Etherton, p. 592.
38. Kidd, 1984b, p. 10.
39. Eyoh, 1986, p. 17.
40. Eyoh, 1986, p. 17.
41. Eyoh, 1984, p. 107.
42. Kerr, 1988. For another example of a theatre process (from Lesotho) which renewed itself over a period of time, see Mda, 1993, pp. 131–41.
43. Kerr, 1988.
44. Quoted in Kerr, 1985, p. 17.
45. Freire, 1972, p. 80.
46. Quoted in Kerr, 1985, p. 34.

9

Popular Theatre
&
Macro-Media

The attempt by development field workers to use drama as a means of communication and conscientization is partly a reaction from 'mass' media such as radio, film and television, which are seen as remote from the interests of specific communities and too easily open to government propaganda.

A useful distinction has been made by the Philippines theatre group PETA between macro-media, which involve 'a highly complex technology... high investment outlays and Western-based expertise that only the rich can afford', and micro-media, which 'follow the principles of intermediate technology and expertise that is appropriate to the poor'.[1] PETA workers feel that micro-media (typified by techniques like seminars, study groups and drama) are inherently more popular than macro-media since people are the channel of communication and because it is less easy for audiences to be manipulated by remote metropolitan bureaucrats.

Nevertheless, I think it would be a mistake to completely ignore macro-media in a book on popular African theatre. Analysis of European popular theatre has shown how it is possible for artists attuned to popular needs and fantasies to transform the formulaic, jaded genres of the multiple media (such as science fiction, westerns and domestic soap operas) to create theatre capable of stimulating relevant discourse with popular audiences.[2]

The strongest argument against macro-media as potential arenas for popular African drama is contained in the 'media imperialism' hypothesis. According to this theory, the multiple media of radio, TV and cinema, owing to their origins in the colonial period, and owing to the persistence of Western values through programming and training (what Peter Golding calls the 'transfer of an ideology')[3] form a self-adapting infrastructure which uses the media in Africa as a blatant form of cultural imperialism.

Oliver Boyd-Barrett makes the useful distinction between media systems which consciously export media influence, and those which unconsciously disseminate them.[4] A similar distinction is to be made between Third World countries which consciously adopt metropolitan media values and those

172

which unconsciously absorb them. Boyd-Barrett makes other useful distinctions between the different modes: 1) the shape of the communication vehicle (such as the one-way transmission/reception model of radio as developed in the Anglo-American broadcasting tradition), 2) the set of industrial arrangements (such as the training and administrative hierarchies inherited by African radio stations from the BBC and SORAFOM), 3) the values of practice (such as the reliance on the domestic serial as a drama staple for radio and TV), 4) media content (notably the reliance of African media systems on films and programmes imported from the West).[5]

These modes of media imperialism arise from the already existing dependence of the African peripheries on metropolitan economic infra-structures. In programming, to use an example cited by Elliot and Golding, 'newly founded broadcasting organizations, lacking resources in money and personnel, cannot afford not to buy popular American films and series'.[6]

From a strictly economic point of view such media imperialism may seem inevitable, but for the Third World viewer/listener forced to consume an alien culture, particularly one who is sensitive to the manipulative potential of the medium, the process creates a mood of frustration and impotent rage.

> These media products penetrated individual and collective domains of African lives, impregnated their tastes, their reflexes, their modes of thought, even their decisions, manipulating them to conform to capitalist requirements and to superfluous or illusory needs.[7]

The power and truth of this indictment by Colette Houeto should not tempt us into seeing media imperialism as a monolithic, all-powerful and static system. Media imperialism is as subject to changing historical forces as is politico-economic imperialism. It takes on many forms and is constantly adapting itself. In radio/TV broadcasting, for example, there is an enormous difference between a vast, centralized, multi-media complex like Cité de la Voix du Zaire (opened by Mobutu Sesse Seko and Valéry Giscard d'Estaing), with its expensive equipment and European technicians, and a decentralized regional system run by local staff, such as one of the smaller state broad-casting networks in Nigeria.

More important still, since independence, theatre artists and broadcasting cadres, despite the Western orientation of their training, have not always acted as passive channels of Western culture. There has been a history of struggle to assert an African popular media culture despite the imperatives towards neo-colonial control. My task in this chapter is not only to outline the structure of media imperialism but also to illustrate the struggle of African artists against that system.

Radio is the dominant medium in Africa owing to its cost-effectiveness. According to one comparative study of Kenyan media, the per capita cost of a single radio show is US\$ 0.008 and of a TV show US\$ 0.40.[8] According to a 1961 UNESCO survey in Nigeria, there were two million radio receivers, but only 60,000 TV receivers, and only 46,000 cinema seats.[9] Of these the radio receivers probably reached an even larger proportion of the population than the 2.8 per cent they appeared to reach, since the communal habits of the extended family allow much more group listening than in a typical Western context.

As pointed out in Chapter Two, the radio services associated with the

A radio drama performance in Gabon

A scene from *Diankha-bi* directed by Mhama Traoré

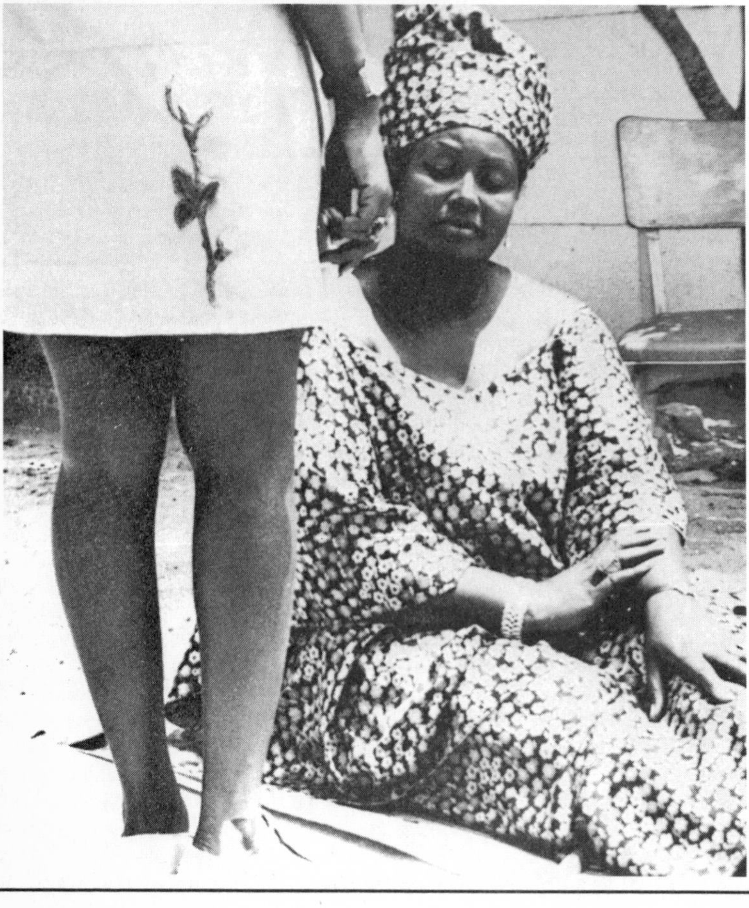

colonial governments had done very little to encourage radio drama in Africa. It's rather surprising to find, therefore, that after independence the ex-colonial government agencies put considerable effort into encouraging African radio drama.

In francophone Africa ORTF (l'Organization Radiodiffusion-Television Française), the successor to the colonial overseas broadcasting service, SORAFOM, and the post-colonial OCAPA, became an important force for encouraging African radio drama. In 1966 ORTF started an annual radio drama competition in French; the best entries were broadcast throughout francophone Africa. The competition was probably modelled on the stage drama competitions initiated just before independence, and served a similar function of legitimating the French language as an important tool of French neo-colonial influence.

In one way the ORTF drama competitions were more subtle than the stage equivalents. In addition to a *grand prix* for the best play chosen by a panel of 'experts', there was a *prix des auditeurs* awarded by ballot from the listeners themselves. This ensured at least some measure of popular acclaim for radio plays independent of the criteria of metropolitan experts. The *grand prix* tended to go to ponderously serious dramas, whereas the *prix des auditeurs* went to more accessible comedies. For instance, in 1969, the *grand prix* went to the symbolic play, *L'Europe inculpée,* by Congolese author Antoine Latambet-Ambily, whereas the *prix des auditeurs* went to a satirical Cameroonian situation comedy, Patrice Ndedi Penda's *Le Fusil,* about a simple farmer grappling with the dishonesty of urban bureaucrats.

In addition to encouraging broadcast drama, ORTF became an influential publisher of African plays. Some of the most illustrious titles in francophone African drama were initially broadcast and later published by ORTF. These include *La Marmite de Koka-Mbala* by Guy Menga, *Notre fille ne se mariera pas* by Guillaume Oyono-Mbia and *Assimilados* by J. B. Obama (all Cameroonian authors) and *Kondo le raquin* by Jean Pliya from Benin.

A similar tutelary role was played by the BBC in anglophone Africa. The BBC's weekly programme, African Theatre, produced during the 1960s and early 1970s by Gwynneth Henderson, became the focus for radio drama. These plays were sold to many African radio corporations, by which they were transmitted to local audiences. Here too, as with ORTF, there was an element of training and competition. In particular, an all-Africa play-writing competition held in 1970, with distinguished African writers as judges, involved a considerable amount of training of would-be authors. The British critic and former head of BBC drama section, Martin Esslin, wrote an instructional pamphlet on radio drama techniques for the occasion. In this way some of the 'classic' radio drama skills developed by the BBC (such as defining space through dialogue, sound effects and 'on-mike/off-mike' contrasts) were transferred to African authors. Where the ORTF competitions, however, encouraged full-length ambitious dramas, the BBC African Theatre series used a short 30-minute format. All the same, some of the plays produced there found their way into anthologies published by Heinemann.[10]

Radio drama provided a useful play-writing apprenticeship and modest source of income for several African authors. One good example is Wole Soyinka, who, after his return to Nigeria at independence, authored a weekly comedy series called *Broke Time Bar*, for which he earned five pounds five shillings per script. The series ran for about two years from 1960 to 1962, and was produced by a dynamic TV and radio impresario, Segun Olusola. *Broke Time Bar* was based on a very accessible trickster formula and was written partly in pidgin English. The main character, with the self-explanatory name, Queen's Broken, is the owner of a bar, and, backed up by his wife Yariabo and his bouncer Girigiri, does his best each week to fleece his various customers. Gibbs describes the series as 'part soap opera, part situation comedy [which] exploits the comedy inherent in coincidence, marital tensions, romantic entanglements, pomposity, confusion over identities and misunderstandings'.[11] The series was very popular with the Western Region listeners, but the programme organizers prevented Soyinka from making the series a vehicle for direct political comment.

The example of Soyinka, especially in the way he transformed the indigenous trickster motif for a mass-media formula, shows that African authors were by no means intimidated by the colonial origins of the radio medium.

Despite the strong links which existed after independence between the ex-colonial broadcasting institutions and the African radio stations, there have been some interesting attempts in Africa to adapt indigenous popular performing traditions to the new medium of radio.

In some ways the radio is ideally suited for preserving African oral traditions, for it too is an oral medium. For example, the West African indigenous tradition of the *griot* – the professional praise-singer, who recorded and interpreted the history of feudal leaders for the ordinary people – has adapted quite well to the radio. In Cameroon and the Gambia, wealthy listeners have hired *griots* to sing their praises on radio, to the accompaniment of the traditional *kora*.[12] Naturally, the fact that the economic base to which the 'radio *griots*' are linked is capitalist rather than feudal causes a considerable shift in content, skills and artistic nuancing, despite superficial similarities of form.

In Upper Volta, the national radio station, Radio Haute-Volta, found that by far its most popular programme was *La Soirée de Larhalle Naba*. This was a variety show in the local language, More, and featuring a skilled *griot*, Larhalle Naba, who recited traditional stories, explained proverbs, and gave a running commentary on the clash between traditional and moral values; the narrative expositions were punctuated by singing and drumming.[13]

The element of teaching in *La Soirée de Larhalle Naba* is important. Didacticism is much closer to the surface in the pre-colonial tradition of theatre than in Western drama. It is not surprising, therefore, that many of the most popular forms of radio performance in Africa mix entertainment with strong doses of instruction. In Tanzania, broadcasters were encouraged to adapt indigenous theatre forms such as oral narratives, songs and the traditional form of dramatized poetry, known as *Ngonjera*, to create radio programmes with a didactic message, in association with the 1975 *Chakula ni Uhai* campaign ('Food is Life').

A rather similar, but more extended campaign took place in Kenya. *Zaa na Uwatunze* (Giving Birth and Caring for your Children) was a 15-minute, Swahili radio drama series, sponsored by UNICEF, and using information supplied by Ministry of Health extension workers. The messages about health and birth control were made attractive by employing a lively format and well-known radio actors and actresses. *Zaa na Uwatunze* proved so popular that it was moved from a Sunday morning slot to prime time on Saturday evening.

Another example of a very popular form of radio performance is the improvised radio play. There were two Swahili programmes on radio Tanzania which captured wide audience appeal; these were *Mahoka* ('Something Funny'), broadcast on Sunday afternoons, and *Pwago na Paguza* broadcast on Wednesday evenings. Pwago and Paruza are the names of two well-known trickster heroes in Swahili oral narratives, and the plays dealt with modernized versions of those stories. *Mahoka* used a formula of an impostor pretending to be someone with skills or high social status (such as a doctor, police constable, musician or mechanic – the role changed each week) being discovered and humiliated. Again, the plot motifs followed an oral trickster narrative pattern. Often the stories had a didactic element, exposing such topical evils as shopkeepers overcharging on the prices of commodities. Although the basic situations were worked out in advance, the actors and actresses improvised the dialogue in the recording studio itself – a technique very alien to Western radio drama, but entirely in the tradition of African improvised oral narrative drama.

A similar type of radio drama has been very popular in Malawi, broadcast in the national language, Chichewa. These improvised plays were called *Kapalepale* (the title is the nickname of the main character), a 30-minute play broadcast once a week, and *Pa Majiga* ('At Majiga's'), a 15-minute play broadcast three times a week; they were sponsored by a building society and a clothing factory, respectively. An analysis of these plays by Joyce Kumpukwe gives insights into the way popular radio drama can build on indigenous traditions but still reflect a contemporary ideology.[14]

One important reason why the *Kapalepale* and *Pa Majiga* plays were popular was that the situations dealt with the everyday problems of a peri-urban proletarian family – problems such as shortage of money, attitudes to strangers, cheekiness of schoolchildren, conflicts at work and marital disputes. The producer of the series, and the main actor in both, was a remarkable artist, Smart Likhaya Mbewe, whose career has not followed a pattern of formal training at the BBC. Mbewe started his career very humbly, as a watchman at the gates of the Malawi Broadcasting Corporation in Blantyre. He had a natural flair for impromptu drama, based on his experience with indigenous improvised oral narratives and dances when he was a herdsboy in the village. His skills came to the attention of an MBC producer, and he was recruited as an actor for a radio drama series called *Kajekete*. In his own words:

> They saw how I behaved and talked to the people at the gate. I chatted a lot, so they decided I would make a good actor.[15]

The imaginative policy at MBC of ignoring the normal Western bureaucracy of recruitment and training paid dividends. Mbewe proved so skilful as both actor and organizer that he completely transformed the radio series, and eventually became producer in his own right, drawing on a tradition of didactic oral trickster narratives for the structure of his plays, and on quick-witted, comic improvisation for the dialogue.

Kumpukwe illustrated the difference between a typical Western process of radio play creation and that of Mbewe's by the following flow charts:[16]

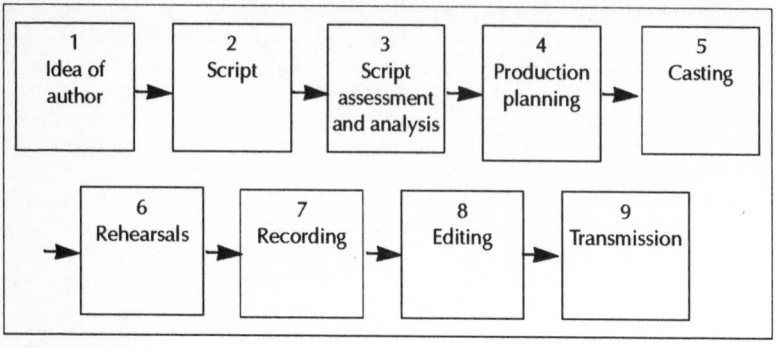

This typical production schedule for a Western radio play is contrasted with that of Mbewe's improvised plays:

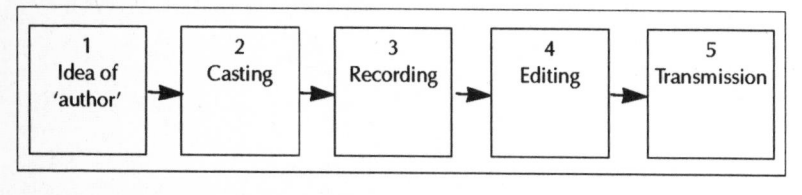

Although Mbewe's technique sounds chaotic (particularly the lack of any rehearsals) it seemed to work; this is partly due to the skilled repertory of actors and actresses he used, who had worked with each other for many years and had an almost instinctive ability at improvisation, play structuring, timing and ensemble creativity.

One of the reasons why Mbewe's plays have been so popular is that they provide moral lessons. As Kumpukwe comments, he 'can be compared to an artist in a traditional African society who functions as a spokesman for the society in which he lives, shares its prejudices and directing its dislikes against what is discountenanced'.[17] Mbewe himself says, 'the aim behind any play is to teach good manners as well as to entertain people'.[18]

The messages behind the plays sometimes dealt with very specific, mundane problems such as informing people not to put charcoal burners in a room without the windows open, or not to allow children to attend football matches unattended. Sometimes they dealt with more general but very pressing problems such as to what extent rural relatives should make demands on urban wage-earners, or whether it is legitimate for wives to hide their housekeeping money from husbands. The plays were listened to very attentively as correspondence and telephone 'feedback' from the audience testified. One reason for this is probably that they provided one of the few arenas where problems could be aired related to the impact of capital. Issues such as urbanization, crime, wage differentials and sexism affect people in Malawi deeply, but, owing to a pervasive system of censorship and government surveillance, they were not aired in public debate.

Mbewe did not need to send his plays (which had no written scripts anyway) to the Censorship Board; instead he did his own censorship. Ideologically, *Kapalepale* and *Pa Majiga* did not, in fact, offer any real oppositional critique of capitalism; instead they offered gratifying pseudo-solutions by imposing a traditional system of rural moral values on a modern urbanized society governed by a wage economy.

The plays followed a fairly rigid formulaic pattern, with the following structural sequences: 1) social blunder, 2) complications arising from the blunder, 3) judgement, 4) resolution. The crucial element is the judgement, which is made by the chief in *Kapalepale* and by the bottle-store owner in *Pa Majiga*. Mbewe defends himself from the implausibility of having a chief settle urban disputes:

> People ask why a chief is found in town, forgetting that there exist even in town people we call 'line-in-charges'.[19]

The 'line-in-charge' refers to a representative of the Malawi Congress Party who was supposed to settle petty domestic issues in a small urban location. There is an ingenuousness, however, in expecting the audience to believe that a 'line-in-charge' or a bottle-store owner could have the same judicial authority as a village chief for settling disputes. What is happening is that the vast social problems caused by the disruptive capitalist relations of production are solved magically and artificially in the plays by appeal to an archaic and respected traditional authority system. In this the plays reflected the ruling Malawian ideology, where appeals to putative pre-colonial moral values of obedience and discipline masked the contradictions of the modern state and coerced people into national consensus. The popularity of *Kapalepale* and *Pa Majiga*, despite the escapism of their solutions to modern problems, arose from them having raised the problems in the first place and providing some kind of artificial solution even at the fantasy level.

A radio series like *Kapalepale* has proved capable of reaching wide popular audiences because the radio itself is a fairly accessible piece of technology. The same is not true of television, which still tends to be a mainly bourgeois status symbol in Africa, and where popular theatre has therefore not taken such strong root.

Even more than radio, television in Africa has been very dependent for training and programming on the former colonial powers, which originally established the television stations in most African countries. A shortage of skilled artists and technicians, combined with the economics of scale, make it far cheaper for an African television corporation to buy a syndicated film from the USA, Britain or France than to make its own. This is reinforced by the expectations of bourgeois consumers for the same 'quality' films which they experienced in Europe; quality, of course, refers to the slickness and sophistication of techniques rather than to the importance of the content.

The effect of this programming policy is one of keeping open the cultural channels between metropolitan values and the African national bourgeoisies, a classic function of media imperialism. George Rebolo, the Mozambican Minister of Culture, has commented on the negative model provided by protagonists in Western film series:

> The hero par excellence is always the middle-class man who acts and achieves his objectives individually ... it is never the working classes who make history.[20]

The hidden objective of such films is to 'reduce the masses to passivity and progressively integrate the worker or peasant ideologically with the dominant structure'.[21]

The use of Western syndicated films can make nonsense out of African TV programming. For example, on Television Zambia a rather serious discussion programme praising the merits of humanism might have been followed by an episode of *Hawaii 5-0*, where the all-American detective hero shows a most unhumanistic disdain for the blacks, drug addicts, Hispanics and other marginals who are identified as the villains.

Kwame Nkrumah was very conscious of the propaganda effect of cultural imperialism:

> One has only to listen to the cheers of an African audience as Hollywood's heroes shoot red Indians or Asiatics to understand the effectiveness of this weapon ... The trade union man, the revolutionary or the man of dark skin is generally cast as the villain, while the policeman, the gum-shoe, the Federal agent – in a word the CIA type spy – is ever the hero.[22]

These comments apply just as much to the TV film as they do to the screen movie.

Ghana was one of the African countries which did not inherit a colonial TV station but which set up its own. At the inauguration of the national television service in 1965 Nkrumah expressed his determination to avoid allowing Ghana's TV service to become an unwitting channel of neo-colonial influence.

> Ghana's television ... will not cater for cheap entertainment nor commercialism. Its paramount object will be education, in the ... purest sense.[23]

This determination proved difficult to fulfil in practice, particularly after the expulsion of Nkrumah. By 1972, 30 per cent of the programming consisted of drama/films; out of this 6 per cent consisted of local drama and 24 per cent cheaply imported syndicated Western material such as *I Love Lucy* and *Mod Squad*. In referring to the Westernized values of Nigerian television programmers, Segun Olusola observed:

> If a half hour of *Highway Patrol* was shown on NTV for as little as 10 naira why should Hubert Ogunde ask 50 naira to bring a half-hour play which did not even include screaming sirens and shoot-outs?[24]

This is not to say that television in Africa has been an unremitting instrument of imperialism. Some countries have experimented with popularizing television; for instance, Ivory Coast has set up TV systems in the primary schools, and Kenya and Zanzibar have experimented with community viewing sets in high-density locations. But these schemes have usually broken down owing to recurrent technical faults.

More significantly there have been some original attempts at creating indigenous television drama programmes within conventional networks. Nigeria was one of the first African countries to make efforts at localizing drama productions. The first television station in sub-Saharan Africa was Western Nigeria Television (WNTV), established before independence. WNTV's first African play, Wole Soyinka's *My Father's Burden*, was commissioned in 1960 by Segun Olusola. Unusually for Soyinka, *My Father's Burden* was written in a very naturalistic style. It deals with the growing realization by Onya, a young Ibo executive, that his comfortable position is based on nepotism. He becomes very disillusioned by the prevalent corruption in Nigerian commercial life, and finds solace through winning support from his Yoruba wife in his decision to resign from the job. The themes of corruption, nepotism and inter-ethnic tensions were considered quite daring at the time. The screening in 1961 was marred by a broadcast delay due to an electricity blackout, which some felt was deliberate sabotage against Soyinka's politically sensitive play.[25]

My Father's Burden was a prestigious example of a whole programme policy at WNTV in the early sixties to indigenize the television service. There were high hopes that such a policy could contribute to Nigerian development, as Chief Awolowo proclaimed in 1959 at the outset of the indigenization policy:

> Television will serve as a teacher and an entertainment and as a stimulus to us all to transform Nigeria into a modern and prosperous nation.[26]

The actual achievements tended to emphasize entertainment rather than teaching, and a considerable amount of Western programming still dominated Nigerian screens.

Where the programme planners at WNTV and later at NTV (Nigerian Television) did succeed was less in specially commissioning literary plays like *My Father's Burden* than in drawing upon the vast repertoire of existing improvised Yoruba Operas. Television became one of the most popular media for Yoruba Opera, not only because it provided income for the artists, but because it was an excellent source of publicity for the Travelling Troupes' stage performances. Duro Ladipo created many popular television sketches such as *Ejagbingba*, *Oyelogbawo*, *Ewe Ayo*, *Ekeju* and *Gbade Gesin*. Some television plays, like *Tiata Yoruba* and *Alawada*, had considerable social impact because they were shown on prime time.

The most popular kind of Yoruba Opera television was the serial. Roy Armes suggests that the popularity of Indian film series in Nigerian cinemas influenced the tastes of Nigerian television audiences.[27] Whatever the origins of the Yoruba Opera series, they became very popular from the late sixties onwards. In the 1970s Ladipo had phenomenal success with his long-running NTV series *Bode Wasimi*, about Yoruba village life in the 1920s. Another very popular series was Isola Ogunsola's crime sketches with NTV called *Aja lo l'eru*. Historical novels or documentaries adapted to the screen proved equally popular genres, examples of which are Ogunsola's *Efunsetan Aniwura* and Oyin Adejobi's *Ekuro Oloja*.

Despite the wide acclaim and financial success which the Yoruba Opera troupes had with television, many of them were not satisfied with the restrictive recording conditions of television without the flexible improvisatory structuring possible in performance to a live and participant audience. Ogunsola complained:

> When you sing in a television production it has to be brief; same for music and drumming. On stage we are completely unencumbered.[28]

Little thought seems to have been given by the play producers to the special requirements of the medium, according to Jeyifo:

> Most of the Travelling Theatre television productions are no more than stage productions lifted into another medium.[29]

Much of the difficulty the Yoruba Opera troupes found in adapting to television came from the entrepreneurial nature of their productions, in which the author dominates the economic and aesthetic shaping of the performance. On television, by contrast, the producer 'is constantly reminded of his dependence on the interrelationship with other interest groups – camera operators, technicians, accountants, supervisors, designers, administrators and TV producers of other programme forms'.[30]

Perhaps more successful was the English language series *Basi and Company* by Ken Saro-Wiwa, a prolific dramatist/novelist as well as controversial anti-government political activist. *Basi and Company*, shown on NTV in 1985, were 30-minute comedies, consisting of linked stories in which one set of trickster heroes tried to outwit another set. The farces used a cast of comic types which included Basi, an unemployed trickster, would-be millionaire, Madam, a ferocious middle-aged landlady, Josco, an escaped convict and drunkard, and Segi, a beautiful, kind-hearted woman about town. *The New York Times* commented that *Basi and Company* was watched by about one-third of Nigeria's population, and praised it for skewering 'national foibles', explaining that 'Basi seems to have struck a chord because it lampoons modern Nigeria's get-rich-quick mentality.'[31]

As early as 1967 Nigeria had set up TV stations in each of the four main regions. The final aim was for nineteen stations – one for each of the nineteen states. During his brief presidency, General Muhammed nationalized 90 per cent of Nigerian radio and television and established a Nigerian Television Authority which had powers to coordinate a networking policy among the different states' TV stations. This meant viewers in Nigeria could view drama presentations from different states as well as telerecordings of indigenous rituals such as the *Atilogwa* Dance, the Hausa Durbar and Pategi Regatta.

The idea of networking provides one possible solution for the problem of the shortage of indigenous TV drama. At present there is almost no regional exchange of drama materials within Africa. If such an exchange could be established it would help cut the reliance on syndicated drama from metropolitan countries.

An ever bigger obstacle to achieving a popular drama on African television is the fact that drama programmes have nearly always been in the colonial languages and often based on Western TV models. In Gabon, for example, much money was spent on a thirteen-part serial in French called *Ou vas-tu, Koumba?*, about a man travelling to Libreville to find work. The series, part-scripted by a Frenchman, was modelled on soap operas popular on French television.

In Zambia, the policy was that only the 'national' language of English could be used on Television Zambia. Consequently the plays on the weekly 'Play for Today' spot were always in English, and tended to have a bourgeois setting (reinforced by the sets, which almost invariably used the luxurious furniture supplied by the sponsoring company, Furncoz). Although some of the English language plays on TVZ, such as Stephen Chifunyise's *I Resign* (1975) and Darius Lungu's *The Man in the Street*, were very popular and requested for several repeat screenings, most of the 'Play for Today' plays did not attain the popularity with Zambian audiences achieved by the Zambian language sketches sneaked into a general arts programme called 'Zamarts'.[32]

Another example of African language TV drama is from Kenya, where a mature comic actress, Aysha Suleman, played the part of Mama Tofi, the tough, jealous wife of a trickster, flirtatious husband, Mzee Pemba, in a VOK Kiswahili radio soap opera, *Heshina Si Utumwa*, in the 1960s. Later she switched to television programmes, using a similar formula in such Kiswahili drama series as *Jamaa ya Mzee Selenge*, and the even more popular *Jamaa ya Mzee Pembe*, a televised version of the original radio programme. A similar popular soap opera, called *The Mukadota Family*, emerged in Zimbabwe. This Shona series built up a large following through the star, Safirio Madzikatire's portrayal of a sexist, rascally trickster-hero, Mukudota.

Such examples of popular African language theatre on television have been comparatively rare, owing to the elitist nature of TV in Africa. The video revolution is making a considerable impact, which may have long-term influence on African television and film-viewing habits. In Ghana, for example, there has been a rapid mushrooming of small video-viewing houses since the mid-1980s. Initially they showed imported all-action martial arts movies. Since about 1990, however, this diet has been supplemented by locally-made Ghanaian-language video plays.

In most of Africa, however, the elitist tendency of television is unlikely to experience substantial change as long as access to TV receivers is restricted to expatriates and members of the local bourgeoisie. In cinema, on the other hand, there has been a rather more complex struggle between African film-makers keen to reach wide audiences and those neo-colonial structures which have maintained obstacles in the path of a popular African cinema.

Rather more than radio or TV drama, neo-colonial structures in the film industry have been challenged by African film-makers attempting to create an indigenous feature film tradition. They have struggled against a film distribution policy whereby Europe and the USA have had a monopoly of films shown in Africa.

The roots of Western domination of African film distribution go back to the colonial period. The two major distributors at that time were Gaumont for the French colonies and Rank for the British colonies. After most African countries obtained their independence in the early 1960s, intermediary companies were established in Africa to distribute films from the major Western film companies. AMPECA (American Motion Picture Export Company) provided films for anglophone Africa, thereby allowing the USA to oust Britain as the dominant supplier of feature films. In francophone Africa, two companies, COMACICO (Compagnie Africaine Cinémato-graphique Industrielle et Commerciale) and SECMA (Société d'Exploitation Cinématographique Africaine), were not only the main suppliers of films, but also owned 70 per cent of the picture-houses.[33]

AFPECA, COMACICO and SECMA have not been totally unmoving agents of imperialism. The history of their attempts to control the African market have been marked by Byzantine shifts of allegiance in the face of pressure from African governments. emergent African film-makers and from the metropolitan suppliers. These manoeuvrings, which have involved the establishment of revamped distribution companies such as AFRAM (Afro-American Films Inc.) and SOPACIA (Société de Participation Cinématographique Africaine) are too complicated to disentangle here. However, it is not difficult to trace the main pattern of Western film distribu-tion policy; it has been a two-pronged strategy of flooding the African market with what Boughedir calls the 'bottom of the barrel' of Western film titles,' and of attempting to discourage or control African film production.

A Senegalese film-maker, Mhama Traoré, has described the impact of this policy on Africa in these scathing terms:

> It's really an imperialist and colonialist assault – those films are vehicles of violence, sex and a culture that is alien to us, a culture into which we are not integrated and into which we in fact refuse to be integrated, because we want to remain ourselves.[34]

Traoré's statement perhaps sounds like an almost paternalist desire to protect young African cinema-goers from Western culture. But there is good evidence that the taste for such films has to be acquired by African audiences. A Burkinabe sociologist, Emile Kargougou, has shown how cinema-going in Ouagadougou is marked by socialization. He explains that most cinemas in Burkina Faso (then Upper Volta) consisted of a covered area at the back for the projector and for the elite members of the audience, and an unroofed area at the front of the auditorium called 'la place des indiennes'. Kargougou divides the 'indiennes' into two groups, the 'neophytes', who are relatively new to cinema-going, and the 'habitués', who have grown used to cinema attendance, and among whom are found noisy commentators monitoring the films for the rest of the audience.[35] In a similar analysis of African viewing habits Bellman and Jules-Rosette felt that African audiences were socialized by poor prints and projection conditions into paying 'more attention to action than to plot [but that] Western education provides a context of meaning for interpreting these films'.[36]

It is this popular audience, easily swayed by the cheap glamour of Western movies, that most concerns committed cineastes like Mhama Traoré. The desire to reach popular, as well as elite, audiences has led to attempts by African film enthusiasts to combat cultural imperialism through the establishment of alternative film distribution circuits.

A pioneering attempt to break the power of Western distributors was made by the Kenyan government in 1967. It successfully withstood a cultural blockade by AMPECA, an action which led to the establishment of a national film distribution company, the Kenyan Film Corporation. Ironically, the Kenyan Film Corporation, once in operation, showed little more imagination than AMPECA in its choice of imported films.

A more substantial attempt to break the power of Western distributors was made by Burkina Faso, which, in 1970, successfully established a national film company, SONAVOCI (Société Nationale Voltaïque de Cinéma), independent of COMACICO/SECMA. The marketing of films by SONAVOCI was so successful that it was able to invest profits, formerly expropriated by the imperialist companies, into financing projects by African film-makers.

It was because of Burkina Faso's brave stand that Ouagadougou was chosen as the centre for FEPACI (Fédération Panafricaine Cinéastes), a pan-African association of film-makers, and the venue for its annual film festival, FESPACO. Though mainly confined to francophone Africa, FEPACI has made considerable headway in putting pressure on African governments to pay attention to local film-makers as well as in publicizing and sharing the skills, ideas and resources of the film-makers themselves. Other festivals established for African film-makers were JCC (Journées Cinématographiques de Carthage), started in Tunis in 1966, and a short-lived anglophone grouping, MOGPAFIS (Mogadishu Pan-African Film Symposium), established in Somalia in 1983.

The purpose in setting up African film festivals was to avoid the 'ghettoization' of African films at metropolitan film festivals, an aim explained by Ababacar Samb:

> We are sick of being 'exhibited' in so many foreign film festivals for the sake of white culture's liberalism, of being given pats on the back, of talking into white microphones, while our films are rotting away on the shelves of so many distributors – the same ones which pat us on the back – both in Africa and abroad.[37]

This struggle to gain control over the material production and distribution of African films is much more difficult than the corresponding struggle for control of African theatre resources.

One of the main obstacles to African cinema independence is the capital-intensive nature of film technology, which makes it difficult to create a 'rough' cinema using minimal resources. Roy Armes suggests that:

> Film-making in Black Africa is less an industry than a craft skill; ... the film-makers are total authors of their work to an extent rare in the West: raising money themselves, organizing the production through their personal companies, directing from their own scripts, and when the work is complete, often themselves promoting the film, and even handling the distribution and exhibition.[38]

The entrepreneurial nature of post-independent theatre forms like Yoruba Opera and Township Musicals was appropriate for stage theatre, where resources were relatively easy to control, but much more difficult in the complex technology of the film industry.

The problem arising from the nature of cinema as an industry and medium has become clear in the careers of individuals film-makers. Most African cineastes were trained in Europe, often using sophisticated professional equipment.[39] However, when they returned to Africa they had to make films with poor equipment, amateur performers, under-trained technicians and shoe-string budgets. The Ethiopian film-maker, Haile Gerima, provides a typical example of the experience. In 1976 he completed a long (150-minute) radical, semi-documentary, *Mirt Sort Shi Amit* (Harvest 3000 Years), on a ridiculously low budget of US$20,000. To achieve this he had to use an almost impossible shooting ratio of virtually 1:1, allowing no room for mistakes in shooting or latitude in editing. On a smaller scale, Diagaye Beye met a similar situation in Senegal. His short film, *Samba Teli*, was started in 1975 with a gift of 850 m of black-and-white film stock. When one of his actors dropped out of the film he had to be replaced by another, regardless of continuity inconsistency.[40] Similar stories of technical hardships could be told by nearly all African film-makers. Malkmus and Armes point out that one unfortunate consequence of such financial constraints is the long gap which normally exists between an African cineaste's first and second feature production.[41]

One effect of these constraints is to make some African films appear rather amateurish or technically deficient for audiences used to the spectacular and lavish professionalism of Hollywood. This creates a dilemma for the African film-maker. One solution is to collaborate with Western organizations by accepting aid, whether of finance, equipment or skilled personnel, in order to create a film with a professional-looking finish. For example, the technical section of the French Bureau du Cinéma de la Coopération assisted in the making of several films in the sixties and early seventies, including Désiré Ecaré's *Concerto pour un exil* (Ivory Coast), Mhama Traoré's *Diankha-bi* (Senegal), Oumarou Ganda's *Cabascabo* (Niger) and Sebastian Kamba's *Mwana Keba* (Congo). Private French film companies helped with the making of Désiré Ecaré's *A nous deux, France!* and Ousmane Sembène's *Le Mandat* (Senegal).

Such assistance has undoubtedly made some contribution to African cinema. The dearth of indigenous cinema in anglophone Africa is largely due to the lack of interest shown by the British colonial administration and the post-colonial aid agencies. Most film-making in anglophone Africa has been restricted to highly instrumental documentaries made by Information Departments. Some typical examples from Tanzania include *Fimbo ya Mnyonge* (A Poor Man's Salvation) about the construction of bamboo water-pipes, and *Amusi wa Miriamu* (Miriam's Wedding), a story concerning the use of modern and traditional medicine. It is rare that such instrumental films get any viewing outside the Ministry of Information's free cinema circuits, let alone outside the country of origin.[42] The Department of Information films have continued in a modified form the tradition of didactic documentaries and simple parables established during the colonial period.

Nearly all the anglophone African films which have been made with Western aid have used private sources. The most celebrated example of this was the Calpenny Company in Nigeria, founded by Francis Oladale with the help of American funds, equipment and personnel. Calpenny made a version of Soyinka's *Kongi's Harvest*, directed by black American Ossie Davies, and *Bullfrog in the Sun*, directed by West German, Jason Pohland, based on Chinua Achebe's novels, *Things Fall Apart, Arrow of God* and *No Longer at Ease*. In addition to artistic opposition (Soyinka disowned *Kongi's Harvest*), Oladale found it difficult to distribute Calpenny's films and the company collapsed. Similar projects involving collaboration between Western companies and African film-makers or performers have been made with little success in Ghana, Kenya and Zambia.[43]

Even in francophone Africa French-aided schemes tended to militate against local film-makers achieving rapport with popular audiences, as Armes explains:

> French aid allowed the production of a great many films which would otherwise not have been made, but these were often highly personal, autobiographical or individualistic works which were in no way designed to meet the entertainment needs of a mass audience for whom an African film remained a novelty. Indeed they existed in a sort of cultural ghetto, more readily available in Paris (through the Ministry's excellent archive) than in Africa where they were restricted to French Cultural Centres.[44]

Effectively this meant that the colonial policy of *la France d'Outre-mer* was being continued after independence in the cultural domain.

Another reason why African film-makers often felt frustrated with co-production was because of the inevitable lack of artistic independence they suffered. Senegalese director, Ababacar Samb, says of the making of his 1970 film *Kodou*:

A scene from Wole Soyinka's *Kongi's Harvest*, directed by Ossie Davis for the Calpenny Company

I got angry with my French editor who was unwilling to follow my directions: my cultural references are not Greek art but black masks! I also took into account the African oral tradition which explains for example the slowness of certain shots.[45]

Samb represents a tendency among African film-makers to turn away from Western aid in order to create an authentic African cinema. Faye Safi from Senegal, the first female African film director, though accepting a small grant from the Bureau de Cinéma de la Coopération, chose not to use it for making a glossy commercial film, but to make a committed documentary about her village. The film, *La Lettre paysanne*, is a kind of radical 16 mm home movie, which allows the rural peasants to talk about their problems.[46]

Several African film-makers have tried to make a virtue out of necessity by building a cinema aesthetic on the very limitations of the cinema infrastructure in Africa. The Mauritanian film director, Med Hondo, has gone out of his way to be independent of Western technological or financial support, believing that an authentic African cinema can only be built on the existing resources, no matter how inadequate. He takes pride in making films 'with my own time and with my own arms, without counting on the force or means of the enemy – the capitalist film industry … and … refusing to utilize the alienating and untruthful techniques of Western cinema'.[47] His masterpiece, *Soleil O*, took four years to make, on account of waiting for funds to buy film stock.

Film-makers such as Samb and Hondo show an awareness of the interconnection between economic independence and aesthetic authenticity. They have a preoccupation shared by many African film-makers with creating an African cinema style as individual as that of Japanese cinema or the Brazilian films of the Cinema Novo school. Unfortunately there is space to discuss only briefly the question of the style appropriate to a popular African cinema.

Considering their relatively small film output, African film-makers display a surprisingly wide variety of styles, ranging from the elegant urbane irony of Ecaré's *Concerto pour un exil*, reminiscent of French Nouvelle Vague films, to the naive parody of American westerns in *Le retour de l'aventurier* by Allassane Mustapha from Niger. Hannes Kamphausen believes that it is so difficult to make films in Africa that only ruggedly strong-willed individuals can accept the challenge – a situation that encourages an idiosyncratic auteur approach to film-making rather than the building of genres or schools.[48]

Nevertheless, I think it is possible to discern two fairly general approaches to film-making, associated with the two giants of the sub-Saharan African cinema, Ousmane Sembène and Med Hondo. Sembène, who has made many famous films, including the full-length features, *Mandabi* (1986), *Emitai* (1972), *Xala* (1974) and *Ceddo* (1978), uses a deep-focus slow-cutting technique which is consciously modelled on the style of the Italian neo-realist cinema of the 1940s and 1950s. He justifies this influence on the grounds that the neo-realist style is suitable for the depiction of Marxist analysis and is accessible to very wide audiences.[49] Another Marxist film-maker, the Malian, Souleymane Cissé, has used a similar neo-realist technique in films like *Le Vent*, a moving account of radical students protesting against a corrupt military dictatorship.

Med Hondo, on the other hand, believes that it is necessary for the African film-maker to destroy the 'classic' grammar of Western film before a truly African cinema can be constructed. Ferid Boughedir gives this useful synopsis of the two viewpoints:

> Supporters of the 'Med Hondo School' think, rightly, that imperialist propaganda doesn't only reside in the content, but also in the form of Hollywood cinema, whence the necessity for an anti-imperialist African cinema to find a different form. Supporters of the Ousmane Sembène school retort that African cinema must be conceived in terms of its destination: the post-colonial African public. That this public is conditioned by a form of 'cinema of distraction' and that one should take account of this conditioning on pain of seeing one's message rejected. [50]

The debate is an important one: whether formal and ideological purity in African cinema should be maintained at the risk of restricting it to an intellectual elite which can appreciate it. Boughedir points out that the popular neo-realist approach adopted by Sembène does not necessarily entail a surrender to Western cinematic and ideological principles. The films of Sembène and those of several others who seem influenced by Western cinematic techniques in fact often display, at a deeper level, a strong allegiance, not only to a radically committed African viewpoint, but also to an African aesthetic. To recognize this it is necessary to examine the dramatic structure of the films as well as the quality of cinematography and editing.

The increasing preoccupation of film-makers since the late 1960s has been with finding an African cinematic style which can appeal not only to a coterie of admirers at international film festivals and cine clubs, but also to the 'indiennes' in the popular cinema halls. Sembène sees a continuity, not a contradiction, between pre-colonial African culture and contemporary culture of the mass media.

> The artist must ... be the mouth and ears of his people. In the modern sense, this corresponds to the role of the griot in traditional African culture.[51]

Many African film-makers have attempted to appeal to the popular imagination of audiences by rooting their films in indigenous narrative formal techniques.

Sembène himself does this in *Xala*, a story about a wealthy polygamist, El Hadji, who becomes impotent on marrying his third wife. The 'xala' (curse of impotence) can only be lifted by suffering humiliation at the hands of a disreputable, prophet-like beggar. The use of allegory (the underlying meaning of the impotence is not sexual, but refers to the economic dependence of the African comprador bourgeoisie) and the folklore motifs of the triple marriage and the ritualistic humiliation of the arrogant protagonist are all based on indigenous African narrative forms and conventions.

There are several other examples of films operating within existing African cultural forms. Ababacar Samb says that he 'threw out all the criteria' he had learned in Rome and Paris when he made his feature, *Kodou*, in 1970.[52] In his second feature, *Jom* (1980), Samb uses a *griot*, Khaly, to tell historical narratives which are relevant to and help resolve problems connected with a modern factory strike. A similar device has been used by Oumarou Ganda from Niger in his 1980 film, *L'Exile*. An ambassador in *L'Exile* uses a traditional tale to illustrate the film's main theme – the importance of keeping one's word.

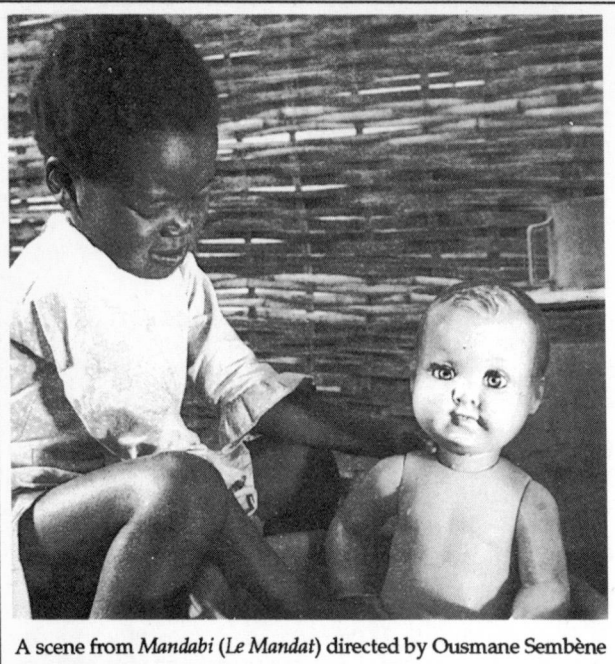

A scene from *Mandabi* (*Le Mandat*) directed by Ousmane Sembène

A scene from Ousmane Sembène's film, *Emitai*

Another way in which African cineastes can base their work on indigenous rather than Western sources is through the use of music. Med Hondo,
for example, attempted to create a 'ciné-opéra' based on African music and
choreography in his 1980 film, *West Indies – Les Nègres marrons de la liberté*.
Hondo has perhaps gone the furthest among African film-makers in
constructing a specifically African film grammar. He justifies this on the
grounds that 'when one has a particular history, a people with its own way
of walking, shaking hands, looking at other people, eating rice, one should
film this in a different way, impose a language and make the film serve this
language'.[53]

The Nigerian film-maker Ola Balogun has experimented with a cinema
based on Yoruba Opera and Concert Party techniques in his films, *Ajani
Ogun* (1975) and *Musik Man* (1976). Other popular films like *Orun Mooru, Ija
Ominira, Aiye* and *Jaiyesimi* used Yoruba Opera artists like Ogunde, Ade
Love, Ogunsola and Fumilayo Ranko. Armes describes these hybrid produc-
tions as follows:

> The resulting films, set in a rural Africa untouched by either colonization or
> modernity, mix traditional songs and dances, folklore and farce, satire and ghost
> scenes.[54]

These films went almost unnoticed among the Nigerian intelligentsia, but
were very popular at the box office, reaping as much as ten times the
producer's initial outlay. It was not only the cinematography of the Yoruba
Opera films which bore little resemblance to European traditions but also the
distribution. Ogunde usually kept the prints of *Aiye* and *Jaiyesimi* himself
and showed them on his travelling tours.

The concern which Nigerian popular film-makers have had with reaching
subaltern audiences has also been shown by francophone African directors
using more conventional distribution systems. Sembène is a crucial example.
He had won a wide reputation in the 1950s for his novels such as *Le Docker
noir* (1965), *Oh Pays, mon beau peuple* (1957) and *Les Bouts de bois de Dieu* (1957),
but he was dissatisfied because these novels were restricted to the literate
intelligentsia.

> When I realized that the rampant illiteracy in my country was preventing my books
> from reaching the masses, I decided to turn to cinema.[55]

Although Sembène's first films, such as *Borom Sarrat* (1963), *Niaye* (1964) and
La Noire de … (1966), made a considerable impact, both in Senegal and in the
West, Sembène was still not satisfied that he was reaching the workers and
peasants, on whose behalf he wanted to struggle through the medium of
film. The main problem was that his first films were made in French and
therefore only appealed to the francophone *assimilés*.

The turning-point in Sembène's cinematic career came with the filming of
his novel, *Le Mandat*, in 1968, a story about an illiterate man trying, without
success, to cash a money order. Sembène decided to do two versions, one in
French (*Le Mandat*) and one (*Mandabi*) in Wolof, the main language of
Senegal. Many people advised Sembène that the Wolof version would be a
total failure; instead the Wolof version was a huge commercial success, and
created a stir within the ruling elite about the advisability of allowing
peasants and workers to see an accessible, honest screen depiction of the

corruption and poverty in Senegal. Sembène continued to experiment with African languages in the later films, *Emitai* and *Ceddo*. *Emitai*, a story about the struggle of a peasant heroine, Sitoe, against the French during the Second World War, was particularly interesting in that Sembène used villagers in the remote Diola-speaking area of Senegal as the principal performers; they participated very enthusiastically and creatively in the making of the film. The final print used Diola dialogue with sub-titles in French.

After the pioneering effort of *Mandabi*, other Senegalese film-makers reached out to wider audiences by making Wolof versions of their movies. These include Nomar Thiam's *Xarim* (1970) and Mhama Traoré's *Diankha-Bi* (1970).

Mandabi not only broke an important linguistic barrier, it also helped to dispose of the misconception, promoted by Western distributors, that African films would not be popular with mass audiences. Since then, several African films have been great box-office successes. *Diankha-Bi*, an attack on customary marriage traditions, was very popular in Senegal and even outside. Over 10,000 tickets were sold in one week in Abidjan for Henri Duparc's 1976 film, *L'Herbe sauvage*, and Balogun's 1979 film, *Aiye*, has been described as 'the biggest box-office success ever known in Nigeria'.[56] Kwaw Ansah's 1980 film, *Love Brewed in the African Pot*, a story about marriage between a motor mechanic and a middle-class girl, played to packed cinema houses, not only in Ghana, but throughout most of anglophone Africa. Such films show that African popular audiences do not necessarily demand the 'ciné-opium' of Western sex and violence, but, if given the chance by distribution systems, are very keen to see intelligent, sensitive films about contemporary African problems.

The interest of African cineastes in popular audiences is not restricted to box-office returns; they have also tried to obtain feedback from the audiences as a way of working towards the participatory creativity which marked pre-colonial theatre. This is partly a question of audience response during the actual screening of a film. Andrew Paquet comments on audience reactions to African films shown at FESPACO in Ouagadougou and Bobo-Dioulasso in Burkina Faso, 'the public really participated – responding strongly to certain scenes, talking back to the screen'.[57] In 1993 I saw a packed audience at a commercial cinema in Gaborone cheering the come-uppance received by a male-chauvinist villain in the Zimbabwean film *Neria*; women in the audience added their own triumphant ululations to those of the screen actresses.

Ababacar Samb rationalizes this type of reaction:

> Our films belong to a culture, a rhythm, even a language, which colonialism and imperialism have tried to stamp out forever. It is only positive that the audiences react the way they do. It means they are judging, that they are taking part, becoming conscious of their own culture.[58]

Samb is talking about film-makers catering for responsive audiences, but some cineastes have attempted to involve audiences even more creatively in the film-making process, not simply treating them as viewers.

Traoré has the habit of going to the working-class 'quartiers' of Dakar and asking audience members emerging from his films for comments. These reactions and suggestions influence the scenarios he writes for subsequent film projects. Hondo made an even more radical move towards collaboration when he directed *Les Bicots-nègres, vos voisins*, a 1973 film about black immigrants in France. The text of much of the film and many of the ideas for its eventual form came from Hondo's interviews with the immigrants themselves.

The film-makers' concern with the audience is linked to the very influential role which art has in Africa in shaping popular opinion. There is a feeling of responsibility towards the public, especially since illiteracy makes literary means of communication difficult. As Traoré puts it:

> Cinema in Africa is actually a school, a social and political school. Cinema, when there is no other means of education at the service of the people, can help them become conscious of themselves.[59]

A similar point is put in an even more openly political context by Sembène. After admitting his allegiance to Marxism-Leninism, but rejecting the idea of a simplistic '"poster" cinema', Sembène asserts:

> I believe that if we African film-makers produce a series of films oriented in the same way, we'll succeed in modifying a little bit the powers that be, and in developing the consciousness of the people.[60]

The 'same way' refers, of course, to a Marxist, class-conscious analysis.

The persuasive power of cinema, noted by Sembène, has not gone unnoticed by the established controlling powers in African states. Most governments have Information or Culture Departments which manufacture documentaries reflecting the state ideologies. Sometimes, even feature films have been made on the same lines, the most notorious example of which is *Demain un jour nouveau*, a very expensive and glossy biography of President Bongo, directed by Pierre-Marie Doug in 1978. The film aroused much opposition at the 1979 FESPACO because of its uncritical homage to the Gabonese head of state.

Most independent African film-makers, however, have refused to allow themselves to be used as props for political despots. On the contrary, they have frankly criticized the injustices and contradictions in African social and political systems. As a result, African films have suffered severely from both overt and disguised censorship.

Hondo's first film, *Soleil O*, which used the theme of African expatriates in France to attack neo-colonialism, was very well received at the Cannes Film Festival, but was not shown in his native Mauritania or elsewhere in Africa. Malian director Souleymane Cissé's *Den Musso* was completed in 1974, but this story of a lower-class girl seduced by an upper-class youth was considered too frank a depiction of sexism and class conflict; distribution was withheld in Mali until 1978. Traoré's film, *Lambuaye*, concerned official corruption in a specific provincial administration in Senegal; when the film opened in 1971 it was restricted to Dakar, and after six very successful weeks it was banned altogether. His later film, *Reou Takh*, which, among other targets, attacked the false image of Africa created by the tourist industry, was completely banned from the outset.

Sembène's films have also had problems with censorship. The French ambassador to Senegal tried to get *Emitai* banned, on the grounds that it was anti-French; although this campaign did not work for Senegal, the film was banned in Côte d'Ivoire. *Xala* was shown in Senegal but only after it had been cut in ten different places. Sembène fought back by distributing a list of cuts to the spectators as they left the cinema. *Ceddo,* a film which exposes the mystifying role of Islam in pre-colonial Senegal, was banned altogether, ostensibly for the spelling of the title, but in reality because of its attack on Islam's colonial role in Senegalese history.

The problems of censorship point to an important contradiction in the African film industry. The technology for film-making is expensive no matter how economical and resourceful the director. In order to avoid dependence on neo-colonial funding or distribution agencies, the most obvious alternative is government support. However, African governments will only be willing to support film-making if they can control them. Most African film-makers are not willing to accept such patronage. For that reason they are left trying to find alternative techniques for raising funds.

The dilemma is the same one which is faced by all African popular dramatists attempting to use the multi-media whether radio, TV or film. If they are to avoid the influence of media imperialism, either they have to accept the ideological confines imposed by national governments, trying to create an independent critique through the obscurity of allegory, or they resort to the difficult task of finding alternative funding, media infrastructures and distribution circuits, at the risk of censorship or artistic persecution.

Notes

1. PETA, p. 13.
2. See, for instance, Barr. Goodlad, and Lawson.
3. Golding.
4. Boyd-Barrett, p. 198.
5. Boyd-Barrett, pp. 199–200.
6. Elliot and Golding, p. 235.
7. Houeto, p. 431.
8. Vincent. See also Kinyanjui.
9. Cited in Kolade, p. 371.
10. See especially Pieterse and Henderson, and Henderson.
11. Gibbs, 1986, pp. 18–19.
12. Head, pp. 101–6. See also Stapleton and May, p. 108.
13. Skinner, p. 290.
14. Kumpukwe.
15. Kumpukwe, p. 14.
16. Kumpukwe, p. 17.
17. Kumpukwe, p. 15.
18. Quoted in Kumpukwe, p. 15.
19. Quoted in Kumpukwe, p. 20.
20. Quoted in Martin, pp. 4–5.
21. Quoted in Martin, p. 5.
22. Nkrumah, p. 246.
23. Quoted in Head, p. 90.
24. Olusola, pp. 373–4.
25. Gibbs, 1986, p. 3.
26. Olusola, p. 373.
27. Roy Armes, personal communication to the author, Cantebrbury, 1986.
28. Quoted in Jeyifo, p. 75.
29. Jeyifo, p. 75.
30. Olusola, p. 376. For other information on Nigerian television drama, see Igbinedion, and Ugbuojah.
31. Quoted in Saro-Wiwa, back cover.
32. *The Man in the Street* earned the distinction in 1978 of being confiscated by the Minister of Culture for its overt Marxism. For a detailed analysis of *I Resign* see Etherton, 1982.
33. Boughedir, 1982b, p. 36. Boughedir's article is my main source for information on film distribution networks in Africa.
34. Traoré, Mhama, p. 33.
35. Kargougou's findings are cited in Skinner, p. 285.
36. Bellman and Jules-Rosette, p. 24.
37. Quoted in Paquet, p. 38.
38. Armes, pp. 2–3.
39. For a good account of such an experience, see chapter one of Vieyra, 1969, where the author explains his excitement at working in the 1940s with famous French film stars and directors.
40. Hennebelle, 1976.
41. Malkmus and Armes, p. 61.
42. One exception is *My Brother's Children*, a film directed by Frank Speed in the late 1960s, using the Yoruba Opera Company of E. K. Ogunmola and funded by the Family

Planning Council of Nigeria. The film contained a lively impromptu speech from the Midwifery Education Specialist. This has become a celebrated example of a film integrating indigenous theatre traditions and an instrumental message.

43. A good account of the failure of Panther Film Productions, an attempted Kenyan–American collaboration, is found in Wa Kyendo.
44. Armes, p. 5.
45. Quoted in Martin, p. 103.
46. Safi.
47. Quoted in Anonymous, 1977. Strong theoretical defences of 'imperfect cinema' as an appropriate film mode in the Third World can be found in articles by Latin American theorists in Getina and Solanas, and Espinosa. See Pines and Willemen for a whole book devoted to the subject.

48. Kamphausen, pp. 36–7.
49. For a fuller account of Sembène's position on neo-realism, see Hennebelle, 1972, p. 207.
50. Boughedir, 1982a, pp. 83–4.
51. Sembène, 1977b, p. 80. For a book-length study of Sembène's films, see Vieyra, 1972.
52. Quoted in Martin, p. 103.
53. Quoted in Martin, p. 100.
54. Armes, p. 3. See also Barber, 1987, p. 25 and Diawara, 1992, pp. 121-4.
55. Interview in Hennebelle, 1972, p. 202.
56. Martin, p. 89.
57. Paquet, p. 38.
58. Quoted in Paquet, p. 38.
59. Traoré, Mhama, p. 35.
60. Sembène, 1977a, p. 27.

10

Populist Theatre & National Ideology in Modern Africa

The problems of censorship faced by African artists in the multi-media point to a fundamental issue of African popular theatre – its uneasy relationship with state hegemony. The insecurity of modern African states, arising from an inadequate infrastructural patrimony bequeathed by the former colonial powers, and from rapid underdevelopment within the world macroeconomy, has led most African ruling parties to seek ways of mobilizing cultural techniques to reinforce national consensus. These types of pre-colonial or syncretic theatre forms which have been transformed for instrumental purposes I term 'populist' theatre.

The roots of modern ideological populist theatre lie in the anticolonial struggle for independence, when many nationalist parties created a political vehicle out of the indigenous performing traditions. In some nations, such as Swaziland, where the post-independence authority was based on the traditional feudal kingdom of the Swazi, that transition of praise and community celebration in such ceremonies as the *Incwala* have simply continued in a somewhat modified fashion after independence. But, even for those republics (the majority in Africa) which were not based on a homogeneous pre-colonial nation-state, it was not too difficult for the performing traditions to make the transition from ritual to politicized function.

Throughout Africa political nationalism was usually preceded by spontaneous movements of cultural nationalism where pre-colonial theatrical, musical or religious forms were revived as a protest against colonialism. Nationalist leaders were not slow to see the advantage of such techniques for creating popular solidarity against colonial rule. In Zambia's Copperbelt, for example, during the late 1950s, there was a strong revival of quasi-traditional funerary rituals. The resurgence was undoubtedly encouraged by the United National Independence Party (UNIP), which was struggling for Zambia's independence. At a time when the Federation authorities banned large political rallies by Africans in the Copperbelt townships, the funeral committees were able to assemble gatherings of over 4,000 for cultural events connected with funerals; these included songs, dances and mimes at which a messianic iconology provided a thin disguise for sentiments of solidarity with UNIP.[1]

During the period immediately before independence, traditional song and dance were commonly adapted to praise public charismatic figures in the nationalist struggle. Leaders such as Jomo Kenyatta in Kenya, Modibo Keita in Mali, Nnamdi Azikiwe in Nigeria, Kwame Nkrumah in Ghana, Kamuzu Banda in Malawi and Sekou Touré in Guinea encouraged indigenous song and dance, transformed for political ends to build up a cult of personality. Such praise songs are psychologically and aesthetically related to indigenous traditions of praise songs and heroic recitations. Heroic forms like the Zulu *Izibongo*, the Chopa *Lithoko* and the Bahima *Kyevugo* have experienced a series of transformations during the imposition of colonial rule, the struggle for independence and the establishment of the post-colonial nation-states which have made them susceptible to instrumental use.

After independence the charismatic leaders continued to consolidate their power bases by encouraging the praise singers and dancers as important organs of ideological control. The transition can be clearly seen in the case of Mali. During the brief Federation of Senegal and West Sudan (1956–60), song and dance played a significant role in educating the masses about nationalist opposition to French rule. Although some of the traditional *griots* were in the pay of the colonial authorities, many others supported the nationalist cause, by performing epics which celebrated great moments in Mali's history, associated with national heroes like Bakary Djan, Da Mouzon, Shellu Ahmadu and Sundiata. Some were even more politicized, composing songs in praise of contemporary leaders of the liberation struggle, such as Mamadou Konaté, Ouezzin Coulibaly or Modibo Keita.

When Mali attained independence in 1960, Keita became president, and his party, Union Soudanaise, favoured a centralized state socialist form of government. The *griots* who had supported Union Soudanaise during the struggle were rewarded by being given paid employment in the National Ensemble, a company of performers under the Commission for Youth and Sports. Other *griots* were organized into the Association for Traditional Artists. These groups were encouraged to praise the policies of Union Soudanaise and to build up the image of Modibo Keita as a champion of the people.

Songs and dances were often created for specific occasions. For example, when Keita returned from the 1963 heads of state meeting of the Organization of African Unity in Addis Ababa, the National Ensemble greeted him at the airport with a dance celebrating the event:

The President said during the conference Africans must unite.[2]

The whole nation was expected to enjoy a vicarious sense of achievement in the president's dynamic foreign policy exploits, in a similar way to the military achievements of the historical warrior heroes.

Comparable ideologically motivated song and dance troupes praising the head of state and his policies were established in many African nations after independence. These troupes did not restrict themselves to praise of the national leader, but also celebrated the achievements of the nation as a whole, and helped mobilize opinion for socio-political innovations. To use

Mali again as an example, the Segou Youth Ensemble composed songs which praised the launching of a steamer on the river Niger, or endorsed the new marriage code abolishing arranged marriages.

This type of exhortatory theatre of national mobilization is probably most closely associated with nations professing socialism, where wide varieties of technique are used to gain popular support for innovative policies.

Tanzania has been particularly enterprising in exploring the way indigenous theatre forms can be modified for political mobilization. The tradition of praise songs flourished after independence in the Makongero and Ng'winamila groups, two professional troupes attached to the Chama Cha Mapinduzi headquarters. The following song by the Makongero group gives some idea of their style:

> The second Five Year Plan
> Tells us that we should eat chicken, eggs,
> vegetables, fish and also drink milk.
> It tells us that we should eat body-building
> foods, it tells us that we should build better houses.
> The Party has lit the torch. Praise to Nyerere.[3]

The praise of the head of state is linked to an exhortatory theme concerning a nutrition campaign, as if the prestige of Nyerere's name could reinforce the message by invocation.

A somewhat more flexible form of politicized entertainment is *Vichekesho*, a form which probably arose at the beginning of the twentieth century in Zanzibar, where it was known as *Tarabu na Vichekesho*. In its origin, *Vichekesho* was a syncretic Kiswahili-language musical farce, which used a combination of improvised sketches and *Tarabu*, the Arab-influenced, neo-traditional, Swahili music. It bore some resemblance to other syncretic forms like Concert Party from Ghana and Yoruba Opera from Nigeria.

Vichekesho was possibly started by street vendors, using comic sketches and music to attract customers. The form was made more commercial by the celebrated Zanzibari singer and actress, Siti Binti Saad, who introduced formal elements derived from Indian musical theatre. *Vichekesho* spread to the mainland and became popular in Tanga, Dodoma and Dar es Salaam. The satirical and didactic potential of *Vichekesho* was drawn out by another popular artist, Bakari Abedi, who, in 1954, founded the Michenzani Social Club, associated with a Zanzibari cultural body known as *Muungano*. According to Bakari, the purpose of *Vichekesho* was to 'make people laugh at the corrupt side of life and in every way convince them to adopt a correct attitude to both work and leisure'.[4] This didactic function was to make the form particularly useful for politically instrumental purposes.

After independence several theatre workers who were militantly in support of the progressive elements in the Tanganyikan African National Union (TANU) and the Afro-Shirazi Party (ASP) saw the potential of *Vichekesho* as a medium of political instruction. Notable among these was Peter Saimanga, who had considerable experience of the art theatre in the Tanzanian Schools Drama Festivals, as well as having attended university extramural courses in drama. In 1964 he started the Friendship Textile Drama Club in Dar es Salaam, which put on *Vichekesho* for industrial workers. In order to expose evils opposed by TANU and ASP Saimanga used the satirical stereotyping which was at the heart of the *Vichekesho* sketches to attack such stock villains as these, listed by Hussein: 'a bourgeois, a false shekh who perpetuates ignorance, a rumour monger, a parasite, a jealous husband who keeps his wives locked, or a miser'.[5]

Because of Saimanga's willingness to perform in factories, and because of his close links to TANU, he was able to adapt his *Vichekesho* to the topical campaigns being promulgated by the Party, and to reach key audiences in the Dar es Salaam proletariat.

The strong tradition of didactic entertainment in Tanzania led to the development of another form of politicized syncretic popular theatre, the *Ngonjera*. Although the form is normally said to have been invented by Matthias Mnyampala, who popularized *Ngonjera* during the 1960s, it is almost certainly associated with a much older tradition of Swahili poetry.

The *Ngonjera* is a poetic dialogue which uses a question-and-answer pattern to disseminate political or social knowledge, somewhat like a Symposium in the Western literary tradition. The following dialogue, an extract from Mnyampala's *Ngonjera-Chama Cha TANU*, in which a wise political cadre explains TANU's policy to a conveniently curious citizen, gives some idea of the genre:

Citizen:	I am asking so that you give me wisdom
	Give me the meaning to console my heart
	I want to hear the truth about the policy of this party
	Tell me TANU's policy, whose Party is it?
Politician:	Listen to me and keep what I tell you
	Keep everything that I will tell you
	Then use what I tell you to avoid blame
	It is the farmers' Party and also that of the workers.[6]

As the *Ngonjera-Chama Cha TANU* continues, the citizen asks more questions in which the politician assures him that capitalists, feudalists and the bourgeoisie have no place in TANU or ASP.

Since the *Ngonjera* relies on fairly serious poetic dialogue and symbolism, rather than on satirical stereotyping, it tends to be a far more direct expression of political propaganda than the *Vichekesho*. One related feature of the *Ngonjera* is that it is capable of assimilating non-theatrical media very easily.

Visual aids like charts, photographs, realia, maps and posters can be included for demonstration purposes. Such pedagogic flexibility has made the *Ngonjera* a popular form for instructors in Tanzania's well-organized and wide-ranging adult education system, who have been keen to find indigenous forms of communication which could be popular outside the formal education framework.

The lusophone nations, which won their independence after protracted wars of liberation against Portuguese colonialism, have also used drama as part of organized campaigns to mobilize the masses for revolutionary change. In Mozambique, agit-prop groups like Grupo Scenico of the FRELIMO armed forces, or the Polyvalent Group of the National Directorate of Culture, have employed collectively produced improvisations to educate the urban proletariat on topical themes such as the reason for food queues and the scarcity of essential commodities. Shortly after independence in 1975, the Polyvalent Group did a series of sketches based on a villainous stock type called Xiconhoaca. The plays were part of an integrated multi-media campaign to eliminate counter-revolutionary tendencies. Posters were stuck up throughout Mozambique, with cartoons portraying Xiconhoaca betraying the revolution, and slogans saying, 'Xiconhoaca is an agent of the enemy', 'Xiconhoaca is a parasite', 'Xiconhoaca is a bureaucrat' and so on.[7] Similar denunciations were made on the radio and in newspapers.

In the Polyvalent plays, according to one description, Xiconhoaca is 'the type of ambitious individualist who joins the Party as soon as he senses the wind is blowing in the revolutionary direction ... Xiconhoaca appears drunk and slothful at work, beating his wives and children at home, and in a particularly harsh light, at a decadent Western style nightclub where all the patrons are drug-crazed, the band has no rhythm, and the dancers are frantic and uncoordinated.'[8] Although the theme is topically modern, concerning Mozambique's struggle to decolonize itself, the play's technique is within a long-established African theatre tradition of using stereotyped negative role models for social control.

The difference between the examples cited from Tanzania and Mozambique and the majority of ideological dance and theatre groups is that the socialist-oriented nations emphasized class distinctions in society, and make some efforts to identify with the subaltern classes in their struggle against imperialism. Such class analysis, however, is fairly exceptional on the continent. Most official, politically motivated cultural groups have actually attempted to cover up any class differences which exist in the newly emergent African nations. A more noticeable preoccupation of the ideological troupes has been that of ethnicity.

In some African nations like Nigeria, Uganda and Benin, where power struggles polarized around ethnic distinctions, dramatized songs played an important part in projecting regional conflicts. For example, in Dahomey (now Benin) shortly after independence, the opposition party, Rassemblement Démocratique Dahoméen (RDD), consisting mainly of Southerners, backed up its motion of censure against the ruling party, Union Démocratique Dahoméen (UDD) (which had strong Northern affiliations), by composing the following song:

> You dress yourself in skins
> You Barîba who never wear
> Trousers or shorts.
> You dress yourself in skins [twice]
> You dress in a hide coat
> You Barîba who never wear
> Trousers or shorts.
> A Gambari will never be our leader.
> It's Apithy who on his return from France
> Brought our proclamation of independence.[9]

Such songs of solidarity through vituperation against ethnic 'enemies' were within an indigenous tradition of semi-dramatized war chants and satirical 'flyting'.[10] The UDD also had its own songs of a similar nature. The putative enemies in the songs tended to change with the vacillations of inter-regional and inter-party political manoeuvres.

These blatant examples of dramatized ethnic conflict tend to be associated with the early period of national independence. Later, during the period when one-party rule became the fashion, artistic expressions of ethnic or regional solidarity were discouraged in the interests of national unity.

The complex relationship between ethnic consciousness and political ideology can be vividly seen in the development of populist dances in Malawi. Traditional dances acted as a powerful vehicle of cultural resistance to imperialism during the colonial period. This was particularly true of *Gule wa Mkulu* ('the big dance'), the masquerade of the Central Region all-male *Nyau* cult, as I explained in Chapter Three.

By the 1950s, however, during the final period of the struggle for independence, the focus of resistance had moved from the cultural opposition of rural chiefs, cult-leaders and spirit mediums towards the well-educated petty-bourgeois national elites. In ethnic terms, most of these intellectual leaders came from the Northern Region of Malawi, not the Central Region, the home of the *Nyau* cult. At that time, as A. C. Ross puts it, 'to talk of witchcraft or the cleansing power of *Nyau* was looked on as siding with the forces of Welensky and the United Federal Party'.[11] This is a good example of the way a folk theatre form which was progressive at one stage of history outlived its radical effectiveness at another.

The conflict between traditional village elites and the modern educated elites came to a head shortly after Malawi's independence in 1964. The leader of the Malawi Congress Party, Kamuzu Banda, who became head of state, was a Central Region Chewa, who had been invited back by younger activist politicians, who were mostly from the Northern Region. These activists became ministers in the new Malawi government, and quickly found that their left-leaning policies were completely opposed to the authoritarian, conservative views of Banda. In the ensuing struggle for power between Banda and the young ministers, *Gule wa Mkulu* masquerades played a significant part in the mobilizing of Central Region ethnic support against the Northern intellectuals. Ross explains this process in detail:

> From December 1964 Nyau groups with their zirombo [zoomorphic masks] were brought from the Central Province area a few miles to the North, in order to terrorize and cow villages which had been reported as supporters of the 'rebel' young ministers. From this time onward these same ministers were referred to as witches whose power Dr Banda had been able to overcome, and were always referred to as fisi i.e. hyenas ... The young men were evil-doers from whose influence the country had to be cleansed.[12]

The process was one whereby Banda appealed to atavistic cleansing and witch-finding tendencies in rural peasant culture, which gave him an important ideological and ethnocentric weapon against the educated Northern radicals in the government. The 'rebel' ministers eventually fled from the country, and Banda was able to consolidate his power from a Central Region base.

After the 1964–5 cabinet crisis, although the *Nyau* cult continued to be an ideological prop, Banda tried to gloss over the ethnicist element in his triumph. He gradually built up a very powerful cultural machinery at a national level, which was designed to pay homage to himself as a way of reinforcing the obedience he needed for national consensus. Ironically, this was a grandiose extension of the patriotic cultural praise dances which the defeated ministers had encouraged to build up Banda's charisma during the struggle against the federation of Rhodesia and Nyasaland. The most powerful expression of the Malawian cultural hagiography industry was an institution known as the *Mbumba*, a mass organization of semi-politicized female dancers. In the Central Region Chewa kinship system, *mbumba* refers to a man's sisters, who need the help of an elder brother (called *nkhoswe*) for their protection and for negotiating marriage. Through the Malawi Women's League, Banda built up the belief that he was the 'Nkhoswe number one' for all the women in Malawi, who were therefore his *mbumba*. In return for his protection, the women honoured him with praise dances.

The *Mbumba* praise dances were backed up by a far-reaching national organization. Each district in Malawi produced its own team of dancers drawn from the Malawi Congress Party Women's League branches in the villages and urban townships. Aesthetically, the drumming, ululations, clapping and choreography were loosely based on indigenous dances such as *Chimtali*, *Mbotosha* or *Chioda*, and were referred to as 'traditional dances', but in fact the authentic music and steps of the individual dances had been transformed in order to create a simplified homogeneous choreography which could be displayed at mass rallies in the national stadia of Blantyre and Lilongwe. Malawian poet, Jack Mapanje, captures very well the sense of aesthetic betrayal caused by these dances when he uses a veteran *Chopa* dancer to comment scathingly on the 'New Platform Dances':

I see my daughter writhe
Under cheating abstract
Voices of slack drums, ululate
To babble-idea-men-masks
Without amulets or anklets.[13]

The choreography of the *Mbumba* dancers was backed up by colourful uniforms, each with a printed photograph of Banda. At the climax of the dances in the stadium the president joined in, like a god descending to the people; and the whole performance was relayed to the nation on the radio. From the state's point of view, the major function of the *Mbumba* dances was to promote national consensus by building up the image of Life-President Banda. Some of the songs offered general obsequiousness, as in the following:

Chorus: Everything belongs to Kamuzu Banda
Leader: All the cars
Chorus: For Kamuzu Banda
Leader: All the houses
Chorus: For Kamuzu Banda.[14] (And so on through trees, chickens, etc.)

These widely known songs were mixed with others especially made up for particular occasions. For example, in 1981, at a time when the late Attati Mpakati, the leader of an exiled political movement, League for a Socialist Malawi, was threatening to infiltrate the country, a young *Mbumba* group known as the Born Free expressed their loyalty to Banda with the following bloodthirsty song:

You just come, Mpakati,
We'll cut you into little pieces.[15]

Although the performers were young schoolgirls, the dances and song lyrics were composed by older cadres creating acceptably orthodox performances on their behalf.

A rather different point about the function of the *Mbumba* dances is made by Landeg White. While acknowledging the dances' basic sycophancy he

Malawian *Mbumba* dance in a
stadium for President Banda

The Kwacha Cultural Troupe
presents

"**CHIKHAKHALI**"

- The Great Laugh -

Programme cover for
Chikhakhali, a dance-drama
created by a Malawian
national theatre group for
performance to delegates at
an international conference.

 A
Traditional Dance
Drama Production

The First COMESA Council of Ministers and Summit Conferences
5th - 9th December, 1994

feels that 'the songs contain muted criticism, making use of the conventions of Praise Poetry that permit comment on the operations of power'.[16] White explains how this aesthetic continuity works in practice:

> The tactic is to claim that Dr Banda 'has found out' what is going on. Dr Banda sometimes 'doesn't know' that money is being embezzled, or that land is being appropriated, or that property has been confiscated, or that famine is prevailing locally, but the song makes all clear ... when after being entertained by the Praise-songs Dr Banda responds with his public speech he refers to the songs constantly ... responding to the indirect and direct pressure.[17]

I believe it should be pointed out that the songs were vetted by MCP leaders so that no real protest was possible. White calls this type of praise song 'a kind of contract between ruler and ruled';[18] in Malawi's case it was a very one-sided contract in which the emphasis was on obedience and conformity.

Another important function of the *Mbumba* dances was to reinforce national unity. After the ethnic tensions which marked the cabinet crisis of 1964–5, the praise dances served to promote a re-asserted unity. There was a regional competitiveness in the stadium performances, each *Mbumba* group vying for the president's attention. In his turn, the president usually acknowledged the dancers from districts known to be recalcitrant. The total performance, with each district taking its turn to dance, in a mood of fierce competitiveness, served as a way of channelling regional rivalries into an expression of national cohesion.

The *Mbumba* dances of Malawi, though exceptional in the extent of their manipulation and mass mobilization, are not unique. They bear some resemblance to a far less eccentric form of para-drama based on pre-colonial African dance – the National Dance troupes. Where the *Mbumba* dances were amateur and aimed at mobilizing mass praise dances by large groups of working-class and peasant women, the National Dance troupes have normally been professional groups which display the dances to mass audiences.

The National Dance troupes first sprang up in some of the newly independent nations like Guinea, Mali and Senegal, formerly governed by French colonialists, though they spread later to anglophone countries such as Ghana, Zambia and Kenya. They probably had their origins in the folklore dance troupes popular in France after the Second World War. These troupes, the most famous of which was Keita Fodeba's Le Théâtre Africain, had African performers, but mostly European audiences. Post-independence African states saw the advantage of creating National Dance troupes which could give an exciting and positive image of the new nation to foreign tourists or official visitors, and to instil feelings of national pride and unity in domestic audiences. There was an element of popularized Negritude here – mediating for mass audiences the sentiments of pride in African history and pre-colonial culture which African intellectuals had responded to in the literature of the 1940s and 1950s.

The Ballets Africains (Guinea) was a famous early example of a National Dance troupe, winning some notoriety in Europe for its bare-breasted girl dancers. One of its most successful dance mimes was a very acrobatic ballet based on the epic of Sundiata. The celebration of pre-colonial heroes such as Sundiata was intended to tap Africa's historical power, to glorify, by analogy, the achievements of the newly independent Guinea. The sense of return to pre-colonial roots was homologous to the theory of communocracy which Sekou Touré tried to establish as the official Guinean ideology.

The revival of pre-colonial culture has been an important element in shaping post-independence ideologies. The variants of 'African socialism', such as Kaunda's humanism, Mobutu's 'authenticité', Nkrumah's conscientism, Sekou Touré's communocracy, and Kenyatta's Harambee spirit, which posit the notion of a classless sharing communal society before the alienating intrusion of capitalism and colonialism, tended to mask the very real class contradictions in modern African states. Here the state ideologies and the subsidized folklore companies have proved mutually supportive. A Zairean critic, Uniamwan Edebiri, has asserted the help which Mobutu's 'authenticité' has given to Zairean theatre:

> Within the sphere of theatre the ideology of authenticity assumes the creation of a dramaturgy which reflects Zairean realities.[19]

By 'realities' Edebiri seems to mean the imagined virtues of rural pre-colonial Zaire – not the poverty and corruption of the modern neo-colonial state.

The organization of the National Dance troupes shows how remote they have been from the realities of rural village life in Africa. The practice of most National Dance troupes was not to employ skilled veteran dancers from the regions to display their own dances, but to employ (or train) professional dancers, who learned the pre-colonial regional dances and modified them to create a sanitized, politically acceptable national repertoire. The leader of the National Dance Theatre of Zaire, Nobyem Mikanza, has explained how the dance drama *Nkenge*, based on a traditional folk tale, which successfully toured the USA in 1981, aimed at cementing the 250 different ethnic groups that comprise Zaire:

> We don't want to convey one cultural aspect of Zaire. We try to bring about unity and since we have a lot of tribes in Zaire it's very difficult. For the performances we have produced since the beginning it's going very well. All the people around Zaire have found themselves in the shows.[20]

Coming so soon after the Shaba Province disturbances the emphasis on unity had clear political implications. The prestige of a foreign tour reinforces the homogenizing aesthetics of a show like *Nkenge* by encouraging the different ethnic groups to identify with a national achievement.

The process of creating a national dance repertoire causes considerable distortion of aesthetic form and social function to the indigenous regional dances. It is always the most spectacular dances and most ostentatious sections of long dances which, after editing, are chosen for presentation, at the expense of subtler, more complex and extended choreographic skills.

The Mali National Troupe provides a good example. Under the leadership of Jules Travelé, Commissioner of Arts and Culture, the Mali National Troupe chose a repertoire of dances from different ethnic groups, such as the funeral masquerades of the Dogon, the song dances of the Peul and the acrobatic dances of the Bambara. Defenders of the National Dance troupes deny that the subordination of regional dances to the ideology of national unity entails loss of authenticity or the nourishment of popular support. Jean Decock, for instance, says of the Mali National Troupe:

Dancers from Zairean National Dance Theatre

Athletic dancers of Sierra Leone National Dance Theatre performing on a proscenium arch stage

Theatre lamps have replaced the evening firelight, but the authentic scenes of ritual and of folkways have been modified only insofar as Western conventions limit performances to approximately three hours.[21]

I believe, however, that the totally transformed economic base and conditions of performance have a far bigger impact on the National Dance troupes' aesthetic content than may be apparent. In the same article, Decock talks about the 'demystifying of the traditional rituals'.[22] By this he means that the pre-colonial dances are stripped of their original religious or moral functions and turned into secular entertainment. In the 'demystifying' process, which is imposed rather than organic, there is a loss of value and complexity.

The aesthetic decline is inevitable when you have such artificialities as 'le folklore Malien' whereby masked Dogon dancers perform 'every hour on the hour during the tourist season' at Sangha, Mali.[23] In that situation the audiences are no longer truly popular – that is, a dynamic and participating community which shares the cultural values of the dance originators. The audiences for the National Dance troupes are either foreign or 'national' tourists; and in either case are alien to the dance's inner meaning or the subtleties of its choreographic skills.

Peggy Harper has observed the difference between the performances of the Nigerian Miango men's dance as presented to tourists and as presented to the home village community:

> The dancers have come to regard their performance for foreign audiences as a necessary but irksome money-making routine. Their dancing has lost much of its attack and precision in performance, and there is less variety of movement patterns and sequence. But when the dancers as farmers and members of the Miango community, celebrate the agricultural seasons, their dancing regains some of its former qualities ... The dance rises towards the level of an immediate expression of the working life of their society.[24]

Harper is not suggesting that indigenous dances should be immune to change; on the contrary she favours the creative transposition of indigenous dance by committed choreographers capable of building new, appreciative African community audiences. But she does deplore the devalorizing process inevitable with tourist performances. Hussein makes a similar attack on the Spear Dance of the Bahima as performed by the National Dance Troupe of Tanzania. He condemns not only its aesthetic poverty, but also its underlying, neo-negritudinal moral vapidity – the 'exultation of African tradition ... romanticizing it without qualifying it'.[25]

The problem which Harper and Hussein point to is that for the ersatz tourist displays of the National Dance troupes, the critical attitudes and moral energy which are the essence of popular theatre are missing: they can only be found in those dances and theatre forms which engage genuine community audiences.

The relationship between audience and performers is crucial for assessing not only the National Dance troupes but the popularity of all forms of government-backed, ideologically slanted dance and theatre. Obviously there are very wide political differences in the theatre forms referred to in this chapter. The theatre of mobilization in Mozambique was perhaps more in tune with the popular interests than the neo-fascist choreography of the Malawi *Mbumba* dances or the blandly domesticating pan-ethnicism of the

Zairean National Dance Theatre. But, even in the Mozambican and Tanzanian examples, there is a sense in which agit-prop theatre workers manipulated audiences by preaching a government-sponsored socialist line, rather than involving them in creative and critical response.

By the criterion of relevant community participation, the ideological dance and theatre forms, however exciting, skilful or relevant, have been instrumental and populist rather than popular folk theatre. The beginnings of a truly popular theatre of the subaltern classes in Africa are to be found in peoples' organizations, which almost always lie outside the state-controlled cultural agencies. As the process of African liberalization which emerged in 1990 grew deeper roots, with its emphasis on civilian rule, multi-party democracy and human rights, the need for a less populist, more participatory theatre gained increasing strength.

Notes

1. Jones, p. 101.
2. Cutter, p. 75.
3. Quoted in Ng'wanakilila, p. 101.
4. Quoted in Hussein, 1971, p. 98.
5. Hussein, 1971, p. 90.
6. Quoted in Leshoai, p. 22.
7. Isaacman, p. 38.
8. Anonymous, 1979, p. 3.
9. Quoted in Hazoume, p. 224.
10. For example, in Togo, the pre-colonial Fon of Abomey used *Avonga* songs at court to insult the Gun people and the Gun used *Avohu* songs at Porto Novo to insult the Fon. See Gilbert, pp. 43–6.
11. Ross, p. 58.
12. Ross, pp. 63–4. See also Short, p. 273.
13. Mapanje, p. 13. For trenchant comments on the significance of such politicized 'theatre',
see Nkosi, 1984.
14. Recorded and translated by the author.
15. Recorded and translated by the author.
16. Vail and White, 1991, p. 28.
17. Vail and White, 1991, p. 28–9.
18. Vail and White, 1991, p. 29.
19. Edebiri, p. 71.
20. Quoted in Bowman, p. 81.
21. Decock, p. 33.
22. Decock, p. 33.
23. Crowley, p. 2.
24. Harper, p. 33.
25. Hussein, 1971, p. 56. For a jaundiced view of tourist dances in South Africa, see Gevisser. For a detailed discussion on the aesthetic implications of commercialization in Tanzanian dance, see Songoyi.

11

Popular Theatre &
the Struggle for Liberation
in Southern Africa

The emphasis in the preceding chapters on the development of popular theatre in independent African countries has neglected those parts of Southern Africa which were subjected to an entrenched form of 'late colonialism' and institutionalized racism. This chapter attempts to outline the way popular theatre in Southern Africa (especially South Africa) has related to the struggle for national liberation. A useful rough division can be made between those popular theatre forms which emerged within the colonial or apartheid hegemony and which mediated some nationalist tendencies in an oblique way, and those which were self-conscious expressions of nationalist struggle. In practice, however, the line between the two approaches has frequently been blurred.

The complex relationship between the liberation movements and wider movements of cultural resistance to colonialism can be rewardingly illuminated by the rich theoretical analysis made by leaders of liberation movements in Angola, Mozambique and Guinea Bissau.

In Angola the importance of supporting indigenous culture against colonial opposition was stressed by MPLA president, Augustino Neto, in 1972:

> We are concerned with keeping and reviving those Angolan cultural practices which have been despised or destroyed through centuries of colonialization. Music, dance and art are not evolving today, because they have been stifled by colonialism in its attempts to force its cultural tradition upon us.[1]

Superficially this statement may seem little different from the cultural nationalism associated with the first phase of the African struggle against colonialism in the 1940s and 1950s. But an important difference emerges later in the interview where Neto distinguishes between those indigenous traditions which should be encouraged (like music and dance), and those which should be discarded (like belief in fetishistic magic).

The rationale for distinguishing between positive and negative elements in pre-colonial cultural traditions was clarified in a 1972 paper given by

Amilcar Cabral, the Secretary General of PAIGC. Cabral recognized the importance of cultural nationalism in Guinea Bissau and Cape Verde, but stressed that it had to be linked to a wider political/economic struggle if it was to move beyond the gratification provided by individual emancipation:

> This 'return to the source' is ... historically important only if it involves both the genuine commitment to the fight for independence and also a total irrevocable identification with the aspiration of the masses, who reject not only the foreigner's culture but foreign rule altogether. Otherwise it is nothing but a means of obtaining temporary advantages, a conscious or unconscious form of political opportunism.[2]

The danger of gaining 'temporary advantages' was that the enemy was capable of eliminating these cultural gains by a subtle policy of co-option.

A common technique used by the oppressor to forestall artistic resistance was that of promoting an ethnic regional indigenous culture in order to discourage the pan-ethnic solidarity required by a national liberation struggle. FRELIMO cadres were aware of the danger in Mozambique, and the following policy document asserts the need to transcend regional culture:

> The dances which are performed today in the liberated regions are no longer dances of Cabo Delgado, or Tete or Niassa. The militants from other regions there bring their way of living, their dances, their songs and from this a new culture, national in its form and revolutionary in content, is born.[3]

This document makes the important observation that revived pre-colonial theatre forms on their own are insufficient to support a liberation struggle, there is a need for a revolutionary theatre which transforms the indigenous culture.

The theoretical debate about cultural struggle in the Portuguese colonies was relevant and helpful to the struggle of the Zimbabwean people against colonialism. One example of a pre-colonial cultural form which became politicized by its exposure to colonialism was the dramatized song. By the use of *madimikira* (parables) and *chibhende* (obscure allusions), it was possible to transform an apparently innocuous traditional song into an allegorical political protest. The following song, which originated during the nineteenth-century wars between the Shona and the Tonga, provides a good example: .

> The thick black forest has a killer lion – beat the drum
> The children of Pfumojena will come and the Tonga will see.[4]

According to George Kahari the song took on renewed significance during the war of liberation. 'The thick black forest ... refers to the urban city and the killer lion is the oppressive police force... The children of Pfumojena are the allies while the Tonga alludes to ...the enemies.'[4]

Songs approached the theatrical by having a leader and chorus taking on different roles. In the following satire, popularized in 1979, the leader takes on the role of a Patriotic Front militant, the chorus that of the 'sell-outs' – the black politicians who agreed to participate with Smith in the abortive Rhodesia–Zimbabwe:

> Leader: You have spoiled the country of Zimbabwe, everything
> Chorus: Yes, please.
> Leaders: You are leaders, there is nothing you refuse, everything.
> Chorus: Yes, please.[5]

Kahari notes that though the song was performed by an urban popular group, The Green Arrows, the use of a participatory chorus was close to the form of traditional Shona narrative drama. This aesthetic 'authenticity' enhanced the song's political effectiveness among the people.

Another pre-colonial theatre form in Zimbabwe which was transformed by the struggle against colonialism was *Bira*, the Shona spirit possession ritual. *Bira* came under ideological pressure after the collapse of the Shona uprising against British settlers in 1896. Since *Bira* appealed to indigenous African religious and nationalist sentiments, the British viewed it as a potential focus of resistance. For example, Nehanda, a female spirit medium who was possessed by the important Shona ancestral hero, Chaminuka, was arrested after she had prophesied the future overthrow of the whites: she was executed in 1898.

During the early part of the twentieth century, however, many of the 'progressive' Zezuru Shona were attracted to the status value of Christianity, and turned away from *Bira*. In the 1960s, after the suppression of the African political party, the African National Congress, and especially after the Unilateral Declaration of Independence (UDI), *Bira* made a remarkable recovery. As Lewis puts it, 'endowed with a new and increasingly politicized content, traditional religion burst forth again, filling the vacuum left by the prohibition of nationalist politics'.[6]

The politicized form of *Bira* involved all-night dancing to the music of drums and *mbira* (hand 'piano'), usually in a specially constructed spirit house known as the *Banya*. At some stage in the performance the spirit medium took off his European clothes and symbolically put on black robes (or less frequently the skin of a wild animal such as a leopard), as a form of commitment to ancestral religion and indigenous African values. According to Berliner, during the performance 'a feeling of solidarity emerges in the community as villagers ritually unite with their ancestors through their common participation in the musical activities of *Bira*. In this respect *Bira* is like a long communal journey through the night.'[7] During the 1960s and 1970s such performances provided important rituals of resistance to the increasingly oppressive UDI regime.

Nevertheless, the relationship between the nationalist parties and *Bira* was somewhat ambiguous. In general, the liberation movements advocated the revitalization of indigenous African arts including *Bira*. ZANU (PF) leaders, in particular, realized the importance of ritual resistance to the Rhodesian Front authorities. The revived interest in such nineteenth-century cult heroes as Nehanda and Chaminuka was expressed in the use of these ancestors as Chimurenga names for combat units. The freedom fighters also encouraged the politicization of *Bira* by linking the power of ancestral spirits to the struggle against the white regime. The following gives an example of such a transformed *Bira* song, where Nehanda, the nineteenth-century heroine of resistance to white settlers, is invoked to give power to the newer struggle of the 1970s:

> We cry to you Nehanda our guardian angel
> Yes, you are that to us
> Yes, you are that to us.
> Please guide our steps in this struggle
> Until we return to a liberated Zimbabwe.[8]

During the early 1970s the 'owners' of *Bira* – the spirit mediums and musicians – were themselves politicized by their cultural contact with freedom fighters and also by the harassment they received from the police. In the mid-seventies, however, the Rhodesian Front regime began to realize the cultural strength of *Bira* and tried to co-opt it. In Marandellas District, for example, the UDI regime enlisted the support of a prominent spirit medium from Makoni, Muchetera Mujura, who had been influential in publicizing the revival of Shona traditional culture. They gave Muchetera financial incentives to build up a network of spirit mediums sympathetic to the white regime; these leaders tried to substitute Shona ethnic loyalties for the Zimbabwean nationalism of the freedom fighters.

In 1977 ZANU (PF) guerrillas killed Muchetera at his home. Afterwards they instigated a policy of linking *Bira* to ancestral cults at a local district level rather than to 'pan-Shona' cults like that of Chaminuka. They used *Bira* to legitimize the 'alien' guerrillas from different areas of Zimbabwe, thereby investing the support of *Bira* for the whole national liberation struggle, not that of the Shona alone. In that way they were able to counteract some of the damage done by cultural agents of the Rhodesian regime.[9]

According to David Lan, who made a very thorough study of the relationship between spirit mediums and guerrillas among the Korekore Shona in the Zambezi Valley, the Rhodesian Psychological Intelligence Unit failed in its attempt to win the Mhondoro mediums, through a misunderstanding of Shona religion and ritual. The guerrillas, on the other hand, were able to fit in with that religion because they conformed to ancestral prophecies as 'the military vanguard of a nation of autochthons, of all the original displaced but authentic owners of the land'.[10] By their willingness to obey ritual taboos (for example, by not killing unnecessarily and by refraining from sex while on military duty) the guerrillas won the support of the Mhondoro mediums, and consequently also of the peasants in the strategically important Zambezi Valley. Lan comments:

> The acceptance of the guerrillas was made easier, quicker, more binding and more profound by allowing this new feature in the experience of the peasantry to be assimilated to established symbolic categories.[11]

The traditional, pre-colonial, earth, rain and ancestral cults found in the Zambezi Valley were not typical of the rest of Zimbabwe. In other areas it was necessary for the guerrillas not simply to conform to existing pre-colonial rituals but to create transformed (and often secular) modes of theatre. Such types of agit-prop drama were created both in the Zimbabwe liberated zones and in the refugee camps of Zambia and Mozambique.

One of the most exciting forms of theatre which was created in response to the war of liberation in Zimbabwe was the *Pungwe*. This was a combination of indigenous Zimbabwean performing arts and attempts by freedom fighters to mobilize peasants against the Smith regime. Kidd, who describes the *Pungwe* as a 'highly participatory form of cultural celebration, learning and mobilization', explains how the form evolved:

> The war effort required an ongoing dialogue with, politicization of, and active effort from the peasants. Long exhortatory speeches turned peasants off. But when the speeches were shortened and combined with songs and dances, or when the same themes were conveyed through short sketches, the villagers responded with

enthusiasm. When the villagers themselves became major actors and co-organizers of the event, their interest and support increased. The skits, songs, dances and poetry became an effective cover for the clandestine meetings and at the time conveyed the ideas and spirit of the revolution. It was highly participatory – villagers and fighters acted out and danced their commitments and built up their morale through collective music-making.[12]

Kidd emphasizes that, although the freedom fighters' cultural experiments were instrumental in creating the *Pungwe*, ultimately the peasants themselves organized as well as participated in the performance; it was in no way imposed upon them. The participatory nature of the *Pungwe* resembled the most advanced methodologies of Theatre for Development, but it was achieved not through the evolution of the international workshops and conferences, but in the cauldron of revolutionary bush war.

The performing arts played a significant part in the lives of the Zimbabwean refugees in Zambia and Mozambique. In December 1978, shortly after the Rhodesian bombing of Chikumbi and Mkushi refugee camps of ZAPU (PF) in Zambia, I witnessed improvised drama performed by Zimbabwean refugees in the ZAPU (PF) Victoria and J. Z. Moyo camps about 30 km west of Lusaka.[13] These performances, mostly by refugees but also including a few guerrillas, consisted of traditional Ndebele war chants which had been radically changed to fit the situation of struggle against the Rhodesian military forces. The refugees did dance mimes depicting such scenes as the shooting down of Rhodesian 'spotter' planes. There was no audience for the mimes apart from the refugees themselves, but they clearly played an important cathartic function in releasing tension and in creating solidarity in the face of the enemy.

Kaarsholm says of such cathartic sketches performed in the ZAPU camps:

> Performances [were] encouraged to evoke a sense of 'life at home' and keep up the spirits of camp members ... A wide-ranging repertoire of 'classical' song and dance genres were investigated and kept intact.[14]

Although the main function of such performances was to reinforce feelings of solidarity Kaarsholm acknowledges another kind of play which allowed somewhat more self-critical analysis of the refugees' plight. For example, praise poetry for Mzilikazi or Lobengula was sometimes given a satirical extension to use 'humour and ambiguous statements' as a way of criticizing teachers, camp leaders, and even political leaders like Joshua Nkomo.[15]

The morale-boosting sketches of ZAPU, even when they introduced an element of allegorical criticism, were restricted by the 'traditional' format of dance drama or heroic recitation. In addition to a theatre of wishful thinking or therapeutic expressions of cultural solidarity and frustration, there was a need for a theatre capable of analysing the problems faced in the revolutionary struggle.

The cultural cadres in ZANU (PF) attempted to create an analytical agit-prop drama in the refugee camps and rehabilitation centres in Zambia and Mozambique.[16] The aesthetic roots of this theatre came partly from the *Pungwe* and partly from the tradition of radical popular theatre emerging in the 'host' countries.

In 1973 Zimbabwean students at the University of Zambia started a drama programme in the ZANU (PF) camps with school teachers and injured combatants. This proved a fruitful combination. Students liked Kufa Chinodza, who had picked up popular theatre with Chikwakwa Theatre (where a ZANU (PF) militant, Fay Chung, was one of the instructors), were able to create authentic dramas about the armed struggle with the help of veteran guerrillas such as Ernest Kadungure and Shiba Tavarwisa. The plays were mainly intended to provide politicization for Zimbabwean refugees, preparing them for the armed struggle, but occasionally they were shown to sympathetic Zambian audiences in Lusaka and the Copperbelt.

In 1976 most of the ZANU (PF) freedom fighters were expelled from Zambia. They set up camps in Mozambique, and agit-prop drama came to play a very important part in the education and mobilization of the refugees. Theatre came under the wing of ZANU (PF)'s Department of Education and Culture. The experience of the Mozambican ruling party, FRELIMO, in the use of drama during the struggle in Cabo Delgado and Niassa provinces proved useful to the Zimbabwean educational cadres. Since, even as late as 1978, there were only nine graduate teachers for 30,000 refugees and combatants-in-training, it was not possible for intellectuals to provide major aesthetic inputs as they had in Zambia. The creation of scenarios was done collectively by the students, and the dialogue and dramatic techniques were arrived at by improvisation.

The popular ZANU (PF) plays provided mostly hortatory, didactic stories giving audiences political and military instruction. An example of such a play is *The People are Invincible* (performed by Form Four students), which offered a somewhat strident condemnation of capitalism and the 1978 Muzorewa settlement. Other plays, however, offered a more complex analysis of problems arising from the struggle. Examples of two such plots were, firstly, a play about a black man pretending to be coloured because the whites had made him ashamed of his colour, and, secondly, a play about the conflict between the traditional submissive role of women in polygamous households and the newer emancipated role of women in the military struggle for freedom.

Aesthetically the plays normally used episodic plots where fairly realistic scenes with improvised dialogue were interspersed with direct addresses to the audience accompanied by drum or *mbira* music, revolutionary songs or traditional dances.

Kaarsholm suggests that two types of theatre emerged within the ZANU (PF) refugee camps, a neo-Maoist type of hortatory, authoritarian drama, and a more democratic, critical mode:

> A tradition of discussion theatre ... dealing with and directly articulating everyday life political grievances, developed in the camps alongside the traditionalist revival of cultural nationalism and alongside the ideologically oriented propaganda tableaux organised by Marxist-Leninist commissars.[17]

He felt that the former provided 'new genres of dramatic activism which came to represent the most potent agents of decolonization and renewal in Zimbabwe after independence'.[18] The best of the revolutionary plays, therefore, not only prepared exiled Zimbabweans for the cultural and military struggle against the Rhodesian Front regime, they also prepared for some of the problems which would arise after the people's victory.

214

A rather different approach is needed for discussing the relationship between popular theatre and the movement towards national liberation in South Africa. The existence of a large urbanized proletariat means that the emphasis is not on rural theatre forms like spirit possession (even though they exist) but on urbanized popular theatre, which is where the cutting edge of artistic conscientization is to be found.

Popular theatre in South Africa has been intimately connected to the musical culture of the people. As early as 1912 there is evidence of a strong African urban brass tradition, with such groups as Modikwe's Band. This vogue gave way to other waves of music and dance styles, such as *Marabi* in the 1920s, *Mbube* in the 1930s, *Mbaqanga* in the 1940s, *Kwela* in the 1950s and *Smanje Manje* in the 1960s.[19] These dances were syncretic musical forms incorporating black American jazz and indigenous dance styles drawn from many rural South African cultures. These township dances served to mediate the new pressures of urban life for workers who were being sucked into the South African metropoles from the rural areas.

Alongside township music arose a vaudeville style of popular entertainment rather similar to Ghanaian Concert Party and Tanzanian *Vichekesho*. The township vaudevilles often presented a comic sketch or mime, performed by popular musicians in between numbers and usually incorporating music into the action. As with Concert Party and *Vichekesho*, the vaudeville sketches relied heavily on stereotyping – making fun of such stock township characters as the naive immigrant, the *tsotsi* (young criminal), the prostitute and the cruel policeman.

Sometimes these vaudeville sketches developed into more sophisticated musical satires. A famous exponent of musical satire was Esau Mtetwa, whose group, Esau Mtetwa's Lucky Stars, performed mostly in Zulu and became very popular during the 1930s. Eventually his talents attracted the sponsorship of a white entrepreneur, Bertha Schlosberg, who introduced the group to white audiences at the British Empire Exhibition in Johannesburg, and even arranged a performance at Sadlers Wells in London. Mtetwa never quite recovered his popular base in the township on his return to South Africa.

Although vaudeville drama did not subsequently achieve the organized skill of Mtetwa's Lucky Stars, it did survive the 1930s. The following is David Coplan's description of a typical vaudeville performance of a *Smanje Manje* group in the 1960s:

> Acrobatic dancing, dancing instrumentalists and comic skits accompany well-choreographed song and dance routines by the 'featured' vocal group. Costumes and comic themes are often symbolic of meaningful social realities, satirizing elite Africans for their 'over-Westernized' and 'over-educated' snobbery as well as poking fun at archetypal township characters.[20]

The reasons why African syncretic popular theatre did not develop any radical critique of South Africa's social structure before the 1970s are quite complex. The development of advanced forms of capitalism would normally be expected to give rise to a politicized class-consciousness. In South Africa, however, that dialectic was complicated by the convergence of capitalist exploitation of black labour and an institutionalized white racist hegemony. This was reinforced by a scattered zoning system for black suburbs, of which

Soweto was the most celebrated example. The establishment of a migrant labour system also discouraged the building of a confident and permanent proletariat. Many of the recurrent cycles of new dance styles, for example, can be traced to fresh waves of labour immigrants into the Witwatersrand, each demanding an uncritical culture of socialization into urban life.

Moreover, the new forms of communication available to black South Africans were scrutinized fiercely by the white authorities, and every step possible was taken to use legislation to obstruct expressions of black solidarity. A whole forest of laws was erected intended to smother any expressions of popular dissent. Prominent among these were: the Entertainment Act of 1931 introducing legal censorship, the 1950 Suppression of Communism Act forbidding quotation from banned authors, the Public Safety Act of 1953 forbidding any activity the Ministry of Justice deemed to subvert authority, the Group Areas Act of 1960 enforcing segregated housing, and the Publications and Entertainment Act of 1963 segregating white and black audiences except under special licence. The State of Emergency declared in 1986 gave the authorities a whole new set of extra-legal powers aimed at preventing assembly of Africans for 'subversive' purposes; anti-apartheid drama could be made to fit those criteria. It was only with the 'thaw' of 1990 that this legislation began to be dismantled.

The heavy-handed legislative machinery mainly reflected the racist ideology of the Boer political hegemony. The 'English' component in the South African white ruling classes tended to project a 'liberal' approach to race relations; but, in fact, the economic control of black entertainment by the white liberal establishment was probably more effective than racist legislation in stunting a critical black theatre.

The relationship between the white controlled entertainment industry and black entertainers paralleled the economic relations between the races. Talented black musicians like the Manhattan Brothers and the African Inkspots in the 1940s and Spokes Mashiyane, Dolly Rathebe and Kippie Moeketsi in the 1950s tried to establish themselves as self-sufficient artists, but ended up being controlled and exploited by white-owned recording and entertainment industries.

There was a similar cultural and economic drive by the white establishment to control African popular theatre. The clearest example of this is the history of the multiracial Union of South African Artists (USAA). The Union, which started in 1953, combined the skills of ambitious black artists with the finance and entrepreneurial drive of white capital. The liberal English group, many of whom had links with industrial giants such as the Anglo-American Company, professed to be protecting black artists from exploitation, but at the same time there was a patronizing desire to protect blacks from 'lapsing' into crime or radical politics.

The theatre production which best exemplified the ideology of USAA was the famous musical *King Kong*, first produced in 1959 with the aid of a 4,000 rand grant from Anglo-American. Written and directed by whites, *King Kong* told of a boxer whose career is destroyed by his involvement in big city crime. Although based on the life of a real boxer, Ezekiel Dhlamini, the story projected a very unfavourable image of African urban life. Robert Kavanagh has convincingly argued that the play helped to crystallize certain white prejudices about African townships, centring on criminal stereotypes such as

216

the prostitute and the *tsotsi*. He criticizes the white liberal producers of the play:

> Because they both romanticized the culture in which the play was situated and underestimated the performers who were to perform it, they simplified, trivialized, even distorted, its content and failed to exploit the real strengths of its form.[21]

King Kong was a commercial success in Johannesburg with both black and white audiences, and became an international hit in London in 1960. Its influence on popular theatre in South Africa was enormous. It paved the way for a tradition of musicals which were financed, written and directed by whites, but which exploited, often to the point of shameless plagiarism, the talents of black singers. dancers and musicians. Later, and much cruder, examples of this tradition were, *Umabatha, Morepa* and *Ipi Tombi*; unlike *King Kong*, these had a mostly rural setting, and projected the stereotype of the 'happy and lively rural African, born with an irrepressible sense of rhythm'.[22] Such theatre acted as a scarcely disguised apology for the Bantustan policy.

A more significant influence of *King Kong*, however, was on black popular theatre, particularly that of the township musical. Much of the dance musical talent tapped by *King Kong* came from the urban African jazz and popular music tradition, which in turn was closely associated with vaudeville theatre. A major achievement of *King Kong* was to establish the idea among black entrepreneurial entertainers that a full-length musical drama, based on the vaudeville tradition, could be popular enough with black audiences to be commercially successful .

The career of Gibson Kente epitomizes the rise of black commercial popular theatre. Kente was born in the Xhosa area of Eastern Cape, and his early cultural influences were Christian hymns and Xhosa traditional music. During the 1950s he worked as a talent scout for the white-owned Gallo Record Company, an experience which exposed him both to the variety of urban popular music, and to the economic demands of a commercial enterprise.

Kente was not satisfied with being an employee of Gallo; he longed for the chance of setting up his own business. *King Kong* gave him the inspiration to direct commercial township musicals for blacks. For that reason he joined USAA so that he could gain stage experience and financial backing. Having failed to find suitable scripts, he decided to create his own plays. The first Kente musical, *Manana the Jazz Prophet,* was not an outstanding success, but his second, *Sikalo,* was not only a commercial hit, but changed the course of black South African theatre.

Kavanagh has given a useful synopsis of the ingredients in *Sikalo*:

> The formula is a simple township tale, featuring the agreeably caricatured stock-types of the townships. There is the shebeen queen, the tsotsis, the brutal but ridiculous policeman, priests who take bribes and preach nonsense. the traditional Zulu boy with pierced earlobes and comical broken English, plus Zionists, the dancing girls and a host of other types to swell the scene.[23]

The music from *Sikalo* became almost instantaneously popular, and the play set the basic pattern for the township musical.

At first, in 1965, USAA supported *Sikalo* (with costumes, rehearsal facilities and administrative backup). But in 1966 the Union called in another director, Mashall Mosia, to replace Kente. This led to severe disputes between USAA

A township dance sequence from *King Kong*

and Kente, which the Union sometimes asked the police to settle. Eventually USAA dismissed Kente and his performers and completely recast the play under Mosia's direction. Kente responded by setting up his own production with the original cast and touring it around the black townships of Johannesburg and other parts of South Africa. It was Kente's version of *Sikalo* which became a big commercial success.

Sikalo was a significant turning-point. It marked the decline of USAA, which became discredited for the heavy-handed paternalism of its white backers, and it was the start of a burgeoning popular black township musical tradition. The black theatre movement was unwittingly aided by the 1963 Publications and Entertainment Act effectively blocking multiracial audiences.

Kente's theatre company was very much a one-man entrepreneurial business; he functioned as financial controller, director. choreographer, play creator, musician and administrator, similar to the role of Bob Johnson in Ghanaian Concert Party and Hubert Ogunde in Yoruba Opera. As a business-man/director Kente was quite ruthless, keeping a tight financial control, and notorious for the demands on his actors and actresses. For that reason many of the experienced performers tended to leave his company. In the plays that succeeded *Sikalo, Life* and *Zwi*, he managed to maintain a few experienced singers and dancers, but by the early 1970s he relied increasingly on training young inexperienced proletarian youths in order to achieve the discipline required for what Kavanagh calls 'ensemble and solo singing and acting of precision and unflagging energy'.[24]

By the early 1970s Kente had built up a large organization of professional and relatively well-paid performers, musicians, administrators, technicians, drivers and labourers. From his petty-bourgeois origins he had managed to build a quite strong capitalist enterprise. His success can be related to the rise of a black entrepreneurial class in Soweto in the late 1960s, which, with the increasingly tighter apartheid laws, came to hold an important position in articulating black consumers with the white-controlled economy. Kente had joined the Soweto elite, whose life style and conspicuous consumption were the envy of the working class.

As would be expected, Kente found commercial rivals. Other entrepre-neurs who put on township musicals included Sam Mhangwane (*Unfaithful Woman* and *Blame Yourself*), Solly Mckgoe (*uLindiwe*) and Boike Mahlamme (*Mahlemola*), but they rarely achieved Kente's artistic or commercial success.

Given their entrepreneurial mode of theatre production and close links to Christian ideology, it is not surprising to find that township musicals in the late 1960s, despite their huge following among the black working class, were fairly uncritical of apartheid. Coplan calls it a theatre of self-realization and suggests that:

> The 'message' of these plays is often confined to the portrayal of suffering, calls to God for deliverance, or at least explanation, and prescriptions for a new urban African social and moral order to aid community survival.[25]

However, the plays did show a great advance on the white-controlled musicals, in that the stereotypes emerged from within the black township culture, and projected the warmth and solidarity of community spirit rather than merely the degradation of township crime.

That sensitivity to community spirit led to radicalization of township musicals in the mid-1970s. As Soweto itself (under the influence of the Black Consciousness Movement) became far more critical of apartheid, theatre entrepreneurs were forced to respond to audience demands. Kente's plays illustrate the change. Kente was also influenced by *Sizwe Bansi is Dead* by Athol Fugard, Winston Ntshona and John Kani, which made him realize the commercial possibilities of committed theatre.

Kente's 1974 play, *How Long*, retained many of the typical township musical ingredients, but there were clear political overtones to some of the situations. The story, about a poor man, Thwala, trying to put his son, Africa, through school, had a politically explosive theme at a time when education was becoming a burning issue in Soweto. The very title, *How Long*, came to have a political significance, and the title song was extremely popular. Although the Publications Control Board, which supervised censorship at the national level, did not intervene against *How Long*, some local authorities demanded a clearance letter from the Censorship Board. The township superintendents of the East Rand and the Vaal Triangle banned performances in their areas altogether. Such restrictions only increased the popularity of *How Long*, and it played to packed audiences in shabby halls in Soweto night after night.

Kente's next play, *I Believe*, was an attempt to change the musical formula by cutting most of the melodrama and burlesque elements. Although it ran into censorship problems because of its political message, *I Believe* proved popular only with militant intellectuals, not with broad subaltern audiences. Kente replaced it in 1975 with *Too Late*, a play which reverted to the politicized musical formula of *How Long*.

Too Late dealt with a cross-section of a township community, including Madinto, a shebeen queen; her crippled daughter, Ntanana; her restless nephew, Saduva; a doctor, Dr Phuza; a priest, Mfundisi; an unemployed layabout, Offside; and a group of young criminals. the Majintas. At the end of the play, after witnessing the evil results of the government's policy, including the imprisonment of his aunt and the death of his cousin at the hands of a cruel policeman (Pelepele), Saduva gives up the chance of education and joins the group of young criminals.

The radical content of *Too Late* came out in scenes such as the one where the officer demands pass books. When Madinto asks how she can be expected to look after her crippled daughter if they are endorsed back to the homeland, the officer exclaims, 'God almighty! Did I make the damn laws?'[26] Even the agent of the regime seems locked in an oppressive but scarcely changeable system. This is where the play falls far short of being revolutionary. The ordinary people in the play protest against oppression but do not organize against it – they merely appeal to the authorities to relax their oppression.

The ideology presented in *Too Late* is a stoical one of an integrated community attempting to defend itself from threats by outsiders, which include whites, sell-out policeman and *tsotsis*. At the end of the play, after Mfundisi has rebuked Pelepele for obeying unjust and cruel laws, Kente has the doctor tie up the play with a much less radical appeal.

> Leaving the law, for now I am afraid unless something is done about this pettiness, the law is going to end up with a hot potato in his hands. Can't something be done to curb the bitterness in both young and old before it's TOO LATE?[27]

The uprising of the Soweto youth a year later must have seemed a confirmation of the doctor's fears.

Trying to analyse the text of *Too Late* is actually unfair, and in some ways rather futile, since the play's impact in performance was much less that of the literary text than that of non-verbal skills – gesture, songs, mime, dance and ensemble movement. Through such techniques a sub-text was established which was far more militant than the dialogue. 'The radical section of the audience', according to McClaren, 'responded to the radical elements in the plays and disregarded Kente's moderate overall meaning.' He goes on to explain that it was the music which was most politically effective since it had the ability 'to fuse an audience of separate divided black individuals in an experience of intense racial/national identity'.[28]

Too Late was at first banned by the Publications Control Board a month after opening. Following an appeal and intense negotiations, a somewhat emasculated version was allowed to be shown. One major change was the ending, which was made even less questioning of authority than the one quoted above. Even so, township superintendents in East Rand and Vaal Triangle prohibited performances of the play in their districts.

Other popular dramatists were also affected by the radicalization of township musicals, including Ridgeway Macu (*A Master of Convenience*) and Rev. Mzwandile Muqina (*Give us This Day* and *The Trial*). *Give us This Day*, based on the parcel-bomb murder of a student Black Consciousness leader, was particularly popular; according to Kavanagh, 'it could pack a hall at a few hours notice'.[29]

In 1976 Kente was arrested while working on a film version of *How Long*. He was released in 1977 and returned directly to theatre work. The musical he created, *Can You Take It?*, steered clear of politics. This and subsequent plays, such as *Mama and the Load*, marked a return to the blander style of *Sikalo* and the 'theatre of self-realization'.

The ideological pressure which had pushed Kente and other popular dramatists into a more radical stance came largely from the Black Consciousness Movement of the late sixties and early seventies. Black Consciousness was a form of cultural nationalism similar to and to a large extent inspired by the Black Power Movement in the United States. It advocated the unity of the black peoples of South Africa (including coloureds and Indians as well as Africans), and the building of black self-respect through psychological decolonization and resistance to white oppression. The leaders of the movement were acutely aware of the importance of culture in building up confidence and solidarity among the black people of South Africa – and theatre was a key medium for them to achieve that conscientization.

One element in Black Consciousness resembled Cabral's 'return to the source' – the desire to assert the value of pre-colonial African culture. An outstanding theatrical example of that sensibility was *uNosilimela* by Credo Mutwa, an epic play with a huge cast which attempted to explore pre-colonial myth and religion. Mutwa was a diligent proselytizer for a return to pre-colonial African values and culture and particularly for the revival of a form of Zulu ritual theatre known as *umlinganiso*. The 1973 production of *uNosilimela* in Soweto by Workshop 71 was an attempt to put those theories into practice by transforming a shabby Soweto hall into a symbolically charged arena for a complex ritual performance. Unfortunately, the technical demands of preparing a stage for *umlinganiso* prevented the kind of touring which was needed for *uNosilimela* to achieve popular success.

There are other reasons why Black Consciousness theatre did not take up the path of pre-colonial ritual theatre. There were strong ideological pressures which prevented radical black artists from making an over-enthusiastic 'return to the source'. The most important of these was that the apartheid regime was actively trying to promote a pseudo-African traditionalism of its own. The promotion of 'Bantu' language and culture, through funding for literature, the school system, film industry and such organizations as Radio Bantu, had the effect of creating suspicions about any 'return to the source' in the eyes of black South African radicals. It even discouraged some popular theatre artists from using African languages in their plays. The following statement by the African National Congress illustrates the distrust.

> South Africa has made much of her protection of separate cultures. What does this amount to? We have in South Africa a government-imposed 'traditionalism' – in fact the use of traditional culture to maintain the legitimacy of a culture of domination. The Republic's protection of culture means for Africans the external trappings of once great cultures reduced to the folkloric and to caricature.[30]

The ANC statement makes the important connection between the government's support of pseudo-traditional culture and its official policy of separate development.

The reaction by Black Consciousness leaders against Bantustan aesthetics led them to a modern urban theatre in English which dealt with topical political issues. The social background of Black Consciousness leaders also impelled them to an urban and fairly literary theatre style. Black Consciousness was closely associated with the South African Student Organization (SASO), which in 1968 broke away from the white-dominated National Union of South African Students (NUSAS). The academic background to Black Consciousness can be seen in the career of Mthuli Shezi, who was student president of SASO at the University of Zululand. He left the university without obtaining a degree, objecting to the institutionalized racism of the university. Shortly afterwards, in 1972, he was elected national vice-president of the Black People's Convention (BPC) an organization which supported Black Consciousness. It was at about this time that he wrote his play *Shanti*.

The plot of *Shanti* deals with a love affair between an African student, Thabo, and his Asian girl-friend, Shanti. The affair runs into problems because of the apartheid laws and because of Thabo's political activism. Eventually Thabo runs away to Mozambique where he joins a guerrilla movement fighting for the overthrow of the South Africa regime, and dies with them. The play uses a montage style, alternating between fairly naturalistic pieces of dialogue and stylized direct addresses to the audience such as the following by Koos, a coloured friend of Thabo:

> I am Black
> Black like my mother.
> Black like the sufferers.
> Black like the continent.[31]

This technique, along with tableau-like grouping, gave Shezi the opportunity to project unambiguously the ideology of the BPC.

Shezi did not live to see a performance of *Shanti*. He was killed by a train in 1973; almost certainly he was pushed onto the track by a white railway official whom Shezi had accused of abusing black women passengers. The death of Shezi inspired some young actors and actresses from Soweto to form a radical drama group called Shiqomo (meaning Spear). The formation of this group almost coincided with that of an even more ambitious group – the People's Experimental Theatre (PET). The two groups merged under the title PET, but with a motto, 'the spear lives on'. According to one of its early newsletters, PET's function was to provide 'a means of assisting blacks to reassert their pride, human dignity and group identity and solidarity'.[32] These aims coincided with Black Consciousness movements such as SASO and BPC.

PET's first production in 1973 was one of poetry readings, music and extracts from black radical writings. Their second production in 1974–5 was *Shanti*. It was performed in Soweto, Linasia and several parts of Natal. Although the style of the play was literary and solemn, initially appealing mainly to students and the radical professional class, eventually the play achieved a much wider popularity. McClaren suggests this was partly because the explicit militancy of the play was so provocative to authorities that it was inevitably going to be crushed; watching the play became almost akin to viewing a 'ritual suicide'.[33]

That fascination did reach its inevitable catharsis. The production received much harassment (such as the confiscation of equipment and the banning of the PET newsletter). Eventually, the whole play was crushed by the arrest of the main actors. To understand those arrests it is probably better to link them to other manifestations of Black Consciousness theatre.

Johannesburg was not the only arena for Black Consciousness theatre; another very important group was the Theatre Council in Natal (TECON), founded by militant black activist, Strini Moodley and Saths Cooper in 1969. In 1972, they helped form the South African Black Theatre Union (SABUTU), organized a theatre festival to celebrate the event and travelled around South Africa proselytizing for black theatre.

The multiracial Johannesburg group, Workshop 71, also responded to the mood of Black Consciousness. Their 1971 play, *Crossroads*, about the eviction of black homesteaders as part of the government's resettlement schemes, was mainly in English, and played to multiracial audiences. Their next play, *Zzi!*, created under the influence of Black Consciousness, used no English – thereby almost eliminating white audiences. The play used a mixture of Zulu, Sotho and Tsotsitaal for performances in Johannesburg, and Xhosa for performances in Cape Town.

One group which had aims similar to Black Consciousness but without close structural links to BPC or SASO was Mihloti in Soweto, which specialized in dramatized poetry readings with music. The audiences for Mihloti's productions tended to be select and highly committed. A critic from the theatre magazine *S'ketch*, described them as 'a small group of conscious brothers and sisters, most of them would-be graduates who go to a play expecting their imaginations to be stirred to thrilling extremes by harassing slogans'.[34] The members of Mihloti formed the core of MDALI (Music, Dance, Drama and Literature – but also meaning 'creator' in Zulu). MDALI arranged regular arts festivals and attempted to be an umbrella movement of black theatre artists in Johannesburg.

Although the Black Consciousness theatre performances were not enormously popular on the scale of the township musical, they were very influential, not only in radicalizing the musical themselves, but also in their considerable effect on the influential group of young students which was to form the catalyst for the 1974 Soweto uprisings. Another important achievement was in the organization of the Black Consciousness groups, which tended to be far more democratic than white theatre companies. In TECON, for example, 'roles were not professionally demarcated; everyone undertook administration, technical direction and acting as required'.[35] Similarly, with Workshop 71, 'all decisions about advertising, budget, pay, venue etc. were taken communally. This emphasis on group democracy was an important and successful exception to the dominant traditions within other theatre groups in South Africa.'[36] The revolutionary nature of Black Consciousness theatre, therefore, was not only in the context of the plays, but in the mode of theatre production, which served as an experiment in non-exploitative social relations.

As might be expected, the radical black theatre groups were not allowed to operate unchallenged. Between 1974 and 1976 they were all crushed or severely restricted during a period of intense unrest which culminated in the Soweto uprising of 16 June 1976 and which rocked the South African hegemony.

The organized harassment of Black Consciousness theatre started in 1973 when several SASO leaders, including the charismatic Steve Biko, were banned. TECON was forced to abandon a projected poetry-reading tour of black schools after headmasters received warnings from police. In the same year, TECON's collage of music, poetry and drama, *Black Images*, was also carefully scrutinized by the police. In 1974, during rallies to celebrate FRELIMO's victory in Mozambique, almost the whole Black Consciousness leadership was detained under the Terrorism Act. These included TECON activists, Saths Cooper, Strini Moodley, and Cooper's wife, Vino, and brother, Revabalan.

Early in 1975 (which was also the year of Biko's detention), Strini's brother Lingan was detained, as were two leaders of PET, Sadeqque Variava and Solly Ismail. The arrested theatre workers came for trial towards the end of 1975, along with other SASO and BPC leaders. Among the charges against them was that they plotted 'to make, produce, publish or distribute subversive and anti-white utterances, writings, plays and dramas'.[37] The script of *Shanti* was attached to the charge-sheet. After suffering solitary confinement, and in some cases torture, several of the theatre activists were released, but Variave, Ismail, Saths Cooper and Striny Moodley were given life sentences on Robben Island, and were only released in the mid-1980s.

Although TECON and PET received the most virulent state oppression, other Black Consciousness theatre groups were also affected. A drama festival which MDALI arranged in 1975 was broken up by the police; the West Rand Administration Board banned several MDALI productions, including Ridgeway Macu's *Matter of Conscience* and two plays by Ismael Matlahabene. In 1976, Mihloti's principal organizer, Molefe Pheto, was arrested. After a year of detention without trial and torture, he was released and went into exile in Britain. These events led to the collapse of both Mihloti and MDALI.

It was not only the official persecution of Black Consciousness theatre which interrupted its full flowering. The transition which took place in July 1976 from cultural mobilization to active insurrection affected popular theatre. As Kavanagh puts it:

> In this situation conventional performances of a play, no matter how militant had become anachronistic; impossible, even a little ridiculous. Events seem to have rendered theatre irrelevant – until the revolutionary struggle is either successful or fails, in which case theatre resumes its social and political tasks.[38]

After the Soweto upheavals were over, popular theatre in South Africa did resume its 'normal' function, but in a rather transformed way.

The persecution of Black Consciousness drama activists had had a decisive effect. Theatre workers realized that blatant provocation of the authorities of the kind made by PET's *Shanti* was perhaps tactically unsound, and ultimately self-defeating. For those groups with the contacts and resources to do it, an overseas tour offered the chance both to avoid self-destruction and to conscientize audiences outside South Africa. This is what happened to Workshop 71. Their 1976 production of the militant play about African life, *Survival*, received considerable legal and administrative obstruction from the state authorities. (One white poet jokingly redubbed the play, *Suicide*.) In 1977, *Survival* re-emerged for a very successful tour in America, where it helped educate American audiences on the evils of apartheid. In 1978 the play was banned in South Africa. Maishe Maponya's *The Hungry Earth* (1979) and *Umongikazi* (1983) are examples of other plays which enjoyed transfers to the radical theatre circuits of Europe, to escape suppression in South Africa.

Although Black Consciousness theatre was not wiped out by the official harassment of the mid-1970s, it did not take on the openly confrontational form of *Shanti* or *Survival*. The dramatized poetry readings to music still flourished, since verse was able to use parable, metaphor and allusion as ways of expressing sentiments that were hard to identify as subversive. Another tendency in the late 1970s was the revival of multiracial theatre.

Several African theatre groups found that having a white manager or director sometimes blunted the edge of state intervention; others found that performing for white or multiracial audiences gave the group a better chance of economic survival. Barney Simon's career is instructive here. During the 1960s Simon, along with Athol Fugard, was one of the white directors most involved with black 'Town theatre'.[39] During the Black Consciousness period, however, Simon found that black theatre had moved against white directors, he therefore exercised his talents in creating plays intended to conscientize white audiences about the evils of apartheid. In the late 1970s Simon returned to multiracial drama. *Woza Albert!*, the play about the imagined return of Christ to South Africa, which he created in 1981 with ex-Kente actors, Percy Mtwa and Mbongeni Ngema, had a phenomenally successful transfer to London's West End.

A somewhat different type of drama has been that of theatre promoting socio-economic rather than political conscientization. Because it presented a less overt challenge to the state hegemony it was allowed to survive the events of 1976.

As early as the mid-1960s Simon had been involved with health education

A scene from *Woza Albert!* by Barney Simon, Mbongeni Ngema and Percy Mtwa

through Theatre for Development projects in the rural areas of South Africa. In the 1970s, several interesting urban projects emerged. One was an unscripted play called *Imfunduso*, created through collective improvisation by women of Crossroads squatter camp in Cape Town. Of this type of almost spontaneous theatre which was not attached to any recognized political grouping, Tomaselli comments, 'Because it is ideologically invisible ... it often escapes the ravages of censorship and other restrictive laws which govern freedom of expression.'[40]

Another interesting example of improvised drama was *Ilanga Le So Phonela Abasabeni*. This play was created by workers at an iron foundry in Johannesburg, under the general supervision of a trade union lawyer, Halton Cheadle. The workers belonged to the Metal and Allied Workers' Union and were arrested for striking illegally. Cheadle encouraged them to use role play in order to reconstruct the events of the so-called strike. The role play proved so imaginative, exhilarating and skilful that before long the workers had created a whole play, which they showed their fellow workers within the Union.

As with some of the Theatre for Development projects, the most consciousness-raising moments occurred in the creation of the play rather than in performance, as Cheadle illustrates:

> At one stage during the re-enactment one of the workers got up and shouted at the 'manager'. In response one old man said to the fellow shouting, 'It's no good saying that now. You didn't say it then. It's too late now.' Humbled the younger worker sat down.[41]

Through such revealing moments the workers were able to explore the potential and the limitations of their power relationships with the management.

This problem-posing element was retained in the finished production through techniques of audience participation. For example, one of the crucial points in *Ilanga* was a confrontation between the workers and a government-authorized representative of the Steel and Engineering Industries Federation of South Africa (SEIFSA). At that moment the actors joined the audience in the front row, and the SEIFSA representative addressed the whole audience. Cheadle explains:

> The crucial thing was to get the audience to participate in rejecting this character [the SEIFSA representative]. Two of the performers never go on stage but sit in different parts of the audience and would heckle and shout ... The response was absolutely spontaneous. We didn't even need those actors to sit in the audience because the whole audience just booed the petty bourgeois sellout as soon as he appeared.[42]

Similarly, at the end of the play, the actors asked the audience what the workers should do, strike or not strike. Whichever answer the audience gave the actors gave alternative arguments, showing the disadvantages of the audience's choice. In that way the debate was transferred from the realm of 'art' into that of real life.

Although *Ilanga* had a cathartic effect on the sacked workers and helped them put their case to fellow Union members, it did not help their legal case. Many of the 'actors' had their dismissal confirmed and were endorsed back to Kwazulu. What happened after that is that actors from Junction Avenue

Theatre group in Johannesburg took over their roles and *Ilanga* became a more conventional 'art play' shown at university theatres and other venues in 1979. This revised, polished version of *Ilanga* appeared 'crudely propagandistic and amateurish' to sophisticated audiences rather than vital, spontaneous and acutely important as it did to the original proletarian audiences.[43] In addition, there was a rather unsettling sense in which the Junction Avenue production fed on the deprivations of the original cast.

The decision to take black workers' theatre away from the institutional support of white liberals is illustrated by the Bahumutsi Theatre Group's play, *Umongikazi*, which was first performed at the multiracial Market Theatre in 1983, but which was later transferred to a nurses' hostel belonging to the Baragwanath Hospital in Johannesburg.

The contrast between *Umongikazi* and *Ilanga* illustrates two different approaches to the problem of creating plays geared to black working-class issues. Maishe Maponya's *Umongikazi* focused on the problem of black nurses in a South African hospital (which the author called 'a microcosm of Apartheid'.) It used the techniques of multiple role play, caricature, flashbacks and revolutionary songs to show the radicalization of a young nurse, Nyamezo. One of the strongest influences on Nyamezo is a committed doctor (Lumumba) who condemns the racist medical training system in South Africa:

> Out of 23 million black people how many qualified black doctors have we got in the country – less than 4,000. And out of five million whites how many qualified white doctors are there? More than 12,000! The education system is rotten! And once you've come to this conclusion – you must start suspecting the teacher, suspect the book he reads from, suspect the school principal, the regional inspector and the whole bloody educational system![44]

The didacticism of this speech is very much in the spirit of the play which was geared to condemning the government-sponsored South African Nurses' Association (NASA) as a racist organization. *Umongikazi* appealed to black nurses to leave white private hospitals and join black hospitals. More to the point, the climax of the play consisted of a meeting of nurses which called for them (and any real nurses in the audience) to abandon NASA and set up an independent union of black nurses. According to Maponya, the Health Workers' Association at Baragwanath Hospital supported the play and encouraged their members to attend and to participate in the assembly at the end of the play.

Despite the strong support which Bahumutsi gave to black nurses in *Umongikazi* and to black miners in the 1983 play, *The Hungry Earth*, it consistently declined to solicit the participation of workers' associations and trade unions, or to become engaged in non-theatrical follow-up activities. Maponya explains why:

> I am not interested in working for another organisation like a trade union or educative body and having my art used as their vehicle. The integrity of my work would be compromised, and I value my independence.[45]

Tomaselli, who was a champion of *Umfunduso* and *Ilanga*, criticized Maponya's position as petty bourgeois for 'seeking individual recognition as an "artist"' without recognizing the 'collective contribution' of audiences and support institutions to his creative achievements.[46]

A scene from Maishe
Maponya's *Umongikazi*

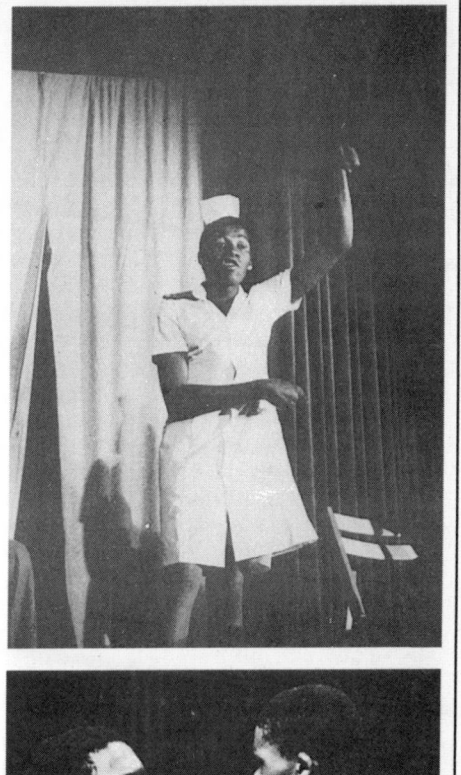

A scene from Matsemela
Manaka's *Egoli*

The kind of theatre which Tomaselli endorsed was represented by the Durban Workers' Cultural Local (DWCL) established in 1983, and not restricted to black members. The DWCL had its origin in the collaboration between Junction Avenue Theatre and the Metal and Allied Workers' Union over *Ilanga* in 1979. The theatre activists of Junction Avenue Theatre were determined to build on the experience, by finding ways of placing more control over the drama production and associated socio-economic campaigns in the hands of the workers.

Two of these early experiments were *Dikhitshening* and *The Dunlop Play*. *Dikhitshening* (In the Kitchen) was a play about domestic labour, which was performed for audiences of maids and their employers in suburban church halls. *The Dunlop Play* was a workshop production involving the members of the Metal and Allied Workers' Union at a Dunlop tyre factory in Durban. The plot, which was created through a combination of scripted scenes and improvisations, loosely followed the experiences of a particular worker, though Coplan comments that 'overall play structure and plotline were hard to establish', with extensive use being made of 'illustrative tableaux which were not plot oriented'.[47]

The rhetorical yet demotic style of *The Dunlop Play* is illustrated by these lines created by foundry worker and principal actor, Mandlenkosi Makhabu:

> I tell you this story to remind you of your life. I tell you this story so you will remember your struggle and the story of the struggle we fight.[48]

No finished version of *The Dunlop Play* was ever created; each performance drew upon audience responses, some of which became incorporated into later versions of the play. Songs which were created through workshops for the play were particularly popular, many of which, according to Coplan, became part of Durban's urban folklore.[49]

Leaders of the Metal and Allied Workers' Union quickly saw the advantage of the theatre activities. Actor Simon Ngubane noted the power of drama as communication. 'It makes a great difference if you can see what's happening rather than just hear it from other people.'[50] Coplan explains that some of the practical effects of *The Dunlop Play* were that 'workshop participants gained a new sense of self-confidence and self-worth, and several became leaders and were elected shop stewards at the next union election. New social networks were created among workers, and resistance to mistreatment stiffened.'[51] Another major advantage was that the mode of theatre production was extremely democratic, with anyone in the workshop able to contribute to the finished production. Thus the theatre, by providing a 'model of democratic, collective procedures of operation',[52] was able to influence the collective decision-making process even in the non-theatrical trade union activities.

After *The Dunlop Play* the DWGL was set up in 1984. The following year the Clairwood Trade Union and Cultural Centre was established, which received some support from radical lecturers at the University of Natal through the Culture and Working Life Project.

In 1986 one of the most spectacular and successful of the DWCL plays, *Mpophomeni* (The Long March), was created by workers at the Sarmcol factory, as a way of strategizing about the need for strike action to support union demands for improved conditions. The play was remarkable for the linkages it created between local factory grievances and socio-political struggles at the national and international levels. It also continued very effectively the audience participation techniques used in *Ilanga* and *The Dunlop Play*.

> At times the division between actors and audience is broken down by shrewd improvised means. 'Scabs' on stage threaten to report the audience (which boos them) to the boss, or the audience is invited to submit 'demands' for a fictional labour dispute taking place on stage.[53]

Such participation techniques were backed up by songs and chanting of slogans.

Not all the DWCL plays were successful. A workshop for Kwa Mashu street cleaners broke up because of divergent political tendencies among the participants. This reflected the violent, highly charged political atmosphere of Natal in the late 1980s. The DWCL, because of its association with COSATU, was identified as an ally of the ANC, even though the Province was a hotbed of support for the mainly Zulu Inkatha Movement. Several DWCL theatre activists were killed by vigilantes, including the road manager of *Mpophomeni* and the major actor, Simon Ngubane. The props and costumes of *Mpophomeni* were destroyed by vigilantes in Natal, as was the touring bus (probably through mistaken identity) by young 'comrades' in Soweto.

Despite these set-backs, the DWCL established itself as a very innovative exponent of economic and political self-advancement in the promotion of culture, through plays like *Mpophomeni* and the equally successful *Bambata's Children*. The impact which the DWCL had on the black trade union movement as a whole can be gauged by the election of its activist Mi Hlatshwayo as cultural coordinator for COSATU.

In a sense the localized nature and apparently economistic perspective of the DWCL plays made their confrontation with the apartheid regime somewhat more oblique than the Black Consciousness plays of the 1970s. This does not mean, however, that the tradition of flaunted theatrical defiance of apartheid completely died in the 1980s. Some groups such as Bopha, The Eye, Asazi and Hamba Dompas emerged in the townships in the 1980s, and made very politicized theatrical analysis of topical events, a genre which has been described as 'theatre of emergency'.[54] They were able to do this through living a marginal artistic existence without any permanent base, rehearsing in private garages, and showing plays on Sunday afternoons. (By 1985, owing to rising township violence, audiences were unwilling to travel to a theatre hall at night.)

Even a relatively well-established group like Bahumutsi lived something of a marginal existence, adapting scripts to local circumstances and finding impromptu solutions to the innumerable practical problems of performing in the African townships during a period of intense political upheaval. Steadman explains those problems:

> Anyone who knows the problem facing the black actor in South Africa will know that to expect a full cast to arrive on schedule is to expect a great deal. This presents no unsurmountable problem to Maponya's Bahumutsi group. To switch roles at a moment's notice, to use a stage manager as an impromptu actor, to cut, adapt, reverse and restructure in accordance with circumstances – these are the realities of performance in black theatre in South Africa.[55]

Such theatre bears the same kind of relationship to Western traditions of scripted theatre as guerrilla tactics do to conventional warfare. To that extent the Theatre of Emergency (or Theatre of the Dispossessed as it has also been called[56]) represented a strategic advance on the more confrontational approach of Black Consciousness theatre.

One group which provided a link between the Black Consciousness theatre of the 1970s and Theatre of Emergency, was the Soyikwa African Theatre Company. Matsemela Manaka, the leader of Soyikwa, established the company in 1976 in the wake of the Soweto uprising. At the outset it was predominantly a student group, and its early plays, like *The Horn*, were influenced by Kente's *How Long*, but it gradually acquired a more working-class character with mature plays like *Egoli*, an exposé of the lives of migrant mine workers. *Egoli* gained notoriety in 1979 when the text, published by Ravan Press, was banned, even though, in the following year, the play was performed at the Erlangen Festival in Germany.

Manaka was a very eclectic drama creator, influenced by indigenous South African traditions such as Xhosa story-telling, West African theatre, particularly that of Wole Soyinka, whose name was echoed in the title of the company, and the 'Poor Theatre' techniques of Polish director, Jerzy Grotowski, from whom Manaka learned the prime importance of the actor's creative bodily and vocal resources.[57] By all accounts Manaka extracted extraordinary performances from his cast of four intensively trained working-class actors. Davis had this to say about one of the actors in *Vuka*:

> Moalusi John Letwaba seems through the responsiveness of a well trained body and a controlling intellect able to change in stature, age, even racial feature with but a slight adjustment of posture, a hint of gesture ... When necessary, he can demonstrate a terrifying energy, filling the stage with not one but an army of the Dubula clan. Then as suddenly he magnifies the space around him, becomes a child, approaching the audience (Baba) with respect.[58]

Owing to such creativity of Soyikwa's actors, Steadman suggests that it would be more accurate to describe Manaka as not so much a playwright as a 'scribe' setting down the fertile originality of his actors.[59]

Another commonly observed feature of Soyikwa was its close relationship with the audience. At about the same time that working-class trade union theatre was learning the importance of breaking down barriers between audience and performer, the Soyikwa theatre was learning the same lesson in their more 'theatrical' productions. *Pula* illustrates the point. This play returned to *Egoli*'s theme of the gold-mining industry in the 1970s, basing its dramatic rhetoric on a contrast between a somewhat romanticized view of pre-colonial organic rural harmony and the deracination of industrial capitalism. Manaka constantly incorporated the audience in the play. For example, in one scene 'actors become customers in a shebeen, weaving in and out of the audience, talking to them, offering cigarettes. asking for money and generally structuring them into the action of the play'.[60] In an even more dramatic scene, illustrating an attack by *tsotsis* on the shebeen, the stage lights were deliberately cut, as if by accident, and actors playing *tsotsis* ran screaming into the auditorium as if to attack the audience, who represented the shebeen customers. Steadman comments:

> Reality and fiction became momentarily confused – in a situation where such

attacks in the township are not uncommon. For the audience there was a genuine concern that the action might not be part of the theatre experience.[61]

The breakdown of the play's frame was a feature also found in another celebrated example of 'Theatre of Emergency', *Asinamali*, created in 1984 by Mbongeni Ngema, one of the actors who participated in *Woza Albert! Asinamali* used an all-male cast to portray through flashbacks the contrasting lives of prisoners. The skilful, multi-language ensemble acting and the raw exposure of the degradations suffered by blacks under apartheid made *Asinamali* an explosively popular play.

What was particularly disturbing to authorities was *Asinamali*'s topicality, and the way it referred to real people and incidents through direct appeal to the audience. For example, one character referred to in the play, Bekani, was the name of a real youth worker who had assisted in the early days of the production. A pickpocket, Bro' Tony, was the name of a real pickpocket known in the townships. Most dramatic of all was a scene in which the characters suspected that there was a police informant in the audience; the actors broke out of role and went into the hall looking for him. In the atmosphere of suspicion and fear in the mid-1980s, this touched a raw nerve in township audiences. During a performance in Clement, a real informant in the audience, sent to spy on the play, became frightened and tried to escape. In an act of rage, disturbing for its blurring of art and life, some of the audience chased the informant outside the hall and killed him.[62] Violence was also instigated by the authorities against the cast and production team. A mob hired by the police to intimidate the performers broke into a theatre in Natal and killed the play's local promoter under the mistaken impression that he was Ngema.

There was bureaucratic opposition too. For a time, the Cape Town authorities tried to get a scene in which workers are forcibly checked for VD cut from the performance, although eventually it was allowed to remain. When the troupe arranged a tour of Zimbabwe in 1985, they were refused permission to leave South Africa. However, they were allowed to take the play to Europe and the USA, where in 1986 it created a large impact in both stage and TV performances. As with the Black Consciousness theatre of the early 1970s, there was strong pressure for the 'Theatre of Emergency' to find outlets outside South Africa, when its radically catalytic nature became too disturbing within.

Since 1974, many of the most committed participants in Black Consciousness and other forms of activist theatre fled to front-line countries and joined the liberation movements. Although in the early 1970s Black Consciousness appeared theoretically closer to the ideology of the Pan-African Congress (PAC) rather than the multiracial African National Congress (ANC), after 1976, the Black Consciousness activists in exile tended to join the ANC because of its more efficient and unified command structure, its wider international reputation, and above all for the far more credible presence and organization enjoyed by its military wing, Umkhonto we Sizwe.

One form that revolutionary drama took was the dramatized poetry reading with music, which became popular in the late 1970s at ANC and SWAPO rallies in Lusaka, Dar es Salaam, Maputo and Luanda. The ANC also made contributions to drama created in solidarity with the liberation struggle by non-South African theatre groups in the front-line states. A good

The Soyikwa players singing to the audience in a production of *Size*, performed in urban and rural venues in South Africa during 1988

A scene from *Katshaa!*, a collaborative play created by Zambuko/Izibuko from Zimbabwe in solidarity with the South African liberation struggle

example of such assistance is the ANC contribution (particularly songs, music, poems and uniforms) to the drama trilogy, *Soweto Flowers Will Grow*, created by Masautso Phiri and the Tikwiza Theatre in Lusaka (1977–9).[63]

Another important form of popular liberation drama which emerged in the front-line states was that of refugee theatre. The flood of young committed refugees arriving in Zambia, Tanzania, Angola, Botswana and Mozambique found a creative outlet for the frustration of exile in role play which cathartically re-enacted the oppression they had experienced in South Africa. For example, in Morogoro in Tanzania, at a school/camp for South African youths between the age of 14 and 22, refugees created a play about Hector Peterson, the first child killed in the Soweto uprising. Although the final message of the play was that youth should join Umkhonto we Sizwe, Anthony Akerman, who witnessed the Morogoro theatre, asserted that 'this is not a dramatized political pamphlet. What the children show on stage is their own story.'[64]

Some of the refugee plays, however, attempted to present situations rather more removed from the lives of the young artists. In another ANC camp in Angola, refugees created a play called *Vuyisili Mini* about a trade union leader who was hanged in 1964 on trumped-up charges of terrorism. To a large extent, the emphasis on documentary drama had an educational function. An even more ambitious project was a play called *Freedom in Our Lifetime*, created by refugees in Morogoro; the play was a kind of epic portraying the history of the ANC from 1955 to 1961. That period was well before the memories of the young artists; but the creation of a play about the crucial period when the ANC moved from peaceful resistance to armed struggle served to link the individual sufferings of the exiles to the broader struggle in South Africa.

Freedom in Our Lifetime dealt with such events as the Freedom Charter, the Treason Trial (of Mandela and others), Albert Luthuli's public burning of his pass book, the Sharpeville massacre, and the formation of Umkhonto we Sizwe. But the play was not a mere arid chronology of public events. As one of the play creators, Vuya Sibeko, commented, 'we tried to portray the history of the liberation struggle in such a way that there was little platform thundering and more emphasis on the musical feeling'.[65] The music consisted of ten revolutionary songs which acted as bridges between the scenes. Excessive didacticism was also avoided by showing the effects of the struggle against apartheid on ordinary people in domestic and work situations.

The play was created through research and improvisation by a six-person group of students. Without any conscious theoretical repudiation of Western art theatre, *Freedom in Our Lifetime* employed appropriate African dramatic techniques. Some parts of the performance, such as the fights, were fairly naturalistic; others were quite stylized, like the use of a rough piece of timber to symbolize a rifle. There was an emphasis on a simple dramaturgy, where the absence of set or complicated props was compensated by mime and ensemble grouping. The sense of collectivity also applied to the characterization, since the play presented 'the story of a people, not a few sharply defined, psychologically "rounded" individuals'.[66] Performances of *Freedom in Our Lifetime* were given in Dar es Salaam and Morogoro to Tanzanian audiences, but, normally, performances were intended for the refugees themselves as a form of self-reliant community education.

The theatre of refugees in the liberation movements was of nature a temporary, *ad hoc* mode of popular drama. Its eventual incorporation into mainstream South African theatre was made inevitable by the radical shift in South African politics which President de Klerk initiated in 1989. In particular the release of Nelson Mandela, the legalizing of the ANC, AZAPO, SACP and PAC, the dismantling of the apartheid legal machinery, and the 1994 democratic elections followed by the formation of the ANC-led Government of National Unity had enormous implications for popular theatre in South Africa. At the time of writing these events were too recent to analyse their cultural impact, but some indications can be tentatively suggested.

The major change was to break the polarized cultural field which had existed before 1990 between government-backed apartheid culture on the one hand and popular nationalist culture of resistance on the other. The legalizing of banned organizations marked the virtual end of exile theatre as well as of the cultural boycott; it also forced the ANC to face up to being the most powerful but by no means sole organ of political struggle for a democratic South Africa.

The impact of this was primarily to reduce the need for a theatre of strident radical rhetoric, which had been initiated in the early 1970s and renewed after the State of Emergency in 1985. Even before the unbannings some critics had questioned the effectiveness of such theatre of radical rhetoric which the South African censors were by the mid-1980s increasingly beginning to tolerate:

> ... we are allowed to watch the honkies being trampled on and the National Anthem being sodomized. We feel the clenched fists of the Azanian warriors, and we will say (with some relief): 'Well, this may not be a totally free society, but at least there is room for this expression' ... In so far as a state tolerates its critical artists it incorporates and disarms them.[67]

That the South African government was aware of this tactic is seen in the findings of the government-sponsored Schutte Commission, which in 1986 recommended the toleration of artistic dissent, since 'the expression of grievances often acts as a safety valve for pent up feelings'.[68]

Bob Mooki described the 'safety valve' theatre mode as 'the cathartic approach where people ... are only given a chance to vent their grievances and frustrations in the course of participating in a performance'. He felt that a genuine popular South African theatre 'should actually challenge the people themselves to look critically at their own situation and inculcate in them a sense of urgency and commitment to changing the situation'.[69] Mooki rejected the cathartic theatre of radical rhetoric in favour of a constructive theatre linked to specific sectoral community and working-class struggles:

> Popular theatre activists must be part and parcel of democratic foundations inside the country. They must find themselves in women's, civic, community, students', teachers', medical, religious organisations and foundations, where the collective experience of the people can be used as a weapon of struggle.[70]

As the exiles returned to South Africa, and the machinery of apartheid became dismantled, the opportunities for such strategic community theatre increased enormously. It was no longer a time for generalized consciousness-raising, but for grappling with a host of complex, localized political, economic, social and psychological problems, and to link those to the broader strategic struggle required to replace the authoritarian apartheid structures of control with those of democracy.

Since Mandela's release there has in fact been little sign of the complex committed theatre called by Mooki. Instead there has been a period of theatrical confusion which Robert Greig describes as 'a state of meltdown if you're pessimistic or fission and diversity if you're optimistic'. He explains:

> When Mandela was released old rigidities started falling away. Theoretically at least it was okay for theatre to be about whatever it liked ... The freedom had been recognized but has not been explored. Our theatre is in shock, dealing with ghosts of the past, nervousness in the present and anxiety in the future.[71]

The radical tradition of combative black theatre has survived, as in plays like John Matshikiza's 1993 production at the Market Theatre of a play from an earlier period, *Prophets in the Black Sky*. Far more popular, however, has been a revised tradition of the musical. A seminal production was Mbongeni Mgema's *Sarafina*, which opened at the Market Theatre in 1987. The plot, set during the Soweto students' revolt of 1976, deals with the radicalization of a young girl, who is embroiled in the riots and tortured by the South African police. In a moving fantasy scene she imagines playing the part of Nelson Mandela for a school musical. The fantasy merged with reality when Mandela was actually released while the play was still running. *Sarafina*, with its upbeat choral hits and glitzy choreography, had a phenomenally successful transfer to Broadway, where it won five Tony awards and was made into a film.

Ngema, who in 1992 married the star of *Sarafina* (Lelati Khumalo) in a big society wedding, became a South African media luminary, a role very different from his days as an actor in *Woza Albert!* or author/director of *Asinamali*. A sign of the change was that his 1993 musical *Magic at 4 am* did not open at the Market Theatre but at the Johannesburg Civic Theatre, which had previously been a bastion of white theatre. *Magic at 4 am* was the story of a miner with ambitions to be a successful boxer, a plot which was used as a peg on which to hang a variety of African dances and messages urging unity between ANC, PAC and Inkatha Freedom Party. Bafana Khumalo has criticized the musical for having an eye on the American export market rather than domestic needs, with scenes which 'resemble an anthropological textbook set to music'.[72]

Other authors who have turned to musicals in the 1990s are Matsemela Manaka with *Coming Home* and Duma Ndlovo (*Sheila's Day*).

The state of theatrical flux in post-1989 South Africa had institutional as well as aesthetic implications. The National Party government set up an organization in 1992, the National Association of Culture, headed by respected academic Njabulo Ndebele, and intended to oversee the introduction of democratic, non-racial artistic and performance traditions. There has been some conflict between the NAC and the ANC's Department of Art and Culture, but also considerable dialogue. This indicates that the controversial role of the performing arts may still continue in 'the new South Africa'.

In perhaps no other African country has there been such rapid transformation of society for theatre to mediate. Despite the problems of the transition, the astonishing fertility and versatility of South African popular performance, as well as the theoretical debates which accompanied the dialectic of theatrical activism, and its linkages to the broader history of anti-

Dancers from Smali Ndaba's 1993 musical, *Ubuntu Bomhlaba*

colonial struggle in Southern Africa, offered many lessons to popular theatre workers in those parts of Africa which had already achieved political independence but still faced domestic dictatorship and the hegemony of international economic-political controls.

Notes

1. Neto, p. 190.
2. Cabral, 1982. p. 201.
3. FRELIMO, p. 194.
4. Kahari, p. 4.
5. Kahari, p. 17.
6. Lewis, p. 147.
7. Berliner, p. 205.
8. Pongweni, p. 52.
9. The information about Muchetera is extracted from Ranger, 1982 and 1985.
10. Lan, p. 171.
11. Lan. p. 165.
12. Kidd. 1984a, pp. 6–9. Among the Korekore Shona the common name for *Pungwe* was *Morari*. The ZIPRA guerrillas had their own equivalent of Pungwe called *Ukwejisa*. For an alternative view of *Pungwe* see Frederikse, pp. 60–1.
13. My purpose in visiting the camps was collecting revolutionary songs for a play, *The War of Liberation*, in which I was part of the production team. The play, about the liberation struggle in Zimbabwe, was created by staff and students at the University of Zambia with advice from ZAPU (PF) cadres.
14. Kaarsholm, p. 255.
15. Kaarsholm, p. 255.
16. The information on exile theatre in the ZANU (PF) camps is mostly based on an interview (6 September 1983) with Fay Chung of the Zimbabwe Ministry of Education and Culture, and formerly a senior information and education officer in the ZANU (PF) camps in Mozambique.
17. Kaarsholm, pp. 259–60.
18. Kaarsholm, p. 260.
19. Coplan, 1979, pp. 186–90, and Coplan, 1985, chapter one.
20. Coplan, 1979, p. 207.
21. Kavanagh, 1985, p. 97.
22. Vanderbrouke, p. 50.
23. Kavanagh, 1976, p. 40.
24. Kavanagh, 1981, p. 88.
25. Coplan, 1979, p. 211.
26. Kente, in Kavanagh, 1981, p. 111.
27. Kente, in Kavanagh, 1981, p. 122.
28. McClaren, p. 252.
29. Kavanagh, 1979, p. 34.
30. ANC, p. 73.
31. Shezi, in Kavanagh, 1981, p. 72.
32. International Defence and Aid Fund, p. 61.
33. McClaren, p. 390.
34. Quoted in McClaren, p. 370.
35. International Defence and Aid Fund, p. 61.
36. Kavanagh, 1981, p. 127.
37. Quoted in International Defence and Aid Fund, p. 61.
38. Kavanagh, 1981, p. 12.
39. McClaren's term for multiracial drama performed in art theatres in downtown areas of major South African cities.
40. Tomaselli, 1981, p. 16.
41. Quoted in Tomaselli, 1981, p. 18.
42. Quoted in Tomaselli, 1982, p. 143.
43. Tomaselli, 1982, p. 144.
44. Maponya, pp. 10–11.
45. Quoted in Tomaselli and Muller, p. 47.
46. Tomaselli and Muller, p. 47.
47. Coplan, 1987, p. 23.
48. Quoted in Sole, p. 117.
49. Coplan, 1987, p. 24.
50. Quoted in Sole, p. 117.
51. Coplan, 1987, p. 24.
52. Sole, p. 119.
53. Sole, p. 118.
54. Ellerman *et al.*, p. 21.
55. Steadman, 1981, p. 8.
56. Davis, p. 38.
57. Steadman, 1988, p. 129.
58. Davis, p. 38.
59. Steadman, 1988, p. 117.
60. Steadman, 1988, p. 118.
61. Steadman, 1988, p. 123.
62. Ellerman *et al.*, p. 23.
63. Phiri.
64. Akerman, p. 41.
65. Quoted in Akerman, p. 40.
66. Akerman, p. 40.
67. Adam and Moodley, p. 157.
68. Peterson, p. 256.
69. Mooki, p. 5.
70. Mooki, p. 7.
71. Greig, p. 37.
72. Khumalo, p. 34.

12

Towards a Theatre of Popular Struggle

The history of popular theatre in Southern Africa is one of struggle by the people to gain control over their own culture. It is a complex dialectic in which new tactics of aggression and cultural control by the forces of imperialism have been countered by the people's own types of cultural resistance. A rather similar but more submerged dialectic towards increased control by the subaltern classes over the forms of popular theatre has taken place in independent Africa.

This book has outlined the double rape of African culture which has taken place in the last hundred years: first, the colonial intrusion which tried to devalue or even crush indigenous culture, and, second, the more insidious neo-colonial attempts at hegemony through co-opting the people's culture. Much of the history of popular theatre in Africa is about the instrumental uses of drama, but there has also been the beginnings of a revolt by the people against manipulatory populist theatre. In this last chapter I want to look at a case history of a genuine popular theatre movement, that of the Kamiriithu Cultural Centre in Kenya, as an example of what I believe, despite the repression it experienced, continues to provide a powerful influence on African popular theatre.

The Kamiriithu theatre had its origins partly in an indigenous tradition of cultural resistance to colonialism, and partly in the radicalization of intellectual popular theatre forms such as Theatre for Development and the university travelling theatre.

The influence of the University of Nairobi Travelling Theatre, though perhaps not ultimately the most important, is easiest to trace. As I pointed out in Chapter Seven, the University of Nairobi Travelling Theatre attempted to radicalize itself in the mid-1970s by using Kenyan languages and pitching plays towards popular audiences. The organizers became increasingly aware that theatre created by petty-bourgeois intellectuals for the people could easily be co-opted by the ruling classes.

One of the most subtle forms of neo-colonial control was through funding. African theatre institutions are nearly always desperately short of money. It seems natural, therefore, to receive funds from any available donors whether private or government. Many of the most illustrious African theatre projects have received funds from Western governments or multi-national companies. The Rockefeller Foundation, for example, was the major donor for the University of Ibadan School of Drama and for the Drama Studio in Accra. Esso contributed heavily to the Mbari Centre in Osogbo and Anglo-American to the Union of South African Artists. The British Council assisted the Makerere Free Travelling Theatre, and the art theatre achievements in francophone Africa would have been almost inconceivable without help from ORTF or the French government.

According to Kanyari Kaguongo the ultimate rationale behind 'the foreign ex-colonial camp's interest in the cultural activities of Africa is a public relations-cum-propaganda drive … Their target is our socio-economic system. They are trying to impose on us their models.'[1] The imposition is not a heavy-handed one, but a negative constraint, using the goodwill created by funding cultural events to forestall resentment against continued neo-colonial spheres of influence.

Kaguongo was a member of the Tamaduni Players, a Kenyan group formed in 1976 as a radical metamorphosis of the University of Nairobi Travelling Theatre. Although their first productions were fairly conventional (such as Césaire's *A Season in the Congo* and an adaptation of Okot p'Bitek's *Song of Lawino*) their Kiswahili version of *The Trial of Dedan Kimathi* (*Mzalendo Kimathi*) and a collectively created play about Nairobi's street urchins, *Portraits of Survival*, indicated a desire to reach more popular audiences. The Tamaduni Players, which included actor Karanja Njoroge and director Kimani Gecau, and which had a close relationship with Ngugi wa Thiong'o, attracted great public interest. In January 1980 the West German Embassy in Nairobi tried to sponsor *Mzalendo Kimathi*, but had their K.Sh 4,000 returned with a note stating:

> We (the Tamaduni Players) have resolved that Kenyan dramatic culture can only be developed in an atmosphere free of foreign involvement or interference; we find it invidious, therefore, to receive money from an agency whose prime activity is to generate and sustain the forms of economic and ideological domination to which we are fundamentally opposed.[2]

The impulse towards self-sufficiency and economic as well as aesthetic independence found a sympathetic chord in the rationale of the Kamiriithu Educational and Cultural Centre.

The background of the University of Kenya's Travelling Theatre is essential for understanding the Kamiriithu theatre, but it was by no means the only influence. The Kamiriithu theatre had its roots in indigenous Kenyan forms of resistance to colonialism. Ngugi wa Thiong'o cites the Kikuyu *Muthirigu* dances and songs of the 1930s as 'voicing people's rejection of forced labour, their disgust with cultural imperialism, their uncompromising opposition to political oppression, and their strong condemnation of Kenyan collaboration with colonialist enemy occupation'.[3]

Kamiriithu's origins as a highly populated community arose from the so-called 'Mau Mau' struggle for national liberation during the 1950s, when the British army of occupation razed the traditional village and created an 'emergency village' in Kamiriithu to house Gikuyu peasants who had been uprooted from their homes. This was an attempt to cut of the guerrillas' lines of support. It was the period in which paradramatic theatre forms played an important part in arousing African solidarity against British colonialism. The most celebrated example of this was the Gicamu theatre movement which the freedom fighter Dedan Kimathi started at Karuna-ini in Nyeri. Kamiriithu shared in similar types of cultural nationalism. Almost the sole amenity in Kamiriithu was a bare community hall built through self-help; in this hall the villagers held discussions and performed indigenous dances such as *Erithi* and *Nyangwicu* as a form of cultural resistance. That tradition was to prove a vital ingredient in the revived resistance to neo-colonialism in the late 1970s.

In 1957, after the containment of the nationalist military struggle, Kamiriithu was made into a permanent settlement. This was the period in which the seeds of class division in Kenyan society were sown. Under the Swynnerton plan, land was given to those Kenyans (such as the home guards) who collaborated with the colonialists, and not to those who resisted. That pattern of injustice continued after independence in 1963, and accounts for the explosiveness in post-independence Kenya of songs, dances and literature which refer back to the struggle against colonialism; they are a constant reminder that 'flag independence' did not mark the end of imperialism.

The period after independence also saw the establishment of the multinational Bata Shoe Company near Kamariithu and the spread of privately-owned plantations, for which the local population provided cheap labour. The overcrowding and economic exploitation created problems of illiteracy, appalling housing conditions and social anomie.

The marginalization effect of Kamariithu's economic and social articulation with capitalism was far from unique. Elsewhere in Africa there have been many educational, cultural and economic projects (often funded by international aid agencies) attempting to create community solidarity to face up to poverty. The Theatre for Development movement examined in Chapter Eight has been associated with meliorative projects of that kind. What was different about Kamiriithu was that the movement towards community revival came from the people themselves. The theatre activism grew out of a wider cultural and economic movement.

A group of peasants and workers got together in 1976 to revive the Community Centre (which had fallen into neglect since 1973). They formed the Kamariithu Community Educational and Cultural Centre (KCECC) – a forum for peasants and workers to discuss and plan strategies to improve adult education in the fields of literacy, health care and agriculture.

The KCECC set up a formidable committee system to tackle the different problems faced in Kamariithu. This operated in a very democratic way with a built-in system of self-criticism, so that even the poorest, least prestigious, most inarticulate member of the community could make his/her views felt. Although a community development officer, Nyceri wa Aamoni, was instrumental in setting up the management committee, it was emphatically not led by petty-bourgeois intellectuals. The committee was chaired by a peasant farmer, Adolf Kamau, and most of the other committee members were villagers.

The KCECC also established a system of regulations about the running of the Centre. One of the most interesting collective decisions was the regulation prohibiting alcohol at the Centre. Within a few weeks Kamariithu, which had previously been notorious for drunkenness, managed to cut down on alcohol consumption and crime – a sign of the self-respect which many community members started to acquire, and of their determination not to be seduced into false forms of escapism.

One of the most important sub-committees in the KCECC was that of literacy. The unusual feature of the Kamariithu literacy programme was that it was planned and organized by illiterates themselves, not by teachers or outside agents. The illiterates built up a syllabus based on problems of the village, such as land shortage, unemployment and the whole nexus of economic and social problems arising from poverty. Remarkably, there were no drop-outs from the 1976 literacy programme; by the end of the course all 56 participants had learned to read and write.

The literacy sub-committee was one of several which sympathetic radical intellectuals were invited to join. Ngugi wa Mirii, an adult educator specializing in literacy, encouraged students to use role play and satirical sketches as part of the 'script-writing' process to generate key words for reading and writing. This experience, along with the popularity of the touring version of *Mzalendo Kimathi*, encouraged the KCECC to think of creating a large-scale community play for themselves.

The sub-committees responsible for literacy and culture met to discuss the content of the play, which was to be based on problems facing Kamiriithu. They then commissioned Ngugi wa Mirii and his well-known cousin, Ngugi wa Thiong'o, to create a script of the play based on the autobiographies written by the newly literate peasants and on themes which had been collectively decided upon. In fact the whole play creation process was not really that of a conventional literary text. By June 1977 the Ngugis had written a draft of *Ngaahika Ndeenda* ('I will Marry When I Want'), which had the stamp of some of Ngugi wa Thiong'o's characteristic preoccupations – class conflict, the seduction of a woman as a metaphor for exploitation, and the comparison between the struggle against colonialism and the post-independence struggle against neo-colonialism. Nevertheless, the script was considerably revised by the KCECC after it was submitted to the cultural committee. For example, the Gitiiro opera sequence in the play was written 'word for word at the dictation of an illiterate peasant woman ... and performed step by step according to her choreography'.[4] Further modifications to character and dialogue in the play emerged during the rehearsals.

The community's involvement in the staging of *Ngaahika Ndeenda* was even more impressive, as Ngugi wa Thiong'o testifies:

> I saw with my own eyes peasants, some of whom had never once been inside a theatre in their lives, design and construct an open-air theatre complete with a raised stage, roofed dressing-rooms and stores, and an auditorium with a seating capacity of more than two thousand persons. Under a production team led by Gatoonye wa Mugoiyo, an office messenger, they experimented with matchsticks on the ground before building a small working model on which they based the final complex.[5]

The finished theatre on a site next to the Community Centre consisted of a raised wooden thrust stage with raked seating in a semi-circular arrangement (somewhat like a Greek amphitheatre) using the natural contour of a hill slope. There was a wooden backdrop with doors for entrances, and the whole complex was surrounded by a rough timbered fence, reminiscent of an African domestic stockade.

Over the entrance was an inscription saying 'Mucit wa Muingi' (Gikuyu) and 'Mji wa Umma' (Kiswahili), both meaning 'A People's Cultural Centre'. The spatial dynamics of Kamiriithu were very appropriate for popular participatory theatre. 'The flow of actors and people between the auditorium and the stage and around the stage and the entire auditorium was uninhibited.' Ngugi goes on to recount how at one performance singers climbed eucalyptus trees outside the theatre to sing, so that 'the entire village of 10,000 was the audience'.[6]

The theatre was not funded by donations either from international agencies or from a local Harambee (where bourgeois Kenyans distribute largesse as a form of ostentatious display of wealth). It was built instead through hard work at weekends by the community in a 'Harambee of sweat'. The creative energy which poured into the building of the theatre and into the rehearsals for *Ngaahika Ndeenda* transformed the whole of Kamiriithu by giving it a common purpose and a vision of a democratic method of community action.

> Everything was collective, open and public and it was fascinating to see a unity gradually emerge which virtually rubbed out distinctions of age, education, sex and nationality.[7]

The lack of discrimination against women was particularly notable. Women suffered what Ngugi termed a double oppression. 'As suppliers of labour in colonies and neo-colonies, they are exploited; and as women they suffer under the weight of male prejudices in both feudalism and imperialism.'[8] At Kamariithu women were prominent in the organizing committees and two-thirds of the whole community were women. Not surprisingly, the problems faced by women featured strongly in the finished play.

Ngaahika Ndeenda deals principally with the conflict between two families, the bourgeois Kiois and the peasant Kiguundas. The families are linked partly by the attempt of Kioi to take over Kiguunda's smallholding, and partly by the love affair between Kioi's son, Muhuuni, and Kiguunda's daughter, Gathoni. Muhuuni and Gathoni are no Romeo and Juliet uniting conflicting families. Their affair reinforces the symbolism of exploitation; Muhuuni impregnates Gathoni and refuses to accept responsibility. This is not only an example of male fecklessness, but also mirrors the central theme of the play – the exploitation of the peasants by the bourgeoisie.

The theme of class conflict is further reinforced by the use of flashback devices. The function of these is partly to show the history of solidarity which the peasants have created in their resistance to colonial oppression, and partly to analyse the false direction which destroyed that unity. An important character is Kiguunda's friend, Gicaamba, who recalls the unity and organization which existed during the struggle against the British from the 1920s onwards, and particularly the vows taken during the military struggle in the 1950s. In Gicaamba's words:

> Our nation took the wrong turn
> When some of us forgot those vows.[9]

Kamiriithu Theatre before its destruction in 1982

A scene from *Maitu Njugira* by Ngugi wa Thiong'o and the Kamiriithu Theatre

The notion of a return to the right direction, which was lost at independence, is crucial to the meaning of *Ngaahika Ndeenda*.

'The wrong turn' has had several manifestations. One is the escapism provided by the twin 'drugs' of alcoholism and religion. Christianity in particular is seen as a form of false consciousness which allows the bourgeoisie to feel justified in their wealth and provides promises of remote happiness in the next world for those oppressed in this.

More seriously disruptive is disunity. The ethnic conflicts, for example, between different Kenyan peoples, which were encouraged by colonialism, have continued to divide people after independence. A less discussed form of disunity exists between the sexes. Gicaamba explains how oppressed men scapegoat their women, instead of treating them as valuable allies against the class enemy.

> Do you think it was only the men
> Who fought for Kenya's independence?
> How many women died in the forests?
> Today when we face problems
> We take it out on our wives,
> Instead of holding a dialogue
> To find ways and means of removing
> darkness from the land.[10]

At the end of the play, after Kioi has swindled the title deeds from Kiguunda, the peasant and working-class characters in the play realize that disunity has prevented them from fighting successfully against exploitation.

> Let's unite and organize
> Organization is our club
> Organization is our sword.[11]

The stirring final song, with its litany-like repetition of 'Ngwatamira' (organization), is intended as a rallying cry for the subaltern characters in the play – but even more obviously for the real peasants and workers in the audience. In a way which resembled some types of pre-colonial theatre, as well as drama of the liberation movements and the more radical examples of theatre for development, the dialectic of *Ngaahiika Ndeenda* did not end with the last song but continued in the consciousness of popular audiences after the performance.

Ngaahika Ndeenda ran for several weeks, attracting an ever wider interest in the community, and eventually even in the national and international news media. The peasants and workers who travelled from neighbouring villages were particularly impressed by the organization and solidarity of Kamiriithu, and several groups started to plan similar community centres and theatres of their own; a budding 'Kamiriithu movement' seemed ready to flower.

On 16 December 1977, the local District Commissioner in Kiambu, even though he had never seen a performance, withdrew the licence for *Ngaahika Ndeenda* on the grounds that it encouraged class conflict, and was therefore a threat to public security. The banning threw into sharp relief the Ideological commitment of the Kenyan regime to neo-colonialism. It was particularly shocking because the production appeared to conform to the official government policy submitted to the 1976 UNESCO General Assembly of encouraging integrated rural development through theatre, song and dance. The problem was that government rhetoric about encouraging rural development did not envisage a vigorous, class-conscious, independent movement which was led by peasants and workers, and which ignored the paternalistic controls of Kenyan leaders.[12]

Ngugi wa Thiong'o expressed disgust that expatriates and wealthy Kenyans were allowed expensive and often decadent imported Western entertainment, 'but the peasants with clods of clay had no right to a theatre which correctly reflected their lives, fears, hopes, dreams and history of struggle; had no right to their creative efforts even in their own backyards'.[13] The prominence of Ngugi as an international literary figure and defender of Kamiriithu's achievements made him a particularly embarrassing figure for the government. Unable to crush the solidarity of the whole Community Centre, they chose to retaliate against its most famous spokesman. On 31 December 1977 Ngugi was detained in Kamiti maximum security prison.

The action partly succeeded in its aim of suppressing the spread of a 'Kamiriithu movement' to other villages and townships. But in Kamiriithu itself the spirit of the community was unbroken. The literacy classes continued with an even higher enrolment, the women's group expanded its economic struggle against employment conditions, and the orchestra and choir which had been founded for *Ngaahika Ndeenda* cut two very class-conscious, popular records.

In August 1978 President Kenyatta died, and one of the new President Moi's first actions was to review the cases of political detainees. On 12 December 1978 Ngugi wa Thiong'o was released. He returned to Kamiriithu, and, since he was unable to take up his old post of university lecturer, was able to devote himself full-time to work with the Kamiriithu theatre.

After the oppression unleashed by *Ngaahika Ndeenda*, the KCECC decided that the next play they worked on should avoid the dangerous material of a contemporary story, but should explore the resistance by the Kenyan people to colonialism. With hindsight, it is possible to see that that decision ignored the explosive nature of colonial history in a nation where the struggle against modern variants of imperialism was still being engaged.

The opera which emerged through the democratic system of play creation and communal song and dance (on the basis of Ngugi wa Thiong'o's original script) was called *Maitu Njugira* (Mother Sing for Me). It used the formal narrative device of a girl asking her mother to teach her old songs (of the 1930s) about the struggle against British imperialism. In the process the daughter learns, through a series of operatic flashbacks, about the resistance of the Kenyan people to such laws as Forced Labour (1896–1919), Native passes (1900), Hut Tax (1901) and Masters and Servants Act (1901). The play, which Ngugi called 'a dramatized documentary' relied heavily on stereotyped caricatures who sometimes merged into each other. These included Kanoru the colonial exploiter; Nyabarara and Mwendanda the sell-outs, Kang'ethe and Kariuki the people's heroes; and Nyatiria the heroic African beauty who resists the rape of the colonialists. The play used non-illusionistic techniques to show how these types kept recurring at different stages of Kenyan history. Bjorkman describes such a transition:

Kanoru finds his workers on their knees singing Christian hymns. He puts his whistle to his lips, but instead of a screech church bells are heard ... he decorates two soldiers with 'Christian Soldier medals'.[14]

At that point the character playing Kanoru assumed the costume of a bishop. The point is, of course, to show the collusion between the armed settler wing of colonialism and the missionaries.

Maitu Njugira was never legally performed in Kenya. The history of its banning by the Kenyan authorities shows the fear which neo-colonial governments have for genuine popular theatre.

The rehearsals for *Maitu Njugira* caused tremendous excitement. Over 400 people applied to audition for only 50 roles. During rehearsals, under the direction of Waigwa Wachira and Kimani Gecau, the community's exploration of its tradition of cultural resistance to imperialism was even more enthusiastic than with *Ngaahika Ndeenda*. In November 1981 the KCECC applied to the Nairobi Provincial Commissioner for a licence to perform *Maitu Njugira*. What followed was a campaign of 'official lies [and] ping-pong tactics from office to office'.[15] The chairman of the Cultural Committee, Ngugi wa Mirii, had to move backwards and forwards from the Provincial Commissioner in Nairobi to the District Commissioner's office in Kiambu, trying to obtain a licence which other theatre groups received without any question. This continued right up to the scheduled opening date at the National Theatre on 19 February. The licence to perform never arrived, and when the group came to the theatre singing songs from the play they were confronted by a patrol of police.

The group refused to give up the play. They moved to the university theatre to continue what were called rehearsals, but what were in effect free performances. For a week the hall was packed, a scene vividly described by Bjorkman:

> There were such crowds that the Uhuru Highway was blocked each afternoon. Rehearsals began at 6.30 pm but by 3 pm all the seats were already occupied; people sat on the stage, in the wings, on the stairs, and even in the light and sound rooms. The corridors and stairways were crowded and those who could not get inside sat on the grass outside and listened through open doors and windows.[16]

One of the performers explained that the audience 'would come on to the stage and take part in our closing song' and he described the whole week as akin to a festival.[17]

It was estimated that for the week of 'rehearsals' about 10,000 people saw *Maitu Njugira* ...

On 25 February the University of Nairobi authorities were told not to allow the university theatre to be used by the KCECC. On 11 March the Provincial Commissioner for Central Province, dressed, as Ngugi ironically commented, 'in the full regalia of his office (exactly the same uniform worn by British colonial provincial commissioners)',[18] revoked the licence for KCECC. On Friday 12 March three truckloads of armed police, led by the District Officer for Limuru, razed the open-air theatre at Kamiriithu to the ground.

It seems incredible that a play set in the colonial era should have triggered off a reaction of such violent iconoclasm. But the oppression was not entirely illogical. The history of the struggle against colonialism has always been a sensitive topic in Kenya precisely because the militant action of the Kenyan people was betrayed by the political compromise which led to Kenya's independence. The forces of imperialism continued to exert power, both through the remnants of the settler class, and through an 'expatriocracy' more subtle but no less powerful than the old colonialists. The Kenyan bourgeoise, in alliance with the expatriates, had a vested interest in not reviving memories about the struggle for freedom. As early as 1963 Kenyatta had told settlers in Nakuru, 'Kenyatta has no intention of retaliation or looking backwards, we are going to forget the past and look forward.'[19] *Maitu Njugira* had the precise effect of encouraging the peasants and workers of Kenya to 'look back' and draw comparisons between the injustice and poverty experienced under colonialism and 'the culture of silence and fear ... now carefully nurtured and preserved as a way of life by ... regimes still in the service of imperialism'.[20]

The creators of the play ensured that the comparative message was not lost on the modern audience. Several linguistic puns helped to overlay modern politics on the colonial story; for example, there were several allusions to the phrase 'Nyayo' which means 'footsteps', a slogan used by Moi to mean that KANU was following the footsteps of Kenyatta. One of the mimes in the *Maitu Niugira* also had a topical reference. An old man kept breaking a single piece of firewood at critical points in the play. Towards the end he put several pieces of firewood together and failed to break them. The message concerning popular unity applied not only to the struggle against colonialism, but to the struggle in the 1980s against Kenya's brutal post-colonial, one-party dictatorship.

The songs were also an effective reminder of modern struggles. The following song was always very popular:

> Come, come, come, everybody come.
> Bring what you have
> Bring your education
> Bring your intelligence
> Bring your generosity
> That we will be able to pull those that are left behind,
> That we will be able to awake those who are sleeping.[21]

According to one of Björkman's informants some of the audience would rush on to the stage at that point singing 'Wake up' along with the actors.[22] The same informant underlined the political significance of such moments.

> The real success of the play is that it made people question. That is why it made some people feel it was dangerous. You are shown history from the 1930s to 1982 and you start asking yourself 'What has gone wrong?'[23]

One diversionary tactic which opponents of *Maitu Nugira* adopted to distract from the political message was to draw attention to the language issue. Although the main spoken language was Kikuyu, the play in fact used very little dialogue, relying mainly on songs, dances, mime, slide projections, and crowds disciplined into scenes of ensemble action. The songs were in Kiswahili, Kikuyu, Kamba, Luo, Luhya and Giriana. As the songs commented on the action even the non-Gikuyu audience members could understand most of what was happening. The visual impact also appealed to those who could not follow the whole dialogue. One illiterate spectator commented on *Maitu Njugira*, 'It moved many people, people who are not prepared to read. Naturally workers and peasants have very little time to read. But there visually was like a whole reading.'[24]

Despite such popular appeal, the Kikuyu dialogue in *Maitu Njugira* led some people to accuse Ngugi and the KCECC of being parochial and 'tribal' ... Joe Kadhi, for example, a feature writer with the *Sunday Nation*, pronounced, '*Maitu Njugira* is just a tribal play and only attracts people who understand the Kikuyu language ... it should only be shown in Kikuyu villages and not at the National Theatre.'[25] Kadhi felt that drama in the National Theatre should only use the 'national' languages of English or Kiswahili.

Kadhi's recommendations were in fact in accordance with the practice of some Kenyan theatre groups. For example, Majitu theatre group, operating from an open-air community theatre in Masemo, did not use the local language (Luo) but Kiswahili. The director of Majitu, Felix Osodi, who produced several plays based on Luo folk-stories in 1982, said, with obvious reference to *Maitu Njugira*, 'dialect theatre will die a natural death since Kiswahili is taking root in Kenya's literature and will soon prove to be the language of the entire nation'.[26]

For Ngugi wa Thiong'o and KCECC, however, the use of Kikuyu was not a symptom of 'tribalism', but an indispensable channel, along with other Kenyan languages, for expressing indigenous culture. For them 'tribalism' was not produced by 'ethnic' languages, but by the class system, which drove people into making ethnic conflict a scapegoat for neo-colonial injustice, and regional patronage a substitute for class solidarity. In any case, *Maitu Njugira* did communicate to many non-Gikuyu, since its medium was less Kikuyu or any other language than the integrated 'total theatre' effects of music and mime.

The language issue was, in fact, a diversion. The authorities' intervention was really not in response to the formal elements of *Maitu Njugira*, but more to the class-conscious organizational skills which the KCECC showed in creating it, at a time of considerable instability in Kenya.

Within six months of the destruction of the Kamariithu theatre, many of the intellectuals who had identified with its brand of radical drama fled into exile, pre-empting the inevitable retaliation against them.[27] Over the following year, the Kenyan prisons did indeed fill with political prisoners, many of them intellectuals. The theatre exiles included Ngugi wa Thiong'o who went to Britain, Micere Mugo who went to the United States, and Kimani Gecau and Ngugi wa Mirii who went to Zimbabwe (to be joined later by Micere Mugo). This diaspora of Kenyan popular theatre activists has given rise to a debate about the role which intellectuals play in popular theatre. One view, fuelled by the reluctance which KCECC has shown to continue with drama since July 1982, is that intellectuals are objectively petty-bourgeois, and are therefore not capable of providing solid leadership to popular theatre movements during periods of intense class struggle. According to such a view, the involvement of highly visible academics drew unnecessary official attention to Kamariithu, and their subsequent exile was a 'betrayal' of the peasants and workers in the community. An alternative less dogmatic view is that the exile of the intellectuals was only in the short run a setback, since it also served to internationalize the popular theatre movement, and to prevent the Kenyan government from restricting it to the field of parochial political repression.

What I believe is not in doubt is the genuine commitment of the Kenyan intellectual theatre mentors. In order to achieve their solidarity with Kamiriithu they had to undergo what Ngugi calls 'an epistemological break'[28] with the neo-colonial linguistic and cultural heritage which they had introjected through years of Western education, in order to re-orient themselves to an indigenous tradition of African culture.

Although petty-bourgeois in class terms, they had gone a long way towards committing 'class suicide'[29] to create what Babu calls a 'new youth' capable of helping older peasants/workers to 'understand the stark realities of post-colonial Africa'.[30] The exile of the popular theatre intellectuals was the price they had to pay for their commitment to the struggle of the subaltern classes.

One of the positive features of the Kenyan theatre diaspora was that it accelerated the process of linkages between different African popular theatre movements, and their resistance to censorship or more violent oppression by entrenched neo-colonial regimes. The persecution meted out to Ngugi wa Thiongo and other Kenyan theatre workers won particular international attention, but it was by no means unique.

This book has already referred to the varied oppression faced by such artists as Hubert Ogunde, Ken Saro-Wiwa and Wole Soyinka in Nigeria, Byron Kawadwa, Jon Male and Dan Kintu in Uganda, and a long list of Black Consciousness activists in South Africa. Sierra Leone has also had a fairly representative history of struggle between theatre artists and the government. Sierra Leone's best-known playwright, Yulisa Amadu Maddy, got into trouble for his theatre activities, particularly his 1976 Krio play, *Big Berrin*, which showed the brutality and degradation resorted to by the inhabitants of an urban slum. In 1977 Maddy was detained; after his release he went into exile in Britain. John Kargbo's plays have also met constant harassment. Armed police discouraged audiences from seeing Kargbo's play on the politically powerful Poro secret society, *Let Me Die Alone*. In the same year, 1979, a second play, *Poyoh Ton Wahala*, an attack on high-level corruption, was banned and Kargbo was arrested at the point when his group, the Songhai Players, were about to perform. Two later plays, *Case of the Pregnant Schoolgirl* and *Ekundayo*, were also banned by the Sierra Leonean government.

The experiences of theatre workers in Kenya and Sierra Leone were shared by artists in other parts of Africa such as Malawi, Zaire and Somalia. But the increasing number of popular theatre exiles encouraged a spread of information, which meant that theatre martyrs had less chance of suffering in total isolation. By the late 1970s, many popular theatre workers were beginning to make links with artists in other countries, partly to share theatre experiences, ideas and strategies, but also to publicize the increasing persecution of popular theatre practitioners. International support organizations such as Canadian University Service Overseas (CUSO) and International Theatre Institute/International Amateur Theatre Institute (ITI/IATA) were very useful for providing funding and infrastructure for such networking. But there was also a growing demand for more direct information and support networks within Africa, and indeed the whole Third World.

The Theatre for Development workshops in Botswana, Zambia and Nigeria already referred to in Chapter Eight had provided focal meeting points for regional popular theatre artists. Such interchange of ideas and

Cover for a class-conscious
pidgin play from Nigeria

Mime dancer imitating President Banda at a
pro-democracy rally in Nsanje, Malawi, October
1993

information within Africa and between Africa and other parts of the Third World led to an influential conference/workshop on popular theatre held in Koitta, Bangladesh, in February 1983. Several popular theatre artists from Africa, such as Ngugi wa Mirii, Mapopa Mtonga, Dickson Mwansa, Penina Mlama and Salihu Bappa, attended the conference, where they were able to share with the rich theoretical analysis and practical experience of theatre workers from other parts of the Third World such as India, Indonesia, Malaysia, Sri Lanka, the Philippines, Bangladesh, Jamaica, St Vincent and Nicaragua. In addition, the workshop in the villages around Koitta allowed delegates to see possibilities and constraints of using popular theatre in the context of a Bangladeshi non-governmental grass-roots organization (Proshika) far more broad-based and independent than those found in most parts of Africa. Towards the end of the dialogue the delegates set up a rather ambitious organization of popular theatre workers, the International Popular Theatre Alliance (IPTA), with a rotating secretariat, intended to provide a support base for networking at the national, regional, sub-regional, continental and international levels.

Another opportunity for African popular theatre networking took place later in 1983 at a workshop in Morewa, Zimbabwe. The three-week workshop did not depart significantly from the *Laedza Batanani* Theatre for Development model, except that it was rather longer, and had a larger support structure. In some ways the Morewa workshop was a substitute for a proposed visit by the Kenyan KCECC in 1982 with *Maitu Njugira*, which had been intended by the Zimbabwe government as a model for the development of a rural community theatre in post-independence Zimbabwe. The Kenyan government prevented KCECC from going to Zimbabwe in 1982, but some of the spirit of Kamariithu was able to travel to Zimbabwe in the exiled Kenyan delegates at the 1983 Morewa workshop.

One significant feature of Morewa was the high number of international delegates from countries such as Kenya, Zambia, Nigeria, Tanzania, Ethiopia, Botswana, Swaziland, Malawi and Ghana, where Theatre for Development was relatively well established, as well as francophone theatre artists from Zaire, Mali and Senegal, to whom Theatre for Development was a rather new concept. It also included Felix Sugirtharaj, a skilled veteran from the community theatre tradition in Southern India.

The high level of international representation, along with rather heavy-handed intervention from some of the Zimbabwean bureaucrats, prevented any very radical, local achievements at the workshop. What was significant was the spread of the popular theatre idea to theatre practitioners from many African countries, and the consolidation of networking infrastructures to support popular drama and the rights of theatre artists. At a three-day conference in Harare at the end of the workshop, another networking organization, UAPA (the Union of African Performing Artists), was established linked to the OAU in Addis Ababa, and serving the interests of a broader spectrum of African performing artists than the popular-oriented IPTA.

UAPA and, even more vigorously, IPTA campaigned in 1983 and 1984 for the rights of the theatre workers suffering detention, harassment or intimidation in such diverse Third World countries as Kenya, Malawi and the Philippines. In the ensuing years, however, owing to administrative and communication problems, IPTA failed to fulfil its promise to mobilize radical popular theatre at an international level. UAPA, though plagued by fierce personality clashes, did continue its more restricted programme of net-working among African theatre enthusiasts, and attempted to establish a college in Harare designed to train artists in performance skills. Despite the modest achievements of IPTA and UAPA their very establishment points to the beginning of transnational solidarity among theatre workers at the base, which provides a potential focus for resistance to state-controlled cultural hegemony.

Some measure of the success of networking within different regions of Africa has been the rapid spread of various theoretical models and strategies of popular theatre activism since the main wave of independence in the 1960s. Sometimes this has been through a conscious application of external theories, as with ABUTC's use of models derived from Latin America and Asia. On other occasions it has derived from a realization that local theatre practice has had much in common with the practice of other regions. This seems to be the case in South Africa, for example, where intellectual workers supporting the DWCL have realized its similarity with the achievements of ABUTC and Kamiriithu.

The political changes which have taken place in many African countries since 1959, following the wind of democratization, have had a cultural dimension. In particular, the tradition of satirical partisan song/theatre has revived. For example, in Malawi the period of political debate before and after the 1993 June 14 referendum on multi-party democracy was accompanied by an explosion of songs which denounced the *Mbumba* system established by the Malawi Congress Party (MCP), and replaced it with songs celebrating the power of the people, parodying the *Mbumba* sycophantic performances, and lampooning the political leadership of the Banda regime.[31]

Whether it is in the arena of formal institutionalized drama, or in the people's own informal performances, a cross-fertilization of ideas has taken place through which a mode of committed popular theatre with an African identity has begun to emerge. It is a theatre which, like some forms of indigenous ritual performance, blurs the distinction between art and reality, or, to put it perhaps more accurately, between metaphor and metonymy.[32] But, whereas the pre-colonial theatre often served to validate existing norms, the post-colonial popular theatre, at its most radical, challenges the values and structures of the new state hegemonies.

Sometimes those challenges have taken on a clearly confrontational form, as with Kamiriithu, but in nations with a more open tradition of dialogue the state reaction has been less repressive. The Paukwa Theatre of the University of Dar es Salaam, for example, has over the years found effective dramatic formulas for criticizing the Tanzanian government's political errors or broken promises. Penina Mlama, the author and director of *Remedy for Rot*, said of that Paukwa play:

> It guaranteed so much debate that the central executive of the national ruling party requested to see it. So we had to have a special show for the Party, the Central Committee and the National Executive Committee. We didn't understand why they wanted to see it. Of course, there was a lot of debate, people were saying things like 'now you are being accommodated' and so on. But the high officials saw and discussed the play and one got the impression that they felt it was important for them to know what the people were thinking even if it was not in their favour.[33]

Although the dialogue between popular theatre artists and government, represented by Paukwa on the one hand and the confrontational tactics of Kamiriithu on the other, seems to represent different poles of radical theatre practice, they both represent a willingness to become committed to a cultural struggle for democratic channels of communication and the empowerment of popular organizations. Kaarsholm has eloquently extolled the virtues of using theatre to cure the collective psychic traumas inflicted by autocracy:

> By furthering articulation theatre may bring about necessary confrontations, but at the same time it helps to heal conflict by exposing wounds to the fresh air, bringing the repressed out into the open and making it available for transformation through discussion and communication.[34]

Despite the promise of community health which drama offers, it seems inevitable that popular theatre workers will not achieve easy victories. Solidarity, whether within communities, trade unions, national groupings or international networks, is only possible through the development of strong democratic organizations at the base, to which popular theatre can provide theoretical, strategic and imaginative nourishment, and from which it can receive economic, social and ideological support. The KCECC, for example, appeared threatening to the Kenyan bourgeoisie precisely because its achievements came not from metropolitan bureaucratic leaders but from the organized energy and skills of the subaltern classes. The experience of Kamiriithu provides a warning of the severity which popular struggle can take even in the domain of art. It also showed that African 'workers and peasants can rise to heights hitherto unknown and undreamt of in the area of modern performing arts'.[35] The full extent of that potential is still to be put into practice.

This chapter is ending on a speculative note about the direction of radical popular theatre in Africa. That uncertainty is, in fact, built into the whole book; the structure of *African Popular Theatre* has a somewhat contrived 'suspense', the dénouement of which is bound to be anti-climactic in its attempt to trace the dialectic of African popular theatre. In my enthusiasm to chart key historical movements, I may have overemphasized a chapter-by-chapter 'narrative' account of popular drama – giving insufficient weight to the continuity of African theatre forms. That, of course, would be a mistake; all the modes of theatre examined in this book, however transformed, have survived the assaults of colonialism, racism, neo-colonialism, capitalism, urbanization, the cash nexus and social anomie. Nevertheless, historical changes have caused a constant interaction between drama practitioners, theatre forms and economic/social imperatives. Such changes mean that my account is dated and inaccurate even as I write about it. In order to transcend the artificial formalism of a critical narrative, *African Popular Theatre* can only refer the reader back to the continuing struggles and durable creativity of African popular theatre praxis.

Notes

1. Quoted in Alot, p. 128.
2. Quoted in Alot, p. 128.
3. Ngugi wa Thiong'o, 1981, p. 65.
4. Ngugi wa Thiong'o, 1981, p. 190.
5. Ngugi wa Thiong'o, 1981, p. 190.
6. Ngugi wa Thiong'o, 1986, p. 42.
7. Ngugi wa Thiong'o, 1983, p. 121.
8. Ngugi wa Thiong'o, 1983, p. 119.
9. Ngugi wa Thiong'o and Ngugi wa Mirii, p. 113.
10. Ngugi wa Thiong'o and Ngugi wa Mirii, p. 105.
11. Ngugi wa Thiong'o and Ngugi wa Mirii, p. 116.
12. A little later, in 1979, partly perhaps as a way of co-opting the Kamariithu ideals, President Moi gave a mandate to the Kenyan National Council of Social Service to survey the idea of converting rural beer halls into community theatres. The chief executive of KNCSS described the project in these terms:

    > It will be an informal theatre in people's own vernacular, a theatre to revive the culture of the people in different areas. They will have discussions on what was the meaning of ritual songs or plays staged to educate them on any problems they face.

    Quoted in Asaru-Otoru, p. 6.
13. Ngugi wa Thiong'o, 1981, p. 79.
14. Björkman, p. 62.
15. Ngugi wa Thiong'o, 1982, p. 137.
16. Björkman, p. 59.
17. Björkman, p. 60.
18. Ngugi wa Thiong'o, 1983, p. 127.
19. Quoted in Leys, p. 62.
20. Anonymous, 1983.
21. Björkman, p. 17.
22. Björkman.
23. Quoted in Björkman, p. 18.
24. Quoted in Björkman, p. 14.
25. Kadhi, p. 6.
26. Quoted in Mutahi, p. 15.
27. A few months before the attempted coup of August 1982.
28. Ngugi wa Thiong'o, 1986, p. 44.
29. Cabral, 1980, p. 36.
30. Babu, p. 36.
31. See Anonymous, 1993, p. 6 and Kerr, 1993, pp. 31-2.
32. For further discussion of this distinction see Tomaselli and Muller.
33. Penina Muhando Mlama, interviewed in James, 1990, p. 81.
34. Kaarsholm, p. 274.
35. Ngugi wa Thiong'o, 1981, p. 189.

Bibliography

(Unless otherwise stated, translations from the French are by the author)

Abah, Ogah and Etherton, Michael, 1982, 'The Samaru Projects: Street Theatre in Northern Nigeria', *Theatre Research International*, 8/3, London.

Abdulaziz, M. H., 1973, 'Tanzanian National Language Policy and the Rise of Swahili Political Culture', in Cliffe, L. and Saul, P. (eds) *Socialism in Tanzania, Vol. I, Politics*, Tanzania Publishing House, Dar es Salaam.

ABU Collective, 1982, 'Popular Drama Work in Northern Nigeria', *Third World Popular Theatre Newsletter*, 1/1, Lusaka.

Achebe, Chinua, 1960, *No Longer at Ease*, Heinemann, London.

Achebe, Chinua, 1974, *Arrow of God*, Heinemann, London.

Achebe, Chinua, 1986, *Things Fall Apart*, Heinemann, London.

Acquaye, Saka, 1970, 'Modern Folk Opera in Ghana', *African Arts*, 4/2, Autumn, Los Angeles.

Adam, Herbert and Moodley, Kosila, 1986, *South Africa Without Apartheid*, UCLA Press, Berkeley.

Adedeji, Joel, 1969, 'Traditional Yoruba Theatre', *African Arts*, 3/1, Los Angeles.

Adedeji, Joel, 1972, 'Folklore and Yoruba Drama: Obatala as a Case Study', in Dorson, R. M. (ed.) *African Folklore*, Garden City, New York.

Adedeji, Joel, 1976, 'Trends in the Content and Form of the Opening Glee in Yoruba Drama', in Lindfors, Bernth (ed.) *Critical Perspectives on Nigerian Literature*, Three Continents, Washington, DC.

Adedeji, Joel, 1978a, 'Poetry of the Yoruba Masque Theatre', *African Arts*, 11/3, Los Angeles.

Adedeji, Joel, 1978b, 'Alarinjo: The Traditional Yoruba Travelling Theatre', in Ogunba, Oyin and Irele, Abiola (eds) *Theatre in Africa*, Ibadan University Press, Ibadan.

Adedeji, Joel, 1985, 'The Theatre and Contemporary African Political Development', *African Theatre Review*, 1/1, Yaoundé.

Adelugba, Dapo, 1973, 'Nigeria Theatre Survey', *New Theatre Magazine*, 12/2, London.

Ahmadu Bello University, 1982, 'Popular Drama in Northern Nigeria', *Third World Popular Theatre Newsletter*, 1/1, Lusaka.

Ahmed, Umaru B., 1985, 'Nau'o' in *Wasannin Kwaikwayon Hausawa/A Taxonomy of Hausa Drama*, Ahmadu Bello University, Zaria.

Aidoo, Ama Ata, 1972, 'Interview', in Duerden, D. and Pieterse, C. (eds) *African Writers Talking*, Heinemann, London.

Akerman, Anthony, 1978, 'Refugee Theatre in Tanzania', *Theatre Quarterly*, 8/30, London.

Alot, Magaga, 1980, 'Kenyan Players Take Independent Line', *New Africa*, October, London.

Alston, J. B., 1989, *Yoruba Drama in English: Interpretation and Production*, Edwin Meller Press, Lewiston, Lampeter, Queenstown.

Amankulor, J. N., 1986, 'Masks as Instruments for Dramatic Characterisation in Traditional Igbo Society', *African Theatre Review*, 1/2, Yaoundé.

Ames, David, 1973, 'A Socio-Cultural View of Hausa Musical Activity', in d'Azevedo, Warren (ed.) *The Traditional Artist in African Societies*, Indiana University Press, Bloomington.

ANC, 1977, 'Against Apartheid Culture', *Africa Development*, 2/4, Dakar.

Anonymous, 1977, 'The Francophone Film Industry', *Africa*, 68, January, London.

Anonymous, 1979, 'The Culture Vulture', *This Magazine*, Spring, Toronto.

Anonymous, 1983, 'Programme Notes for Maitu Njugira', *Lift 83*, London.

Anonymous, 1986, 'Merger Talks: The Dust May Settle But ...', *Theatre Magazine*, 3, Lusaka.

Anonymous, 1993, 'Referendum Songs', *The Monitor*, 1/21, 18 June, Blantyre.

Apedo-Amah, Ayayi Togoata, 1985, 'Les Deux Schèmes-stéréotypes actuelles traditionnels du concert-party togolais', *African Theatre Review*, 1/1, Yaoundé.

Armes, Roy, 1986, 'The Development of Black African Cinema', paper presented to African Studies Association of United Kingdom, 17–19 September, University of Kent, Canterbury.

Armstrong, Robert G., 1978, 'Traditional Poetry in Ladipo's Oba Koso', *Research in African Literatures*, 9/3, Austin.

Arrighi, G. and Saul, J. S., 1973, 'Class Formation and Economic Develoment in Tropical Africa', in Bernstein, H. (ed.) *Underdevelopment and Development: The Third World Today*, Penguin, London.

Asanga, Siga, 1985, 'The Idea of African Theatre', *African Theatre Review*, 1/1, Yaoundé.

Asaru-Otoru, Assumpta, 1979, 'Kenyan Beerhalls to be Turned into Theatres', *Zambia Daily Mail*, 22 May, Lusaka.

Awoonor, Kofi, 1972, 'Interview' in Duerden, Denis and Pieterse, Cosmo (eds) *African Writers Talking*, Heinemann, London.

Awoonor, Kofi, 1973, *This Earth My Brother*, Heinemann, London.

Awoonor, Kofi, 1975, *The Breast of the Earth*, Doubleday, New York.

Axworthy, Geoffrey, 1973, 'The Performing Arts in Nigeria', *New Theatre Magazine*, 12/2, London.

d'Azevedo, Warren, 1973, *The Traditional Artist in African Societies*, Indiana University Press, Bloomington.

Babu, Abdul R. M., 1981, *African Socialism or Socialist Africa?*, Zed Books, London.

Badian, Seydou, 1973, *La Mort de Chaka*, Présence Africaine, Paris.

Bame, K. N., 1968, 'Comic Play in Ghana', *African Arts*, 2/2, Los Angeles.

Bame, K. N., 1985, *Come to Laugh: African Traditional Theatre in Ghana*, Lilian Barber Press, New York.

Banham, Martin, 1976, *African Theatre Today*, Pitmans, London.

Bappa, Salihu, 1979, 'Popular Theatre in Social Education and Community Action', research paper, Ahmadu Bello University, Zaria.

Bappa, Salihu, 1983, 'The Maska Project in Nigeria', *Culture and Rural Development*, 3rd and 4th Quarter, United Nations.

Barber, Karin, 1982, 'Popular Reaction to the Petro-Naira', *Journal of Modern African Studies*, 20/3, London.

Barber, Karin, 1987, 'Popular Arts in Africa', *African Studies Review*, 30/3, Emory.

Barr, Charles, 1974, 'Projecting British Charter at Ealing Studios', *Screen*, 15/2, London.

Batsford, Rob, 1973, 'Zambians Steal the Show at TAZ Festival', *Stage*, September, Lusaka.

Baumann, Richard, 1975, 'Verbal Art in Performance', *American Anthropologist*, 77/2, Boston.

Beattie, John, 1969, 'Spirit Mediumship in Bunyoro', in Beattie, John and Middleton,

John (eds) *Spirit Mediumship and Society in Africa*, Routledge & Kegan Paul, London.

Beier, Ulli, 1958, 'The Egungun Cult Among the Yorubus', *Présence africaine*, 17/18, Paris.

Beier, Ulli (ed.), 1967a, *Three Nigerian Plays*, Longman, London.

Beier, Ulli, 1967b, *Introduction to African Literature*, Longman, London.

Beier, Ulli, 1968, *Contemporary Art in Africa*, Pall Mall, London.

Beier, Ulli, 1981, 'E. K. Ogunmola: A Personal Memoir', in Ogunbiyi, Yemi (ed.) *Drama and Theatre in Nigeria: A Critical Source Book*, Nigeria Magazine Publications, Lagos.

Beik, Janet, 1987, *Hausa Theatre in Niger: A Contemporary Oral Art*, Gorland Publishing Inc., New York and London.

Bellman, Beryl L. and Jules-Rosette, Benetta, 1977, *A Paradigm for Looking: Cross Cultural Research with Visual Aids*, Ablex Publishing Corporation, Norwood.

Ben-Amos, Paula and Omorogie, Osaranrem, 1969, 'Ekpo Ritual in Avbiana Village', *African Arts*, 2/4, Los Angeles.

Berger, Peter, 1974, *Pyramids of Sacrifice*, Allen Lane, London.

Berliner, Paul F. 1978, *The Soul of Mbira: Music and Traditions of the Shona People of Zimbabwe*, UCLA Press, Los Angeles.

Björkman, Ingrid, 1989, *Mother, Sing for Me: People's Theatre in Kenya*, Zed Books, London.

Bloom, Harry and Williams, Pat, 1961, *King Kong*, Collins, London.

Boal, Augusto, 1979, *Theatre of the Oppressed*, Pluto Press, Canada.

Bonneau, R., 1972, 'Aperçu du théâtre ivoirien d'expression française avant l'indépendance', *Annales de l'Université d'Abidjan*, Abidjan.

Boughedir, Ferid, 1982a, 'Aesthetics: The Two Major Schools of Cinema', in Martin, Angela (ed.) *African Films: The Context of Production*, BFI Dossier No. 6, British Film Institute, London.

Boughedir, Ferid, 1982b, 'Controlling the Market', in Martin, Angela (ed.) *African Films: The Context of Production*, BFI Dossier No. 6, British Film Institute, London.

Boulouger, Pierre, 1974. *Le Cinéma colonial*, Segher, Paris.

Bowman, Mark Ralph, 1982, 'Nkenge's Journey from Zaire to Bloomington', *Africa Now*, April, London.

Boxer, R., 1965, *Portuguese Society in the Tropics*, Wisconsin University Press, Wisconsin.

Boyd-Barrett, Oliver, 1977, 'Media Imperialism: Towards an International Framework for the Analysis of Media Systems', in Curran, J., Gurevitch, M. and Woolacott, J. (eds) *Mass Communication and Society*, Edward Arnold, London.

Brink, James, 1977, 'Bamana Kote-tlon Theatre', *African Arts*, 10/4, Los Angeles.

Brink, James, 1978, 'Communicating Ideology in Bamana Rural Theatre Performance', *Research in African Literatures*, 9, Austin.

Burnet, Donald and Njama, Karari, 1966, *Mau Mau from Within*, McGibbon and Kee, London.

Byram, R., Moitse, F. and Boeren, A., 1981, *The Report of the Workshop on Theatre for Integrated Development*, University of Swaziland, Manzini.

Cabral, Amilcar, 1980, *Unity and Struggle*, Heinemann, London.

Cabral, Amilcar, 1982, 'On Culture and the New Man', in de Bragannca, Acquino and Wallerstein, Immanuel (eds) *The African Liberation Reader: Documents of the National Liberation Movements, Vol. 3: The Strategy of Liberation*, Zed Books, London.

Cameron, Kenneth, 1994, *Africa on Film: Beyond Black and White*, Continuum, New York.

Césaire, Aimé, 1973, *Une Saison au Congo*, Editions du Seuil, Paris.

Chambulikazi, Eberhard, 1982, 'Popular Theatre in Tanzania', *Third World Popular Theatre Newsletter*, 1/1, Lusaka.

Chifunyise, Stephen, 1978, 'The Formative Years: An Analysis of the Development of Theatre in Zambia from 1950 to 1970', research paper, University of Zambia, Lusaka.

Chifunyise, Stephen, 1990, 'Trends in Zimbabwean Theatre Since 1980', *Journal of Southern African Studies*, 16/2, London.

Chifunyise, Stephen and Kerr, David, 1984, 'Popular Theatre in Zambia: Chikwakwa Reassessed', *Theatre International*, 11 and 12, Paris.

Chifunyise, Stephen, Dall, F. and Kerr, D., 1978, *Theatre for Development*, International Theatre Institute, Lusaka.

Chirwa, Jacob, 1979, 'Dance in a Changing Society: The Mganda Dance Among the Chewa of Katete District', research paper, University of Zambia, Lusaka.

Chirwa, Jacob, 1988, *The Song as a Medium of Social and Literary Comment: A Study of Songs in the Mganda Dance Practised in Mwase Lundazi 1937–1958*, unpublished MA Thesis, University of Zambia, Lusaka.

Chung, Fay, 1973, 'Critic is Out of Touch with Zambian Theatre', *Stage*, September, Lusaka.

Clapperton, Hugh, 1966, *Journal of a Second Expedition into the Interior of Africa*, Frank Cass, London.

Clark, Ebun, 1979, *Hubert Ogunde: The Making of Nigerian Theatre*, University Press, Ibadan.

Clark, John Pepper, 1964, *Three Plays*, Oxford University Press, London.

Clark, John Pepper, 1966, *Ozidi*, Oxford University Press, London.

Cohen, Robert, 1982, 'Resistance and Hidden Forms of Consciousness among African Workers', in Johnson, Hazel and Bernstein, Henry (eds) *Third World Lives of Struggle*, Heinemann/Open University, London.

Collins, E. J., 1976, 'Comic Opera in Ghana', *African Arts*, 9/2, Los Angeles.

Colson, Elizabeth, 1969, 'Spirit Possession Among the Tonga' in Beattie, John and Middleton, John (eds) *Spirit Mediumship in Africa*, Routledge & Kegan Paul, London.

Cook, David, 1965, 'Report of the Makerere Travelling Theatre, 1965', research paper, University of Makerere, Kampala.

Cook, David, 1966, 'Theatre Goes to the People', *Transition*, 25, Kampala.

Cook, David and Lee, Miles, 1968, *Short East African Plays in English*, Heinemann, London.

Coplan, David, 1979, 'The African Performance and the Johannesburg Entertainment Industry: The Struggle for African Culture on the Witwatersrand', in Bozzoli, Belinda (ed.) *Labour, Township and Protest*, Ravan Press, Johannesburg.

Coplan, David, 1985, *In Township Tonight: South African Black City Music and Theatre*, Longman, Harlow.

Coplan, David, 1987, 'Dialectics of Tradition in Southern African Black Popular Theatre', *Critical Arts*, 4/3, Durban.

Cornevin, Robert, 1970, *Le Théâtre en Afrique noire et à Madagascar*, Le Livre Africain, Paris.

Couzens, Tim, 1985, *The New African: A Study of the Life and Work of H. I. E. Dhlomo*, Ravan Press, Johannesburg.

Crehan, Stewart, 1987, 'Politics and Myth in Recent Zambian Drama', *New Theatre Quarterly*, 3/9, London.

Crehan, Stewart, 1990, 'Patronage, the State and Ideology in Zambian Theatre', *Journal of Southern African Studies*, 16/2, Oxford.

Crow, Brian and Etherton, Michael, 1980, 'Popular Drama and Popular Analysis in Africa', in Kidd, R. and Colletta, N. (eds) *Tradition for Development*, German Foundation for International Development, Berlin, and Institute for Adult Education, Toronto.

Crowley, Daniel J., 1971, 'Folktale Research in Africa', open lecture, 29 April, University of Legon, Accra.

Cutter, Charles H., 1968, 'The Politics of Music in Mali', *African Arts*, 1/3, Los Angeles.

Dadié, Bernard, 1956, *Climbié*, Seghers, Paris.

Dadié, Bernard, 1970a, *Monsieur Thogo-Gnini*, Présence Africaine, Paris.

Dadié Bernard, 1970b, *Béatrice du Congo*, Présence Africaine, Paris.

Dadié, Bernard, 1983, *Les Voix dans le vent*, NEA, Abidjan.

Dall, Frank, 1980, 'Theatre for Development: An Appropriate Tool for Extension Communication and Non-Formal Education in Zambia', *Educational Broadcasting International*, 13/4, Toronto.

Davidson, Basil, 1971, 'Pluralism in Colonial African Societies: Northern Rhodesia/ Zambia', in Kuper, L. and Smith, M.G. (eds) *Pluralism in Africa*, University of California Press, Berkeley, Los Angeles.

Davis, Myra, 1987, 'Vuka: Sharing the Image', *Critical Arts*, 4/3, Durban.

Decock, Jean, 1968, 'Pré-théâtre et rituel', *African Arts*, 1/3, Los Angeles.

Dhlomo, H. E., 1935, *The Girl Who Killed to Save*, Lovedale Press, Lovedale.

Diawara, Manthice, 1992. *African Cinema, Politics and Culture*, Indiana University Press, Bloomington.

Drewal, H. J., 1978, 'The Arts of Egungun Among Yoruba Peoples', *African Arts*, 11/3, Los Angeles.

Drewal, Margaret T., 1992, *Yoruba Ritual: Performers, Play, Agency*, Indiana University Press, Bloomington and Indianapolis.

Duerden, Dennis, 1977, *African Art and Literature: The Invisible Present*, Heinemann, London.

Duerden, Dennis and Pieterse, Cosmo (eds), 1972, *African Writers Talking*, Heinemann, London.

Dunton, Chris, 1992, *Make Man Talk True: Nigerian Drama in English Since 1970*, Hans Zell, London, Melbourne, Munich, New York.

Echeruo, Michael, 1976, 'The Dramatic Limits of Igbo Ritual', in Lindfors, Bernth (ed.) *Critical Perspectives on Nigerian Literature*, Three Continents, Washington, DC.

Echeruo, Michael, 1977, *Victorian Lagos: Aspects of Nineteenth-Century Lagos Life*, Macmillan, London.

Echeruo, Michael, 1981, 'Concert and Theatre in Late Nineteenth-Century Lagos' in Ogunbiyi, Yemi (ed.) *Drama and Theatre in Nigeria: A Critical Source Book*, Nigeria Magazine Publications, Lagos.

Edebiri, Uniamwan, 1976, 'Le Théâtre zaïrois à la recherche de son authenticité', *L'Afrique litteraire et artistique*, 2me trimestre, Paris.

Ellerman, Evelyn, Mollel, Tololwa, Nandwa, Jane and Maclaren, Diane, 1986, 'Asinamali: Theatre of Emergency', *ALA Bulletin*, 12/4, New York.

Elliot, Philip and Golding, Peter, 1974, 'Mass Communication and Social Change: The Imagery of Development and the Development of Imagery', in de Kadt, Emmanuel and Williams, Gavin (eds) *Sociology and Development*, Harper & Row, London.

Epskamp, Kees, 1982, 'Training Popular Theatre Trainers: A Case Study of Nigeria', paper presented to the 7th International Conference of Professors in Theatre Research, NUFFIC/CESO, The Hague.

Epskamp, Kees P., 1989, *Theatre in Search of Social Change*, Centre for the Study of Education in Developing Countries, The Hague.

Espinosa, Julio Garcia, 1971, 'For an Imperfect Cinema', *Afterimage: Third World Cinema Issue*, No. 3, London.

Etherton, Michael, 1973, 'Zambian Popular Theatre', *New Theatre Magazine*, 12/2, London.

Etherton, Michael, 1978, 'Wasan Manoma: Community Theatre in the Soba District of Kaduna State', research paper, Ahmadu Bello University, Zaria.

Etherton, Michael, 1982, *The Development of African Drama*, Hutchinson, London.

Eyoh, Ansel, N., 1984, *Hammocks and Bridges: Workshop on Theatre for Integrated Rural Development*, University of Yaoundé, Yaoundé.

Eyoh, Ansel, N., 1986, 'Improvisation and Traditional African Theatre', *Ideas in Action*, No. 165, FAO, Rome.

Eyoh, Ansel N., 1987, 'Popular Theatre as Integration and Conscientization', *IFDA Dossier*, 60, Nyon.

Fabian, Johannes, 1990, *Power and Performance: Ethnographic Explorations through Pro-*

verbial Wisdom and Theatre in Shaba, Zaire, University of Wisconsin Press, Madison.

Fanon, Frantz, 1967, *The Wretched of the Earth* (trans. by Farrington, Constance), Penguin, London.

Farris, James C., 1978, 'The Productive Basis of Aesthetic Tradition: Some African Examples', in Greenhalgh, M. and Megow, V. (eds) *Art in Society*, Duckworth, London.

Feldman, Seth, 1977, 'Viewer, Viewing, Viewed: A Critique of Subject-Generated Documentary', *Journal of the University Film Society*, 29/1, Philadelphia.

Finnegan, Ruth, 1970, *Oral Literature in Africa*, Oxford University Press, London.

Fischer, Eberhardt, 1978, 'Dan Forest Spirits: Masks in a Dan Village', *African Arts*, 11/3, Los Angeles.

Francis, Pierre, 1982, 'Class Struggle in Mali', *Review of African Political Economy*, No. 4, London.

Frederikse, Julie, 1982, *None But Ourselves: Masses Versus Media in the Making of Zimbabwe*, Ravan Press, Johannesburg/Zimbabwe Publishing House, Harare/ James Currey, London.

Freire, Paulo, 1972, *Pedagogy of the Oppressed*, Penguin, London.

Freire, Paulo, 1978, *Pedagogy in Process*, Writers and Readers Publishing Cooperative, London.

FRELIMO, 1982, 'Revolutionary Education', in de Braganca, Acquino and Waller-stein, Immanuel (eds) *The African Liberation Reader: Documents of the National Liberation Movements, Vol. 3, The Strategy of Liberation*, Zed Books, London.

da Gama, Vasco, 1962, 'Diary', in da Silva, Rego A. and Baxter, T. W. (eds) *Documents on the Portuguese in Mozambique and Central Africa 1497–1890*, Centros de Estudos Historicos Ultramarianos, Lisbon.

Gerard, Albert, 1981, *African Language Theatre*, Longman, Harlow.

Getina, Octavio and Solanas, Fernando, 1971, 'Towards a Third Cinema', *Afterimage: Third World Cinema Issue*, No. 3, London.

Gevisser, Mark, 1995, 'Dances and Trances of "Real Africa"', *Open Africa*, No. 4.

Gibbs, James, 1972, 'Mohammed ben Abdullah and the Legon Road Theatre', *African Arts*, 5/4, Los Angeles.

Gibbs, James (ed.), 1981, *Critical Perspectives on Wole Soyinka*, Heinemann, London.

Gibbs, James, 1986, 'Expose, Reflect, Magnify the Rotted Underbelly: Reflections on Some of Wole Sonyinka's Popular Political Drama', paper presented to the African Studies Association of Great Britain, Conference, University of Kent, Canterbury.

Gilbert, M., 1971, 'Court Songs and Traditional History in the Ancient Kingdoms of Porto Novo and Abomey', in Wachsmann, Klaus (ed.) *Music and History in Africa*, Northwestern University Press, Evanston.

Golding, Peter, 1977, 'Media Professionalism in the Third World', in Curran, J., Gurevitch, M. and Woollacott, J. (eds) *Mass Communication and Society*, Edward Arnold, London.

Goodlad, Sinclair, 1976, 'On the Social Significance of Television Comedy', in Bigsby, C. W. I. (ed.) *Approaches to Popular Culture*, Arnold, London.

Götrick, Kacke, 1984, *Apidan Theatre and Modern Drama*, Almquist and Wiksell International, Göteborg.

de Graft, Joe C., 1976, 'Roots in African Drama and Theatre', in Jones, Eldred (ed.) *African Literature Today*, 8, Heinemann, London.

Graham-White, Anthony, 1970, 'Ritual and Drama in Africa', *Educational Theatre Journal*, 22, Washington.

Graham-White, Anthony, 1974, *The Dance of Black Africa*, French, New York.

Graham-White, Anthony, 1976, 'The Characteristics of Traditional Drama', *Yale Theatre*, 8/1, Cambridge.

Granderson, Colin, 1972, 'The Chief in African Writing', *Présence africaine*, 95, 3me trimestre, Paris.

Greig, Robert, 1993, 'Time to Say Boo to the Bogeyman', *Weekly Mail*, 16–22 July, Johannesburg.

Griaule, M., 1938, *Jeux Dogons*, Institut d'Ethnologie, Paris.

Halas, B., 1953, 'La Goumbé: Une association de jeunesse musulmane en Basse Côte d'Ivoire', *Kongo Overzee*, 19, Antwerp.

Hama, Boubon, 1968, *Katica Nima*, Présence Africaine, Paris.

Harper, Peggy, 1968, 'Dance in a Changing Society', *African Arts*, 1/3, Los Angeles.

Hazoume, Guy Landary, 1972, *Idéologies, tribalisme et nation en Afrique: Le Cas dahomien*, Présence Africaine, Paris.

Head, Sydney W., 1974, *Broadcasting in Africa*, Temple University Press, Princeton.

Henderson, Gwynneth (ed.), 1973, *African Theatre*, Heinemann, London.

Hennebelle, Guy, 1972, *Les Cinémas africains en 1972*, Société Africain d'Edition, Dakar.

Hennebelle, Guy, 1976, 'Deux films sénégalais de Ben Diagaye Beye', *L'Afrique littéraire et artistique*, 3me trimestre, Paris.

Hobsbawm, Eric and Ranger, Terence (eds), 1983, *The Invention of Tradition*, Cambridge University Press, Cambridge.

Horn, Andrew, 1981, 'Uhuru to Amin: the Golden Decade of the Theatre in Uganda', *Literary Half Yearly*, 19, London.

Houeto, Colette Senami, 1975, 'Education et mass media', *Présence africaine*, 95, Paris.

Hurley, Paul, 1977, 'Laedza Batanani: An Integrated Rural Development Communication Case Study', in Balcomb, M. (ed.) *Communication for Social Development in Africa*, UNICEF, Nairobi.

Hussein, Ebrahim, 1970, *Kinjeketile*, Oxford University Press, New Drama for Africa Series, London.

Hussein, Ebrahim, 1971, *On the Development of Theatre in East Africa*, unpublished PhD Thesis, University of Dar es Salaam, Dar es Salaam.

Idoye, Patrick, 1981, 'Popular Theatre and Politics in Zambia: A Case Study of the University of Zambia (Chikwakwa) Theatre', unpublished PhD thesis, Florida State University, Gainesville.

Igbinedion, Joseph, 1982, 'Audience Attitudes towards Film on Nigerian Television', in Nwuneli, Onuora E. (ed.) *Mass Communications in Nigeria: A Book of Readings*, Nigeria Magazine Publications, Lagos.

Ijimere, Obatunde, 1966, *The Imprisonment of Obatala and Other Plays*, Heinemann, London.

Imperato, Pascal, 1970, 'The Dance of the Tyi Wara', *African Arts*, 2/1, Los Angeles.

International Defence and Aid Fund, 1981, 'A New Wave of Cultural Energy: Black Theatre in South Africa', *Theatre Quarterly*, 7/28, London.

Irele, Abiola, 1981, *The African Experience in Literature and Ideology*, Heinemann, London.

Isaacman, Allen, 1978, *A Luta Continua: Creating a New Society*, Southern African Pamphlets, New York.

James, Adeola, 1990, *In Their Own Voices: African Women Writers Talk*, James Currey, London.

James, Frederick, 1986, *Theatre: How Can It Be Used as a Strategy for Rural Development in Sierra Leone?*, Institute of Adult Education and Extramural Studies, Fourah Bay.

Jeyifo, Biodun, 1984, *The Yoruba Popular Travelling Theatre of Nigeria*, Nigerian Magazine, Lagos.

Johnson, Alex C., 1982, 'Ola Rotimi: How Significant?' *African Literature Today*, Vol. 12, Heinemann, London.

Johnson, Hazel and Bernstein, Henry (eds), 1982, *Third World Lives of Struggle*, Heinemann/Open University, London.

Johnston, Harry, 1912, *Pioneers in West Africa*, The Gresham Publishing Co., London.

Jones, P. Harris, 1975, *Freedom and Labour: Mobilization and Political Control in the Zambian Copperbelt*, Blackwell, Oxford.

Kaarsholm, Preben, 1990, 'Mental Colonisation or Catharsis? Theatre, Democracy and Cultural Struggle from Rhodesia to Zimbabwe', *Journal of Southern African Studies*, 16/2, Oxford.

Kadhi, Joe, 1982, 'Ngugi's Play is Tribal', *Sunday Nation*, Nairobi, 28 February.

Kahari, George, 1981, 'The History of the Protest Song in Zimbabwe', paper presented to the Conference on Southern African Literature, University of York, York.

Kamlongera, Chris, 1982, 'Theatre for Development: the Case of Malawi', *Theatre Research International*, 8/3, Paris.

Kamlongera, Chris, 1986, 'The British and the Beginning of Contemporary African Drama', *Baraza*, No. 3, Zomba.

Kamlongera, Chris, 1987, 'A Species of Pantomime to be Deprecated: The Case Against Beni in Colonial Malawi', research paper, University of Malawi, Zomba.

Kamphausen, Hannes, 1972, 'Cinema in Africa: A Survey', *Cineaste*, 5/3, New York.

Kasoma, Kabwe, 1976, *The Fools Marry*, NECZAM, Lusaka.

Kasule, Sam, 1993, 'Traditional and Contemporary Influences Upon Uganda: Theatre Between 1960 and 1990', unpublished PhD thesis, University of Leeds, Leeds.

Kavanagh, Robert Mshengu, 1976, 'Theatre in South Africa', *Ch'indaba*, 2, Accra.

Kavanagh, Robert Mshengu, 1977, 'After Soweto: People's Theatre and the Struggle in South Africa', *Theatre Quarterly*, 7/28, London.

Kavanagh, Robert Mshengu, 1977, 'Tradition and Innovation in the Theatre Workshop', *Theatre Quarterly*, 7/28, London.

Kavanagh, Robert Mshengu, 1981, *South African People's Plays*, Heinemann, London.

Kavanagh, Robert Mshengu, 1985, *Theatre and Cultural Struggle in South Africa*, Zed Books, London.

Kennedy, Jean, 1968, 'I Saw and I Was Happy: Festival of Oshogbo', *African Arts*, 1/2, Los Angeles.

Kerr, David, 1975, 'Report on Western Province Travelling Theatre', *Chikwakwa Review 74/75*, Lusaka.

Kerr, David, 1979, 'Tangled Roots: The Quest for Authentic Zambian Culture', staff seminar paper, University of Zambia, Lusaka.

Kerr, David, 1981, 'Didactic Theatre in Africa', *Harvard Education Review*, 51/1, Harvard.

Kerr, David, 1982, 'An Experiment in Popular Theatre: The Travelling Theatre Tour to Mbalachanda', *Society of Malawi Journal*, 35/1, Limbe.

Kerr, David, 1985, 'Deceiving or Conscientizing the Audience?', *UMSU Magazine*, 3/1, Zomba.

Kerr, David, 1988, 'Theatre and Social Issues in Malawi: Performances, Audiences, Aesthetics', *New Theatre Quarterly*, 4/14, London.

Kerr, David, 1993, 'Ideology, Resistance and the Transformation of Performance Traditions in Malawi', *Marang*, 10, Gaborone.

Kerr, David, 1993, 'The Best of Both Worlds? Colonial Film Policy and Practice in Northern Rhodesia and Nyasaland', *Critical Arts*, 7/1, and 2, Durban.

Kerr, David, and Nambote, Mike, 1983, 'The *Malipenga* Mime of Likoma Island', *Critical Arts*, 3rd Quarter, Durban.

Khumalo, Bafana, 1993, 'Has Ngema's Spell Been Broken?', *Weekly Mail*, 30 April– 6 May, Johannesburg.

Kidd, Ross, 1979, 'Liberation or Domestication: Popular Theatre and Non-Formal Education in Formal Education in Southern Africa', *Education Broadcasting International*, March, Toronto.

Kidd, Ross, 1982, *The Popular Performing Arts, Non-Formal Education and Social Change in the Third World: A Bibliography and Review Essay*, CESO, The Hague.

Kidd, Ross, 1984a, *From People's Theatre for Revolution to Popular Theatre for Reconstruction: Diary of a Zimbabwean Workshop*, CESO/ICAE, The Hague/Toronto.

Kidd, Ross, 1984b, 'Popular Theatre, Conscientization and Popular Organization', research paper, International Council for Adult Education, Toronto.

Kidd, Ross, 1984c, 'People's Theatre, Conscientization and Struggle', *Media Development*, 27/3, London.

Kidd, Ross and Byram, Martin, 1981, 'A Fresh Look at Popular Theatre in Botswana: Demystifying Pseudo-Freirian Non-Formal Education', *Rural Development Participation Review*, 3/1, New York.

King, Kenneth J., 1971, *Pan-Africanism and Education: A Study of Race, Philanthropy and*

Education in the Southern States of America and East Africa, Clarendon, Oxford.

Kinyanjui, Peter, 1980, 'Africa', in Lewis, Peter M. (ed.) *Media for People in Cities*, UNESCO, Paris.

Kirby, E. T., 1974, 'Indigenous African Theatre', *The Drama Review*, 18/4, New York.

Kolade, Christopher, 1975, 'The Role of Mass Media in Maintaining and Propagating a Nigerian Cultural Identity', *Présence africaine*, 95, 3me trimestre, Paris.

Koma-Koma, W. P., 1965, *M'ganda Kapena Malipenga*, Malawi Publications and Literature Bureau, Limbe.

Koné, Amadou, 1977, 'De l'Abissa à l'action politique', *L'Afrique littéraire et artistique*, 2me trimestre, Paris.

Kotchy, B., 1971, 'Discours inaugural', *Actes du Colloque sur les théâtre négro-africain, Abidjan 15-19 Avril 1970*, Présence Africaine, Paris.

Kubik, Gerhart, 1965, *Mukanda na Makisi* (Record Sleeve Notes), Abteilung, Berlin.

Kumpukwe, Joyce, 1983, 'S. L. Mbewe, Creator and Producer of Malawian Radio Plays', *Baraza*, 1, Zomba.

Labouret, Henri and Travélé, Moussa, 1928, 'Théâtre mandingue', *Africa*, 1, London.

Ladipo, Duro, 1964, *Three Yoruba Plays*, Mbari Publications, Ibadan.

Ladun, Umaru and Lyndersay, Dexter, 1970, *Shaihu Umar*, Longman, Harlow.

Lan, David, 1985, *Guns and Rain: Guerrillas and Spirit Mediums in Zimbabwe*, James Currey, London.

Larlham, 1985, *Black Theatre, Dance and Ritual in South Africa*, University of Michigan Research Press, Ann Arbor, MI.

Lawson, Howard, 1977, 'Organizing the Screen Writers' Guild', *Cineaste*, 7/2, New York.

Leshoai, Bob, 1972, 'Tanzania: Socialist Theatre', *New Theatre Magazine*, 12/2, London.

Letembet-Ambily, Antoine, 1977, *L'Europe inculpée*, CLE, Yaoundé.

Lewis, I. M., 1971, *Ecstatic Religion: An Anthropological Study of Spirit Possession and Shamanism*, Penguin, London.

Leys, Colin, 1975, *Underdevelopment in Kenya: The Political Economy of Neo-Colonialism*, James Currey, London.

Linden, Ian and Schoffeleers, Matthew, 1976, 'The Resistance of the Nyau Societies to the Roman Catholic Missions in Colonial Malawi', in Ranger, T. and Kimambo, I. N. (eds) *The Historical Study of African Religion*, Heinemann, London.

Liyong, Taban Lo, 1969, *The Last Word*, East African Publishing House, Nairobi.

Mackenzie, R. J., 1978, *The National Popular Theatre Workshop: Bosele Tshwaraganang*, University of Botswana, Gaborone.

McClaren, Robert, 1980, *Theatre and Cultural Struggle in South Africa: Aspects of Theatre on the Witswatersrand between 1958 and 1971*, unpublished PhD thesis, University of Leeds, Leeds.

McClaren, Robert, 1988, *Katshaa! The Sound of the AK*, Zambuko/Izibuko, Harare.

Malkmus, Lizbeth and Armes, Roy, 1991, *Arab and African Film Making*, Zed Books, London.

Mapanje, Jack, 1981, *Of Chameleons and Gods*, Heinemann, London.

Mapanje, Jack and White, Landeg, 1983, *Oral Poetry from Africa*, Longman, Harlow.

Maponya, Maishe, 1983, *Umongikazi*, Polypoton, London.

Martin, Angela (ed.), 1982, *African Films: The Context of Production*, BFI Dossier No. 6, British Film Institute, London.

Masiye, Andre, 1975, *The Lands of Kazembe* (originally *Kazembe and the Portuguese*), NECZAM, Lusaka.

Masiye, Andre, 1977, *Singing for Freedom*, Oxford University Press, London.

Mbulumwanza, Mudimbe-Boyi, 1975, 'Béatrice du Congo de Bernard Dadié, Signe du temps ou pièce à clef?' *L'Afrique littéraire et artistique*, 1/4, Paris.

Mda, Zakes, 1981, *We Shall Sing for the Fatherland and Other Plays*, Ravan Press, Johannesburg.

Mda, Zakes, 1986, *Morotholi Travelling Theatre*, National University of Lesotho, Roma.

Mda, Zakes, 1993, *When People Play People: Development Communication Through Theatre*, Witwatersrand University Press and Zed Books, Johannesburg, London and New Jersey.

Meillassoux, C., 1964, 'La Farce villageoise à la ville: la koteba de Bamako', *Présence africaine* (NS), 52/4, Paris.

Menga, Guy, 1976, *La Marmite de Koba-Mbala*, CLE, Yaoundé.

Merriam, A. P., 1954, 'Song Texts of the Bashi', *African Music Society Journal*, 1/1, Cape Town.

Messenger, John C., 1962, 'Anang Art and Social Control', *African Studies Bulletin*, 5/2, Lansing.

Mitchell, Clyde, 1956, *The Kalela Dance*, Rhodes Livingstone Papers Number 27, Manchester University Press, Manchester.

Mlama, Penina, 1983, 'Theatre for Development: The Malya Project in Tanzania', paper presented to the Africa/Asia Dialogue, Koitta.

Mlama, Penina, 1991, *Culture and Development: The Popular Theatre Approach to Africa*, The Scandinavian Institute of African Studies, Uppsala.

Mooki, Bob, 1986, 'Popular Theatre and Struggle', *Rixaka: Cultural Journal of the ANC*, No. 2, London.

Moser, Gerald, 1986, 'The Portuguese in Africa', in Gerard, Albert S. (ed.), *European Language Writing in Sub-Saharan Africa*, Vol. 1, Akadémiai Kiadó, Budapest.

Mouralis, Bernard, 1971, 'Le théâtre de William Ponty': Actes du Colloque sur le théâtre négro-Africain, Abidjan, 15–19 Avril 1970, Présence Africaine, Paris.

Mtonga, Mapopa, 1977, 'Interview with Alex Tetch-Lartey', *Arts and Africa*, BBC, London.

Mtonga, Mapopa, 1980, *The Dramatic Elements of Gule Wamkulu*, unpublished MA thesis, University of Legon, Ghana.

Mugo, Micere and Ngugi wa Thiong'o, 1977, *The Trial of Dedan Kimathi*, Heinemann, London.

Muller, J. and Cloete, N., 1986, 'The White Hands: Academic Social Scientists and Forms of Popular Social Science Production', *Critical Arts*, 4/2, Durban.

Mutahi, Wahome, 1982, 'Maseno Group a Unique Venture in Taking Theatre to Rural Areas', *Sunday Nation*, 28 February, Nairobi.

Mutwa, Credo, 1986, *uNosilemela*, in Kento, G. *et al.* (eds) *South African People's Plays*, Heinemann, London.

Mwale, Cuthert, 1973, 'Malipenga Dance in Nkhata Bay District', research paper, University of Malawi, Zomba.

Mwansa, Dickson, 1982, 'Theatre for Community Animation in Zambia', *Third World Popular Theatre Newsletter*, 1/1, Lusaka.

Mwansa, Dickson, 1983a, 'ZANTAA – Off-shoot of Chikwakwa', research paper, University of Zambia, Lusaka.

Mwansa, Dickson, 1983b, 'Theatre, its Place and Influence', paper presented to the Africa–Asia Dialogue, Koitta, Bangladesh.

Mwansa, Dickson M. (ed.) (1984), *Zambian Performing Arts: Current Issues, Policies and Directions*, University of Zambia, Lusaka.

Nazareth, Peter, 1978, 'East African Drama', in Ogunba, Oyin and Irele, Abiola (eds) *Theatre in Africa*, Ibadan University Press, Ibadan.

Ndao, Cheik Aliou, 1983, *L'Exil d'Albouri*, Nouvelles Editions Africains, Abidjan.

Ndedi-Penda, Patrice, 1970, *Le Fusil*, ORTF, Paris.

Ndumbe, Kum'a, III, 1986, 'Le Théâtre sénégalais: un succes bien mérité', *African Theatre Review*, 1/2, Yaoundé.

Neto, Augustino, 1982, 'On Culture and the New Man', in de Braganca, Acquino and Wallerstein, Immanuel (eds) *The African Liberation Reader: Documents of the National Liberation Movements*, Vol. 3: *The Strategy of Liberation*, Zed Books, London.

Ngugi wa Thiong'o, 1972, *Homecoming: Essays on African and Caribbean Literature, Culture and Politics*, Heinemann, London.

Ngugi wa Thiong'o, 1977, *The River Between*, Heinemann, London.

Ngugi wa Thiong'o, 1981, *Detained*, Heinemann, London.

Ngugi wa Thiong'o, 1982, 'A Statement at the Press Conference on 10th March 1982', *Kunapipi*, 4/2, Aarhus.

Ngugi wa Thiong'o, 1983, 'Woman in Cultural Work: Kamiriithu People's Theatre in Kenya', *Current Development Dialogue*, 14/2, Geneva.

Ngugi wa Thiong'o, 1986, *Decolonising the Mind: The Politics of Language in African Literatures*, James Currey, London.

Ngugi wa Thiong'o and Ngugi wa Mirii, 1982, *I Will Marry When I Want* (translated by authors from *Ngaahika Ndeenda*), Heinemann, London.

Ng'wanakilila, Nkwabi, 1981, *Mass Communication and the Development of Socialism in Tanzania*, Tanzania Publishing House, Dar es Salaam.

Ng'weno, Hilary, 1967, 'Letter from Nairobi', *African Arts*, 1/2, Los Angeles.

Nkosi, Lewis, 1982, *Tasks and Masks*, Longman, Harlow.

Nkosi, Lewis, 1984, 'Africa: A Continent of Performers', in Mwansa, Dickson (ed.) *Zambian Performing Arts: Current Issues, Policies and Directions*, University of Zambia, Lusaka.

Nkrumah, Kwame, 1965, *Neo-Colonialism: The Last Stage of Imperialism*, Heinemann, London.

Notcutt, L. and Latham, G., 1937, *The African and the Cinema*, Edinburgh House Press, Edinburgh.

Obafemi, Olu, 1982a, 'Revolutionary Aesthetics in Recent Nigerian Theatre', *African Literature Today*, Vol. 12, Heinemann, London.

Obafemi, Olu, 1982b, 'Political Perspectives in Popular Theatre in Nigeria', *Theatre Research International*, 7/3, London.

Obama, Jean-Baptiste, 1972, *Assimilados*, ORTF, Paris.

Obiechina, Emmanuel, 1975, *Culture, Tradition and the African Novel*, Cambridge University Press, London.

Ogunba, Oyin, 1978, 'Traditional African Festival Drama', in Ogunba, Oyin and Irele, Abiola (eds) *Theatre in Africa*, Ibadan University Press, Ibadan.

Ogunbiyi, Yemi (ed.), 1981, *Drama and Theatre in Nigeria: A Critical Source Book*, Nigeria Magazine Publications, Lagos.

Okpewho, Isidore, 1992, *African Oral Literature: Backgrounds, Character and Continuity*, Indiana University Press, Bloomington and Indianapolis.

Olajubu, Oludare, 1978, 'The Sources of Duro Ladipo's Oba Koso', in Lindfors Bernth (ed.) *Research in African Literature*, 9/3, Austin.

Olusola, Segun, 1981, 'The Advent of Television Drama in Nigeria', in Ogunbiyi, Yemi (ed.) *Drama and Theatre in Nigeria: A Critical Source Book*, Nigeria Magazine Publications, Lagos.

Omotoso, Kole, 1976, *The Curse*, New Horn Press, Ibadan.

Onoge, Omafume, 1977, 'Revolutionary Imperatives in African Sociology', in Gutkind, P. and Waterman, P. (eds) *African Social Studies: A Radical Reader*, Heinemann, London.

Opubor, Alfred, 1975, 'Theatrical Forms of Communication in Black Africa', paper delivered to the Comparative Popular Culture Research Seminar on Traditional Media, East–West Communication Institute, Honolulu.

Orkin, Martin, 1990, *Drama and the South African State*, Manchester University Press, Manchester.

Osofisan, Femi, 1977, *The Chattering and the Song*, Ibadan University Press, Ibadan.

Osofisan, Femi, 1980, *Once Upon Four Robbers*, Bio, Ibadan.

Osofisan, Femi, 1985, 'Drama and the New Exotic: The Paradox of Form in Modern African Theatre', *African Theatre Review*, 1/1, Yaoundé.

Ottenberg, Simon, 1972, 'Humorous Masks and Serious Politics Among Afikbo Ibo', in Frazer, D. and Cole, H. (eds) *African Art and Leadership*, University of Wisconsin Press, Madison.

Ottenberg, Simon, 1975, *Masked Rituals of Afikpo: The Context of an African Art*, University of Washington Press, Washington.

Owomoyela, Oyekan, 1976, 'Folklore and Yoruba Theatre', in Lindfors, Bernth (ed.) *Critical Perspectives on Nigerian Literatures*, Three Continents Press, Washington DC.

Owomoyela, Oyekan, 1985, 'Give me Drama Or ...: The Argument on the Existence of Drama in Traditional Africa', *African Studies Review*, 28/4, Los Angeles.

Oyono-Mbia, G., 1974, *Three Suitors One Husband* (*Trois prétendants, un mari*), Methuen, London.

Oyono-Mbia, G., 1975, *Notre fille ne se mariera pas*, ORTF, Paris.

Paquet, André, 1978, 'The FESPACO of Ougadougou: Towards Unity in African Cinema', *Cineaste*, 6/1, New York.

p'Bitek, Okot, 1966, *Songs of Lawino*, East African Publishing House, Nairobi.

p'Bitek, Okot, 1970, *The Song of Ocol*, East African Publishing House, Nairobi.

p'Bitek, Okot, 1982, 'Interview with David Rubadiri', *Isala*, 1, Ibadan.

Peel, J. D. Y., 1989, 'The Cultural Work of Yoruba Ethnogenesis', in Tonkan, E. *et al.* (eds) *History and Ethnicity*, Routledge, London.

PETA, 1980, *Mamugnaong Dula/Creative Dramatics*, MSPCS, Davao City.

Peterson, Bhehirzizwe, 1990. 'Apartheid and the Political Imagination in Black South African Theatre', *Journal of Southern African Studies*, 16/2, Oxford.

Phiri, Masautso, 1979, *Soweto Flowers Will Grow*, Neczam, Lusaka.

Pietersee, Cosmo and Henderson, Gwynneth (eds), 1973, *Nine African Plays for Radio*, Heinemann, London.

Pines, Jim, and Willemen, Paul (eds), 1989, *Questions of Third Cinema*, British Film Institute, London.

Pliya, Jean, 1969, *Kondo le raquin*, ORTF, Paris.

Pongweni, Alec J. C., 1982, *Songs that Won the Liberation War*, College Press, Harare.

Popular Theatre Committee, 1978, *Laedza Batanani: Organizing Popular Theatre: The Botswana Experience, 1974–77*, University of Botswana, Gaborone.

Pownall, David, 1983, 'European and African Influences in Zambian Theatre', *Theatre Quarterly*, 3/10, London.

Poyner, Robin, 1978, 'The Egungun of Owo', *African Arts*, 11/3, Los Angeles.

Ranganath, H. K., 1980, *Using Folk Media Entertainment to Promote National Development*, UNESCO, Paris.

Ranger, Terence, 1975, *Beni, Dance and Society in Eastern Africa*, Heinemann, London.

Ranger, Terence, 1982, 'The Death of Chaminuka: Spirit Mediums, Nationalism and Guerrilla Warfare in Zimbabwe', *African Affairs*, 81/324, London.

Ranger, Terence, 1985, *Peasant Consciousness and Guerrilla War in Zimbabwe*, James Currey, London.

Ricard, Alain, 1977, 'The Concert Party as a Genre: The Happy Stars of Lome', in Lindfors, Bernth (ed.) *Forms of Folklore in Africa, Narrative, Poetic, Gnomic, Dramatic*, University of Texas Press, Austin and London.

Ricard, Alain, 1986, *L'Invention du Théâtre: Le Théâtre et les comédiens en Afrique noire*, Editions l'Age d'Homme, Lausanne.

Rosberg, Carl and Nottingham, John, 1966, *The Myth of Mau Mau: Nationalism in Kenya*, Praeger, New York.

Ross, A. C., 1965, 'The Political Role of the Witchfinder in Southern Malawi during the Crisis of October 1964–May 1965', *Witchcraft and Healing*, Central African Studies Association, Edinburgh.

Rotimi, Ola, 1968, 'The Drama of African Ritual Display', *Nigeria Magazine*, 99, Lagos.

Rotimi, Ola, 1970, *The Gods Are Not to Blame*, Oxford University Press, Oxford.

Rotimi, Ola, 1972, *Kurunmi*, Oxford University Press, Oxford.

Rotimi, Ola, 1973, 'Interview with Margaret Folarin', *New Theatre Magazine*, 12/2, London.

Rotimi, Ola, 1974, *Ovanramven Nogbaisi*, Ethiope Publishing Corporation, Benin City and Oxford University Press, Ibadan.

Rugyendo, Mukotani, 1973, 'Towads a Truly African Theatre: A Study of the Uses of Some Traditional Forms of Kigesi and Ankole in South West Uganda', research paper, University of Dar es Salaam, Dar es Salaam.

Rugyendo, Mukotani, 1977, *The Barbed Wire and Other Plays*, Heinemann, London.

Sabatier, Peggy R., 1980, 'African Culture and Colonial Education: William Ponty School, Cahiers and Theatre', *Journal of African Studies*, 7/1, London.

Safi, Faye, 1977, 'Interview', *African Women*, 9, April/March, London.

Saro-Wiwa, Ken, 1988, *Basi and Company: Four Television Plays*, Saros International Publishers, Port Harcourt.

Schiltz, Marc, 1978, 'Egungun Masquerades in Iganna', *African Arts*, 3/1, Los Angeles.

Schipper, Mineke, 1982, *Theatre and Society in Africa*, Ravan Press, Johannesburg.

Schoffeleers, Matthew, 1976, 'The Nyau Societies: Our Present Understanding', *Society of Malawi Journal*, 29/1, Limbe.

Scott, Kennedy J., 1973, *In Search of African Theatre*, Charles Scribner's Sons, New York.

Sekyi, Kobina, 1974, *The Blinkards*, Heinemann, London.

Sembène, Ousmane, 1956, *Le Docker noire*, Nouvelles Editions Debresse, Paris.

Sembène, Ousmane, 1957, *Oh Pays, mon beau peuple*, Amiot-Dumont, Paris.

Sembène, Ousmane, 1960, *Les Bouts de bois de Dieu*, Le Livre Contemporain, Paris.

Sembène, Ousmane, 1969, *Le Mandat*, Présence Africaine, Paris.

Sembène, Ousmane, 1973, *Xala*, Présence Africaine, Paris.

Sembène, Ousmane, 1977a, 'Film-Makers Have a Great Responsibility to Our People', *Cineaste*, 4/1, New York.

Sembène, Ousmane, 1977b, 'Film-Makers and African Culture', *Africa 71*, July, London.

Senanu, K. E., 1981, 'Thoughts on Creating the Popular Theatre', in Gibbs, James (ed.) *Critical Perspective on Wole Soyinka*, Heinemann, London.

Senghor, Leopold S., 1965 (translated by John Lee and Clive Wake), *Prose and Poetry*, Heinemann, London.

Serumaga, Robert, 1970, 'Uganda's Experimental Theatre', *African Arts*, 3/2, Los Angeles.

Shank, Theodore, 1974, 'Popular Theatre as Popular Education', *Drama Review*, 18, New York.

Sharkah, Tommy, 1983, 'The Role of Drama in Popular Theatre Programmes', paper presented to the African Popular Theatre Conference Workshop, University of Zimbabwe, Harare.

Short, Philip, 1974, *Banda*, Routledge & Kegan Paul, London.

Simon B., Ngema M. and P. Mtwa, 1983, *Woza Albert!*, Methuen, London.

Sissoko, Fily Dabo, 1955, *Sagesse noir: sentences et proverbes malinkés*, La Tour du Guet, Paris.

Sissoko, Fily-Dubo, 1962, La Savane Rouge, Les Presses Universelles, Avignon.

Skinner, Elliot, 1974, *African Urban Life: The Transformation of Ougadougou*, Princeton University Press, Princeton.

Smyth, Rosaleen, 1979, 'The Development of British Colonial Film Policy, 1927–1939, with Special Reference to East and Central Africa', *Journal of African History*, 20/3, Cambridge.

Smyth, Rosaleen, 1983, 'The Central African Film Unit's Images of Empire, 1948–1963', *Historical Journal of Film, Radio and Television*, 3/2, Abingdon.

Sole, Kelwyn, 1990, 'Review of Organize and Act: The Natal Workers Theatre Movement, 1983–87', *Review of African Politican Economy*, 48, Autumn, London.

Songoyi, Ellias, 1988, *Commercialization: Its Impact on Traditional Dances*, Radet for Folkemusikk og Folkedans, Trondheim.

Sowande, Bode, 1979, *Farewell to Babylon and Other Plays*, Longman, Harlow.

Soyinka, Wole, 1970, 'Interview with Lewis Nkosi', *African Writers Talking*, Heinemann, London.

Soyinka, Wole, 1971, 'Drama and the Revolutionary Ideal', in Morell, K. L. (ed.) *In Person: Achebe, Awoonor and Soyinka*, Washington Institute for Comparative Studies, Seattle.

Soyinka, Wole, 1971b, *A Shuttle in the Crypt* , Rex Collings, London.

Soyinka, Wole, 1972, *The Man Died*, Rex Collings, London.

Soyinka, Wole, 1973, *Collected Plays I*, Oxford University Press, London.

Soyinka, Wole, 1974, *Collected Plays II*, Oxford University Press, London.

Soyinka, Wole, 1979, 'Drama and the African World View', in Rowland, Smith (ed.) *Exile and Tradition: Studies in African and Caribbean Literature*, Longman and Dalhousie University Press, London.

Stapleton, Chris and May, Chris, 1989, *African All Stars: The Pop Music of a Continent*, Paladin, London.

Steadman, Ian, 1981, 'Culture and Context: Notes on Performance in South Africa', *Critical Arts*, 2/1, Durban.

Steadman, Ian, 1988, 'Popular Culture and Performance', in Tomaselli, Keyan (ed.) *Rethinking Culture*, Anthropos Publishers, Belville.

Sutherland, Efua, 1970, *The Original Bob: The Story of Bob Johnson, Ghana's Ace Comedian*, Anowuo Educational Publications, Accra.

Sutherland, Efua, 1975, *The Marriage of Anansewa*, Longman, Harlow.

Thompson, Robert Farris, 1974, *African Art in Motion*, UCLA Press, Los Angeles.

Tomaselli, Keyan, 1981, 'The Semiotics of Alternative Theatre in South Africa', *Critical Arts*, 2/1, Durban.

Tomaselli, Keyan, 1982, 'Theatre, Repression and the Working Class in South Africa', *Kunapipi*, 4/2, Aarhus.

Tomaselli, Keyan and Muller, Johan, 1986, 'Class, Race and Oppression: Metaphor and Metonymy in "Black" South African Theatre', *Critical Arts*, 4/3, Durban.

Tomaselli, Keyan, Tomaselli, Ruth and Muller, Johan, 1989, *Studies on the South African Media*, James Currey, London.

Traoré, Bakary, 1971, 'Le théâtre négro-africain de l'école William Ponty', in *Actes du Colloque sur le théâtre négro-africain, Abidjan 15–19 Avril 1970*, Présence Africaine, Paris.

Traoré, Bakary, 1972 (translated by Dapo Adelugba), *The Black African Theatre and Its Social Functions*, Ibadan University Press, Ibadan.

Traoré, Mhama, 1978, 'Cinema Must Be a School', *Cineaste*, 6/1, New York.

Ugbuoajah, Frank Okwu, 1983, *Mass Communication, Culture and Society in West Africa*, Hans Zell, Munich, New York and London.

UNESCO, 1977, *Ten Year Plan for the Preservation and Promotion of the Performing Arts and Music in Africa and Asia*, UNESCO, Paris.

UNZADRAMS, 1973, 'The Role of UNZADRAMS', *Stage*, September, Lusaka.

Vail, Leroy and White, Landeg, 1978, 'Plantation Protest: The History of a Mozambican Song', *Journal of Southern African Studies*, 5/1, York.

Vail, Leroy and White, Landeg, 1991, *Power and the Praise Poem: Southern African Voices in History*, University of Virginia Press, Charlottesville/James Currey, London.

Valbert, Christian, 1971, 'Le Théâtre négro-africain et le public européen', *Actes de Colloque sur le théâtre négro-africain, Abidjan 15–19 Avril 1970*, Présence Africaine, Paris.

Vanderbrouke, Russel, 1977, 'Chiaroscuro: A Portrait of the South African Theatre', *Theatre Quarterly*, 7/28, London.

Vieyra, Paulin S., 1969, *Le Cinéma en Afrique*, Présence Africaine, Paris.

Vieyra, Paulin S., 1972, *Sembène Ousmane: cinéaste*, Présence Africaine, Paris.

Vincent, P. L., 1977, 'Comparison of Media Costs', in Balcomb, J. (ed.) *Communications for Social Development in Africa*, UNICEF, Nairobi.

Vrydagh, P. André, 1977, 'Makisi of Zambia', *African Arts*, 9/2, Los Angeles.

Wa Kyendo, Muli, 1982, 'What's All This About the Bushtrackers?' *Sunday Nation*, 24 January, Nairobi.

Warner, Gerry, 1974, 'Education coloniale et genèse du théâtre néo-africaine d'expression française', *Présence africaine*, 99/100, Paris.

Watene, Kenneth, 1974, *Dedan Kimathi*, Transafrica, Nairobi.

Waterman, Christopher, 1990, *Juju: A Social History and Ethnography of an African Popular Music*, Chicago University Press, Chicago.

wa Thiong'o, Ngugi & wa Mirii, Ngugi *see entries under* Ngugi wa Thiong'o and Ngugi wa Mirii.

Weare, Tony, 1981, 'Ninety Years of Theatre', *Arts Zimbabwe*, No. 2, Harare.
White, Landeg, 1982, 'Power and the Praise Song', paper presented to Conference of Southern African Literature, York University, York.
Wicomb, Zoe, 1989/1990, 'Secom Calling', *Southern African Review of Books*, 12, December/January, Johannesburg.
Willis, Ray, 1973, 'The Indigenous Critique of Colonialism: A Case Study', in Telal, Asad (ed.) *Anthropology and the Colonial Encounter*, Ithaca Press, London.
Young, Sherilynn, 1977, 'Fertility and Famine: Women's Agricultural History in Southern Mozambique', in Palmer, Robin and Parsons, Neil (eds) *The Roots of Rural Poverty in Central and Southern Africa*, James Currey, London.

Index

Aamoni, wa N., 243
Abafamu Players, 127
Abah, O., 161
Abdulaziz, M. H., 129
Abdullah, bey, M., 138–9
Abedi, B., 198
Abeokuta, 100
Abidjan, 22, 105, 139, 142, 192
Abomey, 208
Abussa Mine, 78
ABUTC, (Ahmadu Bello University Theatre Collective), 161-3, 165-6, 170, 254
Accra, 42, 59, 74, 78-9, 113, 118, 130-1, 138-9, 242
Achebe, C., *Arrow of God*, 186, *No Longer at Ease*, 186, *Things Fall Apart*, 186
Achimota, 34
Acquaye, S., *The Lost Fishermen*, 120, 130
Addis Ababa, 197, 256
Adedeji, J., 12, 14, 42, 44
Adejobi, O., 100, *Ekuro Oloja*, 181, *Ono Ola*, 101
Adeloga, S., 106
Adelugba, D., 58, 134, 148
Afikpo (people), 2, 3, 7, *8*, 9, 42, 46, 50
Afolayan, A., 100
African Inkspots (The), 216
African Inland Church, 158
AFRAM (Afro-American Films Ltd.), 183
Agbor (dance), 97
Agit-prop Theatre, 212, 214
Ahmadu Bello University (*see also* ABUTC), 161-3, 164-6
Ahmadu, S., 197
Ahmed, U., 15
Aidoo, A. A., 118
Aig-Imoukhouede, F., *Muchi Charm*, 133-4

Akan (people and language), 50, 73, 76
Akerman, A., 235
Akintola (Chief), 92
Alarinjo Theatre, 12, 14, 44, 85, 94, 99, 135
Albouri, 117
Alhambra Palace, 23
Amin, I. (President), 127-8
Amon, F. J., 37
AMPECA (American Motion Picture Export Company) 183-4
Amsah, J. B., 76, 81
Amsah, K., *Love Brewed in an African Pot*, 192
Amusi wa Miriamu, 186
Anang (people), 54
Ananse (trickster hero), 57, 72-3
Anansegoro (theatre), 119
Anansesesem (theatre), 72-3, 118-19
ANC (African National Congress – South Africa), 222, 231, 233, 235
ANC (African National Congress – Zimbabwe), 211
Anglican Church, 94
Anglo American Corporation, 215, 242
Angola, 15, 33, 40, 69, 209-10, 233, 235
Aniwura, K. (with Okediji, O.), *Rere Run*, 130
Apedo-Armah, A. T., 103
Apidan (theatre), 12, 15, *48*
Apithy, 201
Apostolic Church, 84
Arabs, 50
Arilogwa (dance), 181
Aristophanes, 18
Armes, R., 181, 185-6, 191
Armstrong, R., 91, 96-8
Arrighi, G., 49
Artaud, A., 127
Arthur, J. (Dr), 35

Asazi, 231
Aseru-Oforu, A., 256
ASP (Afro Shirazi Party, Zanzibar), 198-9
ATPN (Association of Theatre Practitioners of Nigeria), 90
Atwia village, 118
audience participation, 7, *8*, 9, 55, 82, 94, 113, 119, 121, 131, 137, 145, 161, 169-70, 181, 184, 192, 207, 211, 228, 232, 246
'authenticité', 205
Awolowo (Chief), 92, 181
Awoonor, K., 18, 31, 78
Axim Trio, 76, 77, 78
Axworthy, G., 95-6, 133-5
Ayame village, 142
AZAPO (Azanian People's Organization), 236
Azikwe, N., 88, 197

Baba Sala, 101
Babu, A., 252
Badian, S., *Le mort de Chaka*, 117
Baganda (people), 197, 207
Bahumutsi Theatre Group, 228, *229*, 231-2
Baker, B., 135
Ballets Africains, 204
Balogun, O., 100, *Ajani Ogun*, 191, *Musik Man*, 191
Bamana (people/language), 1-2, *3*, 4-7, 205
Bame, K. N., 72, 76, 82
Banda, K. (President), 91, 197, 201-2, *203*, 204, *253*, 254
Banham, M., 41, 91, 95, 97-8, 133, *African Theatre*, 41
Bangladesh, 163, 252
Bantu Dramatic Society, 21, *24*
Bappa, S., 161-3, 252
Baragwanath Hospital, 228
Barber, K., 102

Bariba (people), 200
Bata Shoe Co., 243
Batsford, R., 131
BBC (British Broadcasting Corporation), 29, 173, 175, 178
Beart, C., 18, 36
Beattie, J., 46
BCDS (The Baganda Cultural and Dramatic Society), 127
Beier, U., 89, 95, 97-8
BEKE (Bantu Educational Kinematic Experiment), 26-8
Belgian colonialism, 55
Bell, H., 25
Bellman, B., 184
Bemba (people/language), 64, 147
Beni (dance/mime), 59-62, *63*, 64-72
Benin, 9, 12, 113, 175, 200
Benson, B., 89
Benue State, 166-7
Berlin, 95
Berliner, I., 211
Beye. D., *Samba Tali*, 185
Biafran Civil War, 91-2, 135
Biko, S., 224
Bini (people), 9
Bira (ritual), 211-12
Bisa (people/language), 64
Björkman, I., 248-50
Black (Captain), 68
Black Consciousness, 220-5, 232-3, 251-2
Black Moses, 143
Blantyre, 32, 156, 202
Boal, A., 69, 161, 169
Bobo-Dioulasso, 192
Bobo troupes, 139
Bokalaka, 152
Bomo village, 163
Bongo (President), 193
Borgu (people), 11
Bosele Tshwaraganang, 153
Boshi (people), 55
Botswana, 147, 149, *150*, 151-6, 158, 192, 235, 252, 254
Boughadir, F., 189, 194
Boyaru., F., 111
Boyd-Barrett, O., 172-3
BPC (Black People's Convention), 222-3
Brazil, 22, 149, 188
Brecht, B., *The Threepenny Opera*, 121, *The Trial of Lukullus*, 139, *The Caucasian Chalk Circle*, 139, *The Trial of Zwangendaba* (adaptation), 140
Brink, J., 4-6
British colonialism, *17*, 18-20, 22-3, 25-6, 29-32, 45, *51*, 52, 54-5, 82, 84-6, 125-6, 163, 183, 186, 196-7, 201, 211, 215, 242-3, 248
British Council, 108, 111-12, 135, 242
Broadway, 237
Brooke, P., 127
Brotherhood of Man, The, 155
Budo Mission, 111
Bukurebe, 69
Buntungwa Star Band, 154
Bunyoro (people), 46
Bureau des Echanges Artistiques et Culturels, 108
Bureau du Cinéma de la Co-operation, 186, 188
Burkina Faso, 111, 176, 184-6, 192
Burnet, R., 125

Byram., M., 151, 156, 159
Byron, F.A.W., 29

Cabral, A., 210
Cabo Delgado, 210, 214
CABS (Central African Broadcasting Services), 27, 29-30
Calabar, 54, 134
Calpenny Co., 186, *187*
Cameroon, 108, 112, 117, 175-6
Canada, 154
Cantata, 82, 84-5, 96
Cape Coast, 76, 139
Cape Town, 20, 223, 227, 233
Cape Verde, 210
Carrefour, *107*
CCM (Chama Cha Mapinduzi, Tanzania/Zanzibar), 198
censorship, 88, 179, 182, 193, 196, 216, 220-1, 233, 248
Césaire, A., *A Season in the Congo*, 147, 242
CFU (Central Film Unit), 28
Chakula ni Uhai, 176
Chalimbana, 154-5, 158-9
Chama (dance/mime), 60
Chambulikazi, E., 158
Chaminuka, 211
Changalume, 146
Chaplin, C., 74
Chawama! Chawama!, 154
Cheadle, H., 227
Cheelo Ca Madaala, 144
Chekhov, A., *The Bear*, 136-7
Cherubim and Seraphim (Christian sect), 84
Chewa (people/language), 50-2, 54-5, 177-9, 201-2
Chifunyise, S., 21, 144-6, 148, 154-5, 182, 194, *Mabusisi*, 144, *Blood*, 144-5, *The District Governor Visits a Village*, 144-5, *I Resign*, 182, 194
Chikwakwa Theatre, 109, 139, 140-1, 147-8, 142-5, 214
Chikumbi, 213
Chileshe, R., 144
Chimurenga names, 211
Chinamwali (ritual), 71
Chinodza, K., 214
Chipata, *51*, 143
Chirwa, J., 70
Chopa (people), 45-6, 197
Christianity, 18, 19, 33, 40, 45, 49-55, 69-70, 74, 82, 84-8, 97, 125, 128, 158, 217, 219, 247-8
Chung, F., 110, 131, 214, 239
Church of Scotland, 19, 35
cinema, 23, 24-5, 26, 27, 28, 172-3, *174*, 183-6, *187*, 188-9, *190*, 191-4
Cinema Novo, 188
Cissé, D., *La Derniers Jours de Lat Dior N'Gone*, 108
Cissé, S., *Le Vent.*, 188, *Den Musso*, 193
Clapperton, H., 52, *53*
Clark, E., 84-94, 108
Clark, J. P., *Masquerade*, 114, *Ozidi*, 114, *Song of a Goat*, 114, *The Raft*, 123
Clairwood Trade Union and Cultural Centre, 230
Clement, 233
Cohen, B., 76
Cohen, R., 57
Cole, B., 78

Collins, E. J., 79, 82, 102
Colson, E., 45, 50
COMACICO (Compagnie Africaine, Cinématographique, Industrielle et Commerciale), 183-4
Commedia dell'Arte, 136
Concert Party, 41, 65, 73-4, *75*, 76, 77, 78-9, *80*, *83*, 89-90, 94-5, 101-3, 118-19, 138, 191, 198, 215, 219
Congo (Brazzaville), 108, 175, 186
Congo (Kinshasa – see Zaire)
Congo-Samba Tojass, 89
Coochie Coochie Fantango Dance, 89
Cook, D., 135-8
Cooper, R., 224
Cooper, S., 223-4
Cooper, V., 224
Coplan, D., 215, 219, 230
Corneille, P., 34
Cornevin, R., *Le Théâtre en Afrique noir*, 41
COSATU (Congress of South African Trade Unions), 231
Côte d'Ivoire, 60, 76, 105, 112, 142, 180, 186, 192-3
Coulibaly, O., 197
CPP (Congress People's Party, Ghana), 78
Credit Union, 147
Crow, B., 161, 168-9
CUSO (Canadian University Service Overseas), 154, 252

da Gama, V., 16
Dadié, B., *Climbie*, 36-7, *Béatrice du Congo*, 117, *Voix dans le vent*, 117
Dahomey (*see Benin*)
Dahomey National Theatre, 108
The Daily Comet (Nigeria), 86
The Daily Mail (Zambia), 110
The Daily Service (Nigeria), 87
Dakar, 22-3, *107*, 191-3
Dan (people), 9
Dan, B., 197
Danquah, J. B., *The Third Woman*, 39
Dar es Salaam, 30, 61, 68, 198-9, 233, 235
Dar es Salaam (University of), 129-30, 158-9
Darkest Africa, 24
David, A. B., 84
Davidson, B., 55
Davies, O., 186, *187*
Davis, M., 232
Decock, J., 205
Dede, B., 134
Dhlamini, E., 216
Dhlomo, J.E., *The Girl Who Killed to Save*, 39
Diapare, H., *L'Herbe sauvage*, 192
Diawara, M., 28
Dicko, B., 111
Die Voortrekker, 25
Diola (people/language), 192
Dionysius, 115
Dix Corian Jokers, 78
Dodoma, 198
Dogon (people), 6, 205
Dona Béatrice, 115, 117
Donovan Maule Theatre, 106
Don't Use Big Words, 22
Doug, P. M., *Demain un jour nouveau*, 193
drama competitions, 108-11, 175, 198

Drama Studio (The), 118, 242
Duerden, D., 45
DWCL (Durban Workers Cultural Local), 230-1, *Dikitshening*, 230, *The Dunlop Play*, 230-1, *Mphopomeni*, 230-1, *Bambata's Children*, 231

Easmon, S., *The New Patriots*, 112
Ecaré, D., *Concerto pour un exil*, 185, 186
Echeruo, M., 15, 22, 34, 115
Ecole William Ponty, 34, 36-8, 86, 108
Edebiri, U., 205
Egungun (masquerade drama), 9, 10, 11-12, 13, 14, 50, 51, 82
Ekoe (masquerade drama), 54
Ekon, E., 134
Ekpo (people), 9
Elizabethville (*see* Lubumbashi)
Elliot, P., 173
L'Entrevue de Samory et du Capitaine Peroz, 37
Enugu, 89
Epskamp, K., 166-7
Erithi (dance), 243
d'Estaing, G. (President), 173
Esau, Y., *Don't Say it in Writing*, 134
Espinosa, I. G., 195
Esslin, M., 175
Esso, Co., 136, 242
Esu Ogbin, 14
Etherton, M., 101, 119, 124-6, 142-3, 153, 161-3, 168-9, 194
Ethiopia, 185, 252
ethnicity, 7, 12, 81, 93, 200-2, 204-7, 212, 249-50
Euripides, *Ephigenia*, 37
expatriate theatre, 105-7, 131-2
Eye, The (Theatre Co.,) 231
Eyoh, H. N., 168-9

Fajuyi, F. A, 92
Faleti, A., *Basorun Gaa*, 130, *Won Ro Pe Wara Ni*, 130
Fanon, F., 44, 54
Fanti (people/language), 72
Fatunde, T., *Oye Na Tief Man*, 253
Federation of Rhodesia and Nyasaland, 69, 196-7, 201
Federation of Senegal and West Sudan, 197
Female impersonation, 3, 12, 13, 48, 51-2, 74, 78-9, 80, 81-2
FEPACI (Federation Panafricain Cinéastes), 184
FESPACO (Festival for FEPACI), 184, 192-3
Fiawoo, E. K., *The Fifth Landing Stage*, 39
Fimbo Ya Mayonye, 186
Fipa (people), 57
First World War, 61, 67, 84
Fodeba, K., 37-8, 114, 204
Fon (people), 208
Ford Foundation, The, 156
France, 29, 182, 186, 188, 192-3, 242
Francis the Parisian, 79, 81-2
Fratti, M., *Che Guevara*, 143
Frederikse, J., 239
Freedom Charter, The, 235
Freedom in Our Lifetime, 235
Friendship Textile Drama Club, 198
Freire, P., 149, 151-2, 159, 170-1

FRELIMO (Frente de Libertaçâo de Moçambique), 56, 199-200, 210, 214, 224
French colonialism, 22, 25, 27, 29, 34-8, 173, 175, 183, 186, 192, 197
French cultural centres, 108, 111, 186
Fugard, A., 219, 225 (with Kani, J. and Ntshona, W.), *Sizwe Bansi is Dead*, 219
Fulani (people/language), 92-3
funeral rituals, 15, 196
The Funeral, 147
Fwanyanga, M., *Homecoming*, 144

Ga (people/language), 130-1
Gabon, 108, 174, 182, 193
Gaborone, 192
Gallo Record Co., 217
Gambari (people), 201
Gambia, The, 176
Ganda, O., *Cabascabo*, 186, *l'Exile*, 189
Gatoonye wa, M., 244
Gaumont Co., 183
Gbehanzin, 115
Gboko village, 167
Gekau, K., 126, 137, 242, 249
gender, 7, 9, 13, 19, 45-6, 50, 52, 55-7, 79, 81, 167-9, 178, 192, 202, 203, 204, 244, 246
George V (King), 78
Gerima, H., *Mirt Sort Shi Amit*, 185
German colonialism, 61, 129
Germany, 232, 242
Getina, O., 195
Gevisser, M., 208
Ghana, 18, 23, 31-3, 42, 47, 51, 57, 73, 75, 83, 87, 89-90, 94, 102-3, 112-14, 117-19, 120, 130-1, 138-9, 149, 180, 183, 186, 192, 204, 215, 219
Ghana Brigade Group, The, *Obra Ye Ko*, 83
Ghanaian Institute of Art and Culture, *The Good Samaritans*, 130-1
Gibbs, J., 103, 139, 176
Gicamu theatre movement, 242
Gikuyu (people), 250
Gilbert and Sullivan, 84, 106
Gilbert, M., 208
Giriana (people/language), 250
Glover Memorial Hall, 84, 87-8
Goge (dance/mime), 60
Gold Coast (*see* Ghana)
Golding, P., 29, 172-3
Goldsmith, O., 21, 106, *She Stoops to Conquer*, 21
Gotrick, K., 15
Goumbe (dance/mime), 60
Graft de, J., 15, 112, *Sons and Daughters*, 112
Graham-White, A., 41, 112, *The Drama of Black Africa*, 112
Gramsci, A., xii
Granderson, C., 115
Gregory (Lady), *The Gossips of Ede* (adaptation), 133, *Spreading the News*, 143
Greig, R., 237
griot (epic singer/poet), 117, 176, 189, 197
Grotowski, J., 127, 232
Grupo Scenico, 199
Guinea Bissau, 157, 171, 209-10
Guinea (Conakry), 197, 204-5
Gulbenkian Foundation, 152

Gule wa Mkulu (masquerade), 50, 51, 52, 54-55, 201
Gun (people), 208
Gwassa, G. C. K., 129

Haiti, 130
Halo (mime), 18, 78
Hama, B., *Kutica Nima*, 36
Hamba Dompas (theatre group), 231
Hamujompa, P., *Mucaala*, 144
Happy Stars, The, 79, 81-2
Harambee, 205, 245
Harare, 54, 254
Harper, P., 207
Hausa (people/language), 12, 88, 93, 161-3, 164, 182
Hawaii 5-0, 180
Hazards of Poor Sanitation, 147
Heinemann anthologies, 175
Henderson, G., 75
Henga (people), 64
Heshina Si Utumwa, 183
Hethersett, A. C., 97-8, *Iwe Kika Ekerin li Ede Yoruba*, 98
Hides, 26
highlife (music), 78, 89, 155
Highway Patrol, 180
history plays, 29-30, 85-7, 92, 98, 115, 116, 117, 121, 125-6, 235, 247-8
Hlatshwayo, M., 231
Hodgson, A., 110
Hollinshed, R., 98
Hollywood, 24, 185, 189
l'Homme de Niger, 25
Hommes sans nommes, Les, 25
Horn, A., 15, 127, 142-3, 156
Horniman, R., 17
Houghton, J., 22
Hurley, P., 160
Hussein, E., 129-30, 199, 207, *Kinjeketile*, 129-30
Hutton, C., 76, 89

IATA (International Alliance of Theatre Associations), 252, 254
I Love Lucy, 180
Ibadan, 14, 22, 88, 92, 133-5
Ibadan (University of), 95-6, 114, 133-5, 137, 139, 143, 242
Ibibio (people), 51
Ibsen, H., 132
Idoye, P., 148
Ife, 88, 97, 113, 118, 124
Iganga, 26
Igbimadion, J., 194
Igbo (people/language), 50, 93, 96-7, 115, 181
Ijaw (people/language), 114
Ijimere, O., 96, 139, *The Fall*, 139
Ilange Le So Phoneola Abesabeni, 227-8, 230-1
Ilesha, 88, 92
Ilorin, 92
Imbuga, F., 137
Imfunduso (theatre form), 227
Imperato, P., 6
Incwala (ritual), 196
India, 163, 198, 252, 254

Indonesia, 252
Inkatha Freedom Party (South
  Africa), 231, 237
Ipi Tombi, 217
IPTA (International Popular Theatre
  Alliance), 252, 254
Irele, A., 126-7
Islam, 60, 69-70, 128, 194
Ismael, S., 224
Isola, A., *Kosegbe*, 130, *Aye Yo Won
  Tan*, 130
Italy, 136, 188
ITI (International Theatre Institute),
  154-5, 168, 252
Ivory Coast, (*see* Côte d'Ivoire)
Izibongo (praise poetry), 197

Jacobs, W. W., *The Monkey's Paw*
Jaguar, Jokes, The, 82
Jaiyesimi, 191
Jamaa ya Mzee Pembe, 182-3
Jamaa ya Mzee Selenge, 182-3
Jamaica, 252
jazz, 89, 215
Jeans schools, 31-2, 35-6
Jeffreys, D. W., 56
Jeyifo, B., 84, 100-2, 181
Johannesburg, 17, 24, 55, 59, 65, 215,
  219, 223, 227-8, 237
Johannesburg Civic Theatre, 237
Johnson, B., 72, 74, 75, 77, 81, 87,
  219, *Afei Menu Moho*, 81
Johnson, S. (Rev.), 97
Johnston, H. (Sir), *53*
Jolson, A., 74
Jos, 88
Jules-Rosette, B., 184
Junction Avenue Theatre, 227-8, 230
J. Z. Moyo Refugee Camp, 213

Kaarsholm, P., 213, 255
Kabaka, The, 128
Kabale, S., 132
Kabete, 35-6
Kadhi., J., 250
Kadungule, E., 214
Kaduma, G., 153
Kaduna, 88-9, 96
Kagnongo, K., 242
Kahari, G., 210-11
Kaka II village, 168
Kalanga (people/language), 152
Kalela (dance/mime), 60, 62, 64-6,
  70
Kalingalinga (Lusaka), 155
Kamau, A., 243
Kamba, G., *Mwana Keba*, 186
Kambaa, 68
Kamiriithu Cultural Centre, 113,
  138, *246*, 250-2, 255-6
Kamiti Prison, 248
Kamlongera, C., 156
Kampala, 111-12, 127-8 135-7
Kampala City Players, The, 127
Kampala Shining Star Association,
  127
Kampala Theatre, The, 136
Kamphausen, H., 25, 188
Kamsakala, 145
Kamuli village, 26
Kani, J. (with Fugard, A. and
  Ntshona, W.), *Sizwe Bansi is Dead*,
  220
Kano, 88-9
KANU (Kenya African National

Union), 250
Kanye, 153
Kapumpa, M., 143
Kargbo, J., *Let Me Die Alone*, 250-1,
  Poyoh Ton Wahala, 250-1, *Case of
  the Pregnant Schoolgirl*, 251,
  Ekundayo, 251
Kargongou, E., 184
Karuna-ini, 243
Kasama, 145
Kasoma, K,. 109-10, 143-5, 154, *The
  Fools Marry*, 109, *The Poisoned
  Cultural Meat*, 144-5
Katanga (province), 61
Katete, 66, 143
Katundula, 66
Kaunda, K. (President), 113, 205,
  'humanism', 114, 143, 159, 162,
  205
Kaunda Square (Lusaka), 142
Kavanagh, R. Mshengu, 114, 216-17,
  225
Kawadwa, B., 127-8, 132, 251,
  Oluyimba Lwa Wankoko, 127-8, *St
  Charles Lwange*, 127-8
Kayangu Film Players, The, 127
Keita, M. (President), 197
Kelepile, J., 147, 153
Kente, G., 217, 219-21, 225, 232,
  Manana the Jazz Prophet, 217,
  Sikalo, 217, 221, *Life*, 219, *Zwi*, 220-
  1, *Can You Take It?*, 221, *Mama and
  the Load*, 221
Kenya, 19-21, 26, 28, 30-2, 35, 59-60,
  62, 67, 106, *107*, 111-13, 115, 125-7,
  129, 148, 173, 176-7, 180, 182-3,
  186, 195, 197, 204, 240-5, *246*, 247-
  51, 254-5
Kenya Film Corporation, The, 184
Kenya National Theatre, 106, *107*,
  111, 126, 129, 249
Kenyatta, J. (President), 197, 205,
  248, 250
Kerr, D., 64-5, 70-1, 139, *140*, 144,
  147-8, 156, 208, 213
Kgatleng District, 153
Kgotla, 152
Kheri, S., 68
Khumalo, B., 237
Khumalo, L., 237
Kiambu, 247, 249
Kidd, R., 151-2, 159-61, 168, 212-13
Kikuyu (language), 35, 242-5, 250-1
Kilembe, 136-7
Kimathi, D., 115, 125-7, 129, 243
King, K., 35
King Kong, 216-17, *218*
Kinjeketile, 115, 129
Kintu, D., 250
Kintu Players, The, 127
Kinyanjui, P., 194
Kisimu, 136
Kitsina-Ala Project, 166-7
Kittermaster, M., 30
Kiyingi, W., 127-8, 132, 135
Koitswa, S., 153
Kontjingile, 156
Kojo Brake's Band, 78
Koma-Koma, W., *Mg'ande Kapena
  Malipenga*, 64-5
Konaté, M., 197
Koné, A., *Le Respect des Morts*, 139,
  142
Konye village, 168
Korekore (people), 212, 239

Kotchy, B., 139
Kote-tlon (narrative drama), *3*, 4-6
Krio (language), 251
Kubik, G., 15
Kumpukwe, J., 177-8
Kurame village, 168
Kuyinu, G., 87-8
Kwagh-hir (masquerade/puppet
  performance), 166-7
Kwa Kuta, 144-5
Kwa Mashu, 231
Kwazulu, 227
Kwela (music), 215
Kyevugo (praise poetry), 197

Labouret, H., 18
Lacerda, F., 29-30, *Journey to the
  Lands of Kazembe*, 30
Ladan, U. (with Lyndersay, D.),
  Shaihu Umar, 116
Ladipo, A., 99
Ladipo, D., 90-1, 96-100, 121, 181,
  Moremi, 97-8, *Oba Koso*, 97-9, *Oba
  Moro*, 97-8, *Oba Waja*, 97, 121,
  Alawada, 181, *Bode Wasini*, 181,
  Ejagbingba, 181, *Ekeja*, 181, *Ewe
  Awo*, 181, *Gbade Gesin*, 181, *Oyelo-
  gwawo*, 181, *Tiatu Yoruba*, 181
Laedza Batanani (theatre movement),
  145, 147-9, *150*, 151-6, 159-61, 166,
  168, 252
Lagos, 22-3, 34, 59, 84, 86, 88
Lakoju, T., 161
Lamu, 76
Lan, D., 212
Latin America, 195
Layeni, A. A., 85
Latham, G., 26
Lee, M., 136
Legon (University of Ghana), 118,
  138-9
LESOMA (League for a Socialist
  Malawi), 202
Lesotho, 151, 153, 156, 158. 170-1
Letembet-Ambily, A., *L'Europe
  inculpée*, 175
Letwabe, M. J., 232
Lewis, I. M., 45, 211
Liberia, 9, 22, 76. 81
Libreville, 182
Likoma Island, 64-6
Lilongwe, 155, 202
Limuru, 249
Linasia, 223
Linden, I., 50
Lisabi Hall, 84
Lisbon, 18
literacy, 154, 163, 242-4
literary drama, 29-30, 91-5, 96-100,
  105-31, 133-7, 229
Litumuca, 144
Liwonde, 169-70
Lobengula (Chief), 213
Lo Liyong, T., 45
Lomé, 79, 81
London, 8, *17*, 23, 91, 99, 215
London Shakespeare Co., 108
Loram, C. T., 35
Love, A., 191
Lozi (people/language), 144-5, 155
Luanda, 33, 233
Luapula Province (Zambia), 147
Lubumbashi, 64
Lucas (Bishop), 76
Lucky Stars, 215

Luganda (language), 127-8, 136
Luhamba, A., 158
Luhya (people/language), 250
Lukuku, W., *Drown in a Drink*, 144-5
Lungu, D., *The Man in the Street*, 182, 194
Luo (people/language), 35, 136, 250-1
Lusaka, 30, 109-11, 113, *140-1*, 142-5, 153-6, 214, 232, 235
Lusaka Housing Unit, 153-4
Luthuli (Chief), 235
Luwingu, 155
Luwum, J. (Archbishop), 128
Lyndersay, D. (with Ladan, U.), *Shaihu Umar*, 116

Machinga (District, Malawi), 62-3
McClaren, R., 221, 223, 239
Macu, R., 219, 221, 224, *A Master of Convenience*, 221, 224
Madagascar, xi
Maddy, P., *Big Berrin*, 130, 251
Madzikatire, S., 183
Maghreb, xi, 35
'Maji Maji' Rebellion, 129
Mahlamme, B., *Mahlemola*, 219
Mahoka (radio drama), 177
Mahood, M., 134
Majitu Theatre Company, 251
Makerere Dramatic Society, The, 135
Makerere Free Travelling Theatre, The, 135-8, 143, 242
Makerere (University of), 127, 135-8
Makhabu, M., 230
Makisi (masquerade), 15, 42, *43*, 44
Makongoro Group, 198
Makoni, 212
Makurdi, 89, 166-7, 242
Malawi, 32, 50-2, 54-5, 61-2, *63*, 64-5, 70, 139, *146*, 156, *157*, 158, *164*, 169-70, 177-9, *203*, 204, 207, 252, 253
Malawi, (University of), 139, 169-70
Malaysia, 252
Male, Z., 156, 171
Mali, 1, 4-6, 111, 188, 193, 197-8, 204-5, 207, 254
Malian National Ensemble, 197, 205
Malikopa (radio drama), 30
Malindi, 67
Malipenga (dance mime), 60, 62, 63, 64-71
Malkmus, L., 185
Malya Project, The, 158-9
Manaka, M., 229, 231-2, *234*, 237, *Egoli*, 229, *The Horn*, 232, *Vuka*, 232, *Size*, *234*, *Coming Home*, 237, *Pula*, 237
Mandela, N. (President), 235-7
Mandingo (people), 1
Mang'anja (people), 50
Mangbetu (people), *10*
Mangochi, 70
Manhattan Brothers, 215
Mansola (King), 52, *53*
Manzini, 156
Mapanje, J., 202
Maplanka, M., 153
Maponya, M., 225, 228, *229*, 231-2, *The Hungry Earth*, 225, 228, *Umongikazi*, 225, *229*
Maputo, 233
Marabi (music), 215

Marandellas District, 212
Marionhill School, 34
Market Theatre, 228, 237
Mariage au Dahomey, Un, 37
Masabe (spirit possession ritual), 45
Masasi, 69
Masemo, 251
Maseru, 170-1
Masiye, A., 29-30, 39, *The Lands of Kazembe*, 29-30, *Singing for Freedom*, 39
Maska village, 162-3
Maskiyane, M., 216
masquerade, 1, *3*, 4, 6-7, *8*, 9, *10*, 11-12, *13*, 14, 42, *43*, 44, 48, 50, *52*, 55, 157
Matinga, C., *The False Friend*, 32
Matlahabane, I., 224
Matshikiza, J., *Prophets in the Black Sky*, 237
'Mau Mau' War, 125-6, 242-3
Mauritania, 188-9, 192-3
MAWU (Metal and Allied Workers' Union), 227, 230-1
May, C., 194
Mbalachanda, 156, 158, 169
Mbaquanga (music), 215
Mbari Club, 96
Mbari Mbayo (cultural centre), 97-8, 113, 166-7, 242
MBC (Malawi Broadcasting Corporation), 177-9
Mbewe, S. L., 177-9, *Kajekete*, 177, *Kapalepale*, 177, *Pa Majiga*, 177
mbira (musical instrument), 211, 214
Mbotosha (dance), 202
Mbowa, R., 127
Mbube (music), 215
Mbulumwanza, B., 115
Mbumba (dance), 202, *203*, 204, 254
Mbunda (people), 15
Mbuzi, S. (with Kerr, D.) *The Trial of Zwangendaba*, 149
MCP (Malawi Congress Party), 201-2, *203*, 204, 254
Mda, Z., 156, 171
MDALI (Music, Drama, Dance and Literature), 223-4
Mecca, 162
media imperialism, 172-3, 174-80, 183-5, 189, 194
Meillassoux, C., 148
Mekgoe, S., *uLindiwe*, 219
Men of Africa, 28
Menga, G., *La Marmite de Koka Mbala*, 175
Merriam, A., 55
Mganda (dance mime), 62, 65, 67, 68, 70
Mhloti, 223-4
Mhangwana, S, *Blame Yourself*, 219, *Unfaithful Woman*, 219
Mhondoro, 212
Miango (dance), 207
Micere Mugo, 115, 125-6, 129-30, 252 (with Ngugi wa Thiong'o), *The Trial of Dedan Kimathi*, 125-6, 138, 242, *Mzalendo Kimathi*, 242-5
Michenzani Social Club, 198
Mikanza, N., 205
militaristic mime, 59-70
Mitchell, C., 64-6
Mkalama, 68
Mkangi, G., 59, 67

Mkushi (refugee camp), 213
Mlama, P., 158, 252, 255, *Remedy for Rot*, 255
Mlongoti, E., 30
Mnyampala, M., *Ngonjera Chama Cha TANU*, 199
Mobutu, S. S. (President), 173, 205
Mochudi, 153
Modikwe's Band, 215
Mod Squad, 180
Moeketsi, K., 216
Mogadishu, 185
MOGPAFIS (Mogadishu, Pan African Film Symposium), 185
Molepolole, 153-4, 159
Molière, J. B., 34, 37, 134, *Les Fourberies de Scapin*, 134
Mombasa, 59, 67, 76
Mombasa Times, The, 67
Moodley, L., 224
Moodley, S., 223-4
Mooki, B., 236
Moore, R.J.B., 67
Mopeia, 56
Morake, K. P. (Hon.) 159
morality plays, 33, 40
Morari, 239
More (language), 176
Morepa, 217
Morewa, 168, 252
Morriseau-Leroy, F., 130-1, *Oyo-Ye*, 131
Moser, G., 40
Mosia, M., 217
Mouralis, B., 39
Mouzon, D., 197
Mozambique, 16, 45-6, 50, 55-7, 64, 179, 199-200, 207, 209-10, 212-14, 233, 239
Mozambican National Directorate of Culture, 199-200
Mozart, A., *The Magic Flute*, 111
Mpakati, A., 202
Mphalele, E., 42, 144, *The Return of Nsato*, 144
MPLA (Movimento Popular de Libertaçao de Angola), 209
Mshengu, *see* Kavanagh, and McClaren entries
Mtambweni, 68
Mtetwa, E., 215
Mtonga, M., 52, 54-5, 103, 143, 145, 154, 156, 252
Mtwa, P., *Bopha*, 231 (with Simon, B., and Ngema, M.), *Woza Albert!*, 225, *226*, 233
Muchenje, T., 156
Mudenda, E. H. (Hon.), 159
Mufacheni, 155
Muganda (dance mime), 60, 62, *63*, 64-70
Mugo, Micere, *see* Micere Mugo
Muhammed, General (President), 182
Mujura, M., 212, 239
Mukasa-Balikuddembe, J., *Bones, The Mirror*, 136
Mukadota Family, The, 183
Mulangali, *157*
Mulimi ya Butali, 144
Muller, J., 256
Mulungushi Declaration, 143
Mungoni, E., 30

Muqina, M. (Rev.), *Give Us This Day, The Trial*, 221
Mustapha. A., *Le Retour de l'aventurier*, 188
Mutenga, K., 147, 153
Mutwa, C., *uNosilemela*, 112, 221-12
Muungano, 198
Muwowo, E., 22
Muzorewa, A. (Bishop), 214
Mwacisompola, 156
Mwansa, D., 131, 148, 156, 252
Mwanza, 158
Mwima Trading Centre, 169-70
mystery plays, 33, 40
Mzimba, 62

NAC (National Association of Culture, South Africa), 237
Nadiope, K. (Chief), 26
Nahoubou (King), 117
Nairobi, 59, 61-2, 106, *107*, 125, 129, 242, 249-50
Nairobi (University of), 126, 138, 241-4
Nambote, M., 64-5, 70-1
narrative drama, 15, 57, *73*, 142, 177, 189, 232
NASA (Nurses Association of South Africa), 228
Natal, 223, 230-1, 233
Natal (University of), 230
NATAAZ (National Theatre Arts Association of Zambia), 111
National Dance Theatre of Zaire, 205, *206*
National Dance Troupes, 204-5, *206*
National Party (South Africa), 237
Nazareth, P., 109, 138, 142-3
Nazombe, O., *Kulyabantu*, 144
Ndaba, S., *Ubantu Bomlhaba*, 238
Ndau (people), 45
Ndau, C.A.S., *l'Exil d'Albouri*, 117
Ndebele (people/language), 213-14
Ndebele, N., 237
Ndirande Welfare Club, 32
Ndlovo, D., *Sheila's Day*, 237
Nehanda, 211
neo-realism, 188
neo-traditional drama, 114, 221-2
Negritude, 2, 44, 204, 207
Neria, 192
Neto, A., 209
New York, 89, 91, 237
New York Times, 182
Ngbaisi (King), 115
Ngema, M., 225, *226*, 233, 237, *Asinamali*, 233, *Sarafina*, 237, *Music at 4 am*, 225, *226*, 233
Ngoni (people), 45
Ngonjera, 176, 199
Ngugi wa Mirii (with Ngugi wa Thiong'o), *Ngaahika Ndeenda*, 129, 245, 247-9
Ngugi wa Thiong'o, 19, 106, 125, 129, 137, 242, 245, *245*, 247-51, 253-4, *The River Between*, 39, *Maitu Njugira*, *246*, 248-51, 252 (with Micere Mugo), *The Trial of Dedan Kimathi*, 125-6, 137, 242, (with Micere Mugo), *Mzalendo Kimathi*, 242-5 (with Ngugi wa Mirii), *Ngaahika Ndeenda*, 129, 245, 247-9
Ng'weno, H., 106
Ng'winamila troupe, 198
Ngubane, S., 230-1

Nhlabatsi, D. A., 159
Niassa Province (Mozambique), 210, 214
Nicaragua, 252
Niger, 27, 186, 188-9
Niger River, 198
Nigeria, *3*, 7, *8*, 9, *10*, 11-12, *13*, 14, 22-6, 42, 44, 46, *48*, 49, 52, *53*, 54, 60, 76, 82, *83*, 84-103, 113-15, *116*, 117-19, *122*, 130, 133-5, 149, 161-3, 173, 175-6, 180-1, 186, *187*, 191-2, 194-5, 198, 200, 207, 219, 251-2, 253
Nigeria Daily Times
Njama, K., 125
Njoroge, K., 242
Nkenge, 205
Nkhata, A., 30
Nkhata Bay, 69
Nkhotakota, 70
Nkomo, J. (President, ZAPU, PF), 213
Nkosi, L., 113, 119, 208
Nkrumah, K. (President), 78, 92, 114, 117, 180, 205, 'conscientism', 114, 205
Nkrumah is a Mighty Man, 78
Nkrumah is Greater than Before, 78
NNDP (Nigerian National Democratic Party), 92
Northern Rhodesia (*see* Zambia)
Nouvelle Vague films, 188
Norway, 132
Notcutt, L., 26
Nsanje, 253
Nsenga (people/language), 14
Nsingizini, 156
Ntaja, *63*
Ntshona, W. (with Fugard, A. and Kani, J.), *Sizwe Bansi is Dead*, 219
NTV (Nigeria Television), 181-2
NUSAS (National Union of South African Students), 222
Nwoko, D., 95
Nyame, E. K., 78-9
Nyangwicu (dance), 243
Nyanja (language), 143, 154
Nyasaland (*see* Malawi)
Nyau (ancestor cult), 50, *51*, 52, 54-5, 201
Nyemnego (Princess), 111
Nyerere, J., 4, 34, 114, 136-7, 'Ujamaa', 4, 114
Nyeri, 126, 243, 249

OAU (Organization of African Unity), 197, 254
Obafemi, O., 123
Obame, J. B., *Assimalados*, 117, 175
Obey, A., *Noah*, 133
Obote, M. (President), 128
Obiechina, E., 22
Odets, C., *Waiting for Lefty*, 144
Odwira Festival, 47
Ogun (Yoruba God), 54
Ogunba, O., 39, 49, 54, 97
Ogunbe, A., 100
Ogunbiyi, Y., 15
Ogunde, H., *83*, 84-96, 101, 128, 180, 191, 219, 251, *Bread and Bullet*, *83*, 88-9, *Garden of Eden*, 85, *Israel and Egypt*, 85, *Africa and God*, 85-6, *The Throne of God*, 85, *Nebuchadnezzar's Reign*, 85, *Balthazzar's Feast*, 85, *King Solomon*, 85,

Journey to Heaven, 85-87, *The Black Forest*, 87, 90, *Worse than Crime*, 88, *Herbert Macaulay*, 88, *Human Parasites*, 88, *Strike and Hunger*, 88-9, *My Darling Fatima*, 89, *Portmanteau*, 89, *Beggar's Cave*, *Highway Eagle*, 89, 94, *Princess Jaja*, 89, *Village Hospital*, 89, *Delicate Millionaire*, 89, *Swing the Jazz*, 89, *Gold Coast Melodies*, 89, *Yoruba Ronu*, 90, 92-3, *The Song of Unity*, 90-1, *Keep Nigeria One*, 93, *Mama Eko*, 93, *Oba'nta*, 93, *Ogun Pari*, 93, *Oh Ogunde!*, 93, *Onimoto*, 93-4, *K'ehin Sohun*, 94, *Aiye*, 191-2, *Jaiyesimi*, 191
Ogunmola, K., 90, 94-6, 121, 134, *The Reign of the Mighty*, 95, *The Love of Money*, 95, *The Palm-wine Drinkard* (adaptation), 95-6, 134
Ogunsola, I., 100, 181, 191, *Aja lo l'Eru* (adaptation), 181, *Efunsetan Aniwura*, 100, 181
Oh Calcutta!, 93
Oke Ado, 100
Okediji, O., *Aja la l'Eru*, 101 (with Aniwura, E.), *Rere Run*, 130
Okot p'Bitek, 66, 111-12, 242, *The Song of Ocol*, 66, *The Song of Lawino*, 111, 242, *Acan* 111
Okongu (Chief), *10*
Okumkpa, 2, 7, 9, 46
Okyeame, 118
Oladule, F., 186
Olajabu, O., 98-9
Olaiya, M., 100-2
Olusola, S., 176, 180
Omara, T., *The Exodus*, 136
Omotoso, K., *The Curse*, 123
Ondo, 49, 54
Onibon-Okuta, A., 99
Onimola, S., 85
Operation Feed the Nation, 162
Opubor, A., 21, 31, 131
Ori Olokun Theatre, 113, 118
ORTF (l'Organization Radiodiffusion-Television Française), 175, 242
Orun Mooru, 191
Osofisan, F., 123-4, 128, *Once Upon Four Robbers*, 123, *The Chattering and the Song*, 123-4
Osodi, F., 251
Osogbo, 88, 96-7, 113
Ottenberg, S., 2, *3*, 7, *8*, 9, 42, 46, 50
Ouagadougou, 111, 184, 192
Ousmane, Sembène (*see* Sembène, Ousmane)
Owo, 88
Owomoyela, O., 15, 82, 84
OXFAM, 158
Oyenusi (Dr), 94
Oyo, 11, 14, 52, 88, 92
Oyono-Mbia, G., *Trois prétendants, un mari*, 112, 144, *Notre fille ne se mariera pas*, 175

PAC (Pan African Congress), 233
Pacquet, A., 192
PAIGC (Partido Africano de Independencia de Guine e Cabo Verde), 210
Paiva (song), 56-7
Paiva, A., 56
Palaver, 25

Panther Film Productions, 195
Paris, 18, 29, 36, 38, 108, 186, 189
Pategi Regatta, 182
Patriotic Front (Zimbabwe), 210
Paukwa Theatre, 255
p'Bitek, Okot, see Okot p'Bitek
Penda, P. M., *La Fusil*, 175
People are Invincible, The, 214
Peroz (Captain), 37
PET (People's Experimental
   Theatre), 223-4
Peters, A., 96
Peterson, H., 235
Peul (people), 205
Phelps-Stokes Commission, 35-6
Pheto, M., 224
Philippines, The, 163, 172, 252, 254
Phiri, M., *Soweto Flowers Will Grow*,
   235
Pickering, A. K., 32
pidgin (language), 130, 164, 176, *253*
Pines, J., 195
Plautus, *O Mostelleria*, 144
Pliya, J., *Kondo le raquin*, 175
Plymouth Committee, 29
Pohland, J., *Bullfrog in the Sun*, 184
Poland, 232
Polyvalent Group, 199-200
'Poor Theatre', 232
Poro Secret Society, 251-2
Porto Novo, 208
Portraits of Survival, 242
Portuguese colonialism, 16, 20, 29,
   30, 33, 45, 56-7, 199
Pownall, D., 109-10
Post Office Savings Bank, 26
praise song, 196-8, 201-2, 204
Prétendants rivaux, Les, 37
Primary Health Care, 156, *157, 164*
Proshika, 252
Pungwe, 212-14, 239
puppets, 149, *150*, 153
Pwago na Paguza (radio drama), 177

Radio Bantu, 222
radio drama, 27, 29-30, 127, 158, 172-
   3, *174*, 175-9, 183, 194
Rag-time (music), 76
Ranger, T., 60-2, 64-6, 239, *Beni,
   Dance and Society in East Africa*,
   60-2, 64-6
Rank Co., 183
Ranko, F., 100, 191
Raposo, J. P., 56
Ravan Press, 232
Razha (dance mime), 60
Rathebe, D., 216
RDD (Rassemblement démo-
   cratique Dahoméen), 200
Rebelo, G., 179
refugee theatre, 213-14, 235-6
Reith, J. C., 29
Ricard, A., 79
ritual, 1, 4, 7, 9, *10*, 14, 47, 50, *51*, 52,
   54, 114, 128, 196, 201, 212, 221
Rockefeller Foundation, 133, 241
Roman Catholic Church, 33, 40, 45,
   50-2, 54-5
Rome, 189
Rorke's Drift, 25
Ross, A. C., 201
Rossini, G., *The Barber of Seville*, 20
Rotimi, O., 100, 114, *116*, 117-18,
   Ovanramven Nogbaisi, 116, 117,
   The Gods Are Not to Blame, 117-18,

Kurunmi, 117
Rouch, J., *27*
'rough theatre', *148*, 153
Rubadiri, D., 127
Ruganda, J., 127, 138
Rugyendo, M., 2, 113, 124-5, *The
   Contest*, 124-5
Rumba (dance), 62
Runyoro/Rutoro (language), 136

Saad, S. B., 198
Sabatier, P., 40
SABTU (South African Black
   Theatre Union), 223
SACP (South African Communist
   Party), 236
Sadlers Wells, 215
Sadru-Kassem, *Bones*, 136
Safi, F., *La Lettre paysanne*, 188
Saimanga, P., 198-9
Saltpond, 76
Samb, A., 185-6, 188-9, 192, *Kodou,
   186*, 189, *Jom*, 189
Samory, 37, 115
Senders of the River, 25
Sangha, 207
Sango (god), 11, 99
São Tomé & Principe, 40
Sarmcol Factory, 230-1
Saro-Wiwa, K., 181, 251, *Basi and
   Co.*, 181
Sarraut, A., 36
SASO (South African Students'
   Organization), 222-3
St. Vincent, 252
Sauadogo, M., *La fille du Volta*
'Saucepan Special', *29*
Saul, J., 49
Schipper, M., 15
Schlosberg, B., 215
Schoffeleers, M., 50
Schools Drama, 33-4, 107
Schutte Commission, 236
SECMA (Societé d'Exploration
   Cinematographique Africaine),
   183-4
Second World War, 62
Sea Shanties, 72
Sekondi, 74, 76
Sekyi, K., *The Blinkards*, 23
Seghers, A., 38
Segon Youth Ensemble, 198
SEIFSA (Steel and Engineering
   Industrial Federation of South
   Africa), 227
Sellers, W., 26
Sembène, Ousmane, 186, 188-9, *190*,
   191-4, *Le Mandat (Mandabi)*, 186,
   188, *190*, 191, *Emitai*, 188, *190*, 192,
   Xala, 188-9, 193-4, *Ceddo*, 188, 192,
   Le Docker Noir, 191, *Oh pays mon
   beau people*, 191, *Les bouts de bois de
   Dieu*, 191, *Borrom Sarrat*, 191, *La
   Noir de …*, 191, *Niaye*, 191
Sena Sugar Estate, 56-7
Senanga, 144
Senanu, K. E., 121
Senegal, 34, 36-8, *107*, *147*, 184-6,
   188-9, *190*, 190-4, 204, 254
Senghor, L. S., 44
Serumaga, R., 112
Setswana (language), 151
Shaka, 115
Shakespeare, W., 20, 98, 106, 108,
   133, 138, *Hamlet*, 20, *Richard II*, 20,

Henry IV, 20, *Julius Caesar*, 34,
   136-7, *The Merchant of Venice*, 133
Shalaberi village, 162
Shank, T., 148
Shezi, M., *Shanti*, 222-5
Shiquoma, 222
Shona (people/language), 183, 210-
   12
Shoniwa, G., 147
Short, P., 208
Shumba, M., 139
Sibeko, V., 235
Sierra Leone, 15, 20, 22, 765, 112,
   130, 149, 156, *206*, 251
Sierra Leone National Theatre, *206*
Silele village, *146*
Simon, B., 225, *226*, 227 (with Mtwa,
   P. and Ngema, M.), *Woza Albert!*,
   225, *226*
Simukoko, Y., 143, 145
Sissoko, F.D., *La Savane rouge*, 36
S'ketch, 223
Slaves of Music, The, 143
Smanje Manje (music), 65, 215
Smith, I. (Prime Minister), 168, 210
Soba village, 162-3
SOFACIA (Société de participation
   Cinéma Africain), 183
So Is the World, 79
Soirée de Larhalle Nuba, La, 176
Soja (dance mime), 60
Sokame, 36-7
Solanas, F., 195
Soli (people/language), 154
Somalia, 185, 252
SONAVOCI (Société radiophonique
   de la France d'Outre-mer), 29,
   173-4
Sotho (people/language), 223
South Africa, *17*, 21, 23, 25, 34, 64,
   117, 156, 215-17, *218*, 219-25, *226*,
   227-33, *234*, 235-7, *238*, 239, 254
Sowande, B., 123-4, 128, 132, *The
   Night Before*, 124, *Farewell to
   Babylon*, 124
Soweto, 117, 215, 219-20, 223, 235
Soyikwa African Theatre Company,
   232-3, *234*
Soyinka, W., 91-3., 100, 103, 114, 119,
   110, 121, *122*, 123, 135, 175-6, 180-
   1, 186, *187*, 232, 251, *The Dance of
   the Forests*, 91, 119, 121, *Kongi's
   Harvest*, 92-3, 121, *122*, 123, *197*,
   Jero's Metamorphosis, 93, 121,
   Madmen and Specialists, 93, 119,
   123, *The Strong Breed*, 110, *The
   Road*, 119, 123, *The Bacchae*, 119,
   The Lion and the Jewel, 121, *Death
   and the King's Horseman*, 121,
   Opera Wanyosi, 121, *Before the
   Blackout*, 121, *The Swamp Dwellers*,
   133, *Broke Time Bar*, 176
Speed, F., *My Brother's Children*, 194
spirit possession, 7, 15, 45-6, 64, 211-
   12, 215
Sri Lanka, 163, 252
Stapleton, C., 194
Steadman, I., 231-3
Stephens (Major), 67
stereotypes, 4-7, 12, *13*, 19, 52, 54-7,
   74-81, 94, 160, 198-9, 215, 217
Sujirharaj, F., 254
Suleman, A., 182
Sumer, 115
Sunday Nation (Kenya), 251

Sundiata, 197, 204-5
Sutherland, E., 72, 79, 114, 118-19, 120, *The Marriage of Anansewa*, 118-19, *120*
SWAPO (South West Africa People's Organization), 233
Swaziland, 151, 156, 162, 196, 254
Swynnerton Plan, 243

Taarabu na Vichekesho, 198
Tabora, 61-2, 66, 69
Tafika Theatre, 143
Tomokloe, J., *Joqolo*, 147
Tamuduni Players, 126, 242
Tanga, 198
Tanganyika (*see* Tanzania)
TANU (Tanganyika African National Union), 198
Tanzania, 57, 60-2, 68-9, 115, 129-30, 153-4, 158-9, 176, 186, 198-9, 207, 215, 235, 252
Tavarwisa, S., 214
Target 2000, 156
Tax, 26
Taylor, W. H., 31-2
TAZ (Theatre Association of Zambia), 109-111, 131
TECON (Theatre Council of Natal), 223-4, *Black Images*, 224
Tea, 26
television drama, 30, 127, 172-3, 179-83, 194
Tambuna village, *51*
Tete, 210
That Scoundrel Subaru, 134
Théâtre Africain, Le, 38, 204
theatre architecture, 2, *10*, 17, 20, 111-13, 118, 142, *146*, 152, *206*, 243, *246*
Théâtre David Sorano, Le, 108
Théâtre du la Cité, 142
Théâtre des Nations, 108
Theatre for Development, 31-2, 130, 149, *150*, 151-63, *164*, 227, 252, 254
theatre-in-the-round, *146*, 155, *164*
Theatre Ltd., 127
'theatre of emergency', 231-3
Thiam. N., *Karim*, *192*
Third Party Insurance, 137
Thwaites, D., 69
Tikwiza Theatre, 235
Tiv (people), 166-7
Togo, 79, 208
Tomaselli, K., 227-8, 230, 256
'town theatre', 225
Tonga (people/language, Malawi), 64
Tonga (people/language, Zambia/Zimbabwe), 45-6, 144, 147, 155, 210
Tororo Cement Factory, 136
Touré, S. (President), 114, 197, 205, 'communocracy', 114, 205
tourism, 205, *206*, 207
township musicals, 185, 215-17, *218*, 224
Trader Horn, 25
Traoré, B., 36-7, 40-1, 58, 117, *Le Théâtre nègro-africaine*, 36-7
Traoré, M., *174*, 184, 186, 192-3, *Diankha-Bi*, *174*, 186, 192, *Lambaaye*, 193, *Reou Takh*, 193
Travélé, M., 18

Travélé, J., 205
travelling theatre, 127-8, 130, 133-9, 142-5, *146*, 147-9
Triomphe du griot, 37
Tsotsi, 215, 217, 220, 232
Tsotsitaal (language), 223
Tumbuka (people/language), 64, 143, 145
Turner, L. W., 29
Tutume College, 152
Tutuola, A., *The Palm-wine Drinkard*, 95-6
Twi (people/language), 118
Two Bobs, The, and the Caroline Girl, 76, 78, 81
Tyi Wara, 6

UAPA (Union of African Performing Artists), 254
UDD (Union Démocratique Dahoméen), 200
UDF (United Democratic Front, Malawi), 62, *63*
UDI (Unilateral Declaration of Independence, Zimbabwe), 211-12
Ufipa, 69
Uganda, 2, 25-6, 46, 111-12, 124-5, 127-8, 135-8, 200
Uganda National Theatre, 111, 127
Uganda Theatre Guild, 135
Ugbuojah, F. O., 194
Ujiji, 61-2
Ukwejisa, 239
Umabatha, 217
Umkhonto we Sizwe, 233, 235
Umlinganiso, 221
UNESCO (United Nations Educational, Scientific and Cultural Organization), 25, 149, 168, 247
UNF (United National Federal Party), 201
UNICEF (United Nations Children's Fund), 176
Union Soudanaise (Mali), 197
UNIP (United Indepedence Party, Zambia), 143, 196-7
United States of America, 154, 195, 233
Unity, 144
UNZADRAMS (University of Zambia Drama Society), 109-11, 131, *140*
Upper Volta (*see* Burkina Faso)
Uruwira, 69
USAA (Union of South African Artists), 216-17, 219, 242

Vail, L., 56-7
Valbert, C., 38, 105
Variava, S., 224
Vaudeville, 34, 59-60, 74, 84, 166, 215-16
Victoria refugee camp, 213
video, 152, 158, 183
Vichekesho, 198-9, 215
Vieyra, P., 194-5
VOK (Voice of Kenya), 182-3
Vrydagh, P. A., 42, 46
Vugiri, 26
Vuyisili Mini, 235

Wachira, W., 249

Wa Kyendo, M., 195
War of Liberation, The, 239
Warwick Bioscop, 23
Wasan Bomo, 163, 165
Wasan Manoma, 161-2
Wasan Maska, 162-3
Wasan Samaru, 165
Watene, K., 115, 138
Welch, Dr, 32
Welensky, R. (Sir), 201
Wenger, S., 96
West End Trio, 78
West Indies, 22
White, L., 56-7, 202
'White Face'/ 'Black Face', 65, 74, 75, 76
Wilde, O., 24, 106, *Lady Windermere's Fan*, 24
Willemen, P., 195
Williams, R., 42
Windybrow Theatre, *17*
Winneba, 139
Witwatersrand, 215, 220
WNBS (Western Nigeria Broadcasting Services), 98, 180-1
Wolof (people/language), workshop, 71, 221, 223-5, *Crossroads*, 223, *Zzi!*, 223, *Survival*, 225
work song, 55-7

Xavier, F. (St), 33
Xiconhoaca, 199-200
Xhosa (people/language), 217, 232

Yalley, Master, 74, 6
Yeats, W. B., 132
Yoruba (people/language), 9-14, 22, 49-50, 52-3, 81-2, 84-103, 130, 181
Yoruba Opera, 23, 33, 41, 44, 73, 82, *83*, 84-103, 118, 121, 134-5, 181-2, 185, 191, 194, 198, 219
Yusuf, S., 26

Zaa na Uwatunze, 176-7
Zaire, 28, 55, 61, 64, 69, 115, 117, 173, 205, 208, 252, 254
Zambezi (River), 212
ZANTAA (Zambian National Theatre Arts Association), 110-11, 131
ZANU (PF) (Zimbabwe African National Union, Patriotic Front), 211-12, 239
ZAPU (PF) (Zimbabwe African People's Union, Patriotic Front), 213, 239
Zaria, 88, 161-2, 165-6
Zambia, 15, 20-2, 26-7, 29, 42-5, *46*, 50-1, 54-5, 61-2, 64-9, 109-11, 126, 140-1, 142-5, *146*, 147-8
Zambuko/Izibuko, *Katshaa!*, 234
Zanzibar, 26, 180, 198
Zimbabwe, 20, 45, 64, 152, 168, 183, 192, 211-14, 233, *234*, 239, 252, 254
ZIPRA (Zimbabwe People's Revolutionary Army), 239
Zirimu, E., *Keeping Up With the Mukasas*, 136
Zomba, 156
Zulu (people/language), 25, 115, 197, 215, 221, 223, 231
Zululand, University of, 222